# THE 1000 HOUR DAY

24th JULY 2011

Thanks for an amazing
holiday and for looking
after us.
Love and gratitude,

Hank & Jo. xx

# THE 1000 HOUR DAY

TWO ADVENTURERS TAKE ON THE
WORLD'S HARSHEST ISLAND

Chris Bray

Published in Australia in 2010 by Pier 9, an imprint of Murdoch Books Pty Limited

Murdoch Books Australia
Pier 8/9
23 Hickson Road
Millers Point NSW 2000
Phone: +61 (0) 2 8220 2000
Fax: +61 (0) 2 8220 2558
www.murdochbooks.com.au

Murdoch Books UK Limited
Erico House, 6th Floor
93–99 Upper Richmond Road
Putney, London SW15 2TG
Phone: +44 (0) 20 8785 5995
Fax: +44 (0) 20 8785 5985
www.murdochbooks.co.uk

Publisher: Colette Vella
Designer: Hugh Ford
Project editor: Karen Ward
Map: Ian Faulkner

National Library of Australia Cataloguing-in-Publication entry

Bray, Chris.
The 1000 hour day: two adventurers take on the world's harshest island / Chris Bray.
978-1-74196-967-2 (pbk.)
Bray, Chris—Travel.
Carter, Clark—Travel.
Victoria Island (Nunavut and N.W.T.)—Discovery and exploration.
Arctic regions—Discovery and exploration—Australian.
971.955

Printed in Australia by Griffin Press, an Accredited ISO AS/NZS 14001:2004
Environmental Management System printer.

The paper this book is printed on is certified by the © 1996
Forest Stewardship Council A.C. (FSC). Griffin Press holds
FSC chain of custody SGS-COC-005088. FSC promotes
environmentally responsible, socially beneficial and economically
viable management of the world's forests.

*To my extraordinary dad, Andrew Bray.*
*Without you, none of this could have happened.*
*Thank you.*

# CONTENTS

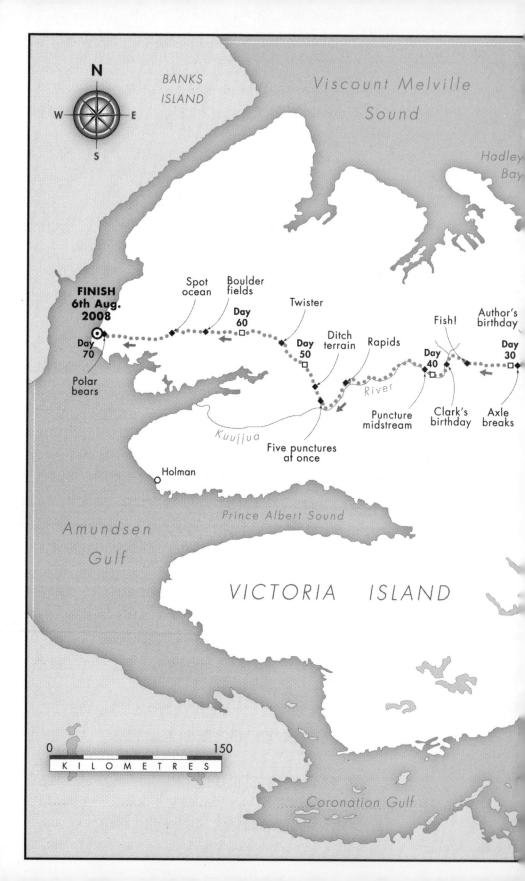

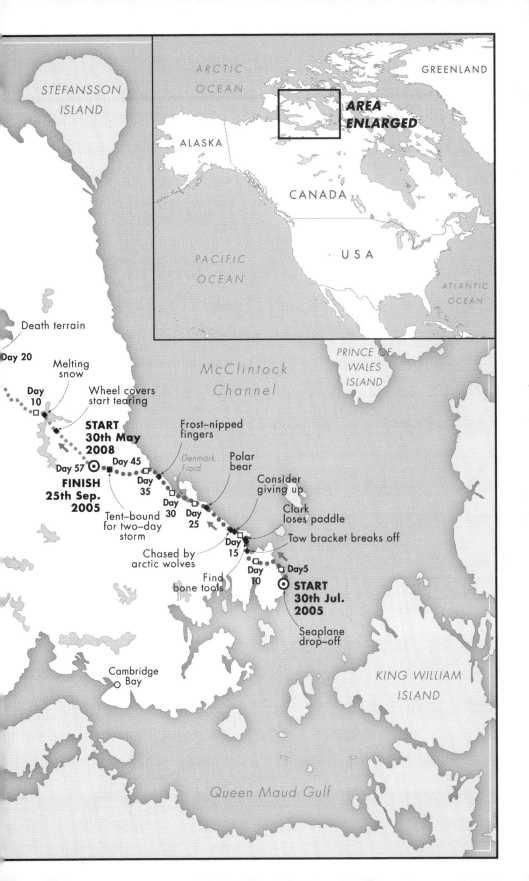

# PADDLEABLE AMPHIBIOUS CART 2005

**Empty:** 88 kg **Full:** 250 kg **Range:** 65 days

## HAULING MODE

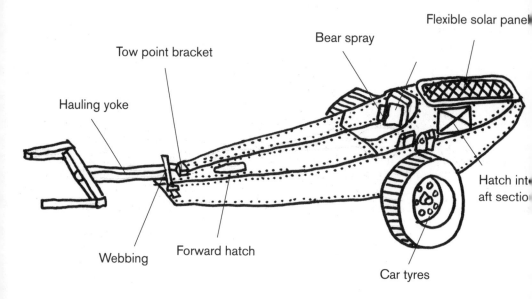

Tow point bracket

Bear spray

Flexible solar panel

Hauling yoke

Hatch into aft section

Webbing

Forward hatch

Car tyres

## KAYAK MODE

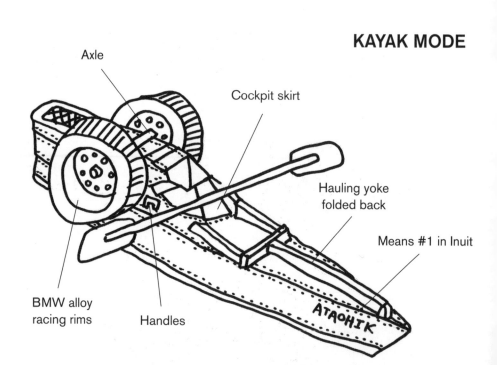

Axle

Cockpit skirt

Hauling yoke folded back

Means #1 in Inuit

BMW alloy racing rims

Handles

ATAOHIK

# PADDLEABLE AMPHIBIOUS CART 2008

**Empty:** 44 kg    **Full:** 249 kg    **Range:** 100 days

## SINGLE HAULING

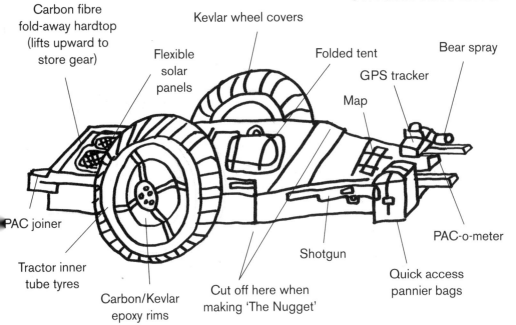

Carbon fibre fold-away hardtop (lifts upward to store gear)

Flexible solar panels

Kevlar wheel covers

Folded tent

GPS tracker

Map

Bear spray

PAC joiner

Tractor inner tube tyres

Carbon/Kevlar epoxy rims

Cut off here when making 'The Nugget'

Shotgun

PAC-o-meter

Quick access pannier bags

## JOINED TOGETHER FOR CAMP/RAFT

(Tents designed to fit on top of joint carts, which float and can be paddled like a raft)

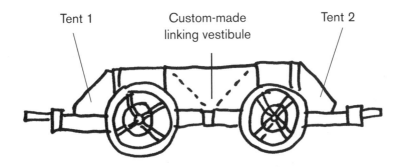

Tent 1

Custom-made linking vestibule

Tent 2

## SHORTENED 'THE NUGGET' FOR DOUBLE HAULING

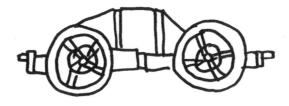

# PART ONE
# GENESIS OF ADVENTURE

# THE PROPOSITION

## JANUARY 2005

*'Good morning, Air Canada.'*

'Hi, could you put me through to someone in your marketing department?'

*'Hold the line for a moment?'*

'Certainly.'

I gulped some water, which instantly seized in my dry throat. My heart was racing. I must have made a dozen similar calls that day already, but the pressure of only having *one* chance to convince a company in *seconds* that they really do want to give you *thousands of dollars* for no apparent reason, is never easy.

*'Good morning, Marketing. This is Ben.'*

'Hi Ben, my name's Chris Bray. I was hoping you'd have time to have a quick chat about sponsorship?'

*'Er ... okay ...'*

'Great. Well, I'm 21, and the Australian Geographic Society's "Young Adventurer of the Year". I'm preparing for a two-man, world-first, unsupported, 65-day expedition across the Canadian Arctic. My friend Clark and I are going to be paddling and hauling our home-made wheeled kayaks through parts of the world that have never been explored before—past polar bears, wolves ... It's going to be pretty crazy, and we're filming a documentary as we go, which could give Air Canada some great exposure ... I was wondering if you'd take a look over a sponsorship proposal I've written for you?'

*'Wow, 65 days? That sounds like a hell of a trip! Yes, please send it through ...'*

I jotted down '65' and circled it on my notepad—now a mosaic of stress-induced, subconscious doodles. 'Thanks very much, I'll post it right away.'

Well, that was easy. My confidence rising, I traced my shaking finger down our list of potential sponsors, and dialled the next number.

*'Welcome to Sony. How can I help you?'*

'Hi. My name's Chris Bray, I'm 65, and Austra—'

Beside me, my mate Clark Carter burst out laughing. So did I.

*'Hello ... who is this?'*

We glanced at each other and shook our heads—nope, this wasn't salvageable. I quickly hung up, hoping she wouldn't remember my voice when I summoned the courage to call again. Enough trauma for one day. Eighteen phone calls: five write-offs, messages left with seven, and I had convinced the remaining six to at least read over the proposals that I'd apparently already gone to all the trouble of writing for them. So that was six proposals we now had to write up and post off.

Flipping through our endless To-Do list, I located the next task: 'Borrow two shotguns from someone in Canada—protection from polar bears'. Like most of the grand, sweeping statements on our list, this was easier said than done. We didn't even know anyone in Canada.

However, biting off more than is comfortable to chew is a skill—or habit—that Clark and I practise regularly. I had only just met Clark a few months prior, and already we had decided to entrust each other with our very lives, alone in the Arctic. To be honest, it was worse than that—somewhat amusingly, 'Meet Clark' was actually on my To-Do list for this expedition. In my defence, I will point out that it was right up there at the top of the list, along with other essentials like 'Tell parents'.

A few months earlier, on 18 June 2004, the usual flood of spam email had found its way into my inbox. There were emails trying to convince me to buy Rolex replicas, money scams, and one entitled 'Proposition'. Assuming this 'proposition' to be a once-in-a-lifetime opportunity to buy two Viagra tablets for the price of one, I almost deleted it, but curiosity got the better of me, and I opened it up:

*Hey Chris,*

*My name is Clark Carter, and I'm a 19-year-old guy from Terrigal, NSW.*

*Congratulations on winning the Young Adventurer of the Year. Your expedition sounded awesome!!!*

*At the moment I'm trying to plan a trip to Greenland to traverse its giant icecap along the Arctic Circle using skis and man-hauling sleds … I have been looking around for someone to partner up with on this 'mission' and to help plan out every detail with me. If this isn't your sort of thing, do you have any advice you can give me on getting a sponsor's attention or know of any other would-be adventurers that would take up this opportunity?*

*Thanks for your time, and hopefully in a year or so we'll be trekking across Greenland.*

*Cheers,*

*Clark*

I read the email again. If this was indeed spam mail, it was certainly very cunningly targeted, using an irresistible combination of key-words, specifically 'adventurer', 'icecap', 'Arctic' and 'hauling sleds'. I fell for it, and replied at once.

I needed no encouragement to chase this proposition—I was in the middle of university exams, halfway through my third year studying Electrical Engineering at the University of New South Wales, in Sydney, Australia. I longed to be somewhere else, far, far away from 'Kirchoff's voltage laws' and 'complex impedances of tuneable antenna stubs'. Greenland, being over 15,000 kilometres away, sounded ideal.

Of course there was more to my decision than simply wanting light at the end of my study tunnel. Most boys, at some point or other, dream of setting off on wild journeys to unexplored lands. Boldly venturing where no man has been before, enduring unimaginable hardships and preferably braving wild animals—these are, after all, the key ingredients for any good adventure. If you subscribe to the Hollywood film definition, then there should also be at least one damsel in distress, to drive the hero onwards—I mean, why else would anyone risk their life in such a way? Unfortunately, historically, these damsel-in-distress cases are few and far between. There was no fair maiden waiting for Sir Edmund Hillary and Tenzing Norgay atop Everest, and although there were several bizarre theories about what early explorers might find at the North Pole—including a giant hole leading to the centre of the earth—finding a princess in need of rescue wasn't one of them. There must then be other factors that motivate humans to embark on such seemingly pointless journeys.

Scientific research? Not as often as you might think. Sir Edmund is famously quoted as saying, 'Nobody climbs mountains for scientific reasons. Science is used to raise money for the expeditions, but you really climb for the hell of it.'

Frostbite, altitude sickness, hypothermia—why on earth would anyone in their right mind want to willingly inflict such things upon themselves? This is the first question on people's lips, and one that I, like many others, sometimes struggle to answer succinctly. I think this is partly because the desire stems from so many different reasons, but also partly because, quite frankly, words fail to convey what it is actually like to be out there. As Sir Douglas Mawson once said, 'If you have to ask the question, you will never understand the answer.'

On a very elementary level, heading off into the 'unknown'—be it 'unknown' to humankind as a whole, or simply 'unknown' to the individual who seeks to push back the limits to his or her own experiences—is what leading a fulfilling life is all about. As the old adage goes, 'Nothing ventured, nothing gained.' The way I see it, you can either spend your life in front of the TV pretending life goes on forever, or you can realise it is in fact finite, and that you'd better get up and make the most of it. Never put off till tomorrow what you can do today. I really believe in that—with a few exceptions. For example, why tell your parents *today* that you're going to walk across an island inhabited by polar bears when you could tell them *tomorrow*?

# AN ADVENTUROUS UPBRINGING

Most boys dream of wild adventures, but these dreams are put on the backburner—if not completely extinguished—to accommodate other more immediate, perhaps more 'normal' desires as they grow up. I count myself incredibly fortunate in having been somewhat freed from 'normality' by a fairly unique upbringing.

Most of my primary school years were spent sailing around the world with my family on our home-made yacht. My father, Andrew Bray—a mechanical engineer turned yachting-magazine writer— and my mother, Victoria, built a total of four yachts together. Some of my earliest memories are of them building *Starship*—a 44-foot (13.5 metre) aluminium cutter with a lift-keel—in our front yard.

We moved on board in 1988, when I was just five years old and my sister Sarah was seven. Early the following year all four of us, together with five years of correspondence schooling paperwork, cast off on the adventure of a lifetime for my parents, and a marvellous upbringing for Sarah and me.

We sailed up the east coast of Australia, then west across the top to Darwin and its crocodiles, and out across the Indian Ocean to Mozambique, via the islands of Chagos and Mayotte. In early 1991 we left South Africa and headed to Ireland via St Helena (one of the most isolated islands on earth), Ascension, the Cape Verde Islands and the Azores. Passing through Scotland's Caledonian Canal, we then sailed across the North Sea to Norway and Sweden, ducking through the top of Germany to spend the winter frozen-in, making snowmen in Holland. Early in 1992 we crossed back to the UK, and by summer we reached the Mediterranean via the beautiful French canals—sailing right through Paris within sight of the Eiffel Tower. After crossing the Atlantic Ocean, we were snorkelling in the

Caribbean by Christmas, and after slipping through the Panama Canal, sailed out into the Pacific Ocean. A myriad of other exotic locations followed, including the Galapagos Islands, where we snorkelled with seals, and Suvarov Atoll, where we swam with sharks and gathered enormous coconut crabs with the islanders. All in all, by the time we returned to Sydney for Sarah to start high school, we'd visited 32 different countries and lived on board *Starship* for over five years.

There is nothing quite like ocean sailing. It has to be said, though, that Sarah and I got the better end of the deal. We didn't have to keep constant watch for ships day and night like our parents did, nor worry about the weather. For us, life consisted of reading, playing Lego and other games, while waiting for the peg clipped over the fishing line trailing astern to go *click*, signalling it was time to haul in another dinner. The excitement of peering down into the sapphire-blue depths trying to catch the first glimpse of the huge fish—as the line audibly 'zinged', knifing back and forth—was just incredible. One gloved handful at a time Dad would pull in the last few metres of piano-wire trace and bring the now exhausted fish alongside. Perhaps a yellowfin tuna (one lasted the four of us a record 24 meals), or maybe a beautifully painted dorado or 'dolphin fish'—or, on a few occasions, perhaps a not-so-exhausted marlin which would then rise to its full 3-metre length above the water and 'tail-walk' defiantly before flinging the hook from its mouth.

On top of fishing there were countless other things to keep us entertained. Tired seabirds would sometimes come on board for a break, and I'd instantly try to adopt them as pets. Dolphins would play beneath our bow, whales followed us, flying fish would litter the deck in the mornings, and on particularly dark nights, the yacht's wake would often burn like blue fire from phosphorescence. To top the whole experience off, we usually only did our correspondence schooling when in port, and even then it took just two hours a day! As it was impractical to 'correspond' our correspondence schooling, we simply worked through the pages at our own pace under Mum's guidance, and when we'd done that day's scheduled work, we were free.

Life was one extended holiday, financially sustained by the rent from our home back in Avalon on Sydney's Northern Beaches, and Dad's ongoing freelance magazine writings. We certainly didn't have money to fling around—we couldn't afford the usual tourist attractions, nor to eat out or hire cars to explore inland (the game parks in South Africa were an unforgettable exception)—but living on a tight budget made it financially *just* possible to continue this dream potentially indefinitely. Without much money to spend, nor shops to spend it in, and no TV to watch, Sarah and I learned to be resourceful and practical too, building the toys and other things we didn't have, and repairing them when they broke—a skill I later relied on in the Arctic.

I was ten when we returned to Sydney, and after five years of sailing, I now had a problem. This adventurous upbringing had led me to believe that constantly travelling—always experiencing new cultures and places—was normal. As you can imagine, it didn't take long before the novelty of remaining in the same place wore off, to be replaced by a burning desire to resume my 'normal' lifestyle of daily adventures.

School back in the real world didn't seem very normal either— for a start it took a whopping six hours each day instead of the usual two. Inadvertently now applying my work ethic of 'if I just plough through it I'll be able to get back out and play' to a full six hours of schoolwork a day, I excelled in my studies, and was awarded dux of both primary and high school. Unfortunately, this achievement combined with my ever-growing interest in everything from technology to entomology, the fact that I wasn't the tallest or sportiest of boys, and my rather pale complexion topped off with an interesting haircut (my mum continued to cut it for me after we returned from sailing), led to me being branded a basket-case nerd. Admittedly, in addition to the usual boyish joys of blowing things up and training my wondrous German Shepherd dog, Gypsie, to 'cut' and other Swiss-army-style functions on command, I did actually start an online business, BlackJackal.com, through which I sold electronics and home-made computer programs—so, yeah, looking back on it, maybe I really was a nerd after all. By the end of high school, an overall leaving mark of 99.2 per cent granted me access to any university course I wanted, and so I was faced with a choice: what did I actually want to do with my life?

I applied for Electrical Engineering at university, not out of a desire to learn the intricacies of circuit theory but because I have always enjoyed doing practical things, and solving technical problems. I saw—and still see—engineering as the degree that would teach me the most about how the world works, while also building problem-solving skills and design techniques which can be applied not only to electronics, but also to everyday problems such as how best to manage time or money, or—although I didn't know it at the time—how to orchestrate a world-first expedition to an unexplored region of the Arctic.

It was in the summer of 2001–2, just before I started university, that I decided to convince my good friend Jasper Timm to come to Tasmania with me for a spot of hiking for two weeks. I was eighteen at the time, and had done a bit of bushwalking, camping and trout fishing with my dad over the years, and occasionally during holidays Jasper and I'd catch the ferry over to The Basin—a popular yet secluded waterfront camping ground in Ku-ring-gai Chase National Park. Once off the ferry we'd then 'accidentally' slip outside the designated camping zones and hide out in the surrounding hills for up to five days at a time, living off hard-core camping foods such as chocolate biscuits and tins of creamed rice. To keep us entertained as we counted off the days, we'd flip through my *SAS Survival Guide* for ideas. For example, did you know that all animal snares fall into one of four categories—'Strangle', 'Mangle', 'Dangle' or 'Tangle'? We failed to catch anything except occasionally ourselves, but succeeded brilliantly in the larger goal which was, of course, to have fun.

Jasper's and my decision to spend two weeks hiking in Tasmania would certainly be taking this style of adventure to a new level, but I had no idea just how profound this trip's impact on me would actually be. Looking back on it, I think our innocent little holiday was a major turning point in my life. Objectively, it was nothing special—we spent six days walking the popular Overland Track (an 80-kilometre tracked route through the Cradle Mountain–Lake St Clair National Park in Tasmania's central highlands), sharing the trail with countless others—but that was all it took to revitalise the travel bug in me.

I found hiking a very satisfying way to travel. It was wonderfully simple—I enjoyed bringing only what we absolutely needed (although for some inexplicable reason we brought an entire bottle of honey we never even opened). It was refreshing to find myself unburdened by many of the things I never actually realised were cluttering my usual daily life—things like mobile phones, emails, alarms, TV ... Out on the trail I woke each morning with a simple purpose: to shoulder my heavy hiking pack as far as I could, taking in all the new sights and experiences along the way. I had started to form a nagging suspicion that 'purpose' was somehow lacking in the busy daily routine of my normal life, and it felt good to now have a simple, solid objective to work towards each day.

When I say the hiking lifestyle is simple, we did not find it easy—it involved extended sessions of some of the hardest physical work I'd ever done—but this only served to amplify the sense of satisfaction at the end. The dictionary definition of 'accomplish' is 'to gain with effort', and we all know this to be true. Very little satisfaction can be derived from doing something that is easy, while much pride can be taken from completing something that was truly hard to achieve. The tangible rewards at the end of each day were meagre at best—some pasta followed by an uncomfortable night's sleep in a wet tent—however, come evening, I found this was all I wanted. Simple pasta never tasted so good, nor was lumpy ground beneath my sleeping bag ever so desirable. Back at home, I'd never known myself to involuntarily grin from simply being able to lie down and straighten my back.

On top of the travel itself, the unforgettable experiences, the purity and immediate reality of life, the fresh air and the excitement, I enjoyed the *challenge* of hiking. What particularly captivated me was that it seemed to have no limits. Unlike school, for example, where I found I could achieve full marks without having to really push myself, when hiking, I got out exactly what I put in. If I pushed myself further, the results just got better—the longer I walked uphill, the better the view; the more hills I walked up, the more vistas I experienced. The only ceiling—besides money and time available—was how much I could endure, how far I could push myself, and for how long. I found the challenge irresistible.

I was awarded a scholarship to study Electrical Engineering, with the only down side being that I'd have to work my summer holidays at various sponsor companies. These sneak previews into what my working life as an office-bound engineer could be like were nothing short of terrifying. Each day I'd head into work and sit among employees who'd proudly clocked up 25, 30, even 40 years of employment in the same firm. I'd ask these more extreme cases what they intended to do when they retired (soon?), and after hearing of my hiking adventures, they'd sometimes say that they too had always wanted to do something like that. 'Absolutely, there's always time,' I lied. I have often thought traditional working life is the wrong way around: working in offices when we are fit and young enough to get out there and enjoy life, only to be freed by retirement later—by which time all that some people manage is to sit and dream of what they would do if only they were twenty years younger. Discussing this later with Australian adventurer Don McIntyre, he told me of a more profound experience he'd had at one of his first jobs. He'd asked an ageing man resembling Sir Francis Chichester if he'd ever done any sailing. In reply, the man led him back to his workstation—in front of a photocopier—and proudly showed him two ruts his feet had actually worn into the concrete after eons of standing in front of the machine. By the end of my first placement, I'd made a promise to myself to find a 'job' that in itself fulfilled my dreams—because they might not be still within reach at the end of my working life.

# THE GRAND PLAN

Fast forward to Clark's email of June 2004. Greenland it was, and we started planning right away. How, When, Where and Why? 'Why' was a given. 'Where' began with the aim to cross the whole island at the 80th parallel. Deciding 'When' took a bit more thought. I was now heading towards the end of my third year at uni, after which my scholarship dictated that I take the following year off to undertake two six-month industry placements before returning for my fourth and final year of studies. If we didn't want to enjoy temperatures of 40 below zero and perpetual darkness in the Arctic, we'd have to go in summer—which of course is winter in the Southern Hemisphere. Starting my first six-month placement as early as possible, and leaving the second one as late as possible would open up about six weeks in between—midsummer in the Arctic. Bingo. And for the final piece of the puzzle—'How'—standing on skis and being pulled across the giant icecap by a huge kite sounded like fun.

Having not even met each other yet, Clark and I plotted away via email for some time, and unfortunately the problems mounted almost as fast as our excitement. Firstly, Clark wasn't too sure how well his parents would react to the whole idea. To be honest I hadn't broached the subject with mine either. Ignoring these towering hurdles, I casually unveiled our grand plan for the first time in the closing lines of a graduation talk I gave to students back at my old high school. To my horror, I didn't realise my dad had snuck into the audience until I bumped into him on the way out. As we walked home together, our conversation danced through every conceivable topic, except Greenland. Could it be that he had fallen asleep during that part of my speech? He must have. Brilliant. That was close.

Late that afternoon Clark and I discovered another problem, and one that we couldn't overcome. In the peak of the Arctic summer—the only time I could get off from work and uni—the surface of Greenland's icecap starts to melt. Temperatures climb above even 10 degrees Celsius—this must be the reason most traverses seem to occur in April or May! We were shattered. Visions of us gliding over pristine snow-covered ice were replaced by scenes of toiling across the top of a giant, half-melted Slushie.

I was a bit despondent over dinner that night, and something was evidently concerning Dad also. Eventually, he carefully put his fork down, and asked, 'In your talk today, what was all that about going to Greenland?' His eyes met mine.

So, he hadn't been sleeping at all. Rather conveniently, I was able to tell him the truth: 'Oh—ah, yes. Yes, I *was* planning on that, but just this afternoon I realised it's actually not possible. So don't worry about that.' While my parents have always been very supportive of all my projects, they have a knack for worrying, as all good parents do. The prospect of such an expedition was something that needed to be strategically introduced, and backed up with conclusive evidence that it was well thought out—not casually brought up over dinner without even a supporting 'Safety Considerations' document!

As Greenland wasn't going to work for us, we had to find somewhere that would, and fast. We opened our respective atlases and began pointing randomly at bizarre corners of the globe. Namibia? Siberia? At one point I got an SMS from Clark saying: 'Hey, do you want to walk across the Great Sandy Desert instead?' It wasn't your average SMS.

We thought of everywhere, even crossing Alaska, south to north following its Canadian border. I had often wondered how countries decided where to draw their boundaries, and now I know. If you look closely, they run right through places that neither country wants. Alaska's follows a horrifying trail of peaks and glaciated, crevasse-filled valleys. We might have been crazy, but we weren't mad.

A couple of days into our research, Clark stumbled across 'Victoria Island', a funny-shaped island tucked up away in the Arctic Archipelago—that tangled mass of islands above Canada. Despite its being the ninth-largest island on the planet, neither of us had ever even noticed Victoria Island before. The more we looked into it, the more excited we became.

Not only did it sport an enthralling array of wildlife including polar bears, muskox and arctic wolves, but the landscape was also incredibly diverse. There'd be no endlessly pursuing the same barren white horizon for weeks as we'd have endured on an icecap traverse. In the height of summer we'd experience everything—both frozen and liquid coastlines, lake-strewn tundra, swampy grasslands, expanses of ice-shattered shale, plateaus, and even massive rivers just starting to thaw. Better yet, the island is largely unexplored. It was absolutely perfect. I stuck in a Post-it note to mark the page, and snapped shut the atlas. At last we had something real to work towards.

By now it was early November 2004, and I was just finishing that third year of uni. We had nine months to go before summer would make its brief appearance in the Arctic. While that may sound like a lot of time, the amount of work involved in organising an expedition of this scale is actually mind-boggling. The dreaded To-Do list which would dictate our lives from then on began to get out of hand and kept on growing. First things first: for the sake of formality, I decided I should probably at least meet Clark ... Everything so far had been conducted via email, SMS and phone calls.

I stood atop the Opera House steps in Sydney, and cast my eyes out over the sea of milling people. My mind kept cycling through the photos he'd emailed me, trying to marry them up with one of the figures below. Bingo—this was him—striding very purposefully up the ... up the ... no. Okay, that wasn't him. People look so different when not posing for a rock-climbing photo, or on holiday, as he was in most of the photographs I'd seen. Okay, this guy's walking right up to me—this has to be Clark. Unless it's some guy about to ask for directions? No, this was definitely him. Clark kept advancing up the stairs, and at last our eyes drew level. Then he walked up the last two steps. Dammit—why is it that all the people I team up with for expeditions have to be so much taller than I am?! Just like Jasper, at over six feet tall, Clark was a comical six inches taller than me. We grinned, and shook hands.

Next up was to find a decent map of the island. The Arctic Archipelago, we'd found, was virtually ignored by just about every atlas we had. Occasionally, some of the islands would creep in at the top of maps of the Canadian mainland, but that was about it. Minutes after our first meeting, we walked into the Reference

Section of the State Library of New South Wales—and pulled out their biggest atlas available for public viewing. When it came to Victoria Island, though, again the atlas contained scarcely more detail than my one at home. Clearly we were going to have to call in the big guns.

We walked over to the elderly lady behind the 'restricted viewing' counter and put forward our case. She slid her glasses further down her nose and, peering over the top of them, whispered, 'Come with me …' Feeling rather important, we followed her into the 'special' part of the library, where she dug out a prehistoric-looking atlas of Canada and placed it on a huge table. Under her watchful gaze we carefully opened it and stared in disbelief for a few seconds before running to the photocopier. Pages of graphs showing average temperature and precipitation for the various Arctic islands, extent of sea ice for each season, even approximate distribution of different animals … It was all there.

We retired to a side room with our wad of photocopying and fell upon it. 'Hey, look at this—it says polar bears range over the whole island.' 'Yeah, but no walruses …' We could scarcely contain our excitement at this glut of information. I glanced at my watch—still another 30 minutes before we had to head off. Plenty of time for a preliminary budget. We brainstormed every conceivable cost, and tallied it up: $15,000, so that's $7500 each—we nodded in agreement; that was expensive, but achievable. Sure, we only had $5000 between us, but we could raise the rest through sponsorship. Too easy. If we'd known back then the final budget for the journey would actually be closer to $250,000 by the time we got to the far side, we'd have immediately gone back to the atlas in search of a more realistic destination. Ignorance is bliss, however, and we shook hands, slapped each other on the back, and went our separate ways home, full of enthusiasm.

Within a couple of weeks Clark left on a short hiking and mountaineering trip in New Zealand with some mates. After undertaking a guided training course, their goal was to climb Mount Aspiring, near Mount Cook in the Southern Alps. I was anxious to see how things would pan out; it would, after all, be his first real taste of serious expeditioning. Clark'd spent much of his childhood growing up in a small mining community in the Great Sandy Desert of Western Australia, and he—like me—retained a love for the outdoors that had surpassed conventional limits and was fast becoming a passion for adventure. He and I both, it seemed, suffered continual gnawing from the 'Why not try something bigger?' bug. So while Clark busied himself gaining a healthy fear of mountains in New Zealand, I kept researching Victoria Island, and two weeks later we both had good news. Firstly, Clark was still alive, and secondly, I hadn't uncovered any impossible hurdles we wouldn't be able to overcome—besides the obvious ones of money, time, logistics, and parents. We were still good to go.

My confidence in Clark had been boosted also—having successfully completed their training course in New Zealand, he and his mates had on the day made the difficult decision not to attempt Mount Aspiring under the conditions then prevailing. Careful risk management and being able to back down when required are probably two of the most important skills to have in this kind of game. To our horror, just a few weeks after Clark returned, news headlines told of another young climber from New South Wales who had just attempted Mount Aspiring and, tragically, fallen to his death. It was both a reality check, and reassurance that Clark had definitely made the correct decision.

Notebooks literally filled with pages of To-Do's were multiplying on my desk like rabbits. There was just too much to do. Every day we'd chew through as many tasks as we possibly could, only to discover that by the time we fell into an exhausted sleep, we'd have added almost twice the number of tasks as those we'd managed to tick off. Reflecting this, our anticipated costs grew to around $25,000—still only about a tenth of our final budget—and already the magnitude of this undertaking was starting to concern us. We now had six months to get it all together, and we were already feeling pushed for time.

We decided to collate all our thoughts into one epic 'Expedition Document'. We fed this beast with every scrap of information that came to light, and gradually our expedition started to take form within the pages. The document was immense, and covered every aspect of the journey ahead—equipment lists (with an exact weight down to the gram for each carefully selected item); first-aid equipment (from the basics through to the inhalable painkillers used in ambulances, and—although we really hoped we wouldn't meet any polar bears this close—'abdominal pads'. Enough said); route maps; descriptions of expected terrain variations and how we'd deal with their ramifications; electricity calculations to determine the size of solar panels we'd need to keep all our electronics running, using NASA data on average cloud-cover and solar energy at those latitudes; search and rescue procedures; a detailed daily meal menu; and so on.

Firstly, we had to decide on a route to take. We figured if we were going to try and cross the whole island, we might as well do it properly, and start from the most easterly tip and head for the most westerly. We wanted to strike a balance between taking the most direct route the terrain would allow, while also visiting the most interesting areas. Our proposed route would take us just over 1000 kilometres—past a frozen coastline, then inland over the tundra, up onto a plateau, down a massive river and, ultimately, across to the far side. Although the prevailing winds are westerly, we opted to start on the eastern side and head into the wind, as partway through we would link up with the extensive Kuujjua River which ran south-west and would, if we brought kayaks, help us greatly on our way.

Victoria Island appears innocuous enough when you first glance at a map, but when you peer closer, the entire island is absolutely littered with a myriad of little lakes. How could we lug all of our food and supplies across this tangled patchwork of land and water? It really was a bit of a conundrum. Ideally, we'd use a kayak for the wet bits, and some form of cart for the dry bits—but clearly we couldn't take both. What we needed was a kayak with wheels. However, as is the problem with such unique expeditions, there was a decided lack of ultra-strong wheeled kayaks on the market—in fact, there were none.

'Take a look at these,' Clark said, pointing at a wheeled kayak cradle in an outdoor catalogue, 'they look like toys!' It was getting ridiculous; all we could find were pathetic little plastic wheels that looked like they were designed to help frail old men roll their kayaks from the garage to the car. Clearly we were going to have to buy a kayak and build the wheel system ourselves. 'No biggie,' we assured ourselves.

Next item on the list was food. Every day out there we'd be burning enormous amounts of energy, and so we'd need ridiculous quantities of food to fuel our bodies. Bringing the right type and amount of food was critical. Unable to afford professional advice from a nutritionist, we went right back to basics. Most importantly, as with every item, we had to keep the weight right down. Per gram, fat gives you the most energy, so it'd be great if we could just live off slabs of butter. Realistically, though, humans can only digest around a 50 per cent fat diet, and we had to balance out the rest with some carbohydrates and protein. An active man burns around 3000 calories per day, and someone hauling a sled to the North Pole consumes more like 6000–8000. This increase is partly in response to the exercise, and partly burnt by the body just to stay warm in the bitter cold. Clark calculated that we'd need about 4500 calories each per day, as we anticipated a similar workload as that of a polar trek, but it wouldn't be anything like as cold, perhaps only down to minus 5 degrees Celsius or so.

Armed with a calculator and our target daily amount of calories for fat, protein and carbohydrates, we walked into the supermarket. I scrutinised the label on the back of a chocolate bar. 'Ten per cent fat? That's ridiculous!' We got solemn nods of understanding from passing weight-conscious shoppers, which changed to horror as I continued, 'We need like … 50 per cent fat, at least! Let's try pure butter.' With 'diet' this, and new 'ulta-slim' that, it was near impossible to find the original lard-injected versions of anything. Eventually we composed our menu, which included 123 grams of chocolate (that's half a family-sized block), 50 grams of butter, 200 grams of nuts, and 50 grams of peanut butter, each, per day.

'How many days do you reckon it'll take to walk across?' It was the question on both our lips. If we travelled for just five hours a day (which we could do before lunch if we really wanted), at a snail's walking pace of just over 3 kilometres an hour, we rationalised it should take no more than 60 days to cross the island. This was deliberately very conservative—we knew we could put in much longer days than that, especially in the 24-hour sunlight that we could expect in the Arctic at that time of year, and paddling down river and even along the coast would be much faster than walking, and 3 kilometres per hour was pretty slow for walking. However, we were intending to film the journey to create a documentary, and so we'd need a bit of extra time along the way for this. 'Sixty days … let's give us another five. Sixty-five days,' I said. It would be difficult squeezing a 65-day holiday into the 45-day break I was allowed between my scholarship work placements, but as with so many other looming hurdles, I adopted the 'we'll cross that bridge when we come to it' approach. I jotted the number down in our notebook, tapping the pen on the page for emphasis. Sixty-five days. Agreed.

'So … 65 days times two people times 123 grams of chocolate is …' I punched the numbers idly into my calculator. 'Oh my God! Sixteen kilograms of chocolate!' We hastily tallied up the total mass of our ultra-weight-efficient diet and shifted our shoulders uncomfortably, already feeling the obscene load we'd be hauling. Over 60 kilograms in food alone, each.

Thankfully, drinking water wouldn't be an issue, as we would never be more than a stone's throw away from a lake. We'd been told that the lakes, refreshed by snow-melt each season, should be safe to drink from. The only other major consumable was fuel. Our two MSR liquid-fuelled stoves drank 'white spirits' (the same thing as 'white gas'), but how much? Again, it wasn't the sort of thing we wanted to run out of—unable to boil our rice, pasta or dehydrated meals we'd soon be in real trouble.

'Well, we're having two mugs of hot drinks a day,' Clark started.

'And we'll have to boil the oats in the morning, and … I'd say about a litre of boiling water for dinner,' I continued. Next we carefully measured out 1 litre of cold water—complete with a few ice cubes—into our saucepan, and fired up one of our stoves outside. By measuring the change in weight of the fuel bottle after boiling, we worked out how many grams of fuel was spent to boil 1 litre of water. After a few more back-of-the-envelope calculations, we pulled out the number we were looking for: we'd need 8 litres of white spirits to fuel our journey. Conscious of the fact that my backyard didn't mimic Arctic conditions too precisely—it was somewhat warmer and less windy for a start—we drastically decided to double our figure, allowing 16 litres of fuel. Better safe than sorry. Besides, a week or two into our trek we could make a much more accurate reassessment and burn any excess fuel to save weight. Ordering extra, on the other hand, would be a little more difficult.

It was now mid January 2005, and I had begun working at Siemens Logistics & Assembly—the first of my two six-month industry placements. Again, I found the dreaded nine-to-five office work was made tolerable only by the knowledge that I was working towards such an exciting adventure at the end of it. While at work, every second I had spare—and, admittedly, more than a few seconds that I didn't really have spare—I continued to plan, organise, research and make notes.

Our Expedition Document was really starting to flesh out by this stage, and it was time for us to put it to the test. It was, you see, a dual-purpose document. While it would be the key to securing the sponsorship we so desperately needed, there was a far bigger hurdle to overcome first. For days I waited anxiously for just the right moment, and then it happened. I sat Mum down, and brought out the semi-complete document. 'I'm going to take a holiday between my two work placements ...' I began.

I thought she took it very well, even the page about the polar bears. When I had finished, Mum slowly looked up, pained concern bleeding through her brave exterior, and whispered, 'Have you told Dad?'

Steady on, I thought, let's learn to crawl before I try and run! I shook my head. 'Ohhhh,' she gulped, visibly squirming under the anguish of not being able to confide in him. 'Just ... please tell him soon. Please don't let him find out by reading it in the paper, or by overhearing a speech like your Greenland idea ... okay?'

I agreed.

I bit the bullet and broached the subject with Dad just a few days later. Remarkably, buried beneath all his immediate concern, words of caution and analysis of foreseeable problems, I detected more than a trace of enthusiasm—excitement even. I was thrilled. I expected to have to battle this one—I was even prepared to put my foot down and make a stand—but listening to his reaction ('The scholarship program won't be happy ... and hmm, what about ...'), even his negatives sounded more like token hurdles put in place to maintain the responsible parent image, while inside he clearly wanted to say, 'What an awesome project!'

Clark's parents, on the other hand, were still recovering from his New Zealand trip. He still owed them money for it, and having realised how narrowly he'd escaped death by deciding not to climb Mount Aspiring, they were not thrilled with the concept of adventuring at all. Clark was getting increasingly nervous as time went on and his parents remained in the dark about Victoria Island. He admitted to me that the main reason his parents had supported his going to New Zealand was because he promised them it would be his last venture before starting university, knuckling down, and getting his degree. 'I just don't know what they'll say ...' He shook his head. His best chance, he decided, would be to wait until university started at the end of February—that way he could sweeten the bitter pill by delivering it at the same time as the good news that his university career was under way. As horrifying as keeping our plans hidden from them for another full month sounded, it would be possible because, rather conveniently, Clark's parents live in America for work.

Like a freight train out of control, we couldn't afford the time to wait for Clark to inform his parents—we just had to keep on planning, and hope for the best. We ordered two Atlas hauling harnesses from Eric Philips's expedition outfitting company, Icetrek. Eric—who along with companion Jon Muir was the first Aussie to ski to both the North and South Pole—was greatly impressed by our plans: 'Distinctly different. Great stuff!' We splashed this endorsement over our promotional poster, and stamped it proudly in our Expedition Document. Others soon followed. 'A chilling trek, guaranteed to set imaginations ablaze!'—Ben Kozel, first Australian to raft the full length of the Amazon ...

'So when do we get to meet Clark?' Mum questioned while Dad listened in.

'I'm meeting with him this weekend,' I admitted, realising as I said it that our meetings no longer needed to be confidential and off site.

'We'll have a barbecue!' Mum announced, and that was that. Clark turned up, and I introduced him, every bit as nervous as if this was a new girlfriend. He sweet-talked his way through a lengthy lunch, and answered all their questions precisely the right way. We were both waiting for the inevitable, 'So, what do your parents think of all this?' But it never came. That was very lucky.

'He's lovely,' Mum gushed later that night. 'He seems very sensible—I get good vibes from him.'

'Yes, he's a nice kid,' Dad added. Relief washed over me. Hurdles were falling like dominoes ...

The arrival of our hauling harnesses was the first tangible evidence, besides the maps we'd bought, that this really was happening. Huge padded waist- and shoulder-straps, and an equally huge price tag— in every way our harnesses resembled a very expensive backpack, with the minor exception that there was nowhere you could actually *put* anything, just two stainless steel D-rings stitched to the sides with reinforced webbing to clip into the sled. They looked very serious.

'Yes, that's right. Just any big old truck tyre will be fine—we just want to drag them behind us as we walk along the beach …'

The guy at the tyre service centre paused, and looked up from the greasy tyre he was working on. 'Wh—' he began, absent-mindedly picking up his socket spanner only to put it down again, obviously having difficulty grappling with the mental image of such an inane idea. 'Sure, but … why?' We were getting this question more and more frequently.

The next morning, a couple out for an early morning stroll along Palm Beach found themselves subconsciously following a carefully smoothed trail, about 1 metre wide, snaking its way along the sand. Abruptly their path terminated at a gasping, sweaty form sitting on a truck tyre. Suddenly realising what they had been doing, the couple turned around and gazed incredulously back along the winding path they had followed, and then turned their eyes, full of confusion, on me. 'I'm employed by the council to smooth the beach,' I explained between gulps of air. 'New OH&S rules … lumpy sand has been identified as a trip-hazard.' They nodded in complete lack of understanding, and wandered away in bewilderment before I had the breath to set the record straight.

Dragging the tyre was as much of a promotional stunt as it was training. So many people stopped us along the way that we soon carried in our pockets a wad of flyers to hand out seeking sponsorship. Our respective local papers even ran a few stories: 'Beach warm-up for Arctic trek' ran one headline. It was much harder than it looked—the tyre would gradually fill up with sand, feeling more and more like we were hauling a ship's anchor. It was amusing watching how young kids reacted—some would run up and throw more sand in the middle (little bastards, they'll grow up to be personal trainers, those ones!), and some would climb on board while their parents called them off in complete embarrassment. Others would adorably trot along beside the tyre, scooping out handfuls to lighten our load. The more ambitious youngsters sometimes asked for a turn, and while they didn't move it very far, it was a welcome break.

At long last Clark received his letter of acceptance into Media Studies at university—the good news he needed before attempting to tell his parents about the expedition.

Halfway across the globe, his mum answered the phone, and Clark swung his carefully scripted plan into action. He delivered the sweeter news about uni, hesitated, and then chased it up with the bitter pill. There was a little noise on the other end of the phone, and then his mum simply hung up on him.

Like a stunned mullet, Clark sat by the phone, dumbfounded, as he came to grips with what had just happened. This wasn't good. Suddenly, the silence was shattered by Clark's phone going off.

'Hello?'

'Hi, Clark,' the melting tone of her voice was reassuring. 'Look, I know you'll be safe, and I think it sounds amazing. I just wish it wasn't my boy who was going, that's all. But if you're decided, then … Dad and I will support your decision.'

An uncontrollable grin spread over Clark's face as he replaced the receiver and texted me the news. Weightless with relief, I flicked back through our To-Do book, and placed a satisfying tick against 'Tell Clark's parents about the expedition', on page one. Below it was listed another equally minor task: 'Organise sponsorship'.

# TASMANIAN WILDERNESS EXPEDITION

Luckily I'd already had some experience organising sponsorship. During my university scholarship industry placement at the end of 2003, I sat at my workstation PC and—trying to keep alive the memories of hiking the Overland Track with Jasper—just happened to stumble upon the website of well-respected hiker John Chapman. Flicking through descriptions of some of his epic hikes, one in particular seized my imagination. This was to be the second turning point in my life, a somewhat exaggerated version of the first. I again convinced Jasper to set off with me, this time on a 30-day trek through Tasmania's extremely isolated south-western wilderness. Only a handful of people had ever done what I wanted to do—hike between Port Davey in the south up to Strahan about 200 kilometres north, following the inhospitable western coastline. There would be no tracks—we'd need to use a machete, and we'd also need two airdrops of supplies along the way. I only had four weeks' break between finishing this work placement and starting my third year at university, and I was determined to make the most of it.

The only problem with this Tasmanian adventure was that it was going to be incredibly expensive. On Sunday evenings I worked as a kitchen-hand or 'dish-pig' in a local gourmet pizza café, and I stuck up a tiny poster on the café window stating that 'Dish-Pigs Belong in the Wilderness', below which I laid out the plans for our adventure, asking for financial support. The odd two-dollar tip occasionally found its way to me, but one day my boss Phil—an enthusiastic (if not partially mad) South African—introduced me to another enthusiastic (and also partially mad) South African,

Andreas. Andreas presented me with a $20 donation to ensure that he had my full attention, then sat me down and told me he'd been on several adventures himself, and knew a thing or two about sponsorship. 'Leave it with me, I'll talk to some people, and I'll see what I can do.'

Meanwhile I'd informed my local northern Sydney newspaper, the *Manly Daily*, about our proposed adventure. Very generously, journalist Liz McDougall ran a half-page story, ending with 'If anyone wants to assist the adventurers, phone Chris on …' But by the end of the day I'd had only two responses to the article, with a total of $20 in cheques apparently in the mail. I needed to do better than that. Liz encouraged me to apply for formal sponsorship with the Australian Geographic Society. I dismissed the idea as absurd— they sponsored real expeditions headed to places like Antarctica, not students going on an extended bushwalk. Partly to humour her, and partly to prove my point, I printed out a copy of the application form and read over the questions. 'Why is this project important to Australia?' I laughed dryly, and shoved it at the bottom of my ever growing pile of paperwork.

Not long after, I heard back from the South African, Andreas. He took Jasper and me to meet the managers of Aktiv8, the Australian importer of a range of high-profile outdoor equipment, including the brands Karrimor, Exped and Ortlieb. I brought with me a lengthy document I'd prepared detailing every aspect of our Tassie expedition—covering everything from the safety precautions we'd be taking, to how we planned to cross rivers, right down to our proposed dinner menu. Together we all chatted about it for some time.

The more the managers understood what we were intending to do, the more visibly worried they became. 'You do realise, for instance,' one began, 'that these rivers you'll have to cross won't be meandering streams. They will be fast-flowing, their banks will be steep and slippery—there will be no wading in, you'll have to hang off tree roots and drop into them and swim for your life. You'll have about 60 seconds to flounder to the far bank—hopefully without being swept onto submerged rocks—before hypothermia will start to set in …' They looked at us with genuine concern in their eyes.

'Umm, yes … we are aware of this,' we lied, trying to hide our alarm. We were asked to leave them for two hours while they thought it over. Jasper and I maintained our confident expressions until we were safely outside, and then gave each other a look that said, more plainly than words, 'Oh my God! What exactly are we getting ourselves into?'

Two hours later we walked back in. They told us up front that they had actually been trying to talk us out of the expedition from the start of our meeting, and they had been surprised at our (blind) confidence—so much so, that they had decided to sponsor us. 'If you're seriously going, then we're going to help you survive as best we can.' We smiled weakly.

They then proceeded to kit us out on the spot with everything they could think of from their warehouse. About an hour later we walked out grinning like idiots, both shouldering Karrimor's top-of-the-line 60-litre (expandable to 100-litre) hiking pack, stuffed absolutely full with everything from bedrolls and waterproof camera bags, to thermals and Karrimor clothing. We just couldn't stop smiling. The packs were next season's model—they were not even released in stores yet! In the space of a few hours we'd gone from two boys wanting to go on a hiking holiday to feeling like two explorers setting out on an epic expedition. It did wonders for our confidence and credibility, and I went home and filled in the sponsorship application for Australian Geographic and posted it off, along with applications to a number of other companies.

To our surprise and delight, our number of sponsors grew. Even Australian Geographic came on board, providing us with funds to buy a decent camera! Clearly either not enough people out there were asking for sponsorship that year, or we were getting ourselves into something much bigger than we realised.

We raided the local supermarket, totally clearing out their pasta and burrito-bread shelves, and put together our two airdrops of supplies. These would be flung unceremoniously out of an aircraft to hit a rocky beach at just over 100 kilometres per hour—unless they overshot the mark, in which case they would be stuck high out of reach in a tree, or worse, landing before the beach, out in the ocean. Needless to say, we went to some lengths to pack them carefully. Delicate supplies like bags of milk power were surrounded by a shield of pasta, which in turn hid behind a protective layer of muesli bars. We then waterproofed each bundle, smothered them in a layer of empty egg cartons to act as crumple zones, and wedged them into four separate 20-litre cardboard wine casks. All done, we sent them on ahead to Tassie by courier.

After three months of planning we found ourselves sitting in the car on the way to the airport, while we frantically stitched 'Australian Geographic' patches proudly onto our matching Karrimor pants. A boy behind us in the luggage check-in queue whispered just loud enough for us to hear: 'Wow, Mum, look—they're from Australian Geographic!' As our plane headed south to Tasmania we still couldn't quite believe all this was happening—we were embarking on a real expedition as professionally sponsored adventurers!

The first oversight in our planning was disregarding the fact that Strahan—where we'd booked a seaplane to fly us into the wilderness at 5 pm that very afternoon—was in fact quite a long way from Tasmania's Launceston airport, where we now stood. Armed with the knowledge that we couldn't afford the once-per-day bus—which had just left anyway—the plan had always been to hitchhike to Strahan. We stood beside the road and took turns, one holding out an Australian Geographic banner to catch the attention of passing motorists, while the other held out his thumb for a ride. It worked like a charm, and we scarcely had to wait between lifts. Nevertheless, the afternoon ticked on.

With about one hour before our seaplane was due to leave, we found ourselves crammed in the back of an old VW Kombi as the driver and passengers—some incredibly boisterous German backpackers hell-bent on getting us to Strahan on time—coaxed the old vehicle to attain speeds and noises I'm sure it was never designed to achieve. Between backfires, we hurtled ever onwards. 'Zis is ze town we were zinking of staying at tonight …' one backpacker commented. 'But … no … it looks iz no good …' the driver lied, barely glancing down the turn-off as we rocketed past.

Five o'clock came and went, and we were still more than an hour away. We had missed our flight. Once this fact had sunk in, the Germans apologetically deposited us on the roadside at Zeehan—the last major town before Strahan—turned around and drove off, presumably all the way back to their intended stopover.

Thankfully, the pilot was unconcerned when I finally got through to him via satellite phone. 'Don't worry about it, I'd prefer to fly you in the morning anyway.' Relief washed over me and, after enlisting the help of several more motorists, we arrived in Strahan late that night. The camping ground was chock-full, so we opted to set up camp in a park across the road, using a street sign to tie our tent to. Morning light revealed this street sign was in fact a large 'No Camping' sign. Hurriedly we packed up and sat in front of the Wilderness Air shed, trying to bring our laughter under control and regain serious explorer composure before our pilot appeared.

An hour later we were high in the air, following the coastline south to Port Davey—the same coastline that we'd hike back to Strahan. I suddenly noticed the pilot was intently studying a map which he'd draped over the steering wheel rather than watching where he was flying. Noticing my concerned glances, he leant over and, above the deafening roar of the engine, shouted into my ear, 'I'm not quite sure where I'm going. I've never flown into this remote area before. I do scenic joy-flights around Strahan.' I tightened my seatbelt still further.

About half an hour later, I gesticulated to a lake below and the pilot orchestrated a rather abrupt landing at our designated starting point near Port Davey. After the plane drifted into the shallows, we waded ashore with our packs and then stood watching the plane take off again and grow ever smaller in the sky until it was lost to sight.

This was it. That plane would now cover—in the space of about 40 minutes—the same journey that would ultimately take us 28 days of pure exertion. We posed for the traditional 'start of expedition' photo and then turned our attention to finding a way through the dense barrier of scrub that surrounded this lake, separating it from local grasslands we'd seen from the plane.

Confidently we strode right into the wall of scrub, only to find that it was alarmingly impenetrable just there. We withdrew, confidence still intact, and tried again 50 metres further along the lake's shore. It was particularly nasty just there also, if not even worse. Still ignoring the disheartening burden of reality, we tried a third location, to the same effect. 'Oh, I see … it's like that, is it?' Clearly, we'd just have to bite the bullet and fight our way through.

Out came the machete, and in we went. Prising apart the gnarled, tight branches in our faces, we'd hack, pull, bend or snap them down, firstly to waist height. From there we could get our knees into it and force the tangled mass down to a height we could climb onto, and trample down. Advancing this way 30 centimetres at a time, we gradually mined our tunnel into this wall of scrub and eventually struggled through to the 'grassland'. All I can say is that the 'grass' looked a lot shorter from the plane. It was, at times, above head height—well, above my head height, anyway, as Jasper enjoyed pointing out. Creeks were invisible until we unceremoniously fell through into them. Ground snakes slithered at eye-level. Come nightfall, it took a good hour to slash and trample the 'grass' low enough for us to set up our tent. Our arms and legs were lacerated by razor-grass, and our bodies ached in shock. Yet we were in the highest of spirits—this was, after all, what we came here for, an adventure that would challenge us.

Over the following 28 days Jasper and I were transformed from boys into young men. We learned a huge amount, and endured a great deal. At times the situation looked near hopeless. Every headland we came to we were faced with either trying to shuffle along the face of a sheer, slippery cliff that plunged directly into the thundering waves of the Southern Ocean below, or climbing up and fighting across an endless mass of 5-metre-high scrub on top. Whenever even remotely possible, we'd opt for the cliff face—which goes some way to revealing the horrors of the scrub lurking on top.

On one memorable occasion, when faced with having to inch our way several hundred metres inland to get around a narrow gulch, Jasper fought hard to try and convince me that the easiest option was to pick a lull in the churning waves, plunge in and swim across and try to climb up the other side before the next set of ocean waves roared through. It was lucky we did not attempt this, however, as a few days later we spotted an enormous shark fin cruising the shallows. Occasionally, rocks we grasped for support gave way—pulling right out of the cliff face like books from a bookshelf. Looking back on it, we were very lucky to have escaped some near-disasters with only minor cuts and scratches.

Tasmania's weather is notoriously wild, and with nowhere to go but onwards, we often found ourselves copping the full brunt of its unpredictability. A day might start out with a crisp, clear blue sky, yet by lunchtime we could be being lashed by heavy, near horizontal, frigid rain and even hail.

To make matters worse, we were constantly—and increasingly—hungry. I had made the fundamental mistake of underestimating the effect of hard work on our appetites, and we'd brought only about the same amount of food as we'd consumed each day on the Overland Track. After 28 days on this near-starvation diet, we came out looking like suitable candidates for World Vision sponsorship: sunken eyes, hollow cheeks, the lot. There were times when we tried to catch seagulls to eat, and pad out our evening meals with whatever we could find—minuscule shells we'd scraped from the rocks at low tide, even tiny fish, barely 10 centimetres in length, that we'd somehow caught with our hands in a rock pool.

It certainly wasn't all bad, though. Sometimes, for example, we'd find ourselves walking along seemingly endless kilometres of pristine beach. Looking back over my shoulder, I'd gaze at our two pairs of footsteps trailing off into the distance until they were lost in the sun's reflection off the wet sand. We were truly free—free to pick our own route, our own campsites, and our own challenges. At times like this as we plodded along, our minds were also freed, and I found myself thinking of nothing and everything—of life, and what really mattered. At home our minds are always so busy with things to do that we don't often get a chance to deeply explore our thoughts. I felt fantastic, experiencing greatly amplified versions of those same feelings I had found so attractive on our earlier hiking holiday. Out there, where decisions suddenly had very real and potentially life-threatening consequences, I felt so much more alive. All my senses became more acute, taking everything in—I could hear the slightest noise in the distance, and detect the faintest whiff of drying kelp washed up on the shore, sometimes several bays ahead.

Unfortunately, sometimes our superhuman sense of smell worked against us. On Day 22 we found ourselves holding our burning noses as we gazed out over a particularly gruesome sight. The shorelines of the next two bays were strewn with the decomposing bodies of 110 long-finned pilot whales and 50 bottlenose dolphins, in a rare mixed-species stranding that had occurred a month or so earlier. Those images will stay with me for a long time, as will the memory of how impossible it is to hike with a heavy backpack—while trying not to breathe.

The same day we stumbled upon on a colony of Australian fur seals, complete with young pups. Conveying this find to marine scientists at the CSIRO later, we were told that unless these pups were freak births, we had potentially discovered the world's most southerly breeding colony of these playful seals. All other known breeding colonies were several hundred kilometres north, in Bass Strait. To my delight, our findings were included in an official population and distribution report for the species.

Returning home from that expedition, I immersed myself in all the various 'post-expedition' tasks with enthusiasm. First there were over 300 photos on transparency film to develop, scan, colour-balance and crop. Then came the first opportunity to try out my writing skills—a two-page article in *Australian Geographic*, a few newspaper articles, and I even had an eight-page article translated into French and published overseas! This, I was sure, was going somewhere.

Public speaking was the next challenge, as the Australian Geographic Society had invited us to present a lecture to the paying public at their Sydney headquarters. To put it mildly, neither Jasper nor I enjoyed public speaking at school, but we soon learned that if you're speaking on a topic that you're genuinely enthusiastic about it's actually kinda fun, and our talk—including an amusing demonstration of how an adventurer (that would be me) has to fight with a machete through a wall of scrub (warily played by Jasper)—was very well received. Other smaller speeches soon followed, including my giving the Valedictory Speech at my old high school for their Year 12 graduation ceremony—a precursor to the talk I did a year later when Dad overheard my Greenland plans. I tapped the microphone and began: 'Well, a few weeks ago when I was invited to give the Valedictory Speech here tonight, I have to admit, I didn't even know what "Valedictory" meant. After asking around, it seems it's supposed to be when someone old and famous returns to their high school and talks about their life. I am obviously neither old nor famous, and in fact I was sitting where you are, just three short years ago.' It served to highlight the fact that there's no time like the present to chase your dreams. It was to be the first of many 'motivational talks' that I would give.

Our biggest post-expedition surprise came when Australian Geographic informed us that we were to be awarded their prestigious 'Young Adventurer of the Year' award for 2004, labelling our trek 'One of the toughest foot journeys in the world'! We were flown down to Melbourne for the award ceremony on 9 June 2004, and we got our first real taste of mainstream media attention. We somehow survived an interview for TV and bluffed our way through our first live-to-air ABC radio interview. We thought the expedition was pretty scary at times—but I promise you, it all paled in comparison to doing a live interview. The only thing more terrifying than a live radio interview is a live TV interview, and luckily I'd have to wait for my next adventure before facing that horror.

During the ceremony, seeing our names and images displayed up there beside well-known adventurers who had been to the South Pole in home-made planes, or who had hauled sleds there on skis, felt incredibly surreal, and even a bit fraudulent. When it was over, the clouds we were walking on eventually led us back to the hotel room that Australian Geographic had paid for. At 21 years old, I had never actually spent a night in a hotel before—my 'holidays' had always involved tents. I lay on the bed scribbling idly away on the two complimentary sheets of letter paper beside the phone. I could get used to this, I decided. There must be some way of making a career out of adventuring.

Make a living out of adventuring: far, far easier said than done. For the remainder of 2004, my third year at university (although I had been so wrapped up in post-expedition work that I scarcely noticed), I pondered this problem. There were many potential sources of income from adventuring—writing articles and books, selling photographs, public speaking, or even making documentary films on my travels. I felt it would be hard to earn a decent living from any of these individual avenues, so instead I started practising them all. In this way, I convinced myself that there was a dim light at the end of the dreaded 'office-work' tunnel—or more correctly, a faint 'exit' light flashing before the tunnel ever really began.

Keen to experience some cold-climate hiking, I teamed up with another mate of mine, Karl Toppler, and he came with me back to the Overland Track, this time in July 2004, right in the middle of the harshest winter Tasmania had experienced in 25 years. The trip was just awesome. There was virtually no one else on the trail—just us and our toes. I mention our toes as a separate entity because there were times when they were so numb from cold that I seriously doubted they were still attached. At times I took my boots off to empty out what honestly felt like a rock in between my toes, only to discover that it was in fact just one of my senseless toes rubbing on those beside it. This hike served as my introduction to sub-zero expeditions, and I fell in love with the concept at once—numb toes and all. I was really keen to take the experience further—to try something longer and colder. The problem was, however, that not all of my friends were as enthusiastic as I was.

It was an uncanny coincidence, then, that within a few weeks of deciding I wanted to try something more extreme, Clark's initial 'Proposition' email had found its way into my inbox.

# PREPARATIONS, PAC BUILDING AND SPONSORS

Clark and I were going to need a hell of a lot more sponsorship for our Arctic expedition than I'd managed to get for Tasmania, but at least this time around I had better contacts and the credibility of an Australian Geographic award, as well as several very positive 'sponsorship reference letters' to slip into the back of our ever growing Expedition Document.

Before we could start chasing sponsors, however, we still had one or two minor details to sort out. For a start, we hadn't yet found a suitable kayak for which we could build wheels. I unfolded our plans to a local kayak manufacturer, and he shook his head. 'Nah. Listen, if you go putting 75 kilograms in each end of a kayak—even the strongest Kevlar-reinforced ones—stick it on a pair of wheels and bounce it across 1000 kilometres of tundra, it's just gonna tear in half!' I chose to ignore him, and presented my plans to another kayak outlet. By the third shop I was starting to detect a pattern, and as I slunk home, I began to worry about what this meant.

That night, Dad, being a mad-keen boat builder, cheerfully voiced what I dared not. 'Well, you'll just have to make your own kayaks then, I guess.'

'No. No way,' I retorted. Clark and I were already drowning under our still-growing To-Do lists—we had no time for this. I counted on my fingers. It was currently April 2005, so we still had May ... and ... yeah. May. It was going to take all of June to send whatever kayaks we chose to Canada by cargo ship, and July was our start date. So, what, we had about seven weeks to come up with a design, get the materials together and build two of the world's strongest kayaks in our garage ...

'Make it out of aluminium, it'll probably only take a few weekends' work in the garage,' Dad said reassuringly. It's true, we did have a remarkably well-equipped garage after all my parents' yacht-building.

'All right, I guess so,' I agreed, adding 'building kayaks' to the list. It wasn't like we had a choice.

Clark and I stared vacantly at my crude sketch of a kayak, unsure of quite how to begin. 'So, we're looking at each needing to float about 170 kilograms of food and equipment …' I started.

'And our weight on top of that,' Clark pointed out.

'Oh, yeah. That's a good point.' I drew a stick figure seated in the cockpit, and waited for further inspiration. That familiar feeling of biting off more than we could chew descended around us. A simplistic hull-design program from the internet allowed me to calculate the buoyancy of various contorted 'yacht' hulls, the front half of which vaguely resembled a kayak—at least it was pointed. Transporting objects longer than 4 metres starts to get difficult as well as expensive, so that defined our length. As for the width, I sat on a bench seat in the garden, and—using a grass-rake as a mock paddle—worked out how wide a kayak could be before paddling became impractical. The last important factor—the height—was simply determined by the displacement we needed to keep the whole contraption afloat under the load, with enough spare deck-height so waves wouldn't just roll over us, but not so much that windage would be a problem. After a week or so playing with curves and buoyancies in my 'spare time', I came up with something that looked like it'd do the trick.

Jumping the gun a little, without a completed Expedition Document, we rushed out a makeshift sponsorship proposal to every sizeable aluminium outlet in Australia. To our great joy, Alcoa—the world's largest aluminium company—became our very first sponsor, delivering us all the aluminium we needed, including doing special production runs of extra-long sheets so we could make the hulls from one strip. 'That wasn't even a polished sponsorship proposal we sent out!' Clark grinned. It certainly was encouraging, and spurred us on to start harassing companies for major sponsorship. We just had a few details to fill in first.

One of these was what to do about the very real threat posed by polar bears. Being Australian, the idea of having to keep an eye out for hunting predators while going bushwalking was completely foreign to us. No matter how disconcerting animal noises can sound right outside your tent at night, you can always snuggle deeper into your sleeping bag and ignore it—it's probably just a kangaroo. Unfortunately, this 'she'll be right, mate' attitude wouldn't work so well for us up in the Arctic. The idea of sleeping with only point-nothing of a millimetre of tent fabric between me and the world's largest land carnivore—the only species of bear that actively hunts humans—was worrying to say the least. Alarmingly, polar bears can and do smell out people—sometimes from over 10 kilometres away—and hunt them down while they sleep, ultimately exploding through the side of the tent onto its unsuspecting occupants. To try and prevent this, or at least give us some warning, I designed a perimeter tripwire alarm system that we'd use each night. Basically this involved hammering in four stakes around the tent, between which we'd run our string tripwire that plugged into a simple circuit. When a bear (or, more commonly, one of us stumbling out to the toilet at night) bumped into this string, the plug would be yanked out, and an ungodly scream would be unleashed from a 110-decibel siren. While hopefully scaring the bear too, the main purpose of this alarm was to wake us up with enough time to defend ourselves.

So what then? After you leap from the tent to confront a bear that can stand a horrifying 4.3 metres tall—that's tall enough to look into a second-storey window, or to look you square in the face when it's standing on all fours—what do you do then? People kept pointing out to us that while they may look big and cumbersome, polar bears can actually run at speeds of up to about 40 kilometres per hour—there was no way I would be able to outrun one. They were missing the point, though: I wouldn't need to outrun the bear—I just had to outrun Clark. Still, there had to be better options, and we spent considerable time researching them.

Most of the Canadian Government texts online recommended that 'when a bear approaches too close, get back into your vehicle and drive away'. Not a lot of help when the nearest car would be hundreds of kilometres away. Failing that, they recommend that you run downhill, because polar bears have relatively short front legs and apparently can't run down a slope. Hmm, yeah—not a great deal of help either, considering Victoria Island would mostly be completely flat. At last we came upon some practical solutions. We'd each carry a can of 'bear spray'—similar to the pepper-mace used by the police, but with a range of up to 9 metres. A nose full of this deters most grizzly bears, but some hungry polar bears have been known to be alarmingly persistent, and have even been reported to enjoy licking off this chilli-dressing before trying again! Still, it was worth carrying.

Polar bears primarily hunt seals, and mostly catch them as they surface at their limited set of breathing holes through the frozen ocean. In summer, however, the surface melts into countless cracks and openings, and the seals are no longer restricted in their breathing locations. This makes life hard for the bears—no longer able to simply lie in wait at a hole, they are now forced to either follow the receding ice northwards, or come ashore and wait out the summer on land, getting hungrier and hungrier. Come the end of summer, these hungry bears congregate on the coastline waiting for the ocean to freeze over once again. Unfortunately for us, this meant the only bears we'd be likely to come across in our summer traverse would be incredibly hungry ones, possibly having not eaten in months. We'd need something to back up our cans of sweet chilli sauce spray.

The ceaseless tap-tap-tapping of keyboards around me at my work placement continued on into lunchtime. I, on the other hand, had been counting down the seconds. 12:29:59 ... 12:30:00. Lunch break. I picked up the phone.

'Good afternoon, my name's Chris, I'm from Australia. I was just wondering how best to defend myself against a polar bear.'

In the workstation cubicle opposite mine, the tap-tap-tapping stopped.

'A twelve-gauge, pump-action shotgun loaded with solid-slug bullets? Fair enough. Thanks.'

I dialled another number.

'Hi, I hear you've done a bit of hunting up in the Arctic? ... Do you know what colour polar bears' eyes reflect when you shine a torch at them in the dark? ... When my bear tripwire goes off at night, it'd be good to know if that's a bear coming at the tent, or just a curious muskox!'

Feeling more than a little self-conscious, I glanced around the deafeningly silent office. I couldn't help grinning at the bewildered expressions of my co-workers, and I continued as quietly as I could.

'A bright white-ish colour, okay, and wolves are orange. And muskox? Green. Okay, great. Thanks very much.'

'White-ish,' I echoed, typing one of the few remaining pieces of the puzzle into our Expedition Document.

The keen interest from the adventure community began to beg the obvious question: has this ever been attempted before? Could it be a world first? Claims like this are often more than a little subjective, I find—I mean, if you define what you're doing specifically enough, the chances are that yes, you probably are the first person in the history of humankind to walk from here to there, following your precisely wandering route. Failing that, you're probably 'the first ever Sydney-born Australian, under the age of 25, who grew up on a yacht' to attempt it. Amusingly, you do hear claims almost as absurd as this from time to time. Why do people bother with such trivial statements? Largely because most sponsors want media exposure, and the media aren't interested in something that has already been done before—it has to be 'new' to be 'news'. Conveniently for us, what we were attempting was absurd enough that the chances of anyone else having ever bothered to try were pretty slim.

We set to work researching the history of the island. It had been visited by some polar greats—Amundsen was there in 1903, and Sir John Franklin visited before he and his men all perished on their infamous, ill-fated expedition to locate the Northwest Passage. Actually, what happened to the Franklin Expedition was one of the most celebrated mysteries of the nineteenth century. His incredibly high-profile expedition, complete with sailing ships HMS *Erebus* and *Terror*, seemingly vanished off the face of the earth in 1845. Many subsequent expeditions were sent out in search of Franklin, and eventually some remains and personal effects—including evidence that the team were driven to cannibalism in their final days—were found at various locations, including on King William Island, just to the east of Victoria Island. It is now believed that the expedition likely wintered on the eastern coastline of Victoria Island as their ships drifted, bound by pack ice in McClintock Channel. It was even possible, locals said excitedly, that we might discover proof of this—caches perhaps, artefacts, even scribbled notes—which would be historically invaluable. We wasted no time in adding that to our 'Interesting aspects of the expedition' section of our document.

So, our island had been visited by early explorers, the Inuit of course lived there for thousands of years, and in the present day there are two small permanent communities on the island: Cambridge Bay and Holman. However, much to our excitement, our research indicated that our route would take us through whole regions probably never before seen by human eyes. Even the local Inuit elders agreed, saying that there was no evidence of their ancestors ever having visited such areas, and they would have had little reason to do so, being away from the caribou migration routes and other resources which the Inuit traditionally followed. Certainly, they would not have tried something as pointless as crossing the whole island from coast to coast in one hit. Despite ever-increasing diamond survey sites from mining prospectors advancing across the island, much of it remains virtually unexplored from the ground, and most map data is derived from aerial measurements. For some form of official confirmation on a newsworthy 'world first' status, I approached the prestigious international Explorers Club, based in New York.

Founded in 1904, the 3000-odd members of this exclusive club have been responsible for many of the world's most famous expeditions. Chaired at the time by Sir Edmund Hillary (who, together with fellow Explorers Club member Tenzing Norgay, was the first to reach the summit of Mount Everest in 1953), other members past and present include the first person to reach the North Pole (Robert Peary in 1909), the first to the South Pole (Roald Amundsen in 1911), the first to the deepest part of the ocean (Jacques Piccard and Don Walsh in 1960) and even the first to the surface of the moon (Neil Armstrong and Buzz Aldrin in 1969). The club's research division pondered my question for a few days, and ultimately informed me that, no, as far as they knew, no one had ever attempted something even remotely similar to our proposed expedition. Bingo! I opened our document: 'Edit' ... 'Search & Replace' ... 'Expedition' with '*World-First* Expedition'. The email from the Explorers Club didn't stop there, however; they suggested that with my background, I apply for membership. It really was an honour, and I wasted no time sending in my application. A few weeks later I got a phone call informing me that I had just been elected as their newest member—by far the youngest of the 30 members in Australia, and the second-youngest in the club worldwide! I felt like a total impostor—absolutely amazed that they accepted me—but it certainly added to the credibility and prestige of our expedition, and I proudly entered it into our now almost complete Expedition Document.

The final touch required coming up with an interesting name for our journey, and an accompanying logo. We agonised over this seemingly trivial detail for days, coming up with every cheesy name under the sun. The sun, as it turned out, was actually the deciding factor in the end. I worked out we'd experience just over 1000 hours of perpetual daylight on our trip before the sun first dipped briefly below the horizon, and so we christened our undertaking 'The 1000 Hour Day Expedition'. The logo simply became the silhouette of a stick figure hauling the words '1000 Hour Day' over some 'tundra' that was formed by the sentence 'Unsupported across Victoria Island—the High Arctic'. We proudly printed our logo onto every document we could find, and that was that.

Over the following days, a total of 56 large, imposing manila envelopes found their way onto the desks of marketing managers all around Australia, and even several offices overseas. Our love–hate relationship with 'The Document' now spanned 48 concise colour pages comb-bound with a black cover. We hoped it would have been a pretty formidable sight as it slid out of its envelope along with a sponsorship proposal uniquely tailored for each company. But would it do the trick? Was it enough? Some of these companies receive literally dozens of requests for sponsorship every single week.

Back at home, Clark and I held our breaths. Absolutely everything depended on what these companies decided over the next few weeks. Everything. It was genuinely terrifying, especially as we'd already spent far more money than we had between us, and were now sinking handfuls of money into building our wheeled kayaks, or PACs (our acronym for Paddleable Amphibious Carts), with every passing day. We were pretty stressed, and on top of all this pandemonium, I was still engaged in full-time work placement, and Clark's first batch of university exams were hurtling towards him at an alarming rate.

The days merged into one continuous blur of delirium, punctuated only by the occasional moment where time stood still—when the post arrived each day. They were easy to spot—the replies to our sponsorship proposals—neat little envelopes branded cleanly with the company logo. 'Nestlé', 'Nike' or 'Cadbury', for example. They looked so innocent lying there on the kitchen table, but the sight of them struck fear into our hearts. What if they said no? Pretending we didn't really care, we'd leave them as long as we could, and then eventually cave in and tear them open:

*Dear Mr Bray,*

*I would like to thank you for your proposal to [name of company], offering us the opportunity to support your 1000 Hour Day project.*

*As you will appreciate, [name of company] receive many requests for sponsorship and support and we have had to develop strict guidelines by which these submissions are evaluated.*

*...*

*It is always difficult for us to decline opportunities such as the one you offer and we appreciate the time and effort taken to contact us. Unfortunately our sponsorship budget and resources are fully commited and we are unable to assist on this occasion.*

'Yeah, oh well,' Clark muttered, reading over my shoulder. 'We never really expected *them* to agree.' Rejection letter followed rejection letter, and we laughed them all off, trying not to see the obvious trend.

'Of course we're getting all the "No"s first,' I said, trying to maintain confidence. 'The ones that *are* interested will take longer, they'll have to run it past higher management.'

'Yeah, I guess. Come on, let's get back to work on the kayaks,' Clark mumbled, 'your dad's already out there.'

On weekdays, I'd come home from work, change my claustrophobic business attire for something more practical and head straight into the garage where our PACs were gradually taking form. It was a painful and slow process. Our hands were lacerated by jagged metal edges, punctured by broken-off pop-rivets, and smeared with Sikaflex sealant which—even after scrubbing with turps and steel wool until our eyes watered—never quite washed off. During the week, my dad would help out too, devoting countless hours in the garage. Clark would work with us all weekend, every weekend, and all three of us gave it everything we had, trying desperately to get them finished in time.

A typical day would see us wake early and deal with quieter To-Do tasks until 9 am, by which time we figured our neighbours would be up, allowing us to return to noisily cutting, grinding, drilling, riveting, welding and hammering our PACs together. Breaking only for hasty meals we'd be back out there again, even after dinner. Just as delirium set in around 10 pm, my mum would invariably appear with mugs of hot chocolate and lovingly baked muffins to keep up morale. Long after everyone else had gone to sleep Clark and I kept at it, trying to be as quiet as we could, until, CLANG!—one of us would accidentally drop something noisily against the enormous metal war-gong that was our PAC hull. Seconds later a bleary-eyed Dad would swing open the garage door and command, 'Christopher! That's quite enough! We need to get some sleep, and so do our neighbours!' We'd then slink inside and busy ourselves again with the silent To-Do's until the wee hours of the morning. When finally we could no longer keep our eyes open even with coffee, we'd sleep like dead men for as little as three or four hours before our alarm clock would jerk us back to life, ready for another day of the same. We just couldn't keep this up. Despite our herculean effort, we were falling further behind schedule each day—at the current rate the last possible cargo ship would leave for Canada weeks before the PACs would be finished. It was hopeless—we were fighting against a deadline that we just could not meet. We simply couldn't work any faster, or sleep any less.

Slumped forward in my chair at work, I didn't hear my boss stride up to my cubicle. 'Chris?' I jumped, my eyes focused, and my mind—which had been a squillion miles away—now wound itself back to the present.

'Hi. Oh … ummm … AutoCAD drawings, where was I? I finished them, that's right. Do you have more?'

I'd been caught napping on the job, and we both knew it. However, he kindly pretended not to notice, and continued, 'Chris, as promised I asked management if they'd sponsor your trip, but apparently they can only sponsor teams, not individuals, I'm sorry.' This was a common catch, and I nodded in understanding.

'However,' my boss went on, 'I may be able to help you in another way.' I looked up, eyebrows raised. 'Would some time off work help?'

I could have hugged him—right then, time was even more valuable than money. 'You've done more than enough AutoCAD drawings,' he said. 'We'll call if we need you to come in next week.' When my expression revealed just how much this meant, he added, 'Actually, you can go home now if you want.' The dull glow of hope that had nearly extinguished inside me now burst back into flames, and I was out the door even before my computer had finished logging off.

'Yes?' My neighbour came to his front door. 'Oh, Chris, hello! Come in, what can I do for you?'

I didn't have time to beat around the bush. 'I'm really sorry to have to ask you this, but would you mind putting up with a bit of late-night garage noise for the next week or two?' A faintly pained look flashed through his eyes. Come to think of it, his eyes looked almost as bleary as mine. Perhaps I should have asked this question several weeks earlier.

'No, no. That'll be okay,' he replied. 'I read about it in the paper the other day, actually—extraordinary. Good on you.'

Left with no excuse to down tools even as midnight came and went, Dad, Clark and I redoubled our efforts, and various friends started dropping around to lend a hand. Ever so gradually, the idea of getting the PACs finished in time began to creep back into the realms of possibility. I skimmed over the final few days' schedule Dad had put together:

*29 May—Build and install seat and handles for PAC no. 2, test both hulls for leaks;*

*30 May—Sand and paint both PACs (today cargo ship starts loading in Sydney);*

*31 May—Build hauling yoke for both PACs, load our supplies being sent by ship and* ~~build wooden crate for kayaks~~ *just wrap PACs in bubble-wrap;*

*1 June—Hire truck and drive PACs to shipping office before 10 am cut-off.*

Clark tapped the grubby sheet of paper. 'That's what I like to see— confidence. I see your dad didn't leave any time for "fix any leaks in hulls after testing".'

He was right—this impossibly crammed schedule left absolutely no time for anything going wrong. Still, some hope was better than no hope, and we gulped the dregs of our third cup of coffee and reached for the pop-rivet gun.

While the hull of PAC #2 started to take shape on the 3D scaffolding of frames we'd constructed, we continued working on the details of PAC #1 we'd recently pulled off the frames: seats; watertight bulkheads; hatches; the wheel system; even fitting a stainless-steel wear strip along the bottom to help protect it from abrasion. My mum sewed together waterproof 'skirts' that sealed the cockpit opening when we sat inside, and also sewed sling holsters in which we'd suspend each shotgun in a convenient 'gun-hatch' behind our seat. The theory was that even when kayaking, we could reach back and rip open this hatch that led into the cavernous aft section of the PAC, right where the shotgun would be hanging, ready to be slid out at a moment's notice. James Bond, eat your heart out.

The next day, although utterly exhausted physically and mentally, we were given reason to smile. W.L. Gore—makers of world-famous Gore-Tex and Windstopper outdoor fabrics—had agreed to sponsor us. We could not believe our luck. At $2000 a pop, we had not been looking forward to forking out for the Gore-Tex Immersion Technology Drysuits we needed for Arctic paddling, but capsizing in ice-strewn water could be fatal without them. 'Consider the suits taken care of,' Isabel, the company's marketing manager had told us. 'And we'll organise a meeting with our boot-fitting expert in the city—he'll find you the very best hiking boots available, no expense spared.'

Finally, all those months of living in denial—forcing ourselves to believe that this expedition really was inexplicably still going to happen somehow, and completely emptying both our life savings— were starting to pay off. Our list of sponsors began to grow, and we suddenly found ourselves at the helm of what was shaping up to be an almighty adventure. Of the 56 sponsorship proposals we sent out, unbelievably, over twenty of them agreed to back us. Among these, the Australian Geographic Society gave us a particularly valuable cheque, Air Canada agreed to cover our airfares, and Ocean Frontiers—the not-for-profit youth adventure organisation started by well-known Aussie adventurers Don and Margie McIntyre—became our naming sponsor. Thus the 'Ocean Frontiers 1000 Hour Day Expedition' was born.

> It is our belief that expeditions of this scale and vision promote the spirit of adventure … We feel that such adventures are vital to the development of a strong national character.
> Yours sincerely
> Rory Scott
> Managing Director, Australian Geographic

Having endorsements like this gave us enormous credibility and enabled us to attract more big names. Nir—the manager of the outdoor gear importer Aktiv8 that equipped Jasper and me for Tasmania—was as eager as ever to help this time around. In what must have looked like a well-orchestrated robbery in broad daylight, I walked around the whole store, while Nir followed closely behind dragging a huge cardboard box. Anything I pointed at on the shelf was thrown into the overflowing box—over twenty Ortlieb drybags of various colours, shapes and sizes, Exped sleeping mats, two more Karrimor backpacks, and even their best tent—an Exped Orion Extreme. 'And, Chris, the sleeping bags and camera bags will come in soon … I'll send them,' Nir assured me. As bewildered customers looked on, I thanked him and proceeded to waltz out the door with the box, without paying.

We had a lot to celebrate as far as sponsorship was concerned, and we still had another month to fish for more, but right now—as my dad bluntly reminded us just as we started to congratulate ourselves—we only had one week left to get the PACs finished, and at the current rate, 'It's just not going to happen, Christopher!' Each evening revealed we'd only achieved half the day's scheduled work, and were forced to divide the remaining tasks between the dwindling number of days left. It was a nightmare. When I found I could count on one hand the days remaining, a sickening fear squeezed us all into overdrive. Suffice to say that the three of us fitted several weeks' hard work into the space of a few days.

Forty-eight hours before the cargo ship was due to depart, we heaved both alarmingly heavy PACs next door, placing them beside our neighbour's swimming pool. 'Shall we see if they float?' It was a critical moment. We gingerly lowered one in, and let it go. Miraculously, it didn't spin upside down and plunge straight to the bottom. Actually, it didn't even list to one side. I gave it a dubious shove from behind, and that familiar sheepish grin—the expression that comes from realising we'd just somehow pulled off yet another miracle—spread across my face as the PAC slid effortlessly through the water to the other side, just like a real kayak. I hopped in, and to my delight the craft was incredibly stable—the car tyres on either side acted like outriggers! A wave of relief and pride flooded over us.

Then I noticed the leaks. There was a pool of water forming in the bow, and it was getting bigger. There was also water collecting in the stern.

I sat inside each PAC in turn, while Clark and Dad proceeded to press down hard at each end, forcing any leaks to reveal themselves in a jet of incoming water. 'There it is!' Clark's finger pointed accusingly to where water was spilling in around a faulty pop-rivet.

'And over there,' Dad added. 'And ... and ... there's one back here, too.'

My mind reeled. This was bad. In fact, for a second there, I couldn't even think of anything mildly reassuring to say in our traditional 'she'll be right' style. Wait—yes, I could. 'Well, we haven't painted them yet, that'll fill in any little holes ...'

'Yes, that's true.' We all agreed.

We heaved them back into the garage and smeared a little extra sealant around. There wasn't even time to re-test them, or, far more worryingly, to see if they floated at all when loaded with the anticipated 170 kilograms of food and equipment—we'd just have to hope for the best.

That evening I uploaded a few images onto our expedition webpage <www.1000HourDay.com> which I'd somehow found the time to build and maintain over the months, preparing it for the live updates we'd be sending back from the Arctic every few days via satellite. I didn't think anyone was watching our site, but the next morning the local newspaper printed a photo of me testing the PACs, along with a brief story informing all of northern Sydney that the PACs had officially been 'declared watertight'! They certainly weren't my words, but hey, I always believe what I read in the paper, so it was a big relief to read that we must have imagined the leaks.

There was now only one minor detail left—building the hauling system—and we had a good half afternoon left to do it. We made the hauling fork out of aluminium angle, attached it to the bow, and ceremoniously rolled the first completed PAC out of the garage. Our neighbours hurried over to squint blearily at the result of all the late-night noise. With the pressure of an assembled audience, we prepared ourselves for the first ever attempt at PAC hauling. Their youngest son Tom—four years old—volunteered to mimic the 170 kilograms we'd load into each PAC, and leapt into the cockpit seat. I shouldered my harness, and took a few tentative steps. Nothing fell apart—definitely a good sign. I strode the full length of the driveway. Tom was loving it, and his dad made some amusing comment about Clark and me having chariot races out on the island. I wasn't laughing, though—I was too busy trying to catch my breath, and also staring, hypnotised, at the way the hauling fork bent and flexed as I leant forward. It actually looked like it was about to break. Oh, well, the Arctic wilderness would undoubtedly be flatter and smoother than our paved driveway. Wouldn't it?

Celebrations were put on hold as we spent that final evening in the garage completely rebuilding the hauling arm. To my horror, Dad dug out an excessively thick, heavy square section of metal tube from under the house. 'We don't have anything else. This'll just have to do,' he said, as I stood there gaping in dismay. 'All the hardware shops are shut.' He looked me square in the eyes. 'You have run out of time, Christopher.'

Several hours later we bolted on a hauling arm that looked like it was designed to restrain a bullock, and declared the PACs—at long last—complete. Through drooping, twitching eyelids, we shoved them full of all the gear we didn't want to have to bring with us on the plane in a month's time, such as tools and buoyancy vests, and then in a scene reminiscent of Shelob's lair in *The Lord of the Rings*, we suspended each PAC from the garage roof, and wound each in 50 metres of bubble-wrap. 'To: Cambridge Bay,

Nunavut, Canada—Ocean Frontiers 1000 Hour Day Expedition.'
I patted the sticker down, and went to bed.

About 30 minutes later it was morning, and we trucked our two mummified PACs to the shipping handlers and watched wide-eyed as a forklift scuttled hurriedly over, levelling its prongs only at the last second so they slid *underneath* our PACs rather than plunging right through their sides. 'Oh, wouldn't that have sucked ...' Clark whispered, grinning.

There was champagne that night, and for the first time in recent memory I allowed myself a decent sleep-in the next morning. The previous month had been so incredibly harrowing, but not only had we learned innumerable metalworking skills, we'd shown that Clark and I got on very well together, even under times of immense stress. We'd need this teamwork to survive out in the Arctic—countless expeditions have set out with teams made up of childhood best friends, only to come back with those rock-solid friendships in tatters. Considering Clark and I didn't even know each other before deciding to embark on this trip, discovering we seemed to get along okay was very reassuring.

# THE COUNTDOWN

Four weeks. That was all the time we had left, now that the PACs were on the ship, to get this expedition together. There was still an enormous amount of work to be done—building those kayaks was only supposed to be a side task—'a few weekends' work in the garage'. We could see that we weren't going to get everything ticked off, so 'prioritising' was the word that first weekend, and a few things quickly filtered to the top of the list.

It was to be a very high-tech expedition—loaded with state-of-the-art High Definition video cameras (virtually unheard of in early 2005), a handheld chartplotter GPS, two satellite phones, digital SLR camera, even a laptop. We'd need a small power station to keep them all charged—or an incredibly long extension cord. We'd already decided solar panels were the obvious solution—the low temperatures and 24-hour sunlight suited them perfectly. The problem with traditional solar panels, of course, is that they are incredibly delicate, encased under a huge sheet of glass. Funded by the University of New South Wales' school of photovoltaics, we opted to buy a revolutionary technology—panels that could literally be rolled up. To my alarm, however, by the time I tried to order the four 32-watt panels that I'd seen advertised earlier, the US military had taken over the company and purchased all stocks worldwide. Miraculously, a chain of frantic phone calls revealed four 'cosmetically damaged' but otherwise perfectly functional panels hiding in reserve in Australia, under the guard of a sympathetic importer.

Luck, we started to realise, was increasingly massing on our side. The harder we tried to overcome insurmountable odds, the more people seemed to come out of the woodwork to help us. This is a phenomenon eloquently summarised by Paulo Coelho in his book *The Alchemist*: 'When you want something, all the universe conspires in helping you achieve it.' This—as it turned out—was one of the biggest life lessons we were to learn over the coming years.

Things were also starting to look up in the documentary film department. At the rather fancy annual dinner for the Australian division of the Explorers Club, good fortune seated me next to Sue—an interesting woman who seemed to have unlimited energy. Over a traditional glass of port—handed around on a silver platter, no less—she explained that she worked for one of Australia's largest independent production houses. 'We produce a lot of documentaries for Discovery Channel,' she said, passing me her card. 'I think they'd be very interested in your adventure.'

My thoughts were interrupted as a man stood in front of me and extended his hand. 'I'm Dick Smith, very pleased to meet you, Chris.' The evening just got better and better—although I still felt like an impostor being part of this club, I was making invaluable contacts.

With less than a week left to go, Clark and I did a lightning trip into the city to buy some last-minute equipment. I pinned my phone on my shoulder and answered it as I slid my credit card across the counter in exchange for some polycarbonate unbreakable camping cutlery.

It was Sue. 'I've just got off the phone with Discovery Channel in Washington, and they are keen for us to get a contract with you guys. Have you worked out an asking price?' she asked. We had. I crossed my fingers, and told her. Her silence either meant I was asking far too much, or far too little. 'I'm sorry, Chris, that's just not going to happen. I was imagining more like a third of that!'

A *third?!* I was devastated, but decided to hold firm. 'Well, this is a pretty expensive expedition, and that's the figure we've come up with ...' Sue indicated she'd be too embarrassed to even ask Discovery for that much, and the conversation came to an awkward end.

The next day she called me back. 'All right, Discovery agreed to it,' she said. We were ecstatic. 'We'll need to spend a day doing some pre-expedition filming with you boys, though,' she added.

And so, with our 'Very High' priority To-Do list still spanning several pages, Clark and I found ourselves—with only four days left—standing perfectly motionless on my local beach, while a five-man camera crew, complete with director and assistant, started off the day with several takes of what they called the 'hero' shot—us staring blankly out to sea, trying to pretend we weren't going blind looking directly into the sun. The next humiliation consisted of us having to lie side by side in some old sleeping bags, directly on the public beach. Why? I can't imagine. 'You're bringing 16 kilos of chocolate?! This is great, we'll film a close-up of you guys stuffing yourself with chocolate as fast as you can.' Unfortunately they weren't joking. After suffering that embarrassment we were filmed dragging our truck tyre along the beach again and again while they got it just right.

'What else do you do to keep fit?' the director asked. Between gasps, Clark mentioned that indoor rock-climbing was a hobby. 'Oh, hey, I know what'd be awesome …' We shot a nervous glance at each other. 'We'll film you rock-climbing, towing the truck tyre up the wall behind you! Do you do that? Is that possible?' We explained that no, it was not. And so the day progressed.

More than a little concerned at exactly what kind of documentary they had planned for us, we were also starting to really panic about all the things we still had to do in the next three days. We didn't even have our sleeping bags yet—we were still waiting for our two Exped waterproof goose-down ones to be imported from Switzerland! Also, the second of our two $1000 submersible Ortlieb camera bags was still in Germany! Shit! Shit! And here we were, being told, 'Can you just lift that bag up and put it down again? The lighting wasn't quite right on that one …'

Just when we thought our stress levels couldn't escalate any higher, Sky News called and asked us to do a live TV interview at their Sydney studio—that very afternoon. 'Live TV interview!?' Clark repeated the three words we'd hoped we'd never hear.

'Great, we'll drive you there and film the whole thing!' The limitless energy of the film crew was starting to wear us down, but we were grateful for the lift, and the opportunity to escape any more of their filming sequences.

Half an hour later Clark and I tumbled into the newsroom. 'The newsreader will be interviewing you from in there,' the usher pointed, 'but,' he swung his arm in the opposite direction, 'you'll be sitting over here.' He pointed to a lone desk in the centre of the office, absolutely bristling with cameras, microphones and monitors. This torture device only had one chair so I accepted my fate as 'expedition leader' and sat down. In case I wasn't already feeling violated enough by our film crew's sticky-taped wireless mic pulling out my chest hair under my shirt, another was now slid inside my collar, and a tiny earpiece wedged in my ear.

'Can you hear me?' A voice boomed from inside my head. Without the faintest idea who was speaking to me, or from where, I simply said 'Yes' to the wall in front of me. 'Good. Now I'll just get you to clap your hands together for me.' Like a well-behaved puppet, I obeyed. 'Okay, audio's levelled. You'll be on in a few seconds.'

Down in Hobart, our main sponsors Don and Margie McIntyre raced into their nearest pub to watch on the big screen. ' ... that was our correspondent, speaking there from Baghdad. In news closer to home, two incredible young Australian men are about to head off on an epic world-first expedition to the Arctic. I'm now joined by Chris Bray, one of the explorers, in our Sydney studio—Chris, thank you for coming in ...' In an excited phone call that night, Don congratulated me, saying that in the pub, people had stopped talking, and some even put down their beers to watch! This, apparently, was quite something.

Utterly drained from the day's shenanigans, Clark and I slept like dead men.

There were now two days to go. 'We should have done this weeks ago,' I shook my head forlornly as I called the fifth sticker manufacturer listed online. 'Yes, hello. Can you print 60 different company logo stickers, in colour, on clear backing, up to one metre long, that will stick to a ... a ... painted surface?'

'Yeah, I reckon so, it'll take about a week. Is this for indoor use?'

'Ummm, no, not exactly. It's rather "outdoor", and we desperately need these stickers by tomorrow evening if at all possible ... Can you do that?'

There followed a familiar silence, after which he took a deep breath and said, 'Yes. We can do that.' Thank God. I doubt our sponsors would have been very impressed with my backup plan of sketching their logos onto the side of our PACs using permanent marker pens.

My room now resembled an overstocked warehouse—the bed, desk and even the floor was strewn with well over $30,000 worth of brand-new expedition equipment. How were we ever going to fit this all into … into … 'Bags!?!' We both exploded simultaneously, 'We don't have anything to put all this in! Shit! Mum'll drive us to the mall; quick, let's go!'

We picked the four biggest sports bags in the shop, agitatedly tapping our feet as the girl behind the counter asked, 'You guys going on a holiday?'

'Yeah, Canada.'

'How awesome! Snowboarding?'

'Ummm …' we glanced at each other, ' … yeah, that's right!' We didn't have the time.

On the way back home I got another call from the film crew. They wanted to know if they could spend another day or two filming with us. 'But we *leave* in two days, guys,' I said, more than a little exasperated.

'Oh, we promise not to get in your way—you just do what you gotta do, and we'll just film.'

'But …' There were, apparently, no 'buts' if we wanted to keep the documentary deal.

The crew showed up at 6 am and shadowed us everywhere we went for the remaining two days. Every time we muttered something between us, the microphones mounted on long boom poles were hurriedly held above us to catch the words.

'Have you checked the satellite phones are charged, Clark?'

'Damn, no! Where are they even!?'

They sat Mum down on the front steps, cameras rolling: 'So how are you coping with having your son about to head off on such a potentially dangerous journey?' She burst into tears.

On the very last day, we were still panicking, and they were still filming. Couriers were in and out of our driveway all day, delivering amongst other things Flag #49 from the Explorers Club that we'd been given the honour of carrying. While it may sound like a simple gesture, it is one steeped in tradition. This very flag, #49, has quite a history, having been carried on several amazing expeditions over the previous 73 years, including that of the famous polar explorer Captain Robert Bartlett in 1932.

A last-minute re-test for the cameras of our bear tripwire system in the backyard was far from reassuring—my dog, Gypsie, either simply crawled cunningly underneath the string or leapt clear over it to get to the tasty Schmackos dog-treat lying in blissful ignorance on the other side. Trying not to draw too many parallels as she hungrily crunched and swallowed the last shreds, we turned to the cameras and declared that bears—surely—weren't that agile.

Dinner on that last night—marking the end of a day that came and went so quickly it might not have existed—was a special occasion. It was to be our last taste of decent home-cooked food, and our last chance to thank my parents for all they'd done. It was also the last chance we had to remember anything we might need during the next three months, and—oh yeah—it was Clark's 21st birthday. I felt a little guilty about this, but my birthday had been just a few weeks earlier, and we had scarcely noticed that one either. We had about a year of missed parties and social outings to catch up on as soon as the expedition was over. Right now, though, we excused ourselves from the table after our second slice of cake, and retreated back into my room for some last-minute, focused panicking.

Two-thirty am saw me sitting atop the last bag, squashing it smaller while Clark slowly coaxed the cheap zipper along its track. I stood up, and we both surveyed our handiwork. Four massive sports bags, each looking like it was only a matter of time before it exploded at the seams. Every now and again, faint popping noises told us that yet another stitch had decided that enough was enough.

The next morning, after just 90 minutes' sleep, my bedside alarm screeched 4 am. Lights and noises downstairs revealed my family were already up. In fact, they probably didn't sleep. I shook Clark awake and we sat down to a hasty hot breakfast that Mum had lovingly prepared. A quick shower—a brief chance to reflect— and then our pre-organised plan of events engulfed us. Right on cue at 4.30, the film crew turned up again. Attempting to ignore the cameras, I tried to bid everyone a sincere goodbye. It didn't feel very genuine, but then again everything had seemed surreal for several months now. I patted my dog, and we all struggled our bags to the waiting airport shuttle bus purring outside. The crew and their cameras tumbled in, and I seized the opportunity to give a more heartfelt goodbye to my family. It was still hard to believe that this moment was finally upon us. Clark and I crammed inside the minibus and sat beside four bewildered passengers who had just unwittingly become extras in the 'airport shuttle scene' of Discovery's epic motion-picture extravaganza.

'So tell us,' the director probed. 'What are you both feeling right now?' Without a moment's hesitation we replied as one: 'Tired.'

# TO THE ARCTIC!

Alone at last in the airport, we wheeled our obscene load of baggage towards check-in.

'G'day, fellas!' It was Ben—the marketing manager from Air Canada. He greeted us heartily, waving us past the main queue to our own private check-in desk, and introduced us to the airport manager, who pulled out a camera. 'Just for a travel industry magazine ...' She smiled and Ben produced an enormous novelty-sized boarding pass and held it in front of us. We lingered with a small farewell party of Clark's friends and then—while doing a live-to-air interview with a breakfast radio show in Queensland on my mobile—we headed off through Customs.

Just as we were about to board the plane, the airport manager turned up and took our boarding passes. 'Excuse me, but I think you'll find these much more comfortable ...' Smiling, she replaced our two hospitality-class seats with the best two in the plane—Executive First Class, front centre.

For the entire twenty hours of flying, we just could not stop grinning. In fact, we had to form a mutual agreement not to look at each other, as it made us burst out laughing. Even if I stretched my legs out as far as I could, I couldn't touch the seat in front. We leant back in our reclined chairs, glass of champagne in hand, nibbling away at a little bowl of nuts while listening to beautiful classical music. I flicked open the four-course lunch menu and glanced at the first option: 'Grilled Fillet of Salmon: enhanced by Parisienne Jus and Red Onion Jam with Truffle Risotto, Green Asparagus and sliced Bacon.'

'Yes, well, that would *probably* be okay ...' Clark commented poshly, 'but personally, I'm going with the Ravioli—next one down.'

Before I'd even finished my bowl of mixed nuts, a beautiful flight attendant materialised in front of me with a replacement. She smiled. 'We think you deserve a little luxury before your expedition.' While I busied myself trying to extend the foot-rest—curious to see just how horizontal the seat could go—the captain appeared and, crouching in the aisle beside us, chatted about our expedition for a good five minutes before going back to the cockpit. Another flight attendant delicately passed each of us a scorchingly hot wet towel. Utterly bewildered, we shifted them from hand to burning hand, until Clark nudged me in the ribs. 'Look, over there …' The man opposite us—obviously a veteran of first-class travel—simply wiped his brow with it before passing the towel back. 'Aha!' Of course. We knew that. We both followed suit. Try as we might, we weren't doing a very good job at pretending we flew first-class all the time. Surrounded by CEOs and trillionaires, we stuck out like sore thumbs, but we no longer cared, and the flight attendants had clearly taken it upon themselves to see just how much they could spoil us. 'And to think that just a few hours ago,' I mused, 'that radio interview guy asked me, "Why on earth would anyone want to do what you guys do?"'

Our blissful journey was rudely interrupted by Hawaii—a brief stopover. 'Why is it that a journey to the Arctic involves a stopover in the tropics?' Clark thought aloud as he pulled off his Windstopper jacket, sweat rolling down his neck. He started filming as I announced, 'Hey, I just got an SMS from Dad …' I read it through again. 'Apparently there's some kind of trucking strike in Vancouver; he thinks we might have trouble getting our PACs from the ship.'

The enormity of this news didn't sink in, and I shrugged to the camera, 'It can't be that bad.' How incredibly wrong we were.

After a few more hours of heaven aboard Air Canada, we touched down in Vancouver on 7 July 2005. Thumbing through our passports, the Customs official asked us the usual, 'So, what brings you to Canada?'

We pressed our mental 'play' button and recited our standard reply. 'What?' he said, incredulous. 'The *real* Victoria Island?'

I should point out here that about 99 per cent of the people we met thought that 'Victoria Island' was the large island just off Vancouver. That is in fact Vancouver Island, which just happens to have a town on it called Victoria. We always found it amusing the way people would try to let us down gently, explaining kindly that we really were very unlikely to come across any polar bears on our trip, 'but there are some good cafés you can look forward to …' This Customs bloke was one of the few people we met who actually understood where we were going. We found it slightly alarming, then, when he looked us in the eyes and said, 'Whoa! You guys are going to die!'

Amusingly, the cheapest way for us to get to our booked hotel turned out to be in a stretch limousine. 'Watch yourself, boys,' the driver warned as we drove over an invisible line, 'we just entered the baaad part of town … and here's your hotel.' We found ourselves deposited outside a single, shabby, closed door fronting the street.

'Well, it *was* the cheapest place I could find online in Vancouver,' Clark reminded me. 'I'll go in and suss it out.' He vanished inside, leaving me anxiously mentally adding up the value of the contents of the bags around me. Thirty-two thousand dollars, oh and the digital SLR camera, that's $35,000, and—

'Hey, you got any spare change, man?' I whirled around, and my eyes met the vacant stare of a junkie standing right behind me. Positively overflowing with valuables, I assured him I had nothing. He lurched onwards down the street.

'Hey, you're not from round here, are ya?' Two girls I hadn't noticed before spoke up, eyeing me while leaning against the next doorway.

'Umm, no—just here for a snowboarding holiday actually …'

Mercifully, Clark reappeared, waving a key. 'Upstairs, room 102,' he said. 'And there's no lifts.'

Once inside the dingy little room, we looked at the beds. The last time we'd slept was 36 hours ago in Sydney—and even that was for less than two hours. Just to test how cosy they were before heading out for some dinner, we flopped onto the mattresses and—fully clothed, shoes hanging off the ends—we lay there motionless until well after midday the following afternoon.

The next day, as we wandered the streets trying to find breakfast and not get mugged, I called up our Vancouver shipping cargo handler.

'No, there's nothing you can do. Your kayaks are going nowhere anytime soon.' I listened in disbelief as she continued, 'Your shipping container will be buried beneath the thousands of others piling up on the wharves by now.' This couldn't be happening.

'Well … when is the trucking strike expected to end?'

'There's no end in sight,' she replied matter-of-factly, adding, 'and, even after it ends, clearing this backlog of containers will take three times as long as the strike itself.' Sitting in a quiet café, we attempted to keep our heads above the rising feeling of panic as this devastating news sank in.

'So what does this mean?' Clark pondered aloud.

I started to count our worst fears on my fingers. 'One: If we don't get them out soon, it'll be too late to start the expedition anyway. Summer just isn't long enough.' Clark nodded in bitter agreement, staring unseeing at his coffee cup. 'Two: We'll have about $100,000 worth of unhappy sponsors …'

'Yeah. Hope they don't ask for their money back—we've spent it all getting this far.'

'They won't do that, but they certainly won't sponsor us again,' I threw back, being less than helpful. 'Nor will any other company. And it's not like we can postpone it until next year either, not with uni and things …' Our despair was rapidly sinking to new depths. 'We just *have* to get them out. That's all it comes down to.' We downed the dregs of our now cold coffee and flicked open our notebook, waiting for inspiration.

I called the only contact we had in Vancouver: Nancy at Diamonds North Resources—a mining company looking for diamonds up north—one of our smaller sponsors. Her office, as it turned out, was less than 100 metres from where we sat. As always, she was full of energy. 'Come right over! Finally we get to meet, eh?' She toured us around the office.

'Yeah, this strike is no small stop-work meeting, boys,' she said. 'It's costing British Columbia $30 million a day. Businesses are running out of supplies, millions of dollars of perishables are going to waste in those containers each day, internationally touring concerts can't get to their instruments; it's affecting a lot of people.' Smiling in spite of her words, she picked up her phone and said, 'But now it's stopping two young Aussies pursuing their dream, and we can't have that!' She turned her attention to the phone. 'Yes, hi, Terrie, I have two Australians here you'd like to talk to …' Handing the phone to me, she explained that it was Canadian Press—Canada's news-collecting centre that feeds all newspapers, radios and TV stations.

Minutes later I wrapped up an interview, and now armed with the mobile number for the lawyer representing the striking truckers, we were escorted by Nancy and the rest of Diamonds North to a pub across the road where they shouted us a beer or three. In between rounds, I nipped outside into a quiet alley and gave the lawyer, Craig, a call. I came back to the table grinning like an idiot. 'He's going to help us out!' More beer flowed as I broke the news. 'They'll hunt down our container from amongst the thousands, pull it out with a crane and allow our trucker to collect it first thing Monday morning!!' Mugs clinked, and our spirits once again soared.

Quite a few people had joined our table by this stage, including a quiet, stern-faced geologist. 'I've been to Victoria Island,' he said, hesitating. 'So you two boys are going to try and travel, alone, on foot?' We nodded, bracing ourselves for another reality check. 'I've been out there,' he repeated, ' … and to be honest, boys, well, I'd be surprised if either of you make it out alive.' The more he heard of our plans, however, the more animated and interested he became, and when we got up to leave he shook our hands heartily and wished us luck. 'Well, good on you for trying, anyway. You've got courage—maybe you won't die after all.'

Later, hungry for dinner, I was about to swing closed the peeling door on our hotel room when I paused. 'Do you reckon it might actually be safer to take our valuables with us, rather than risk leaving our video cameras and stuff here in the hotel?'

'That's a good point, actually,' Clark agreed, 'besides, we should film us "soaking up the last of civilisation".' This decision almost cost us dearly.

Not five minutes after we left the hotel, a voice croaked up from right behind us. 'Hey, they look like pretty special backpacks, boys, whatcha got in them?' The junkie stood tight beside us at the traffic lights. We ignored him. 'I said, what's in the bags?!' he demanded. I decided against admitting 'Two satellite phones, a GPS chartplotter, a digital SLR camera, a $3000 lens, a portable hard-drive, two $7000 video cameras, wads of cash, passports and some airline tickets.' We needed to defuse this situation fast. Our two grey waterproof camera backpacks stuck out like sore thumbs.

The lights changed and we walked off. He followed. We began to wind around a few streets trying to get our bearings—finding ourselves ever deeper in the 'baaaad' part of town. The junkie quickened his pace and once again drew level. 'Where are you guys from, anyway?'

Clark had a brainwave. 'We're just over from Australia to compete in the inter-college kick-boxing championships.' With that, the junkie melted away into the background.

First thing Monday morning I called our cargo handlers. 'Fantastic news,' I told our contact. 'The striking truckers have agreed to let your truck pick up our shipping container!' Silence. 'They said they'll let your driver through the strike picket line …'

Clearly she didn't share my excitement. 'No. I don't think so,' she replied. 'Why should my driver believe you?' She had a point.

'Well, I can get the truckers' spokesperson to confirm it. I'll get him to call y—'

She cut me off. 'It doesn't matter. Either way, I'm not going to ask one of my drivers to go in there. Shots have already been fired at trucks trying to cross the picket line.'

She didn't care. I was desperate. 'Okay, fair enough. *I'll* find a trucker who'll do it, and then—'

Again, she interrupted me. 'It doesn't matter if you do. *We* are the handlers for your container, and it's a lot of paperwork to transfer it over to some other company. You'll just have to wait, like everyone else.'

I was stunned at her attitude. 'Yeah, thanks, you've been a *great help*.' I spat the words and hung up, fuming.

'God, what a rollercoaster this is,' Clark muttered, as our spirits once again took a dive.

'I'll call the lawyer chap, and dob on them: "Daddy—our cargo handler's being mean to us … "' We laughed, but it really was our best option. I dialled the number.

'Yes, Chris? What is it? I'm standing in front of a public meeting of a thousand people here, and I'm just about to speak to them.'

I wavered. 'Oh, er, it's fine, I'll call you back.'

'No, Chris, what is it?' I hastily explained the conundrum. 'No worries. That shouldn't be a problem. Leave it with me. I'll do everything in my power to get your kayaks out. Don't you worry about it. Now I really have to go. Goodbye.'

With our on-again, off-again expedition apparently back on again, we saw no need to further complicate things by missing our scheduled flight north the next morning. Our PACs could follow us just as soon as they were released—meanwhile, we had other things to attend to. As we jetted towards Edmonton—back in the harsh realities of economy class—we went over our shopping list. Edmonton boasts the world's largest shopping mall, and we still had several things to buy.

'West Edmonton Mall? Yes, it's huge!' Our taxi driver beamed, clearly proud of his city's claim to fame. Wedged in the back with our excessive luggage, we took off towards our next surprisingly cheap—and probably surprisingly nasty—hotel. The taxi left Edmonton behind and we found ourselves cruising along what looked alarmingly like some kind of interstate freeway. We would have asked him where he was taking us, but our powers of speech had been temporarily removed as we started in awe at the exponentially increasing cab fare metre. It was like a horror movie—we didn't want to watch, but at the same time we just couldn't turn away. The $50 mark came and went, and still all we could see outside was an open expanse of nothing.

'So, our hotel's not in Edmonton then?' I managed.

'No.' We looked at each other, unsure of how to react to this news. 'It's in *West* Edmonton, next to the mall,' he added. 'Not far now.'

Ignoring the realisation that if we'd factored in the taxi fare to the cost of our hotel we could probably have stayed in a luxury five-star penthouse closer to the airport, we were pleasantly surprised when we arrived. Gazing at the city lights twinkling through the window of our room as we sat munching Pringles chips for dinner, it suddenly occurred to me that this would be the last 'night' we'd be seeing in a long, long time. Tomorrow we'd fly to Victoria Island, bathed in perpetual sunlight for at least the first month.

The taxi ride the next morning back to the 'airport' was even more traumatic than the one on the way in. 'No, no,' the driver corrected us, 'First Air does not fly from the main Edmonton airport, they operate out of a little hangar out of town.' Fair enough—he evidently knew what he was talking about.

Our confidence slowly deteriorated over the next twenty minutes until, looking out of the window, I whispered 'Are we—'

'Going in circles?' Clark finished my sentence. We were, and had been for some time. It soon became apparent that the only thing with a clear sense of direction was the fare metre. $65, $66, $67 …

When he finally pulled to the kerb, it was only to ask a passer-by for directions. 'The First Air hangar? Umm … yeah, I have seen it somewhere. Try a left back at the crossroads.'

After another ten minutes of driving, at last the taxi driver pointed triumphantly behind him, 'There it is!' He threw a U-turn and moments later we found ourselves, with our bags, standing in front of a derelict shed, watching the taxi drive away. He was right, there was a sign saying 'First Air' clinging to the rusting corrugated walls, and so after knocking on all the doors, we sat down and waited.

'We are 30 minutes early, I guess,' Clark reassured anyone who was listening.

I checked our tickets. I looked at the narrow, dilapidated gravel airstrip across the road. I looked back at the tickets. 'Clark,' I began. 'Clark … it says we're going to be on a Boeing 737 jet—they're pretty big.' I glanced at the threadbare windsock swinging limply from a bent pole marking the runway. 'Oh, shit,' I fumbled frantically in the many bags for my mobile, 'this can't be right!'

We didn't have the number for Edmonton taxis; in fact, we didn't have the number for anything in Edmonton, and nowhere was open anyway. 'We've got fifteen minutes … f*#king taxi driver!!'

Desperate times called for desperate measures. I phoned the only place that would be open at this time of the day: Australia. Thirteen thousand kilometres away, my friend started to track down the Edmonton taxi phone number online. 'Here comes someone …' Clark was staring intently at a car driving up the otherwise deathly quiet street towards us. 'Hey—it's a taxi! It's *our* taxi, the same guy!'

The driver stepped out. Our first instinct was to attack him on sight, but before we had a chance, he'd popped the boot and was bodily throwing our bags inside. 'I just realised this isn't the right place, guys!'

We burst inside Edmonton's main airport, just in time to hear our names called over the PA system. 'Mr Bray and Mr Carter, please proceed immediately to Gate 23. Mr Bray and …'

'Oh my God!' We joined the obscenely long queue as it trickled slowly through security check-in.

'Hold up, guys, what have you got in the bags?' The officer patted our submersibles.

'Oh, just, cameras and umm … stuff.' We were sweating. He could tell something was making us *really* nervous. The PA crackled into life again. 'Mr Bray and Mr Carter—your plane is ready for an immediate departure. Please proceed as quickly as possible to …'

'That's *us* they are calling for,' I pleaded.

He didn't believe me—clearly this was a common escape tactic used by smugglers. We flung open our backpacks and the officer's eyebrows rose as he gazed at all our (evidently stolen) electronics. 'Okay, that's fine.' He looked past us. 'Next!'

We ran for it. As we tore towards Gate 23, the attendant pointed through a little door outside. 'It's on the tarmac—hurry!' We scrambled up the staircase onto the plane, to be greeted by a smiling flight attendant.

'Oh, phew … lucky they aren't pissed-off with us,' I whispered, and then, turning the corner we both stared down a plane-length of angry passengers staring right back at us.

The aircraft started taxiing towards the runway even before we'd made it to our seats. We cursed the taxi driver one last time for good measure, and then both hid behind the pages of the in-flight magazine, trying to pretend we didn't exist.

After refuelling in Kugluktuk, our plane left Canada's northern coastline behind, and flew out over the frozen expanse of the Arctic Ocean. Through the cabin window, we pointed excitedly at the great tears in the ice sheets—endless cracks or 'leads' revealing the frigid, inky water below. In the winter when the ice is somewhat thicker, supplies are actually trucked from the mainland to the Arctic Archipelago. Suddenly, I elbowed Clark. 'There it is!' I pointed. 'Victoria Island!'

Until now, our mental image of the island had been based on a total of about ten or fifteen photographs. There were precious few images around and most of ours had been emailed to us by an Australian couple who had been trying to sail their yacht through the Northwest Passage before the oncoming winter forced them to winter-over in Cambridge Bay. As we approached the island now, though, it looked, I thought, very much like it had been used for repeated nuclear testing. A flat, brown, gravel-strewn, featureless wasteland. Clark's mouth hung open. 'I guess that's Cambridge Bay then ...' We began our descent above a tiny clutter of brightly coloured roofs huddled tightly together in this vast void of nothingness.

Just as we were starting to wonder if there was anything alive down there, we caught sight of people busying themselves down at the airport. Moments later, we stepped off the plane and into what nine months ago had been nothing more than a fanciful, far-off dream. It was 11 July 2005, and finally we—two Aussie boys— were standing in the Arctic. We had no kayaks, but we, at least, were here.

# CAMBRIDGE BAY, VICTORIA ISLAND

In my pocket I had one phone number—that of Doug Stern, the legendary 'White Inuit' of Victoria Island. My very first contact on the island had been when I'd called up their general store, Kitikmeot Supplies, months ago. The manager, Keith, had regularly answered my questions on everything from the weather through to mosquito conditions. However, it hadn't taken long before Doug's name came up. 'Oh, yes, he's quite a character,' Keith had told me. 'He spends most of his time out "on the land"; he's even guided expeditions down in Antarctica!'

Doug, as it turned out when I'd eventually got hold of him, was more than just a wealth of outdoor information—he was also an incredibly generous man. 'I'll probably be out managing the national park on Ellesmere Island by July,' he told me, 'but I'll leave you the key to my house, and you can use it as your launch pad.' It was an honour that we were thrilled to accept.

So, not surprisingly then, when I dialled Doug's number from the airport there was no answer. 'Well … I guess we're walking,' Clark said, stretching his arms before shouldering his backpack and picking up one of our four 28-kilogram bags in each hand.

We didn't get very far before a 4WD pulled up beside us. 'Hey, you must be the two Oz-tralians? I'm Frank, hop in!'

Doug's house was just incredible. A dog-sled lay on the balcony, the roof was adorned with countless caribou and muskox antlers, and the doorway dangled with whale bones, hoofs and other decorations we weren't game to even try to identify.

'G'day, boys!' The Australian voice caught us off guard, and we spun around. There, not 3 metres from us, stood Santa—merry twinkling eyes, flowing white beard and all. I guess it's not all *that* surprising, I thought, we're as near as dammit to the North Pole. 'I'm Phil—from the Aussie yacht stuck in the ice over there,' he said, shaking our hands heartily, glancing at Doug's house behind us. 'The only house in Cambridge Bay without running water, flushing toilet or heating,' Phil laughed jollily, 'but Doug doesn't need it, he pretty much lives off the land.'

For a house without heating, it was surprisingly warm inside. Fur lined the doors to seal them, and the rooms were so crammed full of interesting artefacts that we wouldn't have noticed the cold even if we were freezing. Feathers, fossils, fox-pelts, photographs, skulls, bear claws—all with little Post-it notes stuck next to them reminding Doug where each piece in his museum originated from. 'Oh, that's not a part of his museum,' Phil corrected me as I marvelled at some genuine caribou-skin clothes. 'Doug uses them. He made them, too …'

Word that 'the two Oz-tralians' had arrived spread quickly around the little community of 1500 people. Every time we returned to the house after being shown around town, we'd find a multitude of scribbled letters pinned to Doug's door:

*Chris & Clark! BBQ tomorrow night at my place. Alex.*
*Chris & Clark—Just a reminder that you're both invited to my place tonight for a get-together. Matt.*

Everyone—absolutely everyone—was just so incredibly friendly. Quickly we had more dinner invites and offers of accommodation than there were days to allocate them to; however, on that first night Clark and I were itching to test our gear in real Arctic conditions. At around midnight we walked 4 kilometres out of town, unfurled our Exped mats directly onto the tundra, lofted our sleeping bags on top and got in—without the complication of a tent.

A few hours later, I opened a cautious eye. My face felt slightly sunburnt. I checked my watch. It was 3 am, and the sun still hung blindingly in the bright blue sky. Blinking, I rolled over and peered at Clark. He was sound asleep, his sleeping bag encrusted with a thin layer of ice, and 100 metres behind him, a huge shaggy animal was lumbering toward us.

I sat bolt upright. 'Clark!!' It was our first muskox—a massive bison-like animal with dreadlocks. Victoria Island is home to one of the world's densest populations of these ice-age buffaloes. We'd read up on them—if you approach a herd they will usually clump together forming a defensive circle, young hiding in the middle, surrounded by an impenetrable fortress of formidable horns. Lone bulls, however, can be dangerous. They have been known to charge, gore and even kill people, especially ambitious photographers who like to get too close. I glanced nervously around, looking for the rest of this one's family. He was alone, and the single udder hanging beneath him hinted that he wasn't female. Great, and here we were, both incapacitated, zipped-up like grubs inside mummy bags.

Clark flopped himself up into a sitting position, and the woolly beast stopped, put his head down, and instead of charging, started munching idly on the tundra. Relieved, we went back to studying the insides of our eyelids while the sun incessantly bore down upon us.

The perpetual daylight was a little disconcerting. As we lay there trying to go back to sleep, we couldn't shrug the feeling that we were being lazy, sleeping in, and that it must already be mid morning. Who cares? we decided. So long as we'd had enough sleep, it was time to get up and declare the start of a new day. It was quite a revelation—time became meaningless, and we were free to warp it as we wished. If we wanted there to be ten days per week, all we had to do was remember to have dinner more often. As bizarre as this sounds, some expeditions do choose to operate on a distorted clock, enjoying the exaggerated 'daily distance covered' that comes from realising a 36-hour day. As we'd be doing regular live interviews back home while on the trip, we had seriously considered setting our clocks back to good ol' Aussie time to make life easier. This would, however, put us out of sync with any pilots or anyone else we might need to deal with during the expedition, so we'd decided to stick with 'Canadian Mountain Time'. Still, it was awesome to have the freedom to bend time while still in the safety of Cambridge Bay.

This thrill, unfortunately, was short-lived. Having hiked all the way back into town to begin our new day, we stood, insulted, in front of the supermarket that contained our breakfast. 'Closed,' the sign read. 'Open 9 am.' Dammit! If local time governed our meals, then local time governed our lives.

Keeping our fingers crossed that our PACs would be on their way within a day or so, we wasted no time in preparing for our departure. We collected the enormous stockpile of food we'd had sent ahead from Edmonton weeks earlier, and, sitting on the dog-sled on Doug's verandah, started measuring it all out into drybags. Twelve kilograms of milk powder, 6.5 kilograms of rolled oats, 26 kilograms of various nuts—all had to be divided into nine identical weekly portions. Eventually, gorged on handfuls of leftover cashews, we turned our milk-powder-ringed eyes towards our 16 kilograms of chocolate. 'When we said we wanted "blocks" of chocolate,' Clark said to the video camera, 'we didn't mean it literally.' The formidable stack of four solid 5-kilogram slabs truly was a sight to behold, and it didn't take us long to realise we were going to have 4 kilograms left over.

'Break a bit off, let's quality-test it,' I suggested, already salivating. Easier said than done, and over half an hour later we still hadn't found a way to break into it. Banging it against the edge of a large rock barely dented it, and pre-heated knives couldn't cut it. We even tried hacksawing, but only succeeding in gumming up the saw blade. Short of drilling a hole and inserting a small explosive, we were running out of ideas. Exasperated, I brought out our tomahawk and took a hearty swing at it. Brittled by the Arctic's natural freezer, chocolate shrapnel exploded all around us and the small crowd of Inuit children who'd gathered fell upon the pieces with glee before we could react. Eventually, using a hammer and screwdriver as a jackhammer, we finally reduced all 20 kilograms into varying degrees of chocolate rubble. It wasn't until several days later, however, after borrowing the only set of weigh-scales on the island—from the post office—that we managed to finally divide this mess into our 130 individual daily portions, each weighing exactly 123 grams.

We were grossly unacclimatised, wearing almost every layer of clothing we'd brought and still shivering. Rugged up in our puffy goose-down jackets, we felt increasingly ridiculous as we shuffled past girls stripped down to their minimalist summer kit, some even wearing miniskirts, enjoying the hottest day any of them could remember as the temperature soared to a blistering 15 degrees Celsius.

Every day I called up and gingerly pressed the lawyer, Craig, for news on our PACs, and every day our hopes were raised and then dashed. Every potential solution ended in another problem. Even when Craig located a trucker for us who was willing—with permission—to cross the picket line and collect our container, the handling company refused to fill in the paperwork to hand over 'ownership' of the container to the new trucking company. In fact, they were even starting to pretend we didn't exist. 'I'm just leaving messages after messages, and no one's getting back to us …' Unable to look the video camera in the eye, I just stared dejectedly at Doug's little red phone as anger started to give way to despair.

Thankfully, we didn't have much free time to ponder our fate, as each day was filled with meeting new people, learning new skills and getting everything ready. Early on, Alex Stuit—president of the Ikaluktutiak Paddling Association in Cambridge Bay—threw a fantastic welcoming party in our honour, attended by dozens of unfamiliar faces who soon became like family. After we'd washed down thick Canadian T-bone steaks with mugs of beer, Alex ushered us over to meet someone. 'This man,' he began, 'has dog-sledded all the way to the North Pole, using a sextant—before the days of GPS …'

For a member of the first ever confirmed party to reach the North Pole without resupply, Brent Boddy was surprisingly quiet and unassuming, and we warmed to him at once. Although tall and lean, he wasn't exactly built like an ox as I had assumed all polar explorers were, but beneath his greying hair, his eyes burned with an energetic intensity. 'Paddle over to my cabin and we'll go ice-fishing,' he offered. We agreed at once, ignoring the fact that we didn't have any kayaks—we were already starting to adopt the Inuit philosophy of 'Oh, it'll be okay.' Up here, given time, everything did seem to have a habit of working itself out.

Alex chimed in, 'I'll lend you my two kayaks—but tomorrow, you two should go driving.' We assumed the whole lack-of-any-kind-of-vehicle situation would also resolve itself in true Arctic style, nodded, and reached for a second steak.

The next afternoon Alex pulled up the door to his garage, revealing two little 4WD all-terrain vehicles (ATVs)—the island's main form of summer transport when retreating snow grounded everyone's snow mobiles. To our amazement, after giving us a quick 'crash course' on how to avoid crashing, he flicked us the keys, 'Have fun!' Before we knew it, we were hurtling along the dirt road out towards Mount Pelly with the perpetual twilight igniting our dusty wake into a beautiful orange tail behind us.

Mount Pelly is the only hill of any significance around Cambridge Bay, and to the Inuit it has special traditional ties. Inuit legend has it that Mount Pelly is actually the fallen body of Ovayok, a giant that starved to death while wandering around looking for food. We parked our ATVs at the bottom and hiked wearily upwards, reaching the summit at 3 am, where the view from our sleeping bags was spectacular. In the low sweeping sunlight the endless patchwork of thousands of lakes below shimmered like quicksilver out into the distance, sprinkled with the odd herd of silently grazing muskox. Victoria Island, we now realised, is a truly beautiful place.

It was at this moment of inspiration, combined with extreme tiredness and bad planning, that we inadvertently invented 'arctic tea'—a drink we would both come to depend on during the expedition to restore vital energy, morale and warmth after a hard day's hauling. Having forgotten to bring milk powder, we melted a few of our excess chunks of white chocolate into our tea, and the combination far surpassed all our expectations. It was absolutely delicious—it even made the inch of tea leaves at the bottom palatable! After a few hours' blissful sleep, we awoke to sunburnt noses and headed back into town.

More letters stuck to Doug's door invited us to do a radio interview with the local CBC radio, and another gave us directions to find Lawrence, another faceless name who'd been helping organise the loan of the two local shotguns we'd be taking. After negotiating past his hyperactive dog we knocked on the door and waited, and waited. Something we could never get used to was that every house on the island had a double set of doors, the first door opening into a tiny room no more than a metre or so long, fronting immediately onto a second door. Although confusing for two Aussies who'd consider it rude to just march inside the first door without knocking, it was of course a very practical setup—in mid winter it means visitors don't bring a blizzard inside with them, and the inner rooms remain toasty warm. We generally found, though, if we knocked loud enough on this outer door, and waited long enough, the occupant would eventually open the door to peek curiously out.

'Oh! G'day, fellas!' Lawrence's beaming smile and best Aussie impersonation made us feel right at home, and in no time we became old friends, chewing on strips of dried fish and laughing about our misconceptions. 'Oh, yes,' he grinned, 'when I placed the order for the amount of ammunition you guys were after, some people were wondering if you two were planning on starting a revolution on the island! You know, start a war or something!' It was true, we really were taking a small armoury with us—two 12-gauge pump-action shotguns, 20 solid slugs, 30 buckshot, 15 pyrotechnic 'bear-bangers' as well as several pen-flare bear deterrents—we'd had very conflicting reports about the number of polar bears we could expect to encounter out there.

'I think you'll be lucky to see any,' Lawrence predicted thoughtfully, adding, 'although, up where you're going, who really knows?'

As we left, he passed us a bag of frozen fish—arctic char. This absolutely mouth-watering salmonoid fish forms a staple food of the entire community, and racks of drying char hung tantalisingly outside almost every house. We soon became regular char addicts, eating it raw, dried, fried, frozen—it tasted divine whatever you did to it. It seemed that the Arctic Ocean was brimming with these fish, and Wilf, another friend on the island, gave us all the right fishing lures to ensure we'd easily supplement our expedition diet along the way. 'What you really want, though,' Wilf whispered, 'is square hooks. That's the easiest way to catch char. But only Inuit are allowed to use square hooks, it's just too easy to catch them.' Then, ruining my cunning plans of quietly squaring-up all our normal hooks using our trusty Leatherman pliers, Wilf added, 'Square hooks is what we call fishing nets.'

Keen to learn the apparent lack of skill required to catch bucketloads of char with or without square hooks, we jumped at Lawrence's invitation to join his family at their cabin the next day. Almost everyone on the island seemed to have a little 'cabin' out of town, to which the family could retreat for a spot of fishing, hunting or relaxation. Land is uncontrolled out of town, and families just build these little shacks wherever there's a good spot. Lawrence's overlooked a beautiful ice-strewn bay in a place known affectionately as 'Gravel Pit'. The view—when you could see it through the clouds of mosquitoes—was spectacular, looking out over an endless sea of drifting pack ice. It was our first chance to actually go down and touch the grinding mosaic of ice. Some blocks perhaps 20 metres wide had been pushed right up high and dry onto the land, throwing up great bow waves of pebbles, while others tilted at precarious angles, dripping and sparkling in the sun. The air was filled with the sounds of chunks of ice moaning and squeaking against each other, driven by unseen currents, and the whole puzzle was continually drifting and separating, with gaps suddenly opening up to the frigid water beneath.

We were hesitantly walking along the shoreline admiring all this, venturing the odd step onto a grounded berg, when to our horror, Lawrence—apparently hell-bent on suicide—walked casually out onto the floating sheets in front of us and proceeded to leap further and further out to sea, hopping from one bobbing iceblock to the next, fishing line in hand. 'Come on, you two!' he called over his shoulder, grinning.

The fine art of 'ice-hopping', we eventually learned, is not so much physical as mental. It's just a simple matter of ignoring that little voice of self-preservation and common sense on your shoulder that whispers, 'Chris—leaping into mid air over deathly cold water, towards a small piece of ice that you're well aware won't support your weight—that's a bad thing to do,' and instead listening to the darker voice on your opposite shoulder hissing: 'Go on, Chris! It's perfectly safe. Just maybe give the video camera to Clark in case it gets a bit wet …' Many of these ice stepping stones were indeed far too small to support our weight, but the trick was not to stay on those ones too long—run, jump; run, jump; jump, jump, jump. Worryingly, the whole thing depended on the seemingly remote possibility that we'd eventually find a piece of ice large enough not to completely sink under us—only then could we stop to collect our thoughts and plan the route ahead. To add to the excitement, as water tends to lap around the edges of these ice sheets, the sides are all undercut to an unknown extent, sometimes giving way just as we tried to launch ourselves across the open water. Even in these cases, however, I found that the enormous incentive to stay in the air always got me safely to the far side.

'And the most important thing to remember,' Lawrence continued his coaching, 'is to always look over your shoulder to check you can still get back, because gaps have a habit of widening after you jump them.' We both laughed nervously at visions of Clark and me standing on an ever-shrinking iceblock as it drifted slowly away. 'It happens,' Lawrence cautioned. 'People die like that—you can't exactly swim back to shore.'

After cheating death a few more times, our master finally found a suitable raft of ice to fish from, and we all lay down and peeped over the edge, jiggling the lure up and down in the crystal-clear water. After a few minutes, I had to reluctantly let go of my misconception that char were going to flock to the hook like moths to a light. The only thing that happened was my legs went numb and my pants actually froze firmly onto the ice—I nearly tore the front off them as I stood up.

As we had miraculously survived his first lethal trial, Lawrence now seemed determined to finish us off, and strode out of the cabin with not one but two pump-action shotguns. 'Okay, boys …' In a practised motion, Lawrence levelled his shotgun and fired three powerful shots in quick succession out over the ice. BANG. BANG. BANG. The explosions ripped apart the serene silence and we both stood there like stunned mullet, blinking. 'Your turn,' Lawrence said, passing the gun to Clark. 'See that bit of ice sticking up over there? Pretend that's a polar bear. It's coming right at you!'

Neither of us had fired a shotgun before, and after explaining how the thing worked, Lawrence stepped back and offered one final warning: 'It'll have a bit of a kick, so hold it tight …'

BANG. He wasn't kidding. For a moment there, I think Clark was unsure if he'd accidently fired the gun around the wrong way, and shot himself in the shoulder. He missed the ice 'bear'. 'Oh, don't worry, my friend,' Lawrence reassured him cheerily, 'polar bears are huge—you can't miss a polar bear!' Several shoulder reconstructions later, we were both able to at least *scare* the target, most of the time.

'Okay, fellas, that'll do. Let's start up the barbecue, eh?'

Like many Inuit communities, Cambridge Bay is officially a 'dry town', yet many of the parties we attended were positively swimming in alcohol. One house even had its entire attic stashed full with enough beer, presumably, to 'last the winter'. Matt, the local radio presenter who ran the entire branch of CBC radio on his own, threw a party for us the next 'evening'. It was a wild 'night', culminating in 'the two Oz-tralians' being dared to go for a swim. With national pride at stake, we dutifully accepted and were escorted down to the wharf. The wind was offshore and had blown the floating pack ice across to the other side of the bay, but solid or not, the water was still pretty much zero degrees Celsius.

'Go on—jump off the end of the wharf and swim back to shore!' We might have been foreigners—slightly intoxicated foreigners even—but we weren't stupid. Even if we were lucky enough not to have a heart attack when we hit the water, the 40-metre swim back to shore would be near impossible. We announced that in Australia we were used to beaches, and we'd be going in from the shore.

With a cry of 'Not scared, are you?' one guy ran towards the end of the wharf, slipped and tumbled awkwardly into the icy water below. Everyone stopped. He surfaced, and for the first five seconds proceeded to pretend he was enjoying it—floating on his back, a stroke or two of backstroke, and then, sufficiently impressed with everyone's concerned pleadings for him to come back, he turned and headed for shore.

His strokes got slower and slower as his legs started to fail in the cold. Aborting his swim to shore, he turned back to the wharf and tried to reach for a rusty hanging ladder. Having been in the water for over 30 seconds, hypothermia was setting in and he could hardly grip the ladder, let alone haul himself up. After a few failed attempts to get out, everyone crowded to his rescue and eventually heaved him back onto the wharf. It was certainly sobering to see how quickly the water had crippled him, and any last alcoholic haze was smacked from us when we waded into the water ourselves from shore for our more controlled experience. That's certainly one way to sober up.

# HOME AWAY FROM HOME

Taking a break from still more frustrating setbacks in our mission to free our PACs, we borrowed two of Alex's kayaks and slid them into the Arctic Ocean in front of Doug's cabin. 'So how much kayaking have you guys done before?' Brent asked, ready to guide us to his cabin.

Clark considered this question, drew a complete blank and looked at me—I at least had sat in the PACs briefly in our neighbour's swimming pool while they gradually sank under me. 'Umm … well,' I began, 'my uncle took me out for a brief paddle about a year ago.'

It really was pretty absurd. In my defence I will point out that I'd lined up a free kayaking training course for us back at home, but in the final frantic months we'd run out of time to attend.

'That won't be a problem. You guys'll be fine.' Brent had an incredibly calming quality about him, and after a quick run-down of the basics, we found ourselves paddling—with Brent in the lead—out of the bay.

Reaching the seemingly impenetrable pack-ice shelf, Brent led us through a maze of little open-water leads amidst the shifting ice. Eventually, however, our luck ran out, and ice grated hard against the hull on all sides. In kamikaze-like style Brent back-paddled, and then paddled forward as hard as he could, directly at the ice sheet in our way. With a sickening scrunching sound, the kayak struck the ice, and then gracefully slid up onto it, glided frictionlessly across it, and slipped silently back into the water on the far side! Having been gob-smacked in astonishment so frequently in the last week, both Clark and I barely batted an eyelid, and obediently followed suit, effortlessly sliding up and over the barrier. This seal-manoeuvre was as fun as it looked, and we both started actively aiming for ice sheets to practise on.

Inevitably, the ice became so close that progress was, at last, impossible. We were high and dry, essentially punting our way over the top of a layer of semi-submerged ice, wedging the paddle into melt-holes and slushy bits to push ourselves forward. In another kamikaze stunt, Brent simply stood up in his kayak and stepped out onto what looked alarmingly like water. He turned and showed us—with a quick prod of his paddle—that he was actually standing on a transparent ice sheet just below the surface.

As our inner voices of common sense had long since given up trying to advise us, we both recklessly stood up and followed suit. Soon all three of us had our respective kayaks in tow behind us like sleds as we wandered, jumped and shuffled across the ice. All around us bits of ice were breaking, rising up, falling and squealing as they all drifted about. Brent cheerfully commented that the ice was particularly 'religious' today, as in it was very 'holy'—full of massive gaping holes through which we could fall at any moment. It was an insane situation to find ourselves in, and yet boyishly exciting.

We had our Gore-Tex Immersion Drysuits on while kayaking, which was very reassuring, and once at his cabin we tested them out properly—wading into the water and then venturing deeper for a swim, feeling every bit like displaced astronauts as we flapped and bobbed around on the surface in our bright yellow spacesuits. After we lost all feeling in our limbs we floundered back to shore and, *zzzzzip*, stepped out of our dripping drysuits, revealing perfectly dry clothes underneath. 'How cool is that!' Clark said, nodding approvingly.

We helped Brent set out his line of 'square hooks'—a legal activity for him as his girlfriend is Inuit—and then prepared ourselves for some much-needed sleep. Brent retired to the cabin, and Clark and I heaved two enormous muskox hides from storage nearby and each wrapped ourselves in their shaggy folds, promptly falling asleep to the sound of water lapping the shoreline a metre or two just beyond our feet.

By the time we awoke, Brent had already finished chopping a large pile of wood and we joined him beside the fire. Like everyone else we'd met recently, Brent was determined to fatten us up in readiness for our journey, and we were only too willing to oblige, accepting several helpings of a fried substance that tasted like a cross between beef, lard and Spam. Each mouthful probably reduced our healthy lifespan by a year or more, but it was just what our bodies were craving to fuel another day of Arctic training. 'There,' Brent said warmly, scraping the last greasy pile of cholesterol onto our plates, 'that should give you a bit more energy.'

Maybe we replied a little too enthusiastically, because before we knew it we found ourselves bodily dragging a large wooden dog-sled between the two of us, inching it along the shoreline for hours while Brent searched around, piling more and more slabs of rock onto the back. This morning's task was to collect flagstones to drag back and extend the cabin's front patio. The bigger the better—some took two people to lift—and it didn't take long before the sled became completely immovable. 'Have a look over the hill there,' Brent called, 'I think you'll find a smaller plastic sled there that you can use to haul the rocks back a few at a time …' Unfortunately he was right, and we obediently tied ourselves to this new torture device and struggled the first load of rocks back, emptying them beside the door. In the distance we could see Brent adding still more flagstones to the pile.

We shot each other a meaningful glance, and without exchanging a word, seized the opportunity before us. We quickly slipped inside the cabin whereupon I started fumbling for a spoon while Clark tracked down a large jar of peanut butter we'd spied earlier. Spoonful after sticky spoonful we gorged ourselves on peanut butter, Clark digging out his next spoonful from the rapidly emptying jar while I struggled to chew and swallow my own gummy mouthful fast enough to be ready for the next one. I was shocked to find myself doing this, but I'd never felt quite so desperate for energy in all my life, not even half-starved down in Tasmania. Eventually we brought ourselves back under control and replaced the jar into the cupboard and returned for the next load of rocks.

The distant growl of an approaching ATV heralded the end of the stone age for our little slave labour camp. Brent's Inuit girlfriend Jeanie and her son hopped off the buggy and donated it to our cause. Never before had we fully appreciated the impact motorised transport must have had on the world.

'I think we've caught some fish, boys!' Jeanie said, beaming. Overnight, the gentle arc of floats suspending the fishing net had evidently been upset, with some floats now pulled out of line and others submerged altogether. As we watched, a black shadow cruised in towards the net and struck it in a fury of thrashing water. 'That might be a seal!' Brent exclaimed, hurrying down to the shore. Not altogether sure if this was a good thing, we battled inwardly with ethical dilemmas as he paddled out towards the now silent net in his kayak. He untangled one, two, four large char from the net, slipping each one between his legs into the kayak cockpit, pulling himself along the line of floats towards the black giant. Jeanie joined us on the shore, carrying two moon-shaped *ulu* blades. Brent shouted something and we watched in suspense as he reached underwater and heaved a … massive char up onto the deck. Our relief that it wasn't a seal was short-lived, however, as Jeanie—slightly disappointed—tried to cheer us up by announcing that she'd brought some old boiled seal meat with her that we could have for lunch anyway.

Crouching down beside the assortment of char, Jeanie gave us a lesson filleting fish the Inuit way, ready for drying. It was harder than she made it look, but eventually our shredded rag-like fillets improved and we considered ourselves pretty well fully-fledged Inuits. Pleased by our willingness to learn Inuit skills, she delved into the bloody tangle of raw fish guts and pulled out the liver. Hoping for an anatomy lesson, we crouched closer as she sliced it in half with the *ulu* and held it up for us to—look at? The way she pressed it up against my lips in her blood-smeared fingers suggested otherwise. This was no anatomy lesson. I took it in my mouth and swallowed deeply, pushing the liver well below any limit of possible return, and even managed a polite comment on the likeness of the organ's oily, mucus-covered texture to that of fresh caviar.

Boy, was that a mistake. After enjoying watching Clark being put through the same experience, I gurgled in horror as she scraped aside the roe—the egg sac—from inside the spilling gut cavity and proceeded to offer this new delight up to our mouths. We couldn't really say no. Slurp, slurp. Wince. Smile. Swallow again for backup. 'It's good for you,' Jeanie grinned. Good for our hearts, anyway—anything that raises the heart rate up to 200 beats per minute is like exercise, isn't it?

Again she reached inside the fish's frame and next withdrew the intestines and stomach as we desperately looked around for an escape. 'And traditionally, our ancestors also ate the stomach,' she began, 'but I don't normally eat it, unless you really want some?' We at least pretended to give the question due consideration.

The nightmare continued as Brent came over and started trying to push the eyes out of the fish's head. Thankfully, they held their ground and he gave up, remarking that, strangely, 'Some people have difficulty eating something that's looking back at them.' Really? I'd never have guessed it.

Our next Arctic lesson was to learn some respect for the temperature—or lack of temperature—of the water. 'We're going for a swim?' We repeated Brent's words incredulously. This experience was made possible by first sweltering inside his home-made sauna until we had to run out and dive into the ice-strewn water to save ourselves from catching on fire. There's nothing quite as good as a 50-degree temperature differential to reset your heart!

After a lunch of boiled seal which tasted like rubbery, oily tuna, and a bite or two of seal blubber which had an amazingly warming effect as our bodies went into overdrive processing all the energy, Brent took us out to teach us more ice-kayaking skills. Getting in and out of a kayak floating against a sheet of ice was honestly scary. It's a difficult operation when the ice is moving, the kayak's moving, the water's lurching and all that joins the three is your paddle, which grips to ice like water does to a duck's back. Both Clark and I got a few more grey hairs that afternoon. The Arctic certainly is a risky place to live, a view backed up by Brent, who commented that he finds, on average, one human skull each year.

Now competent ice-kayaking experts, next morning Clark and I hopped into our two borrowed kayaks and started the 10-kilometre paddle home on our own. The wind picked up considerably, and the last few kilometres into the wind across the open bay became pretty intense, forever etched into both our minds. Whitecaps—small breaking waves—were growling past on all sides, along with the odd chunk of ice, and despite digging as hard as we could with our paddles, it felt like we were slipping backwards. Our kayaks would slam into one wave, rear up, and plough into or under the next, icy water running back over the cockpit. 'We're not getting any closer, are we?' Clark shouted over the gale. The town looked just as small and distant as it had for the last twenty minutes, and our arms were tiring.

'Yeah, we are … for sure!' I wasn't as confident as I sounded, and directly downwind of us lay the half-frozen horizon of the Arctic Ocean.

That moment was a bit of a turning point: something extra kicked in inside me, and it wasn't fear. My mood swung into being extra positive, extra optimistic, and extra inspired—I felt, strangely, that I was suddenly 'in my element', and actually really enjoying it. Clark, too, had slipped into the right frame of mind and we both transformed into pirates, hollering 'Arrgh … Scurvy … Batten down the hatches!' and suchlike, in between singing 'Row, Row, Row Your Boat'. It was as if we subconsciously realised that we needed to be positive to get through this, not only inwardly confident, but flamboyantly so, to help bolster each other's confidence. It was a strategy that we would become mighty familiar with in the months ahead.

And so the days ticked past—we'd now been on the island for over a week, still without any progress on the kayak hold-up. We even did our first Sky News TV interview 'live from the expedition' over the phone in Doug's house: 'How are we finding it? Well actually we haven't left yet … no …' Great. Remaining ever optimistic, we reasoned that we needed to keep in shape, so we found an old truck tyre at the local tip and took turns dragging it around town, cementing the publicly held belief that 'the two Oz-tralians' were 'a bit funny' if not 'completely mad'. Clark had managed to develop a whopper blister on his heel, forcing him to hobble around like an old man, and we'd both somehow caught a cold that we just couldn't shake. Yep, we're the *sniff* two ultra-fit Arctic *sneeze* athletes who are here to cross the island.

A benefit of our delayed departure was that one day we returned home to find our house had been reclaimed by its original owner— Doug had returned from Ellesmere Island! From all the stories we'd heard of him, we imagined Doug to be a great giant of a man with a booming lumberjack's voice who could beat up a polar bear with one arm tied behind his back.

We were genuinely surprised by the real 'White Inuit'. 'Oh,' he said in a quiet, almost timid voice, 'you must be Chris. We get to meet at last, that's really neat … I'm having a cup of tea, would you like one?'

Doug was an absolute wealth of knowledge on all things biological, geological, geographical and even meteorological. 'Do you like these?' He pointed to the series of semi-transparent fist-sized spheres that decorated many of his windows.

'Yeah, we were wondering what they were! Are they seeds inside them?'

'Very good, yes. They are actually the crop from a pigeon-like bird called a ptarmigan … it's a traditional house-welcoming decoration. You cut it out of the bird, tie up one end, and then blow into the other and the crop fills like a balloon.'

We carefully put it back on the windowsill. 'And the seeds?' we ventured.

'Well, they're already in there, the crop is almost like the bird's first stomach when it's gathering food …' His gaze flicked to a balloon of a different shape hanging from the overhead light. 'And that one, that's a fish bladder.'

Doug was an inspiration. 'Your trip's going to be really neat,' he predicted. 'I wish I had the time to come along with you, at least for the first bit along the coast … you'll discover all sorts of things up there!' In his same quiet manner, he then made another, more disturbing prediction. 'I think you've left it too late in the season, though.' We stared fixedly at the table, not wanting to hear it. 'It doesn't really matter; you'll get part of the way across, I think. Maybe you should treat this one as a trial run, and come back again next year.'

A little deflated, we recited our well-practised line of defence: 'It'll be fine, the delay starting just means we'll finish a few weeks later, that's all. We'll get there.' At least his predictions, refreshingly, didn't involve us both dying out there. We could have sat for days soaking up his wisdom on all things Arctic; however, true to character, after enjoying only two days' respite back in the comfort of home since having just spent three months alone on his remote post, he waved goodbye, setting off on a five-day canoeing and fishing trip with some friends.

'Good luck with your trip,' he said, slipping on his caribou-fur jacket. 'I guess you'll be long gone by the time I get back.' We assured him we would be.

Five days later, we ran down to the shore to welcome his return. The joke had gone on long enough, and I thought I saw a faintly pained expression flit across his face as he saw us. 'You're still here?!' Whether it was sympathetic pain at our misfortune, or inner pain at having us still occupying his house, we couldn't be sure. We herded our sea of gear into one corner of his living room, and so as not to impose any more than necessary, decided to spend our 'nights' camped out of town from then on.

Having been stuck in Cambridge Bay now for thirteen days, the next morning I was due to call Sky News for what should have been our second weekly interview from 'out on the land'. I gazed forlornly at my scribbled list of 'news' to chat about, notably devoid of any information on our kayak's hostage situation, let alone a departure date for our expedition. 'No, actually we're still in Cambridge Bay …' I tried to sound up-beat, but the producer's direct, blunt questions had the effect of unravelling my carefully woven cocoon of optimism, leaving me exposed to the harsh reality of our situation. 'No, we're not sure when we'll … Yes, we're still going to go.'

I don't think she really believed me—hell, I didn't even know if I believed myself anymore. 'Well, I don't think we'll do an interview,' she said. 'We'll look at running one next week if you're on your way by then.' I wondered if 'on our way back home' counted.

As much we tried to ignore it, every passing day drew the end of summer one day closer—our window of opportunity was sliding shut, and had perhaps already closed. Every evening we convinced ourselves that we could wait just one more day, forever stalling the inevitable decision. It was pathetic. Even if we started out the very next morning, our allotted 65 days would push us well beyond mid September, by which time our world would freeze over and lengthening darkness would start swallowing the hours of daylight. The temperature would begin its slippery slope to 50 degrees below zero, accompanied by 24-hour darkness. We just weren't equipped to cope with even the start of the oncoming winter, yet each day we knew the tail end of our trip was extending further and further into this deadly freezer. It was obvious to us what we needed to do. 'We'll just have to get there in under 65 days I guess …' Irrational optimism had got us this far, we figured, and we'd put in too much to give up now.

Thankfully by now we had plenty of supportive friends on the island, and we drew encouragement from what was in fact our own optimism which they now reflected. We even managed to convert a firm disbeliever—Colin. In days past, he'd had an elite dog team, and a real spark danced in his eyes as he related some of his earlier adventures with them. Thinking him a man after our own hearts, we were a little taken aback when he commented over dinner that he thought we were foolish to set out on our adventure, and that we'd almost certainly die an incredibly lonely death out there. As the evening progressed, however—and as details of our trip leaked out—we could see him getting more and more excited by our plans, just like the geologist in Vancouver. By the time we'd brought out some pictures of us building the PACs and traced a finger along our proposed route on a wall map, Colin was as excited as we were. He announced, 'Well, boys! I think what you're doing is just great! What an adventure!' and firmly shook our hands. 'It's my honour to shake your hands. Good on you. I still think you'll probably die, but good on you for trying!' Our soaring egos placed firmly back where they belonged, he humbled us with one final remark: 'You've inspired me, boys, you really have. You know, there are still a few dog-sled trips I'd like to try one day—maybe I'm not too old.'

# ACTION STATIONS!

The next morning I called Craig for our daily dose of bad news. 'What do you mean "it's happening"?' I asked. 'What's happening?' My cautious optimism gave way to euphoria as he explained to my disbelieving ears that he had done the impossible. He'd again met with the spokesperson representing the striking truckers and convinced him to let our trucker-saviour 'Paul' come in and collect our container. Further, they'd already located the container—now buried underneath six others on the clogged wharf—and first thing Monday morning a huge crane would start digging it out for us.

'And the paperwork? The container handling company said that—'

Craig interrupted me, 'It's all sorted, I've found you a decent handling company—Ecu-Line.'

The uncontrollable grin spreading across my face made talking quite difficult, but I carried on, searching for the inevitable catch. 'So, after the crane puts the container aside, how long before—'

Again he cut me off. 'It won't be "put aside", Chris, it'll be placed directly onto the truck, with engines running, ready to drive immediately to Edmonton airport—that'll take nine and a half hours if he doesn't stop. You'd better organise room on that plane.' It was quite definitely the best piece of news I'd ever heard in my life.

We exploded into action. After two weeks of stagnation, obstacles and impossibilities, in the space of about five minutes everything had just fallen into place. We sent an update to our website with the news, and Canadian Press got hold of the story within hours and rang for an interview. Sitting there listening to their pre-interview spiel before they crossed over to me, it really hit home just how impossibly lucky we had been: 'With the trucking strike now in its third week, Vancouver businesses have lost over $500 million, but it looks like an exception is being made for two Australian kayakers … We have one of the boys on the phone now; Chris, how did …' To be honest, I didn't really know how, and while I tried to justify how critical it was that we started our expedition before summer slipped past, I couldn't help but start to feel a little guilty. The media was full of reports of countless people's dreams that had been broken by this strike, and I feared more than a little resentment brewing that somehow these two foreigners had been given special treatment just to embark on a pointless walk. It could have quite easily turned spiteful, but thankfully, the presenter took a positive view from the start.

The good news circulated quickly, and we confirmed with the floatplane pilot that he'd be able to fly us out to our start point in the next few days. 'Oh, sure. No worries. We'll need two planes, and we'll just strap one kayak onto the side of each.' I reminded him they weren't typical kayaks, but he brushed my concerns aside with a sweeping gesture of his hand.

As the passenger jet carrying our PACs appeared in the distance, Clark and I were already crouched with our video cameras pointing skyward on the back of Wilf's truck hurtling towards the airport. He scarcely slowed at the gates to the airport; instead, flicking on the truck's roof-mounted spinning lights he proceeded to drive right out onto the airfield. The plane touched down right in front of us and we stood around like impatient children on Christmas morning, waiting for all the passengers to disembark so the cargo could be unloaded. After what seemed like an age, the massive cargo hatch swung open, and there on top of everything else was our bubble-wrapped present. It was certainly a sight for sore eyes.

Our two toys had been whisked away from us to Canada before we'd had a chance to even play with them, and we couldn't wait to put them together. As soon as the forklift placed the package on the ground we fell upon it, tearing off great strips of bubble-wrap, deaf to the indignant shouts from the handlers that we couldn't touch it until transport had been paid for. Friends turned up to get a look at the PACs, and the local CBC radio presenter pulled a tape recorder from his pocket and recorded an interview on the spot. We were on such a high that I scarcely batted an eyelid when the cargo handlers—who by this stage had realised the only way they were going to get us to fill in any paperwork was to bring it to us—presented me with the $4000 bill. To be honest, I was expecting more like $400, but right then, I think I would have signed away my first-born child to get our kayaks.

'Chris and Claaaark!' It was the local journalist, Helen, waving us dramatically over to her. 'I've been looking everywhere for you! We're all ready for you, come on, the mayor is waiting!' We had all but forgotten—she'd organised days earlier for a traditional Inuit performance for us that very afternoon! Shoving our PACs in an unused hangar, we piled into the truck and headed to a quiet corner of the bay. Her aunt Mary—an Inuit elder dressed head to toe in a traditional caribou-skin gown—performed the most amazing 'drum dance' for us. We watched in awe as this seemingly frail old woman whirled around, chanting, wailing and stamping her feet, while rhythmically striking a large skin drum held in her wrinkled hands. Her dancing was so vigorous, and her wailings so sudden and intense, that several times Clark and I shot alarmed glances at each other, wondering if perhaps she was having a heart attack.

Following this, two Inuit girls, Yvonne and Charlotte, enchanted us with a display of 'throat singing', the most unusual kind of singing either of us had ever heard. They linked arms, facing each other, and 'sang' together in harmony from the very back of their throats. Surprisingly deep and gurgling without any spoken words, it sounded to me a bit like a cross between a bleating muskox and a burping yodeller. That may sound off-putting, but it was actually hauntingly melodious, beautiful even, transporting us briefly into the timeless, spiritual world of the traditional Inuit people. It was a rare privilege and put us in the perfect mindset for heading out to explore their ancient land.

The next 'morning' we were back at the hangar, assembling the wheels onto our PACs and sticking on sponsor logos. We triumphantly wheeled our contraptions, now resembling over-branded Formula-1 racing cars, out onto the road. 'Shall we see how they go over the tundra?' Clark asked hesitantly. Looking back, it was absurd, but we decided not to—the tundra seemed particularly lumpy just here and we didn't want to break anything unnecessarily. We amused ourselves instead by giving each other chariot rides until Brent turned up.

'So these are the PACs, hey? Wow. Boy they look heavy …' This wasn't exactly the comment we were angling for from our Arctic mentor, especially considering the PACs were still completely empty. He swung himself into the harness and led one of our precious unscratched babies off the road and onto the open tundra. We held our breaths. The PAC joggled around behind him, clanking and rattling alarmingly, but thankfully nothing actually fell off. 'I guess it'll settle down a bit under load,' Brent called back. 'I can see a few issues with it, but I kinda like it …'

Once back at Doug's, we immediately sought to answer a nagging question: 'Do you think all this gear is going to actually fit inside the PACs?' We literally had no idea if it would. As we carried drybag after drybag out of the cabin and placed it beside the PACs, we started to have serious doubts. There really was a *lot* of gear and food—we'd never actually seen it all piled together in one place before. It was one of those silent moments where neither of us said much, and we just started stuffing bags inside every hatch, anxious to see how much of it was going to remain sitting on the tundra. 'We don't really need a tripod each, do we?' No, we didn't. We also didn't need the two harmonicas that we'd earlier convinced ourselves would come in handy at the end of a long day of hauling. We left them on Doug's table, along with several other last-minute equipment list casualties.

Amazingly, everything important fitted inside the PACs, just. We shot each other a classic 'well, that was lucky' nod of approval, and unloaded everything back into Doug's house. While all this was going on, we had a constant stream of visitors dropping by to ogle our famed wheeled kayaks and help with the last to-do's.

'Hmm, I was thinking they were going to be more like kayaks …' It was Fred Hamilton, the floatplane pilot, leaning out of his truck. 'I'm not sure how we'll go fitting them on the planes, actually. We'll see, eh?' For a passing comment, it could hardly have been more pivotal, but he seemed content to cross this bridge when he came to it, and drove off before the power of speech returned to us.

'It'll be okay,' Clark managed at last.

'It better be okay!' I added, laughing. 'There's no other way we can get out to our start point!'

'We could haul there …' Clark offered, and while he said it as a joke, we both cringed a little inside. Nothing—absolutely nothing—was certain.

A little after lunch, Clark and I were doing some last-minute provisioning at the supermarket when a group of Inuit girls ran up to us, pointing. 'I saw you on TV last night,' one said, grinning. 'You were on the news.' It was the first we'd heard of it. 'You're setting out on your trip today,' she announced, and giggling, they all scampered away.

'Ha—I wish!' I said to Clark, visualising all the things we still needed to do and test, including checking to see if the PACs even floated under the weight of all the gear, and if they still leaked. 'But maybe we should try and find Fred and see if we can book our flight for tomorrow evening, or the day after?'

'Speak of the devil,' Clark said, nodding as Fred strode out of the store behind us.

'Hey, boys! Been looking for you about that flight, fitting those huge kayaks on the side of the plane—' A mounting, paralysing dread poured into my stomach as he continued. 'I've been thinking, and, argh … I reckon it'll be okay.' A calming relief washed over us, but it was short-lived. 'We'll fly you out at seven this arvo—but bring them down a little early, just in case we need to think of something else.'

'This arvo!?' I echoed, taken aback.

'Seven pm,' Fred confirmed. 'There's a good break in the weather and I've got both planes free this evening so we can do it in one go—can't say if we'll get another chance this week. You are ready to go, right? I saw it on the news?'

I swallowed hard and looked at Clark. 'Yeah. Well, we can be, anyway …'

Panic. 'Let's split up!' I said. 'You run and start shooting the stock footage to send back for Sky News, and I'll fill in that "we've gone hiking" form for the police. Then we'll load the PACs up, and our test paddle can be around to the floatplane base. Let's go go go!'

Clark hobbled off as fast as the near terminally infected blister on his heel would permit, and I wheezed my way to the Royal Canadian Mounted Police (RCMP) building through the drizzling rain. Just what the doctor ordered. Neither of us had been able to shake our colds.

'Yes, that's right,' the RCMP officer said, nodding, 'anyone going "out on the land" should fill in one of these forms stating where you're going, when you'll be back. So how many days are you going … hunting, or, what are you doing again?' She looked at me.

'Er, my friend and I are going to try and cross the whole island; we think it might take about two months.'

'Wow, that's a seriously long hunting trip!' she exclaimed.

'Oh, we're not hunting …'

She looked perplexed. 'What are you doing then? Fishing?'

'Um, no,' I ventured, 'we're just … walking,' I finished lamely, and at once was struck by the complete idiocy of the whole undertaking. Pointless or not, time was of the essence, and I didn't have time to psychoanalyse myself any further. I filled in the form, and hurried back to Doug's, where Clark was frantically loading the PACs.

Eventually we wedged the last hatch closed, and pulled them towards the water's edge. They were impossibly heavy, and, disconcertingly, we had to take it in turns helping each other to roll them to the shore. Once there, we were faced with a new problem. To convert the PACs from wheeled mode to kayak mode, we had to somehow pull the axle out from underneath, gently lower the PAC to the ground, lift the pivoting wheel arms up on each side, and re-slide the axle back through, linking the two now across the top of the kayak. Considering that each PAC now weighed 250 kilograms, simply getting Clark to 'hold it up' while I withdrew the axle just wasn't going to work.

'Damn! We're going to have to unload and re-load both PACs each time we get into, and out of, every single lake? *SHIT!* That'll take forever!' Clearly we should have seen this one coming, and it served as an unwelcome reminder of just how untested our systems were. After lightening the load by a few token bags of chocolate and other supplies, Clark did a pretty good impersonation of Clark Kent by momentarily supporting—and then hastily lowering to the ground—about 180 kilograms as I did the conversion.

'Great, and now we just drag them the last bit into the water …'

Clark said with a wry smile, knowing full well how impossible this would be. With a horrible grinding, screeching noise we struggled them at last into the water, leaving behind a confetti trail of flecks of orange paint and aluminium filings. With a great deal of trepidation, we gently eased ourselves into our PACs and tentatively pushed off.

'God, they sit *so low* in the water!' I commented, balancing myself so water wouldn't lap in either side.

'Yeah, but they do actually float,' Clark observed, 'so that's good. Right, let's get them to the floatplane base, we're already late!'

To our great relief, the PACs did indeed fit alongside the plane's floats, and after giving mine a cursory wiggle, Fred proclaimed, 'It'll be okay,' and clambered up inside the plane. Ahead, Clark's PAC was already lashed to the other plane.

This was it. It was time to go. As we hugged our adopted parents Phil and Liz goodbye, Liz pushed a warm paper bag into my hands. 'I baked you some muffins,' she said. 'They'll be your last taste of homely comfort.' With that, Clark and I squished in beside our respective pilots and clanked the little door closed.

At the push of a button, the engine sputtered into life, quickly rising to a deafening roar, the whole plane humming as we taxied out into the bay. 'All right, let's see if we can lift off with all this load,' Fred shouted, sounding genuinely interested, and flung open the throttle.

Vibrating so hard I could barely see, the plane surged through the water, slowly gaining speed. The sound of rushing water gradually gave way to the slap-slap-slapping of the wave crests as we scampered along the surface like some ungainly bird, before at long last we lumbered into the air.

'Great!' shouted Fred. After eighteen days waiting in Cambridge Bay, we were finally on our way!

As we droned over the barren landscape, I was again struck by just how empty it was. I wasn't expecting great blankets of animals shuffling across the tundra, although I thought I might be able to at least spot a few muskox—but there was nothing. Kilometre after kilometre of nothing. Just a patchwork of lakes and swamp. After twenty minutes or so of this, my eye was drawn along a snaking gravel pathway, raised a little above the swampy tundra. 'What's that?' I shouted, pointing.

'That's an *esker*,' Fred said by way of explanation.

'What's an esker?' I bellowed.

'It's where a river used to flow underneath a glacier,' he shouted. 'The glaciers are all long gone, but what you're left with are these raised riverbeds—like roads.' They were indeed like roads. 'You should follow them, where you can,' he added, tapping his map and passing it to me. Trying to hold the vibrating map steady enough to read, I saw a winding, intermittent hatched trail.

'I thought they were cliffs!' I shouted.

'What?' Fred leant closer.

'Nothing ...' I said, my mind reeling. The esker symbol really did look very similar to those used to indicate cliffs on other maps I'd seen, and Clark and I had laboriously planned our whole route to avoid them at all costs. Great. Yet another shining example of how ignorant and unprepared we were for the situation in which we'd soon find ourselves. Just ahead I could see Clark's plane, and I wondered if he was feeling as insecure as I was.

'There's the coast,' Fred indicated. As we flew towards our start point—the most easterly tip of the island—we could see the entire coastline was jam-packed with buckled sheets of ice. 'We need open water to land,' Fred shouted, straining to see along the shoreline. After a few minutes, he swung the plane around, heading inland again. 'Sorry, Chris, it's going to have to be this lake.'

After a quick fly-over to check the lake didn't look too shallow, he squared the plane for landing, and we swooped in, rattling at last to a halt. 'All right, let's unload!' he said, climbing out of the cockpit. Ahead of us, with their plane already drifted against the shore, Clark and his pilot were ferrying armfuls of gear onto the tundra.

Lastly we unlashed the PACs and pushed them ashore. Both, we noticed, had water sloshing around inside them from our earlier test paddle. 'I guess they ... um ... still leak then,' Clark said brightly.

We posed with the pilots for a photo, and shook their hands. 'Well, boys,' Fred said heavily, 'you've got guts, that's all I can say. This is bear country. I do wish you the best of luck, but, to be honest, I don't expect to see either of you two alive again.'

With that, they turned away, and in a blast of freezing prop wash and spray, they were gone, taking all our confidence with them.

PART TWO
# VICTORIA ISLAND

# DAY 1 (30 July 2005): Alone in the Arctic

The silence was deafening.

We stood there, watching the spot where the planes had vanished, and, all at once, we were surrounded by the vacuum of complete isolation. Neither of us spoke a word for several seconds as reality sank in: we were standing there, completely alone, hundreds of kilometres from the nearest human, and—as the pilot had kindly reminded us—in 'bear country'. We dug out both shotguns from the mountain of equipment lying in front of us, filled our pockets with bullets and munched quietly on Liz's muffins—their comforting warmth all but drained away—all the while continually scanning our surroundings, searching for the polar bears we could feel watching us.

I turned on our GPS and waited for a fix. 'Damn—we're more than 2 kilometres from our start point, ' I said, wincing. 'Oh, and guess what?' I was grinning now. 'You know our wonderfully planned route, carefully avoiding all those cliffs on the maps?'

'Yes?' Clark said, steeling himself for more bad news.

'Yeah, turns out they're "eskers"—like pebble highways—so that's our route plan out the window.'

Our sense of inadequacy and alienation was complete, and there was nothing else we could do but laugh, and laugh. It felt good, actually, and right then, a whole lot of pent-up worry and stress just seemed to fall away.

At long last, after thirteen months of dreaming and planning, after having our hopes smashed and having to rebuild them more times than we can count, we are, finally, here, on our own in the middle of the Arctic, forced to rely on no one but ourselves. Our world has shrunk to simply include ourselves, and whatever we remembered to pack in that pile of gear. The next two months will be a challenge—a great adventure—but unlike some of the incompetent people we've been forced to deal with to get this far, I know that I can trust Clark, and trust myself. Provided we keep alert and our gear doesn't break, I am confident we'll get to the far side of the island. We just have to take it one day at a time.

Clark fumbled with the tent and eventually got it up fifteen minutes later, while I clumsily set up the perimeter bear alarm, trying not to notice the way the undulating ground left some sections of the tripwire skimming the ground, and others strung worryingly high over ditches. Oh well, I thought, a really big bear'd probably still bump into it anyway. I test-pulled the tripwire, and clapped my hands towards my ears to cover them, but no alarm went off. My stomach gave a little lurch of fear. I checked everything, reconnected the tripwire and tested it again. Silence. I couldn't believe it—our bear alarm was broken!

Horrified, exhausted and more than a little scared, just before climbing inside our tent we loaded our shotguns, and Clark test-fired a bear-banger into the sky. We watched it whirl high into the air and explode, the *crack* sounding strangely truncated with nothing to echo off. We had meant it to be a warning—to scare off any bears lurking in the area—but regretted it instantly, now picturing the heads of every polar bear for miles around turning as one to look in our direction. Feeling increasingly vulnerable, we retreated inside the tent and lay there in our sleeping bags, our ears straining to hear approaching noises outside, waiting. Waiting to be consumed either by sleep, or by a fury of claws and teeth tearing through the side of the tent. Thankfully, we were so utterly spent that tranquillising sleep soon found us.

## DAY 2: Sickeningly difficult

My surroundings only gradually filtered through as I rose from the murky depths of sleep this morning: snug inside a sleeping bag ... in a tent ... Arctic expedition ... first night's sleep ... still alive!! With this last realisation came a surge of absolute elation. Never before have I revelled in the surprise of actually finding myself alive. It was definitely a positive start to our first day 'out on the land'.

I set up the video camera and filmed Clark—steaming bowl of porridge in hand—confidently relating the day ahead. 'Today, we're going to pack up, walk a couple of kilometres to the start point in that direction, and organise ourselves ...' We divided the huge pile of gear and food in two, and loaded up our PACs. Each weighs a whopping 250 kilograms—that's a quarter of a tonne, the equivalent of pulling a cart with three fully grown men standing on it. We clipped our harnesses into the hauling yoke, and ceremoniously shook hands—this was it, the moment we'd been waiting for. I shouldered my harness and leant forward.

Nothing moved. I leant further. Nothing. I bent my knees, and leant right over—my nose only inches from the tundra, my arms reached right out in front to give maximum weight leverage, and, bunched like a human piston, slowly forced my legs to straighten. Ever so gradually, my PAC began to creep forward. Pausing, I turned to see how Clark was going, only to discover that once moving, my PAC didn't want to stop, and instead, it flung me to the ground and then proceeded to try and run over me. Thus I quickly learned about momentum.

We thought dragging a truck tyre was hard work, but the superhuman effort required to advance our PACs even a few steps out here is just unbelievable; sickeningly difficult. All humour quickly drained away from the situation as we stood speechless with shock, our minds reeling, unable to come to terms with the thought of having to haul the carts even to our start point, let alone across the whole island. 'One step at a time ...' we kept telling ourselves, 'let's just try and reach that patch of tundra over there ...' The very best we could manage was five, or perhaps ten steps at a time before we'd find ourselves standing groggily, gasping for air, and literally feeling like we were going to be sick.

Some 30 minutes later, I turned on the GPS to discover we'd managed a mere 70 metres. It was all too much. The lurching motion of the PAC snagging and releasing us, constantly throwing us off balance; its rattling, clanking and grinding; my own ragged breath unnaturally loud in my ears; sweat stinging my eyes and running to the tip of my nose, from where it splashed onto the endless sea of shattered limestone; my body almost horizontal with effort.

Both too exhausted and dizzy to go further, we stopped for an early lunch just short of the 100-metre mark, and collapsed against the side of our PACs. It was then that I noticed that the tow point—the part that joins my hauling arm to the PAC—was buckling. We'd built most of the PAC from aluminium, with a few exceptions including this hauling bracket which we'd built from steel, as it was the one thing we certainly couldn't afford to have break. And here we were, less than 100 metres into a 1000-kilometre journey, and it was already breaking.

MacGyver style, I banged a rock in under the bracket to stop it caving in any further, and with nothing else to do we plodded onwards. Soon Clark's tow point was showing signs of buckling too, and then, a few hours later, a crucial bit of webbing that straps the hauling arm down chafed right through. Of course we have spares, but it was horribly disconcerting to be digging into our 'spare parts' bag so early in the expedition.

It wasn't until late in the afternoon that we eventually crossed the one-kilometre mark. I turned the video camera on Clark. 'Well, (*pant*) that was our first one kilometre of hauling …'

'And how was it?' I enquired.

'Well, I almost broke the PAC, broke my toe, broke my back, and I don't know how you went … (*pant*), but we've done 1000 metres and we've got … (*pant*) a million to go. So (*pant*) yeah, it's going good.'

I agreed, and, boosted by each other's confidence—albeit totally unfounded—we convinced ourselves that all was on track. We expected a slow start, after all—our PACs would only get lighter, we'd grow stronger, and each day we'd chip away at the mental hurdle, one kilometre at a time.

We finally reached the coast a few hours ago. It's an eerie place. Hunks of white sea ice scattered hundreds of metres inland (presumably by the tide, which may have interesting implications for our tent site), and a billowing fog has just rolled in, making these crouching white shapes drift in and out of view. 'Over there—' We'd both stare blindly, trying to pierce through the swirling haze. 'Was that a polar bear?' After a few tense moments, we'd manage to pull our eyes away and focus back on cooking dinner. The tantalising smell of our alfredo pasta lured in our first arctic fox! Clumps of white winter fur still hanging from its new brown summer coat gave it a very dishevelled, scruffy look, to which we instantly related.

I'm now lying in the tent, broken bear alarm still coiled uselessly inside the PACs, and the sun has actually swooped low enough to create a stunning 'sunset', splashing beautiful pinks and purples across the sky. Unfortunately, these seductive colours hide a darker truth: the perpetual, 24-hour sunlight of midsummer is already coming to an end out here. And we've not even reached our start point yet—it's still another 2 kilometres up the coast … Considering that today we managed a grand total of 1.3 kilometres after about ten hours of giving it our all, we should get to the start point sometime the day after tomorrow, and the far side of the island in … just over two years and one month's time.

## DAY 3 (1 August 2005): Achievable goals

Surprisingly, we awoke alive again, having miraculously survived two nights without a working polar bear tripwire alarm. I'm sure we're being paranoid, but each night it feels like a game of Russian roulette—spinning the revolver and putting it to my temple, squeezing the trigger as I close my eyes to go to sleep. Will tonight be the night? Being right on the coast here, this is prime bear territory …

Clambering awkwardly out of the tent this morning—every muscle in my body aching from yesterday's efforts—a strange bush about 100 metres away caught my attention. It was quite high, its brown leafless branches swaying in the wind. Odd, I thought, considering there wasn't even the slightest hint of breeze. I pointed it out to Clark and the two of us watched incredulously as it leant over, righted itself and then proceeded to dance towards us. We stared at each other, rooted to the ground like the bush should have been, unsure quite how to react.

As the tree rose higher, we saw it was in fact balanced on top of something, which turned out to be the head of an enormous reindeer, seemingly 4 or 5 metres tall. 'It's a giant caribou!' I shouted excitedly, diving for my camera. Munching the tundra growing along the bottom of a ditch, the animal's body had been hidden from view, and all we'd seen at first were his towering antlers. Now that we could see him in full, he shrank to the size of a normal reindeer. Without the help of surrounding trees, telegraph poles, buildings or other known height references out here to help judge size and distance, it really is confoundingly impossible to judge!

After the apparition had pranced away, we wolfed down our porridge, packed up camp and shackled ourselves back into the hauling harnesses, wincing as we tightened up into the massive bruises we'd already got around our waists. With a prolonged grunt, our human-piston manoeuvre got the PACs rolling, and we plodded painfully onwards.

The terrain we were inching through today was a cross between an African savannah and a Martian landscape with chunks of ice thrown in to add to the surreal feel. A flat, endless expanse of ice-shattered limestone stretched out as far as the eye could see, the ground melting into a shimmering haze in the distance, where refracting light projected up distorted visions of things below the horizon. At first glance, a distant caribou we spotted around lunchtime actually looked like a giraffe—its legs and neck visually stretched to three times their normal height.

Another weird visual effect resulting from the complete lack of landscape reference points out here is that stationary objects, unbelievably, often appear to move: on numerous occasions, no sooner had I convinced myself that a certain chunk of stranded ice was not a polar bear, or that a particular boulder wasn't a grizzly bear, I'd glance away and look back, only to find it crouched in an apparently different location! Occasionally, fixed objects actually seemed to glide across the ground in front of our eyes until one or other of us would stop to stare directly at it, whereupon our PAC's momentum would quickly lurch us awkwardly forward and we'd stumble onwards, still trying to stare back over our shoulders. And our bear paranoia has quickly soared to the point where we have both now adopted the rather fatalistic attitude of hauling on regardless of the ominous white shapes we regularly notice. One of the strangest phenomena we witnessed today was a large grizzly bear about 200 metres away that we both agreed was definitely moving. In the end it turned out to be a stationary rock, only about 50 metres away, and much smaller than we'd thought. The weirdest thing, though, was that it *had* recently been moving. This boulder had somehow smeared its way across the mud, leaving a path some 20–30 metres long behind it. 'What the?' We marvelled at it for a while before realising that it must have been pushed up the shore by pack ice, long since melted.

Just ahead of me, Clark paused for breath and I drew level. 'Time for a … nut break?' he asked, between heaving breaths. One or two minutes of hauling at a time was all either of us could manage, and the idea of hauling all day (let alone across the island) was more than we could cope with, so we decided to break the day into mentally palatable portions. Even 'hauling until lunchtime' was inconceivable, so we split our 200 grams of nuts per day into four 'nut breaks', during which time we slumped beside our PACs and munched quietly on just a few, stashing the rest in our pockets to eat one at a time later, further dividing the otherwise interminably long 45-minute sessions until the next nut break. We aimed for achievable goals like reaching a particular rock, but often found ourselves simply counting down 50 steps before hanging exhausted in our harness, eating a single nut or a bit of our chocolate ration while trying to recover. Another 50 steps, come on, let's go … Fifty. Fffffforty-nine … Fffffforty-eight … And so we struggled towards our 'start point'.

'I reckon that's it,' I announced around dinner time, pointing to a protruding section of the coastline, 'the most easterly tip of Victoria Island!' We agreed, and set up the tent on top of a rotting matt of seaweed—literally the only place where the jagged edges of the shattered limestone wouldn't slice the floor of our tent to ribbons. 'It stinks, hey?' I said, laughing at Clark's feigned retching. 'Maybe it'll help mask our scent from the polar bears!'

Not entirely convinced by this, I spent half an hour after dinner taking apart the bear alarm, and, to our huge relief, after a bit of rewiring managed to get it working again.

For the first time, we are actually going to sleep feeling safe and secure, and even surprisingly comfortable—the squelchy carpet of decomposing seaweed beneath our blow-up mattresses works a treat.


## DAY 4: An expensive lesson

After breakfast we shackled up and pulled arduously away, at last heading towards our destination, rather than just the start of our adventure.

A herd of six caribou raised their heads and gazed at us with bemused expressions as we toiled slowly past. Suddenly, curiosity got the better of them and they started prancing towards us. All of them. It was amazing. Running right at us. Getting closer. Big antlers. 'Get your video camera!' Clark's words shook me from my trance. Just as we were both starting to wonder at what point we should swap the video camera for a shotgun, they paused, turning their heads awkwardly to one side to stare curiously at us from one bulging eye. As with most herbivores, caribous' eyes are on the sides of their head giving them great peripheral vision to watch out for predators, but they can't see directly ahead so well compared to carnivores with their forward-facing eyes. Nostrils flaring trying to identify a whiff of these strange two-legged animals dragging giant orange abdomens, they edged closer and closer, visibly torn between curiosity and fear. Suddenly one spooked, and the whole herd wheeled around and cantered away.

'I got some awesome footage!' Clark beamed. 'I should charge my video camera; have you got the cable?' I handed it over. Charging our electronics out here involves plugging them into our large 12-volt gel-cell 'main battery', which is itself continually kept charged by our giant flexible solar panels draped over the back of our PACs throughout the day. The problem is, of course, that not everything wants to be charged at 12 volts, and so I'd painstakingly built a 'voltage convertor box' that plugs into our main battery.

'That's funny,' Clark said. 'The charging light on the camera only comes on briefly and then starts blinking at me—it must still be fully charged … Cool.' He handed the cable back and I plugged mine in.

'Great battery life!' I commented, waiting for my charge light to come on. It didn't. I unplugged it and tried again. Nothing. 'That's weird,' I muttered. 'Mine doesn't even react when I plug it in. In fact,' I was now frantically trying to turn my camera on, 'it won't even turn on anymore! What's going o—'

And then it hit me. 'Oh, shit!!' I ripped the charge cable out of the camera and stared at Clark in horror and disbelief. 'We just plugged them directly into 12 volts!! We didn't use the voltage convertor box!' Holding my lifeless video camera to my nose, I inhaled. A familiar smell of charred electronics stung the back of my throat. 'How could we be so STUPID?!'

I was more surprised than angry. 'I spent weeks researching, designing and building that charger box,' I mumbled, shaking my head. 'How could I just ... forget to use it?' It was such a basic failing on my part that it was scary.

'Next we'll forget to load the shotgun, and when—' Clark cut his joke short, realising this mistake was no less likely. 'We'd better be careful.'

We heaved our PACs into motion and wearily stumbled onwards in silence. Fifty painfully drawn-out steps, then pause to wipe the sweat away, calm my breathing, swallow the rising urge to vomit, and fence my thoughts from running wild and dashing themselves against the enormity of it all. This is impossible.

Somehow or other, Clark's video camera thankfully survived being electrocuted, but mine wasn't so lucky. It's actually the circuit board that's fried, not just a fuse, so there is nothing we can do to fix it out here, and after discussing leaving several kilograms of now useless video camera behind on the tundra, I didn't have the heart and have stashed it away in my PAC to get repaired when we get home. We learned an important lesson today, though: physical exhaustion leads to mental exhaustion and bad decisions. We think we're making rational decisions, but really, clearly, we're not. And out here, where decisions have very real, potentially life-threatening consequences, we have to realise that we actually can't trust our own judgement—we are going to have to consciously distrust ourselves, and compensate by double- and cross-checking everything, even stuff that seems simple.

As our hauling sessions started to grow shorter and weaker this arvo, we made camp a little early to give our bodies a chance to recover. We've managed 5 kilometres today, which is great—our best yet. We're gradually finding our rhythm out here, but at the same time, it feels like we're getting more and more tired each day. We're also getting hungrier, which is a bad sign so early. Our breakfast, lunch and snacks are the same every day, but dinner is on a three-day rotation menu. One day it's an amazingly tasty dehydrated meal such as Beef Teriyaki with some extra rice, the next day it'll be plain pasta with butter and a few herbs, and the third day—which is unfortunately tonight—it's just lots of plain white rice, with loads of butter and a sprinkle of herbs. Despite each meal being equally (and highly) calorific, this 'rice night' in particular just seems pathetically small compared to our increasingly ravenous hunger. So this evening, while I wrote our first expedition update for our website—focusing on the positive news such as discovering iPod-assisted hauling (but with only one earpiece, so we can still hear bears, etc.)—Clark went for a walk with the shotgun, hoping to bring home an arctic hare or perhaps a ptarmigan to add to the pot. Although we purchased hunting permits for both delicacies (as well as for fish) before we left, we weren't intending to shoot anything unless we really needed to extend our rations towards the end of the trip, but already, serious food cravings are starting to chew away at us.

Unfortunately, Clark returned empty-handed, and after literally licking our bowls clean, we set up the bear tripwire alarm and, feeling hungry and concerned, shuffled deeper into our sleeping bags and fell asleep within seconds.

## DAY 5: More trauma

3.00 am: SCREECH!!! SCREECH!!! SCREECH!!!

The siren sliced through my dreams and I wrenched my eyelids apart, squinting blindly in the sunny tent. My eyes focused on Clark's and for a second, we gazed stunned-mullet style at each other in complete lack of comprehension. It didn't sound quite like our wristwatch alarm, and it couldn't possibly be morning already. Could it? We blinked stupidly at each other. 'The bear alarm!' I yelled, and terror suddenly surged through us. Just outside, a hungry polar bear would now be lumbering towards us, and if it got to the tent before we climbed out, we were about to die a particularly horrible death.

Fumbling frantically for the zipper on my sleeping bag, after what seemed like hours I finally grasped it, tore it open, and scrambled free. Beside me Clark was doing the same, and simultaneously we ripped open the zippers leading to the tent's twin vestibules, grabbed our shotguns and with a final flourish, unzipped the tent fly. Almost out! My heart racing, I crouched down and scampered awkwardly through the flapping doorway, expecting at any moment to be crumpled by a shaggy hulk of yellow-white fur, claws and teeth. I sprang upright, wildly looking everywhere at once.

Worryingly, something big had actually *snapped* rather than pulled the tripwire. Its broken ends trailed in the wind. 'I can't see it!' I shouted above the alarm's ear-splitting wail. 'Neither!' Clark yelled, eyes wide with fear. Where was it hiding? There were no hiding places for a bear. Maybe it wasn't a bear? But there was nothing—not even a fox. Whatever it was had apparently vanished into thin air. We were alone. As the panic subsided, I gradually became aware of icy water wicking through my warm bed socks from the sodden tundra underfoot, and felt the cold wind cutting through my Icebreaker thermals. Clark shrugged. I silenced the alarm, tied together the broken string, reset the tripwire and clambered back inside the tent. 'Maybe it was just the wind,' I suggested, as we both lay there, staring at the inside of the tent. 'We did set the string pretty tight.'

Today endlessly toiled past, much like yesterday, but thankfully without any more major equipment failures.

Snug back in the tent at last, we hooked our little laptop up to our Iridium satellite phone and connected briefly to the internet to check our email. There was a flood of little messages sent to us through our website—wonderfully encouraging emails of support, sympathy, admiration and, generally, enthusiasm—from all around the world. We even got one from renowned polar adventurer Wave Vidmar, who in response to our iPod comment wrote that we needn't bother leaving one earpiece out, as we'd never hear a bear until it was too close anyway. 'So, listen to your iPod with both ears, but keep an eye out on your downwind side,' he advised. Another poignant email was from Eric Philips, well-known Aussie polar explorer, who wrote, 'It's a really inspiring trip—you're breaking new ground with every step. Hang in there—as the muscles harden and the systems streamline, the mileage will begin to increase.' Humbled and cheered by his words, we drifted off to sleep.

## DAY 6: Slow and steady

Late this afternoon we reached the tail end of our very first esker. Unshackling and scampering up its surprisingly steep side we stood on its flat, pebbly top. 'Wow!' I drew a low whistle, impressed.

Clark raised his eyebrows. 'It really *is* like a gravel highway!' Paving our way forward beside a beautiful lake, this wondrous esker looked purpose-built to haul along.

We heaved our PACs onto the esker, and as it was already 5 pm, decided to make camp—it's just too perfect a spot not to. We managed a mere 2.5 kilometres today (a far cry from the 15 kilometres per day we need to start averaging soon to get to the end before our food runs out), but today's poor mileage was the result of several hours testing and improving our systems, durably repairing our PACs and so on this morning. Tomorrow on the esker will be better. We've adopted a 'slow and steady' approach now—we're out here for the long run. We're already forgetting to miss the comforts of home like hot showers and warm dry socks, and with such an incomprehensible number of days still ahead of us, such luxuries are too far off to 'look forward to', so this—what we have here and now—has actually become 'life'. It is what it is, and we're getting used to it.

I shot at (but unfortunately missed) a duck that would have gone superbly with our pasta dinner.

Actually—not feeling hungry—that's something I am increasingly missing.

## DAY 7: Death Terrain

Despite lurching awake several times due to a bird call that unfortunately is almost indistinguishable from our bear alarm—this feathered fiend has been striking fear into our hearts on a daily basis—we had a good sleep, and woke full of enthusiasm for a record day along the esker. Our PACs were steamrollering smoothly along behind us, and for the first time, we could actually maintain a strong, fast, uninterrupted stride. Listening to up-beat music on our iPods and with permanent smiles plastered across our faces, we flew along the esker, spirits soaring. By first nut break, we'd already blazed an astounding 3 kilometres. 'That's further than we got all yesterday!' Clark pointed out, beaming. 'Keep this up and we might even reach our 15-kilometres-a-day target!'

Our map told us it wouldn't last, however, and after only 3.5 kilometres of heaven, we made a gradual descent into hell. It didn't look bad at a distance, but soon we were surrounded by an endless expanse of the worst hauling terrain we've seen to date: horrifically sharp, jagged pieces of limestone, all propped up and poking at impossible angles, each designed to trip, snag and rip. It was as if someone had laid an enormous slab of concrete somewhere, kilometres across, and then changed their mind and jackhammered the whole thing, and hidden it all here. Trying to haul across this stuff is torture. Every step, the unstable plates of rock tip and clank, and all too often one wheel will suddenly snag, and the PACs' momentum then pivots the carts around, flinging us back and forth like rag dolls on the end of a stick. Picture hiking with a heavy pack, with a little brother hanging from it, flinging himself from side to side and jumping, always trying to throw you off balance. To drag the PACs up and over the snagging rocks, we literally have to crawl on all fours—the fabric of our gloves is shredded, and our hands are bleeding from grabbing the knife-edged fragments as we try to pull ourselves forward. It is exacting a horrible toll on both us and our PACs.

'It all used to be nice and flat,' Clark mumbled dejectedly to the video camera, 'with the odd rock sticking up. But now,' he turned a sample in his hands, 'it's every rock sticks up, and the odd flat rock.' Stumbling upon a muskox skull a few hours further into it, we decided to call this kind of terrain 'Death Terrain'.

Spotting a large lake, we made a beeline to it (in slow motion). It was big—3 kilometres across—and rather than tear ourselves apart any further on the Death Terrain surrounding it, we decided to try paddling across. Excited about our first major paddle, we changed into our Gore-Tex drysuits and pushed the PACs in.

And pushed. And pushed. Despite its being so wide we couldn't even see the other side, the entire lake turned out to be only about 30 centimetres deep and we ended up hauling almost all the way across. Still, the soft squelchy bottom was pure bliss, caressing and massaging our traumatised feet through our wetsuit booties, and we actually managed a decent speed too. Clark thinks we should aim for as many big lakes as we can, and I couldn't agree more!

It was 8.30 pm by the time we'd converted to hauling mode on the far bank, and so we set up the tent and tripwire. While Clark boiled up some dinner, I unloaded and inspected the contents of both PACs to check everything was still dry and confirmed thankfully that the hull hadn't sprung any leaks after being bashed around on the Death Terrain all day.

We are both absolutely exhausted—we've scarcely the energy to raise our spoons to eat. It feels as though every muscle in my body has been sprained from the whiplash of Death Terrain hauling. We are in good spirits though, and very satisfied with today's progress—13 kilometres! A record! Almost 15 kilometres! Things are looking up!

## DAY 8: Hiking poles

My watch alarm went off at 7 am. Neither of us stirred. I heard Clark's go off at 8 am and opened a cautious eye, shifting slightly in my sleeping bag to look across at him. My whole body ached terribly. Clark showed no signs of life, and so I decided to close my eyes for another five minutes. At 9 am, both our alarms went off, and as we both silenced them, we knew each other must be awake. 'Guess we should get up then,' Clark's croaky voice drifted out of his sleeping bag, done up so tightly that only his nose was visible.

I considered not responding. 'Yeah, I guess,' I finally conceded.

It was almost lunch by the time we'd eaten brekky, packed up and started rolling. 'It's a balance,' I commented, chewing on my peanut butter tortilla wrap with extra butter. 'If we push too hard one day, then—' the copious amount of peanut butter was gumming my tongue down, making it hard to talk, '—then, we pay for it the next day with a slow one.'

Clark nodded thoughtfully, adding, 'Yeah, there's no sneaking extra hours hauling overall … it evens out. We should just do what we can.'

A large buck caribou with towering antlers followed us for several hours today, circling us, edging closer to get a better look before retreating and starting again. It's fantastic out here—so many animals that basically walk right up to us, having likely never seen humans before. I'm getting some great photos! The birds flying overhead seem equally intrigued. 'Here comes another one—look!' I'd point at a goose or duck flying towards us from the distant horizon. Reaching us, they fly around and around looking down, then head off, right back to where they came from.

In the afternoon the tundra again dissolved into Death Terrain. Having been flung painfully to the ground for the umpteenth time,

Clark suddenly had an idea. 'We should try using the hiking poles.' Up until then we'd been grasping the hauling yoke itself as we hauled in a vain attempt to restrain its violent, thrashing outbursts, and so as Clark extended his pair of Exped hiking poles, I had serious doubts that letting go of the yoke could result in anything apart from bruised sides and possibly even kidney damage. I watched as he lurched the PAC into motion, and clattered his way forward like some giant four-legged insect. 'It's great!' he called back, looking genuinely delighted, 'Really helps you balance!'

I dug my pair out and gave it a try. He was right. Not only do they greatly add to our stability and prevent us being flung around so much, but we can poke and prod rocks in front before we get to them to see if they're stable, use them as crutches to step over muddy pockets, and even lean against them when we're tired. Now we can't haul without them! We learn something new out here every day.

## DAY 9: Anger management

Around 4 am I woke to find the jagged rocks beneath me had punctured my air mattress, and as blowing it up only provided temporary relief, I soon gave up and lay there, waiting for my watch to tell me it was morning, while the sun continued to blaze relentlessly through the tent fabric.

We hauled to the first of several lakes for the day, unloaded, and for some reason found it even harder than normal to withdraw the axle to convert to kayak mode. After much cursing, we eventually got it, repacked everything, and theatrically paddled into the fog. Having heaved the PACs onto the bank at the far side, we then unloaded all the heavy gear again, and Clark performed the 'Clark Manoeuvre'— briefly hoisting the stern up—while I lowered the wheels.

It has been getting harder for days, but now the axle bluntly refused to slide through. Without the axle clamping the wheels together, when Clark could no longer hold the back-breaking weight of the PAC, the wheels would simply splay out sideways and we'd have to start over again. 'Stupid bloody thing!!' Clark swore harshly, voicing my own anger, 'Is it full of grit or what?' Rinsing it in the lake didn't help.

Ten minutes later we were still trying, my hands were covered in bruises from attempting to bang the axle home, and Clark could only hold it up for increasingly short intervals. 'F&%king thing!!' We were both starting to lose it—I could tell Clark was getting inwardly frustrated with my inability to get it through, and me at Clark for always letting it go just when I almost had it. 'Why does everything have to be so fuc*%ing hard?! Why won't you just,' I was kicking it now, 'GO (*thump*) … IN!!' Bang! With a final unnecessarily vicious kick from my hiking boot, the axle slammed home. Instantly, all our anger and frustration melted away, and we were left standing there silently reflecting upon the rage we'd so easily worked ourselves into. 'It probably just needs re-greasing,' I murmured.

Hauling onwards, I couldn't help wondering how we'd cope with seven more weeks of this kind of pressure. So far we'd always managed to laugh it off, or at least direct our anger towards the situation itself, rather than each other, but we'd come pretty close to snapping at each other just then. I could tell Clark was pondering the same thing, yet neither of us spoke about it.

We are clearly being pushed to our limits out here—mentally as well as physically—and I think it's going to take an enormous amount of self-control to keep it together. Being stuck with the same one person—and no one else—for 24 hours a day, seven days a week, for eight or nine weeks, would be enough to seriously stretch the sturdiest of lifelong friendships to breaking point. But mix this with the kind of stress, sleep deprivation and hunger we are facing out here, and we've got a recipe for disaster. I dread a falling-out. We depend on each other's cooperation to survive.

The rest of the day passed uneventfully, and morale in the tent tonight was unnaturally high, perhaps in a subconscious effort to help lift each other out of earlier thoughts. We chatted openly about this and that, about girlfriends (specifically our lack of—and how we'd make up for lost time in the social scene once we returned home), about our dogs, our friends. 'I've been thinking …' Clark commented. 'It's kinda good that we haven't known each other for all that long, hey?'

I knew where he was coming from. 'Yeah, it gives us heaps of stuff to talk about, and … ' I hesitated.

'Means we haven't already gotten on each other's nerves!' Clark added, and we both laughed, trying to pretend that it wasn't the crux of what we had both been worrying about all day.

## DAY 10: More lake paddling

After re-greasing the axle this morning, converting to kayak mode at today's first lake was a delightful anticlimax, and we were soon paddling into quite a strong headwind. The landscape through which we're travelling is fast becoming a patchword of lakes, and in the wind some of them were large enough to form small whitecaps—crumbling waves that constantly slammed over and rushed along the top of our PACs, spilling either side of the cockpit. Sealed inside my drysuit and with hood drawn down snugly over my snow-mask, I felt quite invulnerable—detached from the situation, almost as if I was playing some kind of virtual reality game. It was actually a lot of fun. Crunching through waves, iPod playing in my ears ... Sure, the PACs aren't all that hydrodynamic, and it's a bit like paddling a freight train at first—paddling the water madly while the PAC only very gradually picks up speed—but once she's moving again, the momentum just keeps her going. Checking my GPS I was thrilled to see I was doing 3 kilometres per hour—even with a headwind—much faster than hauling!

It was hard to keep track of Clark, as turning my head to the side merely gave me an unparalleled view of the inside of my drysuit hood, and eventually I had to put my paddle down, pull my hood down and look back. Clark was a long way back, paddling hard. Whoops, I thought, that's not going to be good for team dynamics ...

Soon reunited—aided by the fact I was blown halfway back across the lake while I waited—we pulled alongside each other and I apologised. 'No, that's all right,' he assured me, 'but we should try and stay together, in case one of us gets into trouble.'

We agreed on an ingenious communication system for paddling. Every so often whoever was in front would look back, and raise his paddle horizontally in both arms, signalling, 'Everything okay?' We'd hold this pose until the other spotted, and either replied with the same signal, indicating, 'Yes, all is okay,' in which case we'd carry on paddling, or, if we held our paddle up vertically, 'No, wait up.' It's a great system, and prevents the dangerous and infuriating situation where the person behind wants to stop for some reason (to bail out water, fix something, or because they've seen something amazing), but then has to spend twenty minutes trying to first catch up to the leader, just to ask them to wait.

By the time we'd paddled along our second lake for the day, we were absolutely spent. For the first time Clark actually cooked dinner inside the tent vestibule to shelter from the icy wind. I had my reservations about this practice, having heard of plenty of tents burning down, but Clark made a point of tying the tent flap wide open to appease my pedantic safety qualms, and it seemed to work fine. It was actually really nice having dinner in bed.

## DAY 11: Mud pits

The wind's now so strong that the waves on the lakes have actually churned the surface into froth, which blows across and builds up in great rafts on the downwind side. Foamy clumps keep breaking free and tumbling across the tundra. We can't paddle into this wind, so we've had to haul around all the lakes today.

We had lunch looking down into a lush swampy valley that looked like Sir Arthur Conan Doyle's 'Lost World'—herds of caribou shuffling around lakes dotted with birdlife. It was amazing. Smugly thinking we were starting to be able to read Victoria Island's terrain, we cunningly opted for a drier-looking deviation ahead. How wrong we were.

Gradually at first, so we failed to notice, we started passing more and more dried patches of dirt. Anywhere from one to two metres across, they were actually pretty good to haul over, being flat and hard, and we were soon inadvertently linking them up, hauling dot-to-dot.

'How good are these!' I called back to Clark enthusiastically. No sooner had the words left my mouth when my foot plunged through the dried crust and sank boot-deep into thick brown mud. The PAC's momentum carried me onwards, planting my other foot in, the viscous goo still sucking hold of my first. Thrown forwards, my gloved hands sank into the mess and the PAC then rammed into me from behind. 'Back out!! Back out!! IT'S A TRAP!' I shouted, already laughing, despite the pain.

The comic nature of the situation soon died away as we carefully negotiated the minefield. It was impossible to tell the difference between the solid patches and those harbouring deep mud. The latter increased to the point where, after veering right and left, hopping over and stepping around, eventually one wheel of my PAC squelched down, sinking up to the hull into mud. 'Give me a hand—I'm stuck!' I called.

'Same here!' Clark's reply drifted across from nearby. We teamed up, and with an almighty effort managed to drag my PAC up and out, but not before the other wheel, and me hauling at the front, sank into an even deeper slurry. It actually felt like quicksand—if I stood still, I felt myself sinking—I had to keep lifting each foot in turn up through the slop, forcing gravelly mud inside my boot as I pulled free, by which time the other boot had sunk so deep that I had to try and lift that one, basically marching on the spot in slow motion. The more we moved, like wet cement the more liquid it became, and the more it spread.

After several hours, we'd progressed perhaps another 100 metres, when both PACs became hopelessly bogged, again. Heaving together to free Clark's, we succeeded in getting both wheels bogged at the same time, and the whole PAC hunkered down into the slurry. 'AAARRGGHHH!! F*#KING MUD!!' I swore, my suppressed rage finally boiling over. We tried again. 'One … two … three … and PULL!!' We smeared forward an inch, the wheels not even turning, just ploughing into the mud like anchors. 'And, PULL!!' Nothing.

'Damn you, Victoria Island!' Clark clenched his fists.

'All right, let's unload everything,' I said, defeated. Even entirely empty—with all our possessions scattered about on the mud—we still couldn't pull it free.

'This is ridiculous …' Clark fumed, exasperated. Over a nut break, we paved the mud in front of each wheel with slabs of nearby rock, and with Clark throwing his weight into the harness and me lifting and pushing behind, making noises like I was going into labour, the PAC slurped forwards and up onto our little pavings.

'Go! Go! Keep going!' I urged, and while Clark played hopscotch with smaller mud pits in front, we scurried all the way across to the base of a dry-looking hill before we dared pause. 'Nice one, guv,' I panted. 'Now let's go back and get all the gear.'

It was almost dusk (i.e. midnight) by the time we had finally relayed all the gear and both PACs to the hill, and together we wearily clambered up. 'Hey, is this an esker?' Clark said excitedly. Raised smugly above the surrounding muddy swampland, a winding, flat-topped pebbly path snaked tantalisingly northwards into the distance. To the west—towards our goal, the far side of the island—an endless patchwork of mud, lakes, spongy grasslands and swamp extended as far as the eye could see.

Still starving after dinner, we pored over our map and filmed a video diary relating our predicament. 'This tail end of the esker we're on here … it goes all the way up to the coast, a good 30 kilometres, and if it stays like it is out there—' I couldn't help splitting a grin '—that could be … well, *quite a lot easier* than our planned route.'

## DAY 12: Fresh meat and disasters

Looking at the problem with fresh eyes in the morning, there really was no decision to make. There quite simply was no way we were going to descend from this gravel highway, back down into the hell of yesterday. Our plan is now to follow this esker north to the coast, and then hopefully we'll be able to kayak along the coast to cover some westward kilometres after that.

Rolling by 9.30, our spirits soared as we made fantastic progress along the esker, watching kilometre after kilometre of marshland pass by on either side. 'Eskers are so the way to go!' We morphed our kayak paddle communication system to our hiking poles, and marched ever onwards, glancing back every so often and raising a hiking pole merrily into the air until receiving the 'all okay' signal. It's interesting—the tempo of our iPod music seems to directly affect our hauling speed. If I'm listening to some upbeat dance track, I seem to stride ahead, until some chilled-out reggae track comes on, and I sag back, to be overtaken by Clark. One thing's for sure though: without our iPods to take our minds off things, we wouldn't be going anywhere fast.

Mid morning I stumbled across strange circular groupings of rocks on the esker. 'Hey, check this out!' I called back to Clark. 'Tent rings!' We'd seen photos of such things in the cultural centre at

Cambridge Bay—the Inuit used rocks to weigh down the edges of their circular caribou-hide tents in the summer. We were standing in the middle of an ancient Inuit campsite. Patches of orange lichen growing on the rocks suggested that these boulders had been in this position for possibly a thousand years or more. It certainly was an ideal campsite, commanding a wide view of the surrounding tundra from atop the esker, and judging by the amount of animal bone fragments around, must swarm with caribou during their yearly migration. The Inuit Heritage Society asked if we could take photos and record GPS locations for any such sites as they don't have much data from out here, and so after we'd documented the find, we lurched our PACs into motion and headed on, full of enthusiasm for further discoveries.

BANG!! Just after lunch—when we were both still feeling weak with hunger—a nice fat ptarmigan came too close to resist, and I shot it dead. Running over and picking it up, I was at once filled with a mixture of adrenalin and euphoria, but also shame.

'I feel kinda bad,' Clark murmured, looking at the chunky pigeon-sized bird, its head hanging limply to one side.

'Yeah, me too,' I agreed, battling the balance of ethics versus my gnawing hunger.

'But ... I bet it tastes good!' Clark said with a grin. 'What do we do with it?'

It was surprisingly easy to convert the feathery feast into two hearty breast fillets and a pair of wing and leg muscles, and by the time I was done, we were feeling altogether better about our sin. 'Mmm, mmm! Ptarmigan burritos tonight!' Clark laughed, rubbing his hands together gleefully while I salivated at the thought.

'Come on, let's keep hauling,' I said. 'Maybe we can stop early!'

I had noticed earlier that the webbing strap on my hauling yoke was almost worn through again, but not wanting to spend the time converting it to the fancy chafe-free pulley system we'd fixed for Clark's, I'd decided to ignore it and see how long it would last. And so when rattling our way across a tussocky break in the esker highway, as I knew I eventually would, I felt the bow of my PAC suddenly nose-dive into the ground behind me, dragging me to a stop. 'Dammit!' I cursed, pulling out my earphones and coiling them away. Looking back, I could see that the webbing had indeed finally worn through, but to my absolute horror, I also saw that the entire steel tow bracket—joining me to my PAC—had literally torn in half!

'Oh, F&\*K!!' I shouted, 'CLARK!'

Drawing level, Clark stared at the damage and slowly dragged his eyes up to meet mine, dismay etched across his face. 'That's … not good,' he whispered, and then after a pause, added, 'Can we even fix that?'

It was serious. The hauling bracket cops the biggest stress loads of the PAC, and we built it from the strongest metal in the entire cart, and I'd simply torn it in half—I'd literally torn through a total of about 100 millimetres of 3-millimetre-thick steel plate.

'Goes to show how hard we're hauling,' Clark commented wryly. We didn't have anything even vaguely as strong to replace it with, and there was no way we could repair it. A mosaic of thoughts began forming in my head. It's over—we get to go home! Or perhaps we could load all the gear into Clark's PAC and take turns hauling—or double-haul, even—that might work! Or I could just push my PAC instead of hauling it …

'I dunno,' I said, standing up, 'let's think it over. But we're not going any further today, that's for sure—let's make camp.'

We talked over the options while Clark cooked our scheduled dinner, and then with great ceremony, fried up the ptarmigan with some precious garlic powder. 'Oh my, that smells good!' I said, unable to shift a stupidly large grin plastered across my face. Clark agreed, dishing it out and passing me a bowl. Our first real meat in weeks, it tasted absolutely amazing. 'For rubbery little knots of meat,' I said, 'these things are bloody awesome!'

It was agreed: the lows of hunger outweigh the highs of morality in the case of ptarmigans, and we'll bag any that are silly enough to come too close in the future. Convincing ourselves that tonight we should make the most of the opportunity for our bodies to recover, we decided to also eat half of tomorrow's cashew nut ration.

'I almost feel full,' Clark announced cheerily.

'Almost!' I agreed.

## DAY 13: Major repairs

Waking early, I staggered wearily over to Clark's PAC and discovered that, as I feared in my sleep, his steel tow bracket was about to tear off also—fatigue cracks had worked their evil along both sides, and the metal was already paring. 'There goes the idea of just using your PAC,' I grumbled over brekky.

We removed my hauling system entirely and tried tying the bow of my PAC directly to my harness—but that resulted in the PAC repeatedly hammering into the small of my back with each step. 'No way!' I said, wincing. 'We're just going to have to fix that torn bracket somehow—modify it or something.'

We stared blankly at it for some time, until eventually inspiration struck. 'Maybe we can bang the torn-off bit flat, on a rock, and then re-pop-rivet it back to the hull ... and we'd also have to drill a big hole in the deck for the nut to recess into ...'

'Do we even have a drill bit that big?' Clark said, looking up.

'Nope! But we can always drill a ring of little holes, and then knock it out—like tearing along the dotted lines,' I said.

'Sounds good to me!' Clark said, impressed.

'Oh, but hang on,' I faltered, 'the bow won't be watertight anymore with a hole in it.'

'Was it ever?' Clark laughed. 'Let's do it.'

It was mid afternoon before we'd finally got mine fixed, and although it took several hours, we managed Clark's conversion more smoothly than our first attempt. Our spirits were buoyed by a gorgeous little arctic fox that bounced curiously up and stood staring at us while we worked. I took some great photos with the 400-millimetre lens that I had borrowed from Canon, and—full of enthusiasm to be a filmmaker and wildlife photographer respectively—Clark and I shackled up, heaved our PACs into motion behind us and plodded onwards.

After only about 100 metres, Clark's fancy anti-chafe pulley system holding his hauling arm down chafed through, and it was his turn for his PAC to nose-dive into the tundra and snag him to an undignified stop. Thankfully, however, our newly repaired tow bracket held firm.

'Let's just make camp. It's already 8 pm,' Clark said, smiling in spite of himself at the comic pathos of it all. 'Clearly, we just weren't supposed to get anywhere today!'

# DAY 14: Losing hope and paddles

'Let's do this!' We were up swiftly with our alarm at 7.30, and soon on our way, aiming for an epic day of at least 15 kilometres to re-establish confidence in our ability to get to the far side before our food (and the season) runs out.

Mid afternoon, just after passing another tent-ring site—complete with broken bits of old bone harpoon heads—Clark shouted something I couldn't hear. I waited for him to catch up. 'My paddle fell off!' he repeated. I glanced past him to where his paddle should have been clipped onto the deck of his PAC. It wasn't there.

'Where did it fall off?' I asked, still failing to grasp the calamity.

'I ... I don't know,' Clark managed, unable to meet my eye. 'I actually can't remember when I last saw it. It could have been ... well ...' With a jolt, I suddenly realised what he was saying, what this meant. I grabbed my camera and started cycling through all the photos I'd taken that day, searching for a glimpse of the paddle still clipped onto his PAC. It wasn't in a photo I took at lunchtime. Scrolling back through time, my stomach started to knot in despair. I reached a photo from yesterday's campsite—the paddle wasn't clipped on Clark's PAC then either.

I swore, and Clark visibly squared himself ready to cop a barrage of abuse. I looked at him.

'I'm really sorry, Chris,' he said. 'I just didn't notice it was missing.'

I was speechless with despair. 'We'll leave the PACs here and go back and look for it,' Clark suggested.

'And look *where?*' I murmured, still coming to grips with the impossibility of it all. 'We don't even know where we walked, there's no footsteps to retrace.'

Clark shot a look back over the expanse of lumpy tundra opening out behind him, and said, 'We could try ...'

'Even if we thought we could find it,' I murmured, 'we can't leave our PACs here and go back—what if a bear came and trashed the PACs to get to all our food, or what if we meet a bear along the way and need our guns, or our medical or emergency stuff, or if we still can't find it and it's late, we'd need to bring food, tent, tripwire—'

'All right,' Clark retracted the idea, 'I can see that. Well, what are we going to do then?' We both knew the expedition depended on us both being able to paddle. We were counting on being able to paddle long distances along the coast in a few days' time, and partway across the island we're intending to link up with the Kuujjua River and kayak for hundreds of kilometres—not to mention the patchwork of lakes and rivers we have to kayak before then.

'We'll build a new paddle,' I said, an inspirational idea forming as I spoke. 'We can just pop-rivet our spare patch of aluminium onto ... one of the bear alarm poles?'

Taken aback almost as much as I was by the idea, Clark looked at me. 'Umm ... okay. Let's do that.'

The satellite phone cut out midway through our weekly live TV interview with Sky News, and I briefly called my dad and asked him to apologise for us. When I told him about the paddle, he plunged into despair. 'No!' he insisted. 'You must haul back and look for it!' He dismissed building a paddle as a joke. 'Oh, Christopher—don't be stupid—you won't get anywhere with a little toy paddle!'

'There is NO WAY we're going to haul our PACs back the way we've come!' I said, begging him to see the reason in our decision. 'It could take days, and we might still not find it, and then what?'

'Ah, well, it's your decision, Christopher,' he said heavily, in the end. 'But I think you're making a big mistake.'

Even though collapsing here at 8 pm we've racked up 13 kilo-metres—one of our best days yet—we don't feel like celebrating. We are far more exhausted and drained than we've ever felt so far. I actually feel quite dizzy as I try to walk around camp, and Clark feels sick from exertion. Dad's foreboding really put a dampener on our morale this evening too. We only keep going out here propped up on positive thoughts and self-belief in the face of overwhelming odds, and to lose something as critical as our paddle, and then to also lose the mental encouragement from my dad—it's torn a gaping hole in our carefully constructed veil of optimism, and through it we now can't help but see despair and failure.

'We gave it everything today,' Clark muttered dejectedly in his sleeping bag. 'Everything! And it was probably some of the best terrain we'll ever get—we pushed on way past normal dinner time—and all we managed is 13 kilometres.'

I didn't want to talk about it. I was hoping Clark wasn't going to bring it up. The reality is—and we both know it—that there really is no way we can make it to the far side anymore, paddle or no paddle.

We'd need to somehow haul further than we did on our ungodly push today, every single day from now on, for over a month, to get to the west side of the island. 'Yeah,' I said at last, voicing what neither of us wanted to hear. 'There's just no way we're going to make it, is there?'

I glanced over at Clark. He was nodding sadly to himself as he heard the words. 'Not really, no,' he finally agreed, 'and it's stupid to keep trying like this—our bodies just can't cope.'

Our feelings couldn't sink any lower.

'And by pushing on like madmen every day,' I continued, 'without the time or energy to even look around or stop to explore or take photos, we're missing out on what we came here for really—we're here for the adventure, surely, not just to get to a particular point on the map?'

It was a pivotal moment. 'That's right,' Clark said, and after a lengthy discussion, during which our morale escalated enormously, I summarised our new philosophy.

'Right, so from tomorrow onwards, we'll keep going, get as far as we can each day *but* when we see something interesting, we'll take the time out to investigate it—guilt free. Yep?' I looked at Clark.

'Yep,' he agreed, smiling for the first time all day.

## DAY 15: We're not going to make it

We slumbered until 9 am this morning, then treated ourselves to brekky in bed, revelling in our new-found freedom. We even took the time to photograph and film the breakfast procedure, something we'd been meaning to do for a while. While both secretly nursing guilt at having accepted our 'failure' already, externally our morale has never been higher, and we are actually excited again about heading onwards, to see and explore new places, rather than dreading waking to the continued, impossible struggle each day.

Hauling along the esker we came upon a decaying muskox. After nervously checking around for lurking predators, we took some photos and headed off. 'The wind's finally shifted ...' Clark noted brightly, the breeze now blowing at our backs. Some twenty minutes later we paused, confused.

'Where's the esker go now?' I dug out our GPS, marked a waypoint, and got a direction. It pointed behind us. Our brows knitted together trying to understand what was going on.

'What, we're supposed to be going ... back that way!?' Clark said incredulously.

We checked again. 'Um, apparently,' I managed, utterly bewildered and disorientated. 'But we just came from that way. Didn't we?'

We decided to trust the GPS, turn around, and head back the way we'd just come. It felt all wrong for the first few hundred metres but gradually started making sense. 'Wow!' Clark gasped. 'We must have totally walked off in the opposite direction after filming that muskox!' It was hard to believe. 'So I guess the wind didn't shift at all, then.'

Six kilometres later, the esker petered out as the land gave way to ocean on the north-eastern shoreline of the island's eastern flange. 'The coast!' Clark shouted in an attempt to sound elated. 'It's not quite what we imagined, is it,' he added, visions of us paddling along the shore fading as we gazed out over a haphazard mudflat punctuated by shallow pools and stranded hunks of ice as far out as we could see.

'Bummer!' I laughed. 'It looks like a cool place to explore, anyway!' Moments later I found a fossil ammonite and Clark a fossilised bit of coral while setting up the bear alarm around the campsite.

I set off towards the distant 'ocean' to fish, can of bear spray in my pocket, but after spotting a large shaggy brown mass lumbering towards me, hurried back to camp, tail between my legs. Binoculars revealed it only to be a muskox, so I set out again, but this time bringing my shotgun. One day we're going to get caught out. Half an hour later I still hadn't found anywhere deep enough to fish, and returned empty-handed, my stomach growling with hunger.

After dinner—dehydrated 'savoury Italian pasta with beef'— we checked our emails. We received a lot of encouraging emails, and one not very encouraging one from my dad. Huddled in our sleeping bags we both leaned inwards to read the letter. Backed up by a plethora of calculations and averages on our distances so far, he basically pointed out that there was zero chance we would make it to the far side of the island, and went on to list various reasons for our getting picked up by seaplane in the next few days.

It was a very gentle, logical email, but it was still painful to read. 'Luckily we've already accepted that we're not going to make it!' Clark said, a little indignantly.

'But why on earth would we get picked up now, though? We may as well keep going until our allotted 65 days run out—getting all the photos and videos we want, and live the experience!'

'Your dad's just being a dad, Chris,' Clark grinned. 'Of course he wants us home!'

## DAY 16: Enough's enough

We actually went for a walk this morning, leaving our PACs back at camp. Not being shackled to a quarter of a ton makes a huge difference. This really is a beautiful part of the world. We justified it as a recce trip to check out terrain conditions ahead, but really we just needed to escape for a while, to clear our heads.

Hopping out onto some pack ice, we dangled the fishing lure pathetically in about 60 centimetres of water. It's all so shallow around here. Clear blue skies, temperature about 3 degrees above zero—the ice all around us sparkling as it melted in the sun. 'If we just keep hauling for 65 days, though,' I said, suddenly thinking aloud, 'I wonder where we'll be when we need to get picked up.'

'Yeah,' Clark joined in, 'and *how* we'll be able to be picked up.'

Dad's email last night raised some important issues. With all the seaplanes on the island leaving in a few weeks, the only option would be chartering a large Twin Otter—if we could find somewhere for it to land—and failing that, a helicopter. Both very expensive and non-guaranteed options. 'We really need to sit down and work out what we're going to do,' I said, reeling in the fishing line.

'Okay,' I began, snug back in the tent. 'We can't make it to the far side of the island, that's clear.' Clark nodded. 'And really, we're here for the experience, not the destination.' Clark nodded again, although more slowly, knowing full well this was really just our own excuse to make us feel better about the former. 'So …' I went on, 'we can either pull out right now, which is just a waste—we could get picked up on the third of September when the last floatplane leaves—or we could stick it out for the full 65 days and just see where we end up.'

We drew up a list of pros and cons for the two latter options to help us decide:

## Stick it out to 65 days and see where we are

| Pros | Cons |
| --- | --- |
| Longer experience | Weather/location could hamper pickup |
| Can say 'we went as far as we could' | Risk being forced to have emergency type pickup |
| Get further—doesn't look as bad | Stay hungry |

## Get floatplane out in 20 days' time

| Pros | Cons |
| --- | --- |
| Less pressure to go go go! | Sponsors may be disappointed |
| More spare time to experience the Arctic | |
| Get more photos and film footage | |
| Lots more food to eat each day | |
| Ditch some food & lighten PACs | |
| Seaplane saves lots $s | |
| Save $s on shorter communications bill | |
| Looks responsible, rather than inflexible and dangerous | |
| Guaranteed pickup—easy | |
| Still have some uni holidays when we get home | |

'Well, it seems pretty clear which one has more pros and less cons,' I said, grinning.

Clark was already laughing. 'Seems we suddenly have 30 days of extra food,' he said. 'Shall I go and get some?'

'Definitely!' I replied, already salivating.

Clark raided the PAC, dumping bag after bag of food into the tent, and clambered in after them, eyes blazing with excitement and anticipation. Grinning like idiots, we melted an entire day's chocolate ration into a mug of hot chocolate, and dug into handfuls of cashew nuts. We were as happy as kids in a candy store. But then, as Clark lifted a tortilla thick with peanut butter to his mouth, guilt came crashing down around me.

'Wait … wait a sec,' I urged, and I could see Clark battling inwardly whether or not to close his mouth around the tortilla before turning to me. At last he put it down.

'This doesn't feel right,' I murmured, 'after all the time and dedication we've put in for a 65-day expedition, all the sponsors' money and everything, to cut this once-in-a-lifetime experience short—almost in half—basically just to save a few thousand dollars with a cheaper plane pickup and things like that … I think we'll regret it. Imagine us back at home in a few short weeks, sitting there, knowing we could have been still out here on this adventure.'

Clark's expression fell, and he nodded. 'You're right. That would suck.'

We sat in silent reflection for a time, horrified at what we'd just almost done.

'So we'll carry on,' Clark stated, 'and just … get as far as we can while still taking the time to experience and film it all.'

'Yeah,' I agreed, 'I think that's the right thing to do.'

We both sat looking at the pre-made peanut butter tortilla. 'I guess that'll have to wait until lunch,' I said, hating myself as Clark forlornly packed it away.

We filmed building our new paddle this afternoon. It only has a small single blade and has a pretty short handle, but it's a paddle nonetheless, and we're quite proud of it.

We snuggled into our sleeping bags, for the first time ever camped in exactly the same place as yesterday, but finally with a guilt-free conscience, and a clear philosophy for the days ahead: to have an adventure.

# DAY 17: Don't run

So long as we hugged the tidal red algae band and didn't veer into the boggy greenish algae areas, progress along the mudflats was good. Frustratingly though, Clark didn't seem to have picked up on this, and he'd invariably wander into the green regions and squelch to a halt. 'Why didn't you go around it?' I asked incredulously.

'Well, I didn't see it,' he explained. Fair enough. Moments later he aimed for another.

'Clark!' I called, gesturing wildly, 'go around it!'

He gazed back at me blankly. 'Around *what*?' he said.

'The *green* bit!' I said, drawing up beside him, '*there* …' I pointed.

He looked from me to the green patch. 'What green bit?' he said, now looking concerned for my sanity.

'*There*!' I said, laughing in disbelief, 'that's all *red*—there, and that's *green*. Yeah?'

'Red!?' he said. 'That's RED? It *all* looks green to me!'

I stared at him. 'I'm colour blind,' he said. 'I am actually red–green colour blind, Chris.' He wasn't joking. 'That is pretty funny,' he started laughing, 'I've been wondering why you've been zigzagging around all morning …'

After a good day's hauling, at 5 pm we set up tent and I decided to go fishing. Ice-hopping out to deeper water, I started jigging the lure up and down in the crystal-clear water, expecting at any moment a silvery char to flash past and grab it. Glancing along the shoreline, I spotted a bunch of white rocks—or perhaps hunks of ice—scattered across the mudflats some 300 metres back along where we'd just hauled less than an hour earlier. I continued fishing. Scanning around as I idly flicked the rod tip up and down, I fixed my gaze once more on these white objects. I stopped jerking the fishing rod. Were there more of them now? Were they *closer*? I stared at the motionless forms for some time before shaking my head, laughing at my own paranoia.

However, just as I turned away, out of the corner of my eye I saw movement. Whipping around to stare, I watched transfixed as more and more white objects seemed to appear from nowhere and fan out across the mud. They must be caribou, I thought—they looked about the right size. There was something odd about the way they were walking, though, they weren't prancing or trotting as deer do, they were more … loping along … like huge dogs! My blood ran cold as I suddenly realised what was happening—I was standing there, with nothing but a fishing rod between me and a pack of six, seven, eight arctic wolves, all pacing closer, and closer!

'CLARK!' I shouted. 'WOLVES!' Over 100 metres away, there was no movement from the tent, my yell snatched away on the bitterly cold wind streaming over the pack ice. The wolves heard me though, and stopped dead, all eyes on me, their ears as upright as the hairs on the back of my neck.

I'd read up on arctic wolves before we left, and the general consensus was that they shouldn't pose much of a threat. Apparently, no one has ever reported a fatal wolf attack; however, as one of the wildlife officers in Cambridge Bay had bluntly put it to me, 'There's a reason for that—because they're fatal, aren't they!' And considering that wolves can bring down fully grown muskox, and that these ones had just been *stalking* me, I decided that now wasn't the time to test out just how amiable this particular pack of highly intelligent, adaptable, opportunistic predators was going to be.

Deciding I'd better get back to camp, I frantically reeled in my fishing line and moved to ice-hop back to shore. The moment I took a step, the whole pack started advancing as one. 'CLARK!' I shouted loudly every few paces, staring mesmerised at the multitude of wolves—clearly visible now—steadily closing the gap. 'CLARK!!'

Finally reaching the shore, there was now nothing but 150 metres of mud separating me from the advancing pack, and panic lurched into my stomach. Various thoughts started flashing through my head. Don't run from dogs. Keep walking. They can run a lot faster than you can, don't give them an excuse. I shot a terrified glance over my shoulder—they weren't running, just swiftly gliding towards me, but gaining fast. I'm actually going to be torn apart. Don't think that—dogs can sense fear. How could I do this to Clark? 'CLARK!?' There was a hint of pleading in my voice now, and it scared me. Another glance back. Shit. They're going to get to me before I get to the tent. Don't run. Okay—run. Run!

With one last wild glance over my shoulder, I saw—as I knew I would—the whole pack shift into high gear, their broad paws digging into the soft ground as they accelerated, now bounding after me as I sprinted up the embankment towards camp. 'CLARK! GET THE GUN!!'

About 50 metres away, the vestibule sliced open and Clark exploded from the tent, shotgun in hand, eyes wide with fright. 'WOLVES!!' Vaulting our perimeter tripwire alarm, I saw Clark lower the gun and I looked back. The wolves had stopped, and now stood watching. As I dived for my camera, the lead wolf advanced a little closer, hesitated, and then turned away, with the rest of them following.

'When I came out they all slackened and stopped,' Clark said. 'What ... what happened?' A chorus of spine-chilling howls cut off my reply, and we both watched in awe as the pack—now a few hundred metres away—lifted their muzzles to the sky and cried long, mournful howls. 'That's awesome,' Clark breathed.

'They keep looking at us,' I said, trying to hold the binoculars steady in my still-trembling hands. 'There's nine of them ... all pure white,' I relayed. And with that, they turned tail and vanished over the skyline.

## DAY 18: Bear tracks

It rained last night—a first. We've been pretty lucky so far, but then again, Victoria Island is actually classified as a desert. Thankfully it didn't turn the mudflats too sloppy, and after some repairs, we headed off.

But it wasn't long before I suddenly stopped dead. The PAC lurched me forward a few more steps, but digging my heels in, I ground to a halt, now standing right on top of the unmistakable tracks of a bear. I spun around, scanning our immediate surroundings and then the horizon more carefully.

'Polar bear tracks!' Clark said as he drew level. 'The tracks lead in from the pack ice.' They looked very fresh, too; unpitted from this morning's rain. 'He must have walked past while we were having breakfast in the tent.' It was a sobering thought, our campsite easily within sight some 700 metres back. We kept our eyes peeled as we hauled onwards.

'I hope we get to see one,' Clark admitted of our biggest fear.

I nodded. 'Yeah, me too, secretly. It'd be amazing.'

# DAY 19: Darkness descends

Weak and battered after an endless day of nightmare terrain hauling, we finally clambered into the tent several hours after we'd normally stop. Clark was poring over the maps from within his sleeping bag, and I'd started writing my diary, when I realised I was squinting. I suddenly put down my pen and looked at Clark. 'Hey, what's different?' I asked, fixing him with a quizzical grin. Blank. 'Having trouble reading the maps?' I hinted.

'Oh, yeah! Hey, it's *dark*! Well, dark-ish anyway—wow!'

It seems summer is coming to an end.


# DAY 20: Muskox visit

We spent the afternoon hauling towards a distant esker 6 kilometres away, tripping wearily, waiting for knock-off time. During a nut break, a large, particularly shaggy old bull muskox wandered slowly towards us. 'Wooo, look out,' I jeered, 'Grandpa's coming right for us!' Sitting there munching our cashews, we wondered at what point he'd spook himself and flee like they always do. But he didn't stop. He just kept lumbering towards us.

We stopped chewing. We grabbed our respective cameras. 'We've got moments left to live, I think,' I said, grinning excitedly into the video camera. 'Shit—he's getting really close, actually!' My humour faltered slightly. We watched in silent amazement as he ambled to within about 40 metres, paused and considered us with his bulging cow-like eyes. Great clumps of his soft inner hair (called *qiviut*) hung untidily from his long shaggy skirt of matted hair, swaying gracefully in the breeze. The Inuit actually collect and make clothing from *qiviut*—it's the world's warmest and most expensive natural fibre, eight times warmer than sheep's wool and softer than cashmere. After a lengthy five minutes or so, the old muskox seemed satisfied, and unhurriedly turned and shuffled away.


# DAY 21: Coastal mudflats

I woke at 7.30 and again at 8. I donned my drysuit and waded out into a nearby lake, casting the fishing lure again and again until

I lost contact with my numb legs and had to wobble awkwardly back to shore, empty-handed again. Where are all the fish? We're so hungry now, all the time.

Toiling from esker tail to esker tail, across the muddy bays crisscrossed with wolf, bear and caribou tracks, we've got quite a rhythm going. Each raised esker gives us something to aim for, and as we can't see past it, it helps compartmentalise the day's challenges into manageable portions. We've also learned not to look over into the next depressing expanse of mud until after we've finished enjoying the nut break atop each esker. It's a silly little system but it helps keep us positive.

Sheltering from the wind, crouched behind my PAC's wheel, I did our weekly live TV interview with Sky News, which was pretty exciting—it's actually been a really eventful week, with wolves and bear prints ...

We have decided not to tell anyone yet that the far side of the island is no longer our goal. I think people would feel we were giving up early. We'll announce it later. Besides, we're still struggling on out here, giving it our best.

We watched the full moon rise over the tundra tonight—it looks strangely squashed and glows surprisingly orange-red. The wind has died and it's beautifully serene out here.

## DAY 22: Rolling, rolling, rolling

We filmed the whole lunch procedure today—tick that off the list—and by 5 pm we had covered an impressive 9.5 kilometres as the crow flies, reaching a perfect campsite atop an esker just as Clark's iPod battery ran out. Putting it on charge as we lay in our tent, we both melted some leftover chocolate ration into our mugs (the reward for near-inhuman self-control all day), pressed 'play' on our respective favourite tracks of tranquil music, closed our eyes and each escaped to our own world of bliss for just a few moments, wrapping our cold hands around our mugs and sipping our sinfully rich hot chocolates. It has become quite the ritual of late—the moment we look forward to all day.

# DAY 23: Bear!

The quality of the kilometre-wide mudflats spanning the esker ridges deteriorated today, hauling was arduously slow and, unable to build up any momentum, we found each step a drawn-out effort. Two large muskox stood atop our first esker this morning, glaring at us as we toiled slowly towards them. 'Are they going to run away or what?' I panted, as we grunted our PACs up the side of the esker. Trying not to look at them, I couldn't help marvelling at their horns—huge battering rams clamped tightly over their shaggy heads, sweeping up into sickeningly sharp points at their tips.

Suddenly one lowered his head and started rubbing it against his foreleg. Simultaneously, Clark and I shouted 'Stop!'—we'd been warned this rubbing was a sign of extreme agitation and often preceded a charge. Our hearts racing, the pebbles under our feet started to grind and pop as the weight of our PACs started to drag us awkwardly backwards down the slope.

'We can't stop here,' I managed through gritted teeth, struggling down on all fours so as not to lose control. 'Let's just ... aim to pass them ... keep going!'

It was a tense moment for all involved. In my mind I ran through my strategy if they charged, starting with fumbling for the quick-release toggles on my harness. Would I be quick enough? After what seemed like an eternity we reached the top beside them, and under their angry stare quickly carried on down into the next mudflat without pausing for a nut break.

'That was dodgy,' Clark grinned in spite of himself.

Passing more bear and wolf tracks scribbled across the mud, we eventually made it onto the day's second esker where, grabbing our handful of nuts, we wandered ahead to inspect the next bay. Clark had just commented, 'Oh, whoops—we forgot to bring bear spray' when, looking around, I suddenly caught sight of a large animal silhouetted against the sky on the next esker.

'BEAR!!!' I shouted, instinctively, almost before I'd even realised it myself. 'There! It's a polar bear!' Clark thought I was joking, until looking where I pointed, he saw it too.

'Oh my God—it IS!' Striding confidently along the esker perhaps 400 metres away, the huge white bear just exuded power and authority, clearly king of his domain. After a few transfixed

TOP: Chris, aged eight, sailing the family yacht, *Starship*, across the English Channel.
RIGHT: Chris on his Tasmanian wilderness expedition, using a machete to cut a path through dense scrub.

OPPOSITE PAGE, CLOCKWISE FROM TOP LEFT: Let's walk across Victoria Island—how hard can it be?; Building the frames for the PAC hulls; Starting to look like a kayak; Noisy late-night work in the garage—cutting sheet aluminium with jig-saw; More late-night work—poor neighbours; Pre-drilling over 1000 holes for the pop-rivets; Assembling the skeleton of the frames. THIS PAGE, CLOCKWISE FROM TOP LEFT: Chris supervises from inside while Clark drills out faulty pop-rivets; Testing if the PACs float in our next-door neighbour's pool the day before the sea-freight cut-off date; Putting on the final touches with mere hours left; With Dad, wrapping completed PACs in bubble-wrap ready for shipping; My dad also put in countless hours in the garage.

THIS PAGE, CLOCKWISE FROM TOP LEFT: Seaplane pilots just before they shook our hands and told us they didn't expect to see either of us alive again; Disaster—the steel tow bracket completely torn in half; Clark learning how to ice-hop, carrying a $7000 video camera, Cambridge Bay. OPPOSITE PAGE, TOP: Chris setting up the polar bear perimeter tripwire alarm system around camp. OPPOSITE PAGE, BOTTOM: Hidden mud pits suddenly turn to swamp and suck in the PAC's wheels.

OPPOSITE PAGE, FROM TOP:
An esker, formed by the
action of ancient glaciers–we
followed these raised gravel
'highways' wherever possible;
Fully grown Arctic fox in
summer coat–these playful
and curious mammals often
walked right up to us. THIS
PAGE, TOP: Keeping up morale,
we often laughed at the silliest
of things–here Clark pretends
to be a muskox, while Chris
pretends not to be concerned
for his sanity. BELOW: Chris
struggling to haul his PAC
through seriously thick, smelly
mud.

RIGHT: Our 30 cm ruler dropped pathetically inside these enormous polar bear tracks—I can't imagine how big the bear must have been. BELOW: Clark paddling his PAC through a maze of icebergs. OPPOSITE PAGE: After being chased by wolves, we take safety more seriously—Clark with toilet paper in one hand, shotgun in the other.

FOLLOWING SPREAD: The shimmering curtains of the Northern Lights burn green above my PAC.

OPPOSITE PAGE, TOP: Towing the PACs up river. BOTTOM: Muskox–Victoria Island has one of the world's densest populations of these shaggy beasts. Lone bulls like this one do charge and kill people. RIGHT: Alpha male arctic wolf fearlessly comes in to investigate camp, less than 3 metres from us. BELOW: I kept a handwritten diary throughout the 2005 trip. BOTTOM: Hauling our PACs up onto the final esker as winter sets in—getting this shot with a 10 second timer took many attempts.

OPPOSITE PAGE: The maze of shifting ice eventually became so thick we had to turn back
ABOVE: Ancient Inuit harpoon head carved from bone–a sealskin rope attaches through the hole and a sharp rock or blade wedges in the front slot.
LEFT: Summer comes to an abrupt end in the Arctic.

TOP: Legendary Arctic pilot Willie Laserich flies in to pick us up on Day 58, one-third of the way across the island. RIGHT: In Willie's Twin Otter aircraft, on our way back to civilisation and unrationed food.

seconds, I turned and bolted back to our PACs, shouting, 'You grab the cameras and I'll get a gun!' We filmed the bear plodding along, occasionally pausing to reach his long neck high into the air, drawing in some scent (not ours, as he was thankfully upwind), before he eventually lay down—half curled up like a dog—and apparently went to sleep.

'I wonder if he's even seen us?' I thought aloud. I've seen bears at the zoo before; however, when there is no fence between you and a bear, there is an optical illusion called 'bear-and-me-and-nothing-in-between' that makes the bear seem at least ten times normal size, and leaves you feeling very small and vulnerable indeed.

It was now almost 5 pm and with the mist already rolling in, we decided it safest to camp rather than slog on through the mud, the only possible route forcing us towards the bear. Even if we made it past him, we'd then be upwind of him and he'd surely smell us. We set up the tripwire alarm with just a little more care than usual, and cautiously cooked dinner well away from camp in case the bear was drawn to the kitchen smells during the night. Sipping a mug of arctic tea, I watched the bear through binoculars. He was lying with his massive head upon his paws, looking directly at us.

Over dinner, Clark broke his unbreakable polycarbonate camping spoon. After we'd stopped laughing, I was able to melt the two bits back together with our trusty lighter and although shorter and reeking of burnt plastic, it seemed to do the trick.

As the bear hadn't moved for over an hour, we eventually crawled inside the tent as evening fell. I wrote a website update relating our exciting predicament, and after agreeing to wake every two hours to check the bear alarm was still operational and that the string hadn't snapped, we wedged a can of bear spray in each tent pocket, actually loaded the shotguns before laying them in the vestibule, wriggled deeper inside our sleeping bags and tried to sleep. With the binoculars, I can literally see the polar bear's distant head while lying in the tent!

## DAY 24: Lunchtime archaeology

After the terrifying seven hours of darkness during which we repeatedly scampered out to check the bear alarm and anxiously waved our torches into the inky blackness at every sound, we eventually decided to 'call it a night', and packed up. Training my binoculars on the bear, I saw him stand, scent the air, and then vanish. About an hour later when the hairs on the back of my neck settled down, we headed off down into the next muddy expanse. Quite hard going. We hauled cautiously up onto the bear's esker, and then onwards, down into more marshy ground.

Lunch was one of those perfect Arctic moments. No wind, clear blue skies, a group of muskox ambling past the shore 100 metres away, passing in front of deep blue hunks of multi-year ice. It really was beautiful. Further along, Clark spotted strange piles of rocks ahead, and we unclipped to investigate. 'They look like caches,' Clark shouted over, 'as if they were piled on top of something big, but now they're just hollow inside …'

I clambered over. The lichen and other plant life around and inside each of these caches was prolific, as if whatever was in there had perhaps decomposed and greatly enriched the soil at each site. 'Maybe they were food caches?' I wondered aloud.

'Or tombs, even …' Clark added. We documented some very unusual-shaped stone tent rings and other features before shackling back up and hauling onwards.

'This is what it's all about!' I said excitedly, 'I love that we can look around and explore a little now.'

'Yeah,' Clark said, nodding, 'I don't feel guilty anymore, actually—it's not like we've "given up"—we're still giving it our all!'

Rather annoyingly, we both realised today that a few days ago— we can't for the life of us remember when—we paused for a nut break on an enormous square-section length of wood that had washed up on the muddy shore. It was so large and conveniently shaped like a bench seat some 10 metres long that we couldn't resist sitting on it and admiring the ice-strewn coastline in front of us. It only just occurred to us tonight that unlike the usual hunks of driftwood, this one was clearly manufactured, and looked remarkably like a section of a wooden mast from an old square-rigged ship, just like the *Erebus* and the *Terror*—Franklin's missing ships! I wonder …

# DAY 25: Denmark Fiord

After repairing our tripod, which had broken a few days ago, and re-wiring our failing laptop charger, we were off in good time this morning, keen to try for Denmark Fiord, a lengthy region of what should be open water, where the crushing pack ice of McClintock Channel is kept out by a long spur—an island, almost, connected by a land bridge.

The prospect of several days' uninterrupted kayaking (and a chance to test out our new paddle) encouraged us onwards today, and despite sluggish terrain that greatly sapped our energy—and one group of aggro muskox that vehemently refused to give way, forcing us to double back and take an even slushier route—we were eventually rewarded with a distant expanse of blue. 'It's open water!' I pointed excitedly. 'Denmark Fiord!'

The last muddy bay we had to cross was immense, and already feeling drained and having eaten our last nut break ration for the day, we wearily stumbled down into it and inched our way towards our goal. The further we went, the stickier and deeper the mud became, and the more we struggled. 'Keep … going,' Clark gasped beside me, eyes glazed, 'It's getting closer …' In the end we had to double-haul onto the final esker, where Victoria Island played another cruel trick on us. It wasn't the final bay after all—yet another muddy expanse now opened up in front of us. Weary and broken, we didn't even have the energy to complain, and simply marched slowly onwards down into our next torture session.

I made it to the final esker—and to the shore of Denmark Fiord—with enough time to quickly set up the tent and watch the joy spread across Clark's face as he crested the rise and gazed out over the expanse of open blue water. It's a magic campsite here, positioned right at the base of the land bridge out to the picturesque 'island' that we've so often stared at on our maps and satellite images from day one of planning, imagining what it'd be like to be here. It's a real landmark, and we are absolutely thrilled to have arrived. What's more, the wind is blowing gently south-easterly, ready for a brilliant day's kayaking tomorrow down the fiord! Life is good!

We enjoyed a rehydrated meal of sweet and sour pork tonight—one of our favourites—while relaxing against our PACs, taking in this magnificent view. It's all bathed in a beautiful evening light, and there's even muskox wandering in the distance. We really are privileged to see such wild beauty. Neither returning empty-handed from fishing, nor reading a particularly graphic email from Dad warning us about the abilities of polar bears, could come close to denting our high morale tonight.

## DAY 26: So much for that idea

A particularly violent gust of wind slamming against my side of the tent woke me at 4 am and I lay there in my sleeping bag, feeling the tent thrash around wildly. The act of unzipping the vestibule and poking my head out caused an icy wind to explode into the tent.

'What's happening?' Clark's dazed and muffled voice escaped his sleeping bag.

'It seems,' I began, utterly crestfallen, 'that not only has the wind swung 180 degrees and is now roaring onshore, but it's also got a lot stronger. There goes our beautiful dream of kayaking merrily down the fiord.' It was a real blow, and we both ate our porridge in silence, staring morosely out at the whitecaps and waves dashing themselves onto the shore, and pondering what to do.

One more week and we'll be halfway through our allotted 65 days. What an eternity it seems. Two months would flash past back home, barely noticed, yet out here each day is a lifetime of experiences, a sea of challenges to overcome, hardships to endure, moments of bliss, beauty and awe to savour forever. In fact, so much seems to happen out here that, come afternoons, we can almost swear that the morning's incidents happened days ago— it's as if our brains struggle to fit in so many experiences into one 'day-sized' compartment. 'That was this morning!?' It's a real shock sometimes.

We decided to spend today filming and photographing a whole list of things on our list, such as converting to/from haul/kayak mode. It's just too heartbreaking to start hauling along the muddy coastline when on a good weather day (tomorrow?) we could easily paddle three times the distance.

Amazingly it was 6.30 pm by the time we finished filming and dragged our PACs back up to camp. We got a lot done, and were so busy that we didn't even pause for lunch, or half our nut breaks!

Even our day's chocolate ration remained untouched in our pockets! Clambering inside the tent, we quickly had lunch, two nut rations, a mug of ridiculously rich hot chocolate, and dinner in quick succession. Having just eaten basically a whole day's ration in the space of about 30 minutes, I actually feel full for the first time in a long time! It's great!

## DAY 27: Kayaking the fiord

Miraculously, the wind swung back 180 degrees during the night, and after breakfast we hauled our PACs down to the water's edge, changed into our drysuits, converted to kayak mode and pushed off. Without even paddling, the wind blew us onwards at almost 1.5 kilometres per hour, as small tumbling whitecaps scurried past. 'How good is this!' I called out, thrilled that the weather—although cold, grey, increasingly windy and even starting to spit rain—was for once helping us on our way.

Hearing no reply from Clark, I pulled my hood back and looked around. He was a fair way back already, madly digging at the water with our little makeshift paddle. 'This thing's shit!' he grumbled bitterly when he finally caught up.

'Well, we'll take it in turns,' I said, holding out my paddle which he accepted gratefully.

While it was certainly awkward to use, I got a rhythm going with the little paddle and got quite used to it, happily scooping my way along at the same rate as Clark was kayaking. Whenever we swapped back, however, Clark would fall behind. To relieve his growing frustration, I decided to permanently swap my paddle for his makeshift paddle. 'Besides,' I said, trying to keep up morale, 'I think it looks cool—all metal and pop-rivets—it's got the same rustic charm as my PAC.'

The further from the windward side of the fiord we paddled, the larger the waves grew, and soon we were surrounded by huge rolling, breaking, churning waves—lifting and spinning our PACs, surging over the stern and sides and emptying bucketloads of icy water across the cockpits. For our first nut break of the day we pulled onto a tiny island and sat side by side, backs to the buffeting wind, and decided to eat lunch instead. 'It's pretty crazy out there,'

I nodded, 'I wonder if anyone has ever been on this island before?'

It somehow took us an hour to get under way again, and by the time we'd managed another 3 kilometres and ducked behind a point for shelter, Clark was flagging. 'I'm just not a kayaker, I guess.' He shrugged apologetically. Strangely, I felt I could paddle on for hours.

After a revitalising nut break and bailing several litres of water out of our PACs, we again pushed out into the washing machine and headed for a spit of land in the distance. Over a kilometre out from shore, paddling our home-made PACs through this bracing weather, muskox on the shoreline, potentially a bear around the next corner, I suddenly felt a real sense of pride and accomplishment. We really are living the dream out here—this is a real adventure!

## DAY 28: Interview from an iceberg

In true Arctic style, the weather changed dramatically again overnight, and we awoke to a perfectly still day without a breath of wind. Heavy mist and cloud was still hiding the sun, and so we decided to go easy on charging our electronics as the solar panels would be struggling. Worryingly, our GPS doesn't seem to accept charge anymore anyway, as its supposedly waterproof charge connections have corroded away, and so we've been checking our position on a 'need to know only' basis for the last few days. Thankfully this morning, however, after doing some serious surgery on it I got it functioning again, and with the tide by then having slid conveniently up to our tent door, we didn't even need to drag the PACs before hopping in them and pushing off into the mirror-like fiord.

We paddled past an increasing number of small icebergs—all shapes and sizes. 'This is awesome!' I said after a time.

'Maybe we should get some pics?' Clark agreed enthusiastically, and after performing a hair-raising balancing act—easing ourselves out of the cockpit and up onto the stern of our PACs—we withdrew our large padded, waterproof Ortlieb camera bags from inside and set ourselves up. We spent several hours drifting around, paddling back and forth in front of the most picturesque bergs getting some great shots.

'We could try and get some footage of us both kayaking past,' Clark said, 'if we could find a suitable iceberg.' I knew what he was thinking, and we soon found a large, stable-looking berg with a bit of an alcove melted into it. We gingerly paddled into the berg until our PACs bottomed out on invisibly clear submerged ice.

'This should be interesting,' I grinned, as I hesitantly stood up in my PAC and, trying to brace myself on the slippery ice with my paddle, gingerly stepped out into what looked like water. Climbing up onto the berg itself was incredibly slippery, and I had to take my gloves off so I could dig my fingers into the frosty surface as I shimmied up on top. Clark joined me and we set the video camera up, pressed 'record' and tried not to rush as we slid back down the iceberg, clambered back into our PACs and reversed our way back down the alleyway of ice. The two of us then paddled back and forth past the video camera's field of view for as long as we could bear, before returning to collect the video camera from on top of the berg. 'That'll l-look … a-awesome,' Clark said, through chattering teeth as he clumsily folded the tripod away.

Dialling in for our weekly Sky News interview, we were put on hold, listening to world news as we shuffled endlessly around and around in circles, stomping our feet and jiggling our arms in a bid to keep warm while we waited. At last I was live: 'Yeah, things are going well out here,' I began, 'we're currently standing on top of an iceberg, saw our first polar bear this week …' The interview went really well—the sat phone even conveniently cut out just as they asked the unanswerable 'Why do you do it?' question—but by the end we were both shivering wrecks.

Chilled to the core, we just couldn't seem to get warm as we paddled along the shore looking for somewhere to camp. Nothing but flat, tidal mudflats. Getting noticeably weaker from the cold, we at last spotted a bit of a drier-looking patch ahead and well inland: the lesser of many evils. We pulled ashore and stepped out into boot-deep, sucking mud. 'This is going to take forever,' I groaned, shackling up as Clark wearily splashed over to help push.

It turned out to be the longest stint of double-hauling we've done so far. On and on, slowly ploughing great wheel ruts into the muddy slurry behind us as we strained and strained to gain each step. Finally we made it, turned around and sloshed back to Clark's PAC. Cold, wet, numb and delirious, we didn't exchange a word as

Clark shackled up while I leaned into the PAC from behind. It was late by the time we were back staggering around camp setting up the tripwire, and past midnight before we finally lay flat in the sanctuary of our tent, gradually coaxing our knotted back muscles to relax.

## DAY 29: Stocktaking

We awoke at 8, 8.30, 9, and eventually came to again at about 10.15 am. Rain lashed the sides of our tent, the windchill taking the 4 degrees Celsius down to minus 8.8 degrees. We independently began a few chores inside the tent and ate breakfast, all the while each quietly revelling in the fact that it seemed the other showed no sign of wanting to get out, haul the PACs all the way back to the fiord and keep going. Without a word, we agreed that today would be our first rest day. We deserve it. Today makes this journey now one day longer than Jasper's and my Tassie wilderness trip.

By 'rest day' I just mean we didn't haul anywhere—we crammed the day full of jobs that have been piling up. I culled photos on the laptop to free up space while Clark snaked his iPod earphone wire along our trail drawn on paper maps and held it against the scale on the side. 'We've done about 180 kilometres so far!' he announced proudly. Not bad. As our other unbreakable polycarbonate spoon has also broken, I set about carving a new spoon from a muskox horn I'd picked up a few days ago. Doug had referred to horn as 'the Inuits' plastic' and after heating it over the stove to soften it (inadvertently filling the tent with the pungent odour of burning hair) and whittling away at it with my Leatherman, I proudly held it out for Clark to inspect. Wrinkling his nose, he kindly said he'd stick to using the broken unbreakable one.

Next we decided to go through all our overall food rations, to check if we have been eating through them at the correct rate. Motivated by the possibility of having to correct any oversupplies, we emptied the PACs of food and inspected them one at a time. The sugar bag was first, and after literally measuring out the number of spoonfuls we had left, Clark gleefully reported that we had enough to have an extra spoon per person, per day! 'Oh, yeah!!! That's going straight into our breakfast porridge!' I grinned. Currently we're only allowed half a spoonful.

Oats were next, and after re-checking twice, Clark delivered a bombshell. 'We ... um, have to cut back on oats a bit, I'm afraid. We're going to have to make do with about half what we've gotten used to.'

For two hungry men, this was devastating news. 'I half-wish we hadn't just checked the rations,' I commented.

'Better half rations now than no rations later,' Clark observed. Butter, peanut butter, rice, chocolate, pasta and dehydrated meals were all on track, he reported.

An evening thunderstorm rolled in and, curled up inside our sleeping bags, we could hear thunder above the rain.

'What'll we do if it hails?' A little pang of apprehension begged an answer.

'The tent'd be shredded ...' Clark thought aloud.

'I guess we'd have to drop the tent, and ... crawl under the PACs?' I suggested, and picturing this dismal scene in my head, added, 'I'm sure it won't hail.'

## DAY 30: Beaten by the wind

Clark somehow managed to pad out our new half-quantity of breakfast oats with enough water that it almost seemed normal, and with a whopping one and a half spoonfuls of sugar, it tasted amazing! After brekky we bit the bullet and agreed to press on today—although the wind's in our face, it's not too strong. We drysuited up and began hauling our PACs across the mud to the coast, passing the largest wolf tracks we've seen. I couldn't resist taking photos, but soon my battery ran out. We have lots of empty batteries at the moment—there's been no sun to charge anything for days.

Ten metres further on I stopped dead in my tracks, staring in shock and amazement, trying not to fall down *into* the biggest polar bear tracks I have ever seen! Talk about feet the size of dinner plates—our 30-centimetre ruler dropped pathetically inside the enormous imprints! 'These things are massive!' Clark said to the video camera, 'I—I can't even *imagine* how big the bear must have been ...' They looked fresh too—no sign of the rain or tide having smoothed them.

'Wow,' I breathed. 'It'd have been well within sight of our tent, too.' It served to ram home, again, the very real threat and terror of being hunted out here, just as we were starting to become a little less nervous. Nearby, we also found tiny bear cub prints no larger than those of a wolf. Huddling together for a nut break, our backs to the wind, our fingers were too numb to pick up individual nuts, and we were forced to eat from our cupped, muddy hands.

Launching our PACs, we began paddling along the shoreline into the wind. Around 1 pm we decided to push on, to have lunch at an island looming ahead. We struggled doggedly onwards as the wind blew harder and harder. The island vanished behind an ominous veil of rain and mist that bore down upon us, soon engulfing us completely. The sea grew steadily rougher, forming 1-metre waves and whitecaps all around us, and the bitterly cold wind lashed the rain hard into our faces, making it difficult to see through our goggles as each wave crashed up over the bow, ran along the deck and poured into our cockpit skirts, necessitating constant draining. I was giving it my all; grimacing, even grunting with effort through gritted teeth with every stroke. Two pm came and went, and snatching glimpses of the shore through the mist, using rocks (bears?) and herds of muskox as reference points, I realised we were actually slipping backwards! I raised my paddle above my head, signalling to Clark that it was hopeless, and we swung sideways and headed directly for shore as the water raced past. I was utterly exhausted and losing coordination—sometimes failing to grasp the paddle as I changed sides, only realising when my hand slammed into the deck.

Eventually we grounded and I stumbled clumsily out, staggering in the buffeting wind and rain until I finally gained my balance and went to join Clark with the lunch things. 'There's no way we can paddle in this,' I groaned.

'And there's no way we can camp on this,' Clark added gloomily, looking around the tidal mudflat on which we were marooned. We tried hauling, but we almost threw up with the exertion, and we didn't have a point to aim for, anyway.

Fumbling with another nut ration we wandered aimlessly ahead looking for somewhere dry enough to camp, and somewhere to collect some water. We found several small pools, but all were disgustingly salty. At last, 1 kilometre on, we found a small dry gravel patch. 'I guess we'd better go back and get the PACs then ...' We turned and mechanically staggered towards our distant PACs, shackled up and hauled them back along the imprint of our earlier muddy footsteps, passing wolf tracks everywhere.

Having finally dragged them both there, we sank to the ground. 'Oh, no,' Clark put a hand to his head, 'we still need water ...' Binoculars revealed what looked like slightly higher ground (less salty water?) way off in the opposite direction, so we grabbed our water bladders and a saucepan to fill from, and walked wearily towards it.

Eventually we came upon a large but rather stagnant-looking pond, full of whirling critters. 'Still pretty salty,' I said, spitting it out, 'but it'll have to do.' It was crazy—the wind was now so strong that when I tried to pour the water from the saucepan into the mouth of the bladder, the stream of water just got whipped away horizontally and dissolved into a fine spray. I tried to turn my back to the wind to create some shelter, but the whirling air around me now caused the water to pour *upwards* right into my face! Eventually we filled the bladders and squelched back to our PACs, each carrying what looked disconcertingly like the kind of clear plastic bag people carry home from the pet shop, ready to start an aquarium—it had that many little bugs and whirligigs swimming around in it. 'Yum!' I laughed. 'Extra protein!'

It was a real battle to get the tent up—the howling wind trying to rip it out of our hands as we slid the poles in and nailed it into the ground with every tent peg we had. As soon as it was up, we both clambered inside, slipped straight into our sleeping bags and blocked out the world with Vivaldi and a hot chocolate at first, and then with alfredo pasta. 'What a day,' Clark mumbled. 'I'm totally shattered.' Today was, as Clark commented, definitely 'one of those days you wouldn't wish upon your worst enemies, but glad you've experienced it yourself and survived', to use as a yardstick in the future when days seem 'hard' ...

## DAY 31: Stuck in the mud

I woke early and lay there, feeling the howling wind buffeting the tent as sheets of rain pelted noisily against the fabric. My wind-speed watch showed a steady 49 kilometres per hour, and in the distance the fiord was a seething body of churning white water. With nothing but sloppy mud to haul over, it seems we're pinned here for the day.

After brekky we busied ourselves with random tasks, filling the time between food breaks. 'My heartbeat's 41 bpm!' I announced proudly. It was 61 bpm when we left home.

Opening the zipper into the vestibule on his side of the tent, Clark said suddenly, 'There's a bird in here—look!' Sure enough, wedged tightly in between our warm inner-tent, our camera bag, and our detergent bottle cringed a small sandpiper bird.

'It must be sheltering from the storm,' I said in astonishment, as the tiny bird blinked up at us, making no effort to escape. 'You know your tent's good when wild animals prefer it to their own natural shelter!' I laughed. 'Or goes to show how bad the storm is …'

I rugged up and went for a walk to collect some water at 5 pm. 'It's 1.5 degrees Celsius out here!' I shouted above the wind. My fingers had never felt so cold before—it felt like they had been frozen inside a block of ice, and then suddenly run under hot water while being struck repeatedly with a mallet. On my way back, I checked the temperature again: minus 0.2 degrees. I dived inside the tent, ripping my gloves off and sticking my hands between my legs in an effort to re-warm them.

'Here it comes,' Clark said, grinning, 'the Arctic winter!'

## DAY 32: Winter approaches

'Wow! Clark … Check it out!' I breathed, peering outside. He woke and joined me gazing out over a completely different world. A blanket of snow smothered the tundra, the little ponds nearby had frozen over, and even our water bladders were crispy around the edges. 'Minus 2.2 degrees,' I said, tapping the thermometer.

We only have a few more days of paddling along the north-eastern coastline of this eastern flange of the island before we strike inland, and anxious to leave these mudflats behind, we packed up camp and hauled to the shore as snow flurried around us.

'Have a look, Clark,' I called him over. There on the ground was one of the little sandpiper birds—just like the one that tried to shelter inside our tent—curled on the tundra, frozen solid. 'Wow,'

I mumbled, 'I guess that's what happens if you don't migrate south in time.'

Snow goggles wrapped firmly around our balaclavas, drysuit collars lifted well up and hoods pulled well down, we felt impervious to the gale and launched our PACs into the angry, breaking water. It was quite the experience, paddling into an Arctic gale, the wind thick with snow, paddling past icebergs as the odd icy wave exploded against the bow. So long as we kept paddling hard, we stayed warm. The moment we stopped—for nut breaks or lunch—our core temperatures dropped and, shivering uncontrollably, we'd have to cut it short and keep paddling.

Spotting an ideal dry campsite at about 5 pm, we pulled in to shore, set up the tent and piled inside. 'It's so quiet and warm in here,' I whispered, wrapping my agonisingly frozen fingers around a particularly rich hot chocolate,

'Cheers, mate!' Clark said, clinking his mug to mine. 'Happy halfway day! Halfway to 65 days!' We only have to survive what we've already endured again, and then we'll be home! It's a wonderful thought, but the now sub-zero temperatures hint that we are in for some hard times ahead.

Pouring an extra hot drink and dividing up our instant just-add-water 'dark chocolate cheesecake' that we brought for this very moment, we spent a pleasant evening reading a swag of lovely emails and website messages while intermittently noting the temperature outside, which was once again plummeting: 0.1, 0.0, minus 0.1, minus 0.2, minus 0.6, minus 1.2.

## DAY 33: Frost-nipped fingers

At minus 2.2 degrees, it became a challenge to do almost anything this morning. After shaking snow off our drysuits we changed into them, and then wedged our already painfully cold feet inside the deformed, frozen solid wetsuit booties—like zipping our feet into a shoe-shaped chest-freezer.

But this trauma was nothing compared to donning our gloves. As usual they were waterlogged after paddling yesterday, and we'd simply left them in the PACs, where they had now frozen absolutely solid. Prising mine out of the cockpit, I had to repeatedly thrash them against the tyres to smash the ice inside them enough to wedge my fingers in.

At first they just felt f*&king cold, and we actually grinned at each other, laughing at the discomfort of it all, but then as we pushed our PACs down to the water's edge, my smile slid away as my fingers reached a level of pain I've never experienced before—my fingers by this stage totally senseless, as if made of plastic. I put them between my legs desperately trying to warm them up, I whirled them around and around trying to force blood-flow back into them, all the while in the most excruciating pain I've ever had to endure. It was all I could do to make little noises behind my balaclava and grit my teeth so as not to cry out. I thought that maybe the shards of ice inside had somehow totally sliced up my fingers, and I ripped my gloves off expecting blood, but no, it was just the nerves in my fingers screaming out that they were dying. Ten hours later they are still burning, and look slightly blistered! Scary, considering it was only minus 2 degrees Celsius.

Paddling out into incessantly slamming waves eventually got the blood flowing again, and after a few hours of giving it my all, I called out to Clark. 'I don't think we're actually moving anymore! Let's head for that hunk of ice on the shore over there!' It was about 150 metres ahead, and we powered towards it. A good 15–20 minutes later it was still no closer. Defeated yet again, we swung broadside and headed for shore.

Unable to spread the butter even with our fingers, our lunch consisted of fragments of butter and toffee-like peanut butter on flat breads, dusted with snow. A quick GPS check revealed we'd only come 900 metres all day. 'What?' I exclaimed. 'That's bullshit!'

It was a real psychological blow. 'We're never going to get out of this place,' Clark groaned. Unable to kayak, unable to camp, we accepted our fate and shackled up. Broken men, we toiled through the boot-sucking mud, head down in our own little world of suffering, no longer caring enough to walk around ponds of water or aim for slightly drier ground. Just one foot splashing, squelching in front of the other, slowly forcing each leg muscle to straighten in turn, thus dragging the PAC forward, one step at a time. It was soul destroying.

I called my parents tonight to wish them a happy anniversary. As soon as Mum realised it was me, she started crying and asked me to come back early! 'Are you warm enough?' she asked.

'Oh yes,' I lied, cradling the sat phone in my throbbing hands.

Dad had some good news. 'The weather forecast for Cambridge Bay shows it warming back up tomorrow ...' Please let it be true. Please let this only be a passing cold front, and not the beginning of the end.

## DAY 34 (1 September 2005): Perfect paddling

The temperature read a balmy 2.2 degrees outside. 'Now's our chance!' I said to Clark as we enjoyed oats and coffee. 'Let's paddle as far as we can today, and get past all this coastal mud!'

Although it was still overcast and we were padding directly into a headwind and current, it was nothing like yesterday, and we made good progress. The current racing past the larger grounded bergs actually kicked up a bow wave, and it sometimes looked like they were charging ahead.

After lunch, a seal popped its head up in the distance and regarded us, before withdrawing back under the surface. We paddled on, and every few moments, the seal would surface, closer and closer. I stopped paddling, and slid to a halt. A huge dark form passed underneath my PAC, and then suddenly the large round face of a bearded seal poked up right beside me, staring at me with curious black eyes, while I stared back, equally amazed.

We had to keep going, but to our delight the seal followed us for almost half an hour, during which time the weather eased, and then, seemed to literally 'turn off'. Without a ripple disturbing the crystal-clear water, and with the stones on the bottom sliding past well below, it really looked as if we were suspended in mid air, paddling through space past hovering chunks of ice, each sculpted into beautiful mushrooms and flutes—some white and some pale blue with cracks revealing an iridescent, electric-blue interior. A single delicate feather rested curled upon the surface of the water as I paddled past, and small, transparent lumps of ice occasionally clunked against the bow and gently tumbled their way down the length of the hull.

'Isn't this just ... magic!' Clark had silently slipped alongside. We ceased paddling for a while and spun gradually around in space, taking it in. I was listening to some tranquil Inuit music at the time, and the whole experience blossomed into an almost surreal dream.

Pulling into shore for the evening, I discovered quite a lot of water in my PAC. 'I think my PAC's got a hole in it somewhere, guv,' I noted to Clark, but not even this could dent our morale tonight.

## DAY 35: The ice maze

It was actually *warm* in the tent this morning! Four degrees Celsius outside, quickly rising to 7 degrees as we examined our maps and decided to head for a river inlet 8 kilometres up the coast. 'Yeah, that looks like a good place to strike inland,' Clark agreed, 'Let's go for it!'

As we packed up camp, sunlight suddenly burst through the thinning clouds. 'The *sun!*' I shouted—our first glimpse for almost a week.

It was brilliant paddling today and our solar panels greedily lapped up the sunshine. The wind and the current were now in our favour, and we tore along, past still more miraculously carved icebergs, some overhung, some forming impressive archways and tunnels, and others convoluted underwater forms. It was just beautiful, pausing occasionally to eat some nuts as the PACs spun silently, then effortlessly gliding ever onwards.

I suddenly noticed, late afternoon, that we were not so much 'paddling past' hunks of ice anymore, but rather threading our way around and in between them. 'It's turning into a bit of a maze, hey!' I shouted over to Clark.

We proceeded for another half an hour or so, as the gaps between bergs became so narrow that our PAC wheels started scraping along the sides—shaving off ice as we squeezed through. The once blissful silence was now filled with the continual groaning, squealing, crunching and splashing of shifting masses of ice around us. Increasingly we became jammed and had to back up and nose into a different opening in the labyrinth. 'This is getting a bit dodgy actually,' I called, fending off from another towering wall of ice. 'It's going to get dark in a few hours ...'

It was a sobering thought. Over a kilometre from shore amongst shifting ice, with nowhere to set our tent or tripwire—in fact, nowhere even to get out of our PACs. And, my PAC was starting to feel particularly sluggish and heavy, gradually leaking and sinking beneath me. 'Let's head back out,' I pressed, 'and follow the shore instead.' Clark agreed and, pushing off with our paddles from the ice that now virtually surrounded us, we manoeuvred our PACs around 180 degrees. The ice looked just as impenetrable behind us. Visions of Shackleton's *Endurance* disaster flashing before my eyes, I headed for a gap, paddled hard and slid up and over a shallow sheet of submerged ice and slipped back into the water on the far side, swerving to avoid another wall of ice.

We eventually wound our way back out of the maze, and headed for shore where we found a narrow ice-free passage and followed that up the coast. Nearing the river mouth, the muddy terrain at last gave way to genuine tundra and stones, a convenient haul-out point on the shore.

Thrilled to be back on solid, dry land, Clark picked up a spiral fossil, and then crouched down to look at a small plant. 'So many things to look at!' he said excitedly. It was sensory overload after the endless oozing brown mud and the silent water.

'Over here!' I called, 'I just found a whale skull!' Surrounded by scattered vertebrae, it looked like the skull of a beluga, the Arctic's famous 'white whale'.

'Hey! Back off!' Clark suddenly shouted behind me, and turning, I saw him running at a large, ungainly bird that was attacking the zipper tassle on our camera bag. 'Don't touch what you can't afford!' It looked like a young glaucous gull, and it couldn't have cared less about Clark comically flapping around trying to scare it off.

I scooped up and tasted some water from a pond at my feet—it was the purest, most unsalty water I'd tasted all week. 'This is an amazing place!' I grinned, feeling all my pent-up worry and stress from the last few days draining out of me. 'Let's take the day off tomorrow and explore!'

## DAY 36: A well-earned break

We woke at 9 am to a blissfully sunny day, and an unusual sensation. 'It's almost *hot*!' Clark commented, reaching for the thermometer. 'Wow! Ten degrees!' We made the most of our rest day today: charging batteries, filming and photographing various things on our lists including shots for sponsors, writing a website update and even loading some essentials into our camera bag and going for a wander inland, carrying both a shotgun and fishing rod.

'I thought Victoria Island was supposed to be teeming with char,' I frowned in frustration, casting again into a snaking river. 'It's rice night again tonight, too … come on, just one fish?'

Just before dinner, I happened upon a lemming. 'Clark—come and look!' Suddenly feeling vulnerable, the little rodent scurried towards me and wedged itself between my boots.

'That's so adorable,' Clark laughed. Every time I lifted my foot to try and walk away, it scampered directly beneath my lowering shoe as a place to hide. Not the brightest of animals …

## DAY 37: At last, we've seen the light!

Revitalised after yesterday's break, we rose early, packed up, clipped ourselves back into our hauling harnesses and heaved our PACs into motion. 'It feels good to be hauling again,' I said, genuinely. After a week of either paddling or soul-destroying double-hauling through thick mud, it was great to be lurching independently over reasonable tundra.

Heading towards the river that we are to follow inland from here, we came across a small, steep esker. A flock of ptarmigans suddenly alighted upon the tundra in front of us. Clark had already seen them and stopped, while I quietly unshackled, loaded my shotgun and snuck up on them, closer and closer, my heart pounding. The instant they took flight I fired. BANG! Two of them lay dead on the ground. I picked them up, waiting for the guilt to flow, but as I looked back to see how Clark was taking it, I saw him already hurrying over with a Leatherman.

'Three-course dinner tonight!' he said, beaming. 'Pasta, then rice, then ptarmigan burritos!' Placing each bird on its back, I pulled a pinch of skin, slit an opening and neatly peeled the whole skin away, feathers and all, revealing two smooth, unbloodied breast fillets beneath.

Our three-course dinner was literally to die for (poor little birds), and our bodies were craving it. By the time we'd finished our mug of arctic tea for dessert it was midnight, and I climbed outside in the pitch dark to hang a leak before bed. We're now experiencing over nine hours of darkness each night, and the daylight is shortening by about eight minutes each day.

While staring absent-mindedly up at the stars, something caught my attention. Patches of the sky were glowing green. The harder I looked, the brighter they became. Shimmering green curtains of light were waving slowly across the night sky. I dived back inside the tent, shouted, 'The aurora!' and re-emerged with my camera and tripod.

It was beautiful to watch, but excruciatingly cold outside, and soon Clark retreated to the warmth of his sleeping bag, while I tried not to freeze to death in pursuit of a photo. It required a three-minute exposure, and unable to do this without a remote, I had to switch to 'bulb' mode and somehow hold the camera's shutter button down for three minutes without holding and wobbling the camera. Feeling in my pocket, I found a shotgun bullet and, using a rubber band, wedged it in to depress the shutter button—it worked like a charm! After each exposure the cold had sucked all the life out of the camera battery, and I had to take it out and, although freezing myself, warm it up under my armpits before trying again.

## DAY 38: Heading inland

It's funny how rare and important big rocks are out here—providing something tangible for us to aim for, and shelter behind. It seems animals out here are also drawn inexorably towards them; most have wisps of muskox hair rubbed off on them, feathers on top of them and plenty of fox, wolf and lemming scat all around. 'It's like they just want *something* to go to the toilet behind, hey!' Clark grinned. We have noticed this amusing phenomenon ourselves too. When the need strikes, we grab the toilet paper in one hand, shotgun in the other, and start walking until we find something—anything—to crouch beside, even if it's just a shoebox-sized rock that provides neither shelter nor privacy. Interestingly, the cumulative effect of so much attention is particularly nutrient-rich soil around such boulders; consequently they are always bursting with plant life, even flowers. Little oases in the desert.

We eventually reached the elusive river and after lunch we converted the PACs to kayak mode and dragged them in. We've been worried it'd only be a shallow creek, but it is a decent river, 6–10 metres wide, shallow with rapids in parts, but mostly deep enough to paddle.

We spent all afternoon trying to work out how best to progress up river. Paddling against the current got us nowhere, and hauling, wading in drysuits was slow and became impossible in deeper sections. We tried tying a long rope to the bow and walking along the riverbank well ahead of our PACs, but they invariably became snagged on the shore. Pondering this conundrum over a nut break, we both suddenly had the same brainwave.

'Let's tow them up the middle of the river, with—' Clark began.

'—one of us on each bank!' I finished. Shoving my remaining walnuts into my mouth I rigged up the rope and we gave it a try.

It worked a treat! One PAC tied in tow behind the other, we just walked along opposite banks, each holding a rope, guiding the PACs through the deepest channels in the river. There was the occasional shallow bit or rapids that we had to walk back and manhandle them past, but for the most part, it was little harder than wandering around during a nut break. I even fashioned a comfortable handle for the end of my rope from a caribou antler we passed!

We didn't get all that far today, but now that we've finally worked out the ultimate way to travel upstream, we're hopeful for good progress tomorrow.

## DAY 39: Hauling up rapids

Although increasingly windy, the first few hours of river travel went well today, and we even ran well ahead and set up the video camera to film us lining the PACs up the river. As we pulled closer and closer, however, trying not to look in the direction of the camera and ruin the shot, I couldn't help noticing that I couldn't see the camera and tripod at all. Across the other side of the river, I could see Clark straining to see over to my side where we'd left it, right on a bend in the river. It wasn't there. Staring now, I could see one thin stick poking up at an angle. It was the leg of a collapsed tripod.

'Oh, *shit!*' I shouted, unshackling and running over, sick to the stomach, while Clark flailed across the river behind me. With my video camera already electrocuted, and this one having just fallen from about shoulder height, our documentary hopes would be ruined.

Lifting up the battered camera that had detached from the tripod and tumbled across the tundra—thankfully not quite reaching the water's edge—I saw its little red 'recording' light still glowing. Unbelievably, it had survived. After scraping out all the mud and grit from its hinges and buttons, we excitedly reviewed the footage. A particularly violent gust of wind had simply blown the whole thing over. 'We're so lucky ...' Clark breathed, shaking his head in disbelief.

By lunch we were having to painfully lift-pull, lift-pull the PACs an inch at a time over more and more rapids. Pushed to our limit, again and again we almost decided to convert to wheel mode and haul along the horribly bumpy, soggy riverbanks instead, but always just ahead the river seemed tantalisingly deeper, at least until it had lured us around the next corner, where we'd be faced with *just one more* rapid, then coaxed around the next bend by seemingly deeper water. It was exhaustingly slow, and at each rapid the slippery rocks twisted our ankles and bruised the soles of our feet.

Having just heaved our way up a particularly bad rapid, my patience was wearing thin. 'Oh, for f&%ok's sake! There's *another* one!' I cursed harshly and Clark too spat the dummy. 'That's *it*– we're hauling.' It actually took some time to lift our PACs up out of the now rather steep-sided river, and by the time we'd converted to hauling mode it was 6 pm and we didn't have an ounce of strength left in us. We decided to call it a day.

## DAY 40: Getting hungrier

Miserable weather, overcast, windy and rainy as we hauled beside the river over tedious, shockingly lumpy, tussock-studded terrain. One consolation we did notice was that hauling is starting to get a little easier—probably a combination of the PACs getting lighter and us growing stronger. While it's still impossible to build any kind of momentum on this ground, meaning that achieving any progress is a constant grind, we are at least able now to doggedly absorb each brutal lurch from the PAC and just force our way steadily onwards.

We made it to a large lake we'd been aiming towards for days and, climbing a small rise beside it during a nut break, gazed out over the view below. 'I wonder if anyone's ever climbed this before?' Clark mused. It is certainly possible we are the first. We haven't seen any sign of Inuit tent rings for over a week, indicating we've crossed out of their usual haunts, which followed the caribou migrations and other sources of food. 'Imagine if we're the first people ever to look down over this view ...' It was an exciting and humbling thought.

I trolled my fishing line behind me for the first 4 kilometres as we paddled across the lake, but apart from catching the line on the bottom a few times, I got nothing. Having almost had an argument earlier today when Clark lost sight of a ptarmigan while I dug out the gun, we have noticed that food—or the lack of it—is starting to test us as much as the terrain.

## DAY 41: Getting colder, too

With a series of long lakes to cross before things start to freeze over again, we pushed hard today, paddling several more. During a break I called the pilot who was originally going to try and find somewhere to land and pick us up from the far side of the island. I chatted to him about the possibility of getting a plane from Cambridge Bay to land on a long esker we're hoping to reach in a week or two, and pick us up from there.

'That's a possibility, yes.' I could picture him chewing it over. 'There's not much else around, but the plane would need tundra tyres even to land on that esker, and I don't think they have any planes equipped with tundra tyres. Not in Cambridge Bay.' This was unfortunate news. 'I'll ask around for you, Chris, but you might have to charter a plane all the way from Resolute instead. But that might be expensive,' he added.

It's now a record low of minus 3.5 degrees outside, and we're camped snugly beside yet another lake as I warm my hands around a mug of hot chocolate. Whenever it's cold now, my fingertips still burn painfully where they got frost-nipped before. I really hope they return to normal one day. Rehydrated 'Chicken Gumbo' tonight—whatever that is—smells good though!

## DAY 42: Sub-zero paddling

The temperature stayed below zero all morning and many of the puddles we hauled past were frozen over, and even the mud pits felt firm underfoot. Just when we'd started to get our heads around the various types of terrain out here, it's all changing! As Clark hauled past what he took for a shallow frozen puddle, one of the wheels on his PAC broke through, sinking in so deep it took both of us to heave it out. Snow lurks in most of the crevices and shadows now and our condensed breaths have even started to freeze onto our moustaches and beards, forming little beads of ice.

We ate lunch overlooking the first of three major lakes between us and the distant start of the esker, still a week or more away, and which we have to reach for a plane to pick us up. Hauling down to the shore, I made to start unloading some weight ready to convert to kayak mode. 'Wait,' Clark interjected, 'let's see if I can lift it without unloading—it's got to be getting lighter by now.' It certainly was, and without having to unload and re-load, the entire conversion took only a couple of minutes, including donning our drysuits.

We paddled across the lake, and opted to stay in our drysuits to haul the 750 metres across to the start of the next lake, which involved a hot sweaty uphill climb, and then a fairly worrying descent, with our PACs forever trying to push us forwards, faster and faster.

'Whatever you do,' I shouted ahead to Clark, who was leaning backwards in his harness trying to brace himself so as not to be steamrollered from behind, 'just don't let it make you run!' He shot me back a wry grin, and I knew he was imagining the same disaster I was.

Miraculously, we made it down to the next lake without any broken legs or arms, converted once again to kayak mode and pushed off. As the temperature fell, I saw splashes of water on the deck of my PAC freeze before my eyes. By the time we pulled out on the far bank some 3.5 kilometres later, mini-icicles had started to form.

We lowered the wheels down for another short haul before slipping into the third and final lake for today, this one 2 kilometres wide. My watch alarm reminded me to call Sky News for another live TV interview partway across, and so I dug out our Iridium satellite phone and chatted away as the now quite gentle breeze spun me slowly around, and a handful of ducks circled overhead quacking excitedly about this curious intruder. Incredibly, Sky News still haven't asked the obvious: 'So, looks like you're not going to make it to the far side then?' Brilliant. When I at last hung up, my paddle had frozen to the kayak.

## DAY 43: Frozen shoelaces

I woke to the sounds of frosty sheets of snow sliding down the side of the tent over my head, melded with the tinkling fall of fresh snow. Today was the coldest hauling yet, and passing a herd of caribou, I noticed their old brown summer coat now hanging in ribbons from a fresh grey-white coat ready to blend in with the snow of winter. Overhead, huge Vs of migrating geese now constantly honk their way southward, while we still trudge steadily north-west. 'Maybe this time it's not just a cold snap …' Clark commented, reading my mind. All the animals here either seem to be leaving, or battening down their hatches ready to face the Arctic winter. All except the lemmings, that is; they seem content to remain conspicuously brown year-round, and we both almost keep treading on them daily as they dart from their holes.

Exhausted at the end of the day, and now within striking distance of the esker, we found that our shoelaces were so frozen that we literally had to get out our Leatherman to work them free. 'Yep,' Clark said, grinning, 'you know it's winter when you need a pair of pliers to get your shoelaces undone!'

## DAY 44: Frozen in

By 8 am it was blowing a screaming gale, snow building up in a long tail behind our tent. 'Bad weather day off?' Clark enquired hopefully.

'For now, anyway!' I replied, glad he didn't want to head outside just yet either.

'Bags not going out and collecting some water for breakfast!' Clark added, a smug smile on his face as he wriggled comfortably in his sleeping bag.

Outside was *surprisingly* cold at minus 7.2 degrees—the coldest yet—and minus 31 degrees if we include windchill effects. Despite all my layers, it took my breath away, and burned my nose and throat. The large lake beside our tent—which only yesterday had been lapping water—had now almost completely frozen over.

Staggering over to the edge with a tomahawk, I took a swing at the surface. With a loud *chink* a split appeared, and after a series of strikes, I managed to wedge out a hunk almost 5 centimetres thick, only to find that the lake had frozen solid all the way to the bottom here in the shallows. I gingerly took a step out onto the ice, and shuffled my way out a few steps towards where I hoped it would be deep enough to find liquid water underneath. The wind, roaring past me, increased, and I suddenly found myself sliding—being blown—out across the ice towards the centre of the lake, where in the distance I could see open water, and a particularly chilling death.

I crouched down but on the frictionless smooth ice I was still accelerating! Using the tomahawk as an ice axe, I slammed it hard into the crust of ice to anchor myself. Fragments of ice flew into the air and screamed past me like shrapnel in the wind.

Using the tomahawk in this way, I eventually managed to crawl my way back to shore, and found a place where I could chip through the ice, revealing about 3 centimetres of silty water beneath. I hastily scooped up a few cups, one thimbleful at a time, before hurrying back to the tent and diving inside, a shivering wreck, my fingertips feeling like they were being crushed in a vice.

We passed the intervals between meals playing games of boxes and writing to-do lists while the wind continued to howl, explosively shaking the tent. When even hangman failed to keep me entertained, I ventured outside for a brief ptarmigan hunt, but returned soon after, frozen to the core, without anything to show for it. After a mug of arctic tea, we finally ran out of food for the day, and thus reasons to stay awake.

# DAY 45: What if it doesn't get any better?

Looks like another day stuck in the tent—it's just far too cold outside in this wind. How long can it last? I had to smash through about 8 centimetres of ice to get some water today! In the afternoon we grew restless and decided to go for a walk to find some ptarmigan. We ended up staggering about 3 kilometres around the lake, and found nothing. The whole world seems to be devoid of life now.

Between food breaks I backed up some photos, culled some others. Clark set up the video camera on a tripod outside and we did a video diary, until a particularly savage gust of wind blew the whole thing over just as I was trying to relate how crazy the wind is out here. Miraculously, the video camera survived, again.

After dinner we lay in our sleeping bags trying to go to sleep as the wind raged against the tent. 'I'm worried that this isn't just a passing storm,' I said, voicing both our thoughts. 'We've spent two days waiting for it to get better, and it's just … not.'

Clark nodded, 'If anything, it's getting gradually worse. Maybe this is just the way it is from here on in.'

It was a disturbing thought. 'If it is,' I said glumly, 'we'd better try and make it to that esker fast, while we can. We can't get a plane to land anywhere around here!' We've solemnly agreed to head on tomorrow, storm or no storm, else things could start to turn a little desperate.


# DAY 46: Facing the storm

Nineteen days left till our 65 are up! We've decided that our pickup date is now close enough that we can start writing our food craving lists without it just being a cruel torment. However, with more pressing matters at hand, we rugged up and faced the storm outside, our sights set on reaching the first part of the esker, only 6 kilometres away. 'So let's hope we get there,' Clark confided to the video camera.

The wind had eased a little, reducing the windchill to around minus 20 degrees Celsius. At last, all packed and ready to go, I walked up to where I'd casually jabbed my hiking poles into the ground three days ago, and tried to pull them out. They were stuck fast, frozen solid into the now concrete-like ground. I literally had to cut them out of the ground with the tomahawk. The PACs themselves had also frozen to the ground and it took both of us to break the wheels free.

'All right, let's do this!' I shouted, throwing myself forwards into my harness, and beginning the slow march across the increasingly frozen, barren white landscape as wind and snow tore around us.

'Now *this* is the *real* Arctic!' Clark shouted back, his voice muffled by layers of balaclavas, hoods and collars. It was a whole new learning experience with the terrain; once mostly soft tussocks and easy to wheel over, each tussock is now as solid as steel, jerking the PAC around as each wheel snags. Mud pits at last have all finally become as firm as they always looked like they should have been, and we even tried hauling across the thicker edges of frozen lakes but found it impossible to get any traction with our feet on the glassy surface, and the odd splintering cracking noise underfoot was a little disconcerting. The most confusing thing of all is that the patchwork of lakes—which we use to orientate ourselves on our map—are all now frozen and as white as the land around them, making them very hard to see. We ended up getting disorientated and finally agreed to turn on the GPS (we don't have any spare batteries now, and it is no longer accepting charge), which revealed we needed to backtrack almost a kilometre to avoid a large semi-frozen lake.

By 6.30 pm the temperature was dropping fast, along with the visibility, and with the esker still 3 kilometres away we decided it'd be safest to call a halt and do the last bit tomorrow. We set up camp on a blanket of snow, praying that as our body warmth melted it during the night we wouldn't find ourselves deposited upon sharp rocks. Clark had the brainwave of pulling out the two tiny foam cockpit cushions from our PACs—each about 30 centimetres square—and using them as a 'mattress', as our air mattresses had long since failed on us. It worked a treat; positioning one under the bum, and one under the shoulder, they comforted the worst of our bruises.

## DAY 47: Getting serious

Determined to get to the esker today, I called our pilot for an update, and he said he was looking into diverting a scheduled flight from Resolute to Cambridge Bay to pick us up somewhere on the esker. That'd be brilliant, and would save us a fortune. 'I assume he's not talking about their regular passenger flight?' I said, grinning at Clark. 'This is your captain speaking, we are just making a bit of a diversion now to try and land on a strip of boulders and ice in the middle of nowhere to pick up some other passengers ...'

The pilot also suggested that as our food rations only last until 2 October, we should aim for a pickup no later than 25 September—just over ten days from now—else freak bad weather could easily delay plans, leaving us stranded out here without food.

By the time we set off, the weather had deteriorated further—we couldn't even see 50 metres in front of us, so we basically had to go the long way, feeling our way along the shores of lakes and following their interconnecting streams rather than trying to walk in a straight line. With snow blanketing the ground, we can't even see what we're hauling over anymore, and our PACs' wheels keep dropping into holes and getting wedged between rocks. It's impossible. With no other option, we again tried our luck walking on the frozen edges of the lakes, but again our feet just slid around on the slippery surface, unable to get a grip.

In a moment of inspiration I put on my Yowie snowshoes, which have spiky metal cleats on the bottom, and it worked a charm! Soon we were clink-clink-clinking our way along the wonderfully flat ice, laughing at all the horrible terrain just metres beside us. Then, with a horrible cracking sound, Clark's wheel broke through the ice, plunging his PAC over onto its side. We knew the water was only shallow and so we were in no danger, but it proved quite difficult to get close enough to the floundering PAC to help Clark haul it free, without causing more ice to break around it. We got it eventually, and marched determinedly onwards.

There was a lull in the biting wind and driving snow, and through the haze I spotted the tail end of the esker now only 500 metres away from us, stretching like a white road into the distance. Desperately hurrying towards it, we were suddenly presented with a horrendous swathe of the most atrocious rock-strewn mess we had ever seen. 'There's no *way* we can haul over that!' Clark groaned, and I was inclined to agree. We spent a good hour trying to find a way left and right around it, but always we were cut off by the same nightmare terrain. The gale rose again, and flurries of snow were swept across the ground, coils of spindrift whirled across patches of open ice and jets of powder streamed around and over the jiggered hunks of rock in between.

'F*&k it! Let's just go for it. This is getting crazy!' Clark roared and swung forward headlong into the rocks. Again and again we were flung to the ground, tripping and falling, being pushed and shoved by our lurching PACs as they bounced and snagged on rock after rock. Clark's hiking pole managed to jam itself between two boulders and, unable to get his hand out of the wrist-loop in time to let it go, his hand got wrenched backwards as the momentum of the PAC surged forwards and ran over the pole, bending it badly and spraining his wrist. 'F&%k you Victoria Island!' he swore into the gale, and onwards we struggled. The icy fingers of desperation were starting to clutch at us, and things were becoming very full-on, very quickly.

We finally stumbled wearily up onto the much-anticipated esker. 'It's not much of an esker, really, is it?' I mumbled, staring in alarm at the jumble of rocks on which we stood. 'It had better improve further on, or we've got a serious problem. No plane is going to land on this stuff.'

Hauling onwards for another 500 metres, things did not improve, but spying a convenient little flat spot for our tent, down a slope and out of the worst of the wind, we decided to call it a day.

It proved nearly impossible to hammer our tent pegs into the frozen ground, and I ended up splintering several of our metal pegs, and banging my senseless fingers with the tomahawk, which did not improve my outlook on the world. After some 30 minutes I gave up, having only managed to get a few pegs in, and most of them only 2 or 3 centimetres deep. 'It's unlikely to blow away if we're in it,' I reasoned, and we piled inside, incredibly thankful for being able to get out of the wind and slowly warm back up.

## DAY 48: Surely they're not still out there?

I woke with my alarm at 1 am to check if I needed to take aurora photos, but thankfully the lack of stars across the inky black sky indicated total cloud cover, so, feeling quite relieved, I went back to sleep. The darkness gradually lightened to the dull grey we've become used to, and still we lay there. Ravenously hungry and also feeling weak, bruised and battered from the efforts of getting to this esker, we decided to reward ourselves with a rest day. 'Maybe at least this incessant wind will die down by tomorrow,' I justified.

We spent the day doing still more repairs to the PACs' hauling system, chipping through increasingly thick ice to find water, and writing expedition update #22 for the website. In this update I finally mentioned the obvious—that we aren't going to make it to the far side, but that we're okay with that, as we're out here for the journey not the destination. Clark sanity-checked it for me as usual, and I uploaded it and downloaded our emails.

We received several interesting emails tonight; all, it seemed, with a common theme of concern. I hadn't written an update for several days since reporting the start of the icy weather, and some of our followers have been growing anxious. It turns out winter has well and truly struck Cambridge Bay too, and the talk of the town had turned to us two poor souls presumably still out in the worst of it. My dad had even got a surprise call in the middle of the night from the Royal Canadian Mounted Police who, tipped off by two separate anxious locals, had riffled through their 'I'm out on the land' files, and found ours, dated as heading out almost two months ago. The alarmed officer could find no record of us having returned, and dialled the first emergency contact number—my dad. I can only imagine what must have raced through Dad's mind as he took the call.

Dad convinced them that we are alive and well, with food and shelter, and have a pickup organised for the coming weeks. In his email to us, Dad did stress, however, that he got the impression from the RCMP that if something does happen to us out here, we are essentially unreachable even by helicopter in weather like we've been enduring this week. It's a sobering realisation. 'Imagine if our tent blew away or tore or something,' Clark pondered aloud, as the sides bowed in around us.

## DAY 49: One last lake

The wind had eased by the morning, and the temperature climbed to minus 2.8 degrees—almost balmy! We shackled up and hauled along the esker, keeping our eyes out for potential airstrips. 'It's not looking good,' I frowned over a nut break. 'Maybe on the other side of that giant lake it's better?' The section of esker we were hauling along—nothing more than a series of rocky, interconnected hills—was eventually cut off by a very large lake. We'd seen it on the map, but had hoped to find a potential landing site well before reaching it. It seemed we were out of luck.

'The problem is,' I considered aloud, 'that being a large lake, it's probably not going to be frozen all the way across …'

Clark knew where I was heading, and continued, 'So we won't be able to haul across it, and we won't be able to kayak across it either. We can't exactly walk out until the ice breaks under us and then quickly convert to kayak mode and paddle!' We laughed bitterly, picturing this in our heads. 'But it's such a convoluted, weird-shaped lake that to haul around it will literally take days!' We both knew it was our only option, and figured we'd better get a move on—deadlines are starting to creep closer.

It was already getting late as we hauled over the last rise and the big lake came into view. Funny-coloured, textured ice seemed to stretch all the way across to the far side, some 3.5 kilometres away. As I stared at the ice, wondering if it'd be solid enough to haul over, I noticed the texture on its surface was moving. It wasn't ice after all, but water. Open water, the whole way across—we could kayak! 'It's not frozen!' I shouted back excitedly as Clark drew level. We couldn't believe it. 'Quick, let's paddle it!' I urged, and Clark took little convincing. With the temperature already falling—heading at least in Cambridge Bay for a record low of minus 9 degrees Celsius and worse up here—it would likely start to freeze over by morning, making it impossible to cross.

Converting my PAC to kayak mode by the shore, I changed into my drysuit and dug out my kayaking gloves and booties. Not expecting ever to have to paddle again, we'd rather carelessly shoved them down inside the cockpit, where they had absolutely frozen solid in a horribly contorted mash. I managed to separate out my gloves and beat them against the PAC wheel in a bid to break the ice inside them enough to make them malleable, but they remained as hard as rock. I even tried sloshing them in the lake as the water must at least be above zero degrees, but nothing could soften them, and there was no way I was going to force my fingers back into that icy torture chamber. I opted for my thinner hauling gloves.

We slid the PACs across just one metre or so of firm ice rimming the lake—marvelling as we did so how easily they glided across the ice—and climbed aboard our bobbing kayaks. 'We should have done an icecap traverse to the South Pole with a sled,' I grinned. 'Whose stupid idea was it to come here and use *wheels*?'

Kayaking the 3.5 kilometres across this lake was unforgettable. As we paddled, the temperature plummeted and our paddles started scooping through a semi-frozen slurry forming on the surface. Every splash froze onto the deck of our PACs, building up thicker and thicker. Every time I swapped sides with my little paddle it had frozen firmly to my gloves and I had to break it free.

We headed for a little alcove opening up in front of us, where two steep hills plunged directly into the lake, forming a beautiful little 10-metre wide entrance that we paddled through into a quiet lagoon off to the side. It was like paddling through a scene in *The Lord of the Rings*, surrounded by towering snow-capped peaks. We scrunched our PACs through a thin crust of ice already stretching out from the bank, and nosed into shore right beside where the esker continued on again. The scenery is unbelievably beautiful.

'What a fitting end to our paddling!' I said as I stood up. 'Oh, look at this!' As I tried to straighten up, I found my entire drysuit had turned into a rigid suit of armour—as if someone had poured a vat of clear epoxy glue all over it. As I bent my arms and legs, whole sheets of ice peeled away from the fabric.

We set up camp on a beautiful little patch of snow tucked in the lee of the esker, and I called Sky News for our weekly interview. They had clearly read my update last night, but to my delight, instead of having to field questions about why we're not going to make it to the far side, the newsreader was full of support: 'It's the adventure that counts. Keep going!'

We tried in vain to convert the PACs to hauling mode, but the axle has literally frozen in place holding the wheels up, so we'll deal with that tomorrow. We clambered wearily into the tent, but glowing inside with relief at being here.

We were inundated with beautiful emails tonight, in response to my 'we're not going to make it but we're okay with that' website update last night. It was so wonderfully warming to read them all—it filled us with pride and happiness; all trace of guilt or failure just melted away. Messages from people we knew, and people we didn't. Some Cambridge Bay locals wrote to say, 'You are true explorers.' 'You are a credit to all who have explored the barrens before you.' And 'No one in Nunavut would even try to do what you have done ... I am proud of you.' Many of these messages come from respected Inuits and people who have spent their life in the Arctic—it means a huge amount to us. A pilot who apparently works around the Arctic said that we had opened his eyes, and that he now feels that he knows this land much better than ever before. Although it was well after dinner, we made ourselves another lunch and lay in our sleeping bags savouring it, brimful of happiness, just enjoying the moment, and thinking about all the good things we can now start looking forward to.

We just need to find somewhere for a plane to land.

## DAY 50: Seen any tarmac airstrips around lately?

I hung up the phone, and Clark looked at me expectantly. 'Well?'

'It's going to cost $10,021 for the pickup,' I said bluntly, still in shock myself. Clark gaped at me as I tried to explain. 'Apparently there are no scheduled flights to divert, so we're going to have to charter a Twin Otter plane all the way from Resolute!'

'Ten grand!?' Clark repeated. 'That's ridiculous!'

'And it gets better,' I added, grinning at the incredulity of it all, 'they need us to find 350 metres of flat, level, solid, non-rocky, straight ground to land on.'

'Oh, great, so we'll just keep our eye out for a *tarmac* then, shall we?' Clark snorted, ''cause there's heaps of them round here.'

We couldn't help grinning, but inside, a little jolt of fear had just shattered last night's comfortable feeling that we'd made it, that we'd crossed the lake and were almost home. 'Shit, I hope we can get picked up,' Clark mumbled, 'there's blatantly nothing like that around here, or anywhere else, for that matter.'

'I'll give that other pilot a call,' I said, thumbing through my little notebook to where I'd scribbled down the number for Willie Laserich from Adlair Aviation—a local Cambridge Bay company that we knew didn't have tundra tyres on any of their planes, but might know someone who did.

I dialled the number and a warm, grandfatherly-like voice answered with a thick German accent. 'Yes, I am Willie.'

I explained our predicament, finishing with, 'So … is this something you can do?'

He thought it over. 'Vot is your GPS position?' he inquired. 'Hmm, yar … this will be fine, you just call me one day before, and I will come over. Okay?'

Surely it couldn't be that easy? 'Sure,' I managed, 'and, er, how much will that cost?'

'About $4,200, is that okay?'

Clark saw my eyes light up, and he started grinning in anticipation. 'That's great!' I said, and remembering the final snag, added, 'Oh, and a runway … We've been told we need 350 metres of flat, level, solid, non-rocky straight ground.' I held my breath.

'How long did you say?'

'Three hundred and fifty metres.'

I heard Willie chuckle and there was laughter in his reply, 'You won't find that out there … No, no, we should be okay with about 100 metres.'

'What a legend!' Clark burst out after I relayed all this to him. 'Let's have a second breakfast to celebrate!'

We eventually got out of the tent, and began our day surrounded by such breathtakingly wild and picturesque surroundings that several times we found ourselves just standing there in awe at the raw beauty of it all. The snow was littered with ptarmigan, fox and lemming tracks, and walking to the shore of the lake we saw ice now stretched way out towards the middle.

'We made it across just in time!' I said, and wiping snow off the ice with my boot, marvelled at how flawless and transparent it was. 'Hey, look at this!' Encased by solid ice for the winter, the ripples on the lake's sandy bottom were visible, complete with a wandering line of wolf tracks through the pattern.

We headed over to the edge of what looked like a wide, snow-filled valley, but walking down into it revealed its true scale—merely 5 metres across. Our 'Boys' Own' adventure day revealed still more amazing discoveries, including whole towering sand dunes apparently made of frozen sand, set hard like cement until I chipped out a hunk and warmed it in my hand, at which it 'melted' back into powdery grains. We climbed one of the hills looking down over the 'gateway' through to the larger lake that we paddled, and took in the beautiful scene. We are so lucky to be here, on this particular day. It's absolutely perfect.

Tomorrow we'd better start looking for a landing site.

## DAY 51: Searching

After waking to find a lemming snuggled cosily beside my neck just underneath the tent fabric, we packed up camp in the morning, shackled up and heaved our PACs up onto the esker. 'Right, let's find ourselves a runway!' I said, and set off. We found a place that looked almost suitable right away and pacing it out, it seems to be about 250 metres long, pretty flat but with a few frozen tussocks that are essentially like rocks growing intermittently across the 'tarmac'.

'It might be okay, though,' Clark shrugged. 'Let's leave our PACs here and explore on foot.' We've become so conditioned to PAC hauling—always walking the 'wheelchair access' route up the most gradual slopes, and avoiding all ledges and ditches—that it actually took a while to realise we were free. Soon we began deliberately scrambling up ledges, just because we could, and it felt great.

We came upon another potential landing site a kilometre or so further along, but although flatter and broader (allowing for different wind direction landings?) it's only about 150 metres long—still long enough by Willie's standards, though. We took some photos, noted the GPS location and headed back to the PACs. It started to grow dark early tonight—possibly bad weather coming—so we set up our tent back at Airstrip #1, and climbed inside.

## DAY 52: No more hauling!

I called Willie and explained both runway options to him. 'I'm sure they'll be okay … both of them,' he said reassuringly.

I repeated what I'd told him about the frozen tussocks. 'Aren't they going to be a problem?' In his warm, kindly way, he dismissed my concerns. 'What if you fly all the way out here and find out that you can't land?' I pushed.

'Oh, that's not a problem,' he assured me, 'I'll just land somewhere nearby and wait.'

I wasn't even sure if I should be taking him seriously. 'R-right. Okay. So, if you land somewhere nearby you'll just give us a call?' I asked. 'What's your satellite phone number?'

Again he brushed these complexities aside. 'Oh, I don't have a satellite phone. If we need to communicate, you can, er, write in the snow ... and I'll drop messages out of the plane.' I was dumbfounded, but I liked his style. 'Don't you boys worry,' he said genuinely. 'We'll get you out of there.'

'Do you know what that means?' Clark said, turning to me, 'We don't need to haul any further! This is it! We're done!' He was right. Definitely cause for a second breakfast! Afterwards, we gathered the GPS, sat phone, EPIRB, shotgun, chocolate, nut rations, camera, and the tiny little 50-millilitre hotel minibar-size bottle of Grand Marnier liqueur that we had bubble-wrapped and dragged 300 kilometres across the Arctic for this very day, and set off to find a suitably scenic place to sit, indulge and reflect. We found a spot perched on the side of a precipitous slope overlooking what must be one of the most stunning views, if not *the* most stunning, I have ever had the privilege to see. Below us a silvery frozen lake lay neatly rimmed by snow-clad mountains and the sweeping, curved tail of the esker upon which we stood. Shafts of sunlight swept across the landscape from patches of bright blue sky overhead, and overall the effect was magical. We took a photo, arms draped across each other's shoulders, holding the tiny bottle aloft, and, sitting on a snow-covered tussock, took turns sipping lidfuls between mouthfuls of chocolate. We have been dreaming of this moment for so long. Everything was perfect, the air was still, and the occasional perfectly star-shaped snowflake drifted down upon us as we proposed toasts and drank to many things. Amusingly, having not had alcohol for months and having burnt off most of our body fat, we managed to get a bit tipsy drinking half each of the contents of this minuscule bottle!

Back at camp before dinner we both fired our shotguns under the guise of checking that they still worked, but really just to hear the amazing echoes reverberate for almost ten seconds. It's not everywhere in the world where you can fire a bear-killing bullet in any direction you want! The freedom out here is complete. We prepared for our celebratory dinner, bringing out the packet of dehydrated Thai Satay Beef which we'd identified as our favourite early on, saving the last for today. It tasted so good, and following this, our second and final 'dark chocolate cheesecake'. 'I think today ranks as one of the best of the whole expedition,' Clark murmured comfortably from within his sleeping bag.

## DAY 53: End-point ceremonies

Minus 8 degrees this morning, and the world is getting increasingly white and barren. It's amazing how cold it feels, most ski holidays are 'colder', but out here, with the wind, and when there's no warm shower and raging fire to warm you back up at a ski lodge or something at the end of the day—it's seriously cold. Some friends in Cambridge Bay have also been complaining of the cold, which, considering they're headed for minus 45 degrees Celsius in a few months, sounded a bit strange until they explained that the beginning of winter up here is actually the worst, because it's a 'wet cold' which feels far colder than the much colder but 'dry' climate of mid-winter.

We decided to leave a small memento of our expedition in the form of a hand-written note wrapped in our Australian Geographic flag, sealed up and wedged inside one of our hollow aluminium bear tripwire poles. We'll plant it at the summit of our 'Gateway mountain' that forms the passage we kayaked through.

'What do I say in it?' I turned to Clark lying next to me on his sleeping bag.

'I dunno ... formal but not too wanky, I guess. "This marks the end of our trip" kinda thing?'

I dated the top and began:

*Here lies the Australian Geographic Society's flag, proudly carried with us on the 'Ocean Frontiers' 1000 Hour Day Expedition—our two-man, world first, unsupported journey undertaken by Christopher Bray (22) and Clark Carter (21) to cross Victoria Island.*

*We started our adventure on 31st July 2005 at 69 deg 51.696 min N, 100 deg 53.668 min W—the most easterly point of Victoria Island, from where we gave ourselves 65 days to get as far as we could*

*towards the most westerly point, while dragging/paddling/hauling some
250 kg of equipment and supplies each in our home-designed and built
PACs (Paddleable Amphibious Carts)—essentially a wheeled kayak.*

*This point, atop this unnamed mountain, overlooks the spectacular
endpoint of our expedition. A very fitting end to an unforgettable journey.
We have arranged for a plane to fly in and collect us and our gear,
leaving behind only this note and a flag as a monument to this adventure
of a lifetime.*

We signed it, slipped it in a cliplock bag with the flag which we also
signed, and hiked up the mountain. Even after hacksawing the bear
pole into a point and pouring boiling water down it to soften the
soil, it proved impossible to drive the pole into the frozen ground, so
instead we formed a cairn of piled stones to hold it upright.

'That's not going to last two seconds when a muskox comes along
and tries to run itself against it!' I laughed, enjoying a steaming mug
of hot chocolate on the summit as we surveyed our handiwork.

## DAY 54: Time to get out of here!

For a change of scene and to get some last-minute pics and video
footage of us hauling along, we packed up camp this morning and
hauled gradually along the esker, leapfrogging the camera to get
numerous 'haul towards' and 'haul away' shots. The finale came
with us hauling from the distance and pausing in front of the
camera to announce, 'Well, this is it—this is as far as our journey
takes us—our landing site is just (erm) over there …' (point off into
vacant space behind the cliff that the video camera is sitting on)
'So we don't need to haul any further!' Handshakes, etc. It feels a
bit fake mocking up these scenes, but hey, I guess that's how it has
to be done—without a film crew ahead of us, there's no way to
legitimately film such 'moments', is there?

It legitimately was the most westerly point we've reached
though—some 300 kilometres from the start, and cause for genuine
celebration. In the evening after a mug of arctic tea we both fired a
pyrotechnic bear-banger, which are a good substitute for fireworks,
and managed to suck enough life out of the laptop battery to check
emails. Dad reported a huge weather system brewing over in Siberia

that is apparently headed our way, and he urged us to get out of here by 23 September—that's in just two days' time—as after that we might not be reachable for days.

## DAY 55: Dancing with wolves

I called our pilot Willie this morning for his thoughts about the incoming gale. 'Oh, hello Chris! How are you two boys getting on out there? It's getting pretty cold back here!' He predicted that there'll be no gale for at least 24 hours, but without elaborating, said 'I'll pick you up tomorrow after dinner. Call me in the morning and let me know what the weather's like.'

With the end suddenly in sight, we went into overdrive ticking off all our last-minute to-do's, and hauled back to Airstrip #1. The weather has eased (calm before the storm?) and is absolutely stunning. A perfect day in the Arctic. 'This is such a fitting end,' Clark said, speaking my thoughts.

After setting up camp, I turned to Clark. 'We always meant to sleep one night on the tundra, without a tent …'

'The weather's good,' Clark agreed, 'and it's tonight or never!' We decided to leave the camp set up so we could retreat inside if the storm hit early, but what better way to enjoy our last night in the Arctic than sleeping out in the open? The idea scared us a little, but as Clark pointed out, 'It's not like a tent gives us any real protection from bears anyway.'

'We'll look alarmingly like two big fat seals, though,' I added, 'wriggling around in our black sleeping bags on the snow …'

While pondering this, I suddenly spotted movement on the distant hill behind us. 'A wolf!' I pointed, before diving for my camera. I've been hoping to see another one—there are so many tracks around here. It was a long way away, and even with the telephoto lens it looked small. As we watched, all of a sudden the rest of the pack just materialised beside the one we'd seen. It was amazing—just like my last wolf encounter—the rest of the pack didn't 'walk into view' they just suddenly started moving and then we saw them, and realised they were there all along, motionless, watching us. The alpha male—the only pure white one in this pack of five—steadily jogged down the hill towards us while the rest hung back. Still in the distance he suddenly dropped out of sight and moments later just appeared, right there, on our slope, not 10 metres from us and our tent! We couldn't believe it. When I swung my camera towards him, he now more than filled the viewfinder and I fumbled to change lenses and focus in the fading evening light, while at the same time we both edged closer to our tent, grabbing a can of bear spray and a large knife.

Watching the wolf was just awe-inspiring. This enormous white dog, perhaps 1 metre tall at the shoulder, strode confidently right around our camp. 'Strode' is perhaps the wrong word: although he certainly exuded confidence and power, his motion across the snow was more akin to gliding, effortlessly moving with such fluid grace that his back and head—even his shoulder blades—remained perfectly level while his tall legs and broad, snowshoe feet blurred silently beneath. Intent on investigating our camp, he paid not the slightest heed to our calls or noises; drifting right up to our PACs, our bear alarm, places where we'd stood, he sniffed, scratched, looked around fearlessly—less than 5 metres from us.

When he finally turned his gaze upon me, I could not look away. I was completely transfixed by the intensity of his dark, almond-shaped eyes as he scrutinised me. Staring into them, I could read calm curiosity, but more than anything else, startling intelligence. He was working us out, weighing things up, double-checking things, testing how close he could pass before we withdrew, and suddenly he padded off, perhaps 10 metres back towards the rest of his pack on the opposite hill, cast one look back at us, lifted his muzzle into the air and howled. A long, drawn-out, baleful howl, curling his tail around his flank in the final moments, as if squeezing out the last few seconds of air. Rooted to the spot, I felt the hair on the back of my neck prickle as I lowered my camera. Beside me, Clark too was motionless.

'It's like he's calling them over,' I whispered as he howled again. The distant wolves shuffled around but did not advance, as if unconvinced. Finally they returned his howl, and after exchanging what can only be described as a howled conversation, with our wolf's cries becoming increasingly pleading, he pierced us with one last, lingering stare, and padded silently off to join his pack. Reunited, all five then proceeded to lope away, at last disappearing over the distant skyline.

'That was ...' Lost for words, Clark and I just stood looking at each other, shaking our heads in disbelief. Some 30 minutes later when we'd calmed down, we slotted back into routine, and wandered together the 500 metres to the (now thoroughly frozen) lake, and laboriously chipped through the top 15 centimetres of ice, withdrew the square 'window' plug of ice and filled up our water bladders. Laughing and chatting, we began walking back towards camp, when suddenly I saw two of the darker wolves appear again on the distant skyline. I turned to tell Clark, 'Hey, look there's ... BEHIND YOU!!!' Wheeling around, Clark locked eyes with the huge white alpha male wolf, less than 4 metres behind him.

His surprise blown, the wolf simply stood there, waiting to see how we would react. My mind reeled. After the initial nanosecond of paralysing fear released me, my reaction was to stride calmly and confidently over and stand beside Clark. 'How the f*&k did he get there?' Clark whispered as we both flicked off the safety pegs on our cans of bear spray—the only thing besides the tomahawk we could use to defend ourselves. 'What do we do?'

His eyes still fixed on us, the wolf began circling us, closer, further away and then closer still, at times coming within 3 metres of us. Easily close enough, I sensed, to reach us with a sudden leap forward. Holding my can of bear spray between us, I dared him to make any sudden movements. But he didn't. He just kept circling.

Determined to show no fear, we advanced towards him, talking loudly. 'Hey, Wolf! Get outta here!' Unfazed, he held his ground, and it became a stand-off—every time we feigned a move left or right, he'd do the same, as if to cut us off. Unwilling to take a step back, we made a sudden lunge forward ourselves, testing him out. He flinched and ran a short distance, but quickly returned, and his behaviour switched. Right in front of us, he stretched out his front legs in a mock crouch, but poked his bottom high in the air, playfully wagging his bushy white tail above him. It was unfathomable. 'It's like he wants to *play* with us?' Clark whispered incredulously.

I kicked a clump of snow towards the wolf and he pounced and caught it in mid air, before re-assuming his position, tail wagging in delight. 'It's a classic "go on, throw me a ball" kinda pose!' I said, still not sure how to take it. Incredibly, the three of us then 'played' in the snow for perhaps a minute or more, teasing each other, with him bouncing towards and away, tail always wagging, catching clumps of snow.

But it soon became clear that while we might have been *playing* with the wolf, he was in fact only *toying* with us. Every 30 seconds or so he'd suddenly stop, all sense of play gone, and stare intently over in the direction where the rest of his pack should have been. They had vanished, and that worried me. While we could keep track of one wolf as he danced around us, and spray him if we had to, a whole pack would have been another story altogether. We got the feeling he was merely distracting us, waiting, while the rest of the gang were closing in, and he kept checking how this trap was proceeding, before flicking back to 'play' mode and bounding around us. 'Let's head back,' I urged, and Clark agreed, sensing the same nightmare unfolding.

Careful not to show any anxiety, we turned and walked towards camp, turning every three or four steps to confront the wolf and burst into a bit of a 'play' session, to which he always responded 'playfully', yet the instant we turned away, he'd fall into silent step behind us, sinisterly sneaking closer and closer. In the end, we turned to find him less than 2 metres away—we could have reached out and touched his shaggy white coat—and unwilling to turn our backs anymore we exploded into a very boisterous 'game' of mock charging and shouting, which startled him and made him back right off while we edged ever onwards towards the tent.

Again he drifted closer, then again he froze and turned to the side to watch something we could not see. Waiting. Wondering—it seemed—why his friends weren't showing up.

When our tent came into view ahead, and our intentions became clear, he suddenly bounded ahead. 'Is he trying to get between us and our camp?' Clark wondered aloud as we hurried behind him, looking all around for the rest of the pack. He reached camp well ahead of us, and seized the opportunity to explore it unhampered, sniffing inside the tent and everywhere. Still alone, he didn't try to prevent us reaching it, and when we did, he kept his distance and after staring intently for a long time at the distant hill, he silently padded off into the ever-darkening twilight without so much as a backward glance.

'Yeah, how about we *don't* just sleep under the stars tonight?' Clark said, grinning. Crawling inside the tent we ate our dinner, and lay there, unable to sleep—minds buzzing from the experience.

## DAY 56: Home time!

Expecting a pickup this afternoon, we woke early and made our celebratory 'last breakfast', consisting of our original full ration of oats, and our final ration of coffee that we've been saving especially. It was divine. Mid morning we gave Willie a call and relayed the good news that the weather still looked fine—no sign of the giant storm yet.

'I'm really sorry, Chris, I can't pick you up today,' he said. 'A local hunter's gone missing overnight—I'm just about to start searching for him in my plane. It could take a while ...'

'Oh, that's fine!' I reassured him. 'We're fine out here, weather's good and we've got food.'

'Good, good ... well, give me a call in the afternoon, okay, and if I've found him, maybe I can pick you up before dinner.'

We spent the day ticking off the final few to-film and to-photograph lists—quite an achievement, actually, almost as hard as the expedition itself! In the afternoon we gave Willie a call back, and he explained that the search was still on—with helicopters and all, now—but that it was raining freezing drizzle and so his plane was grounded until the next break in the weather, at which point he'd get back out there searching. 'Give me a call tomorrow morning, and we'll take it from there.'

With nothing left to do and the wind now picking up, we huddled in the tent and checked our emails and got a weather prediction. 'Looks like that storm's due to hit Cambridge Bay tonight or tomorrow morning ...' I waved the mouse over the numbers, '70 kilometres per hour wind—yikes.' It doesn't seem hopeful for a pickup tomorrow then, and who knows how many days the storm will rage for. We digested this news for some time. Far from being picked up this afternoon as planned, we may have to survive out here for another five or six days. 'Maybe we should go on half-rations,' I said, 'just to be safe.' It was agreed, effective immediately. After sharing a single dinner, we slipped into our sleeping bags and lay there listening to the wind blowing snow against the tent. 'At least people know where we are, and we have a tent,' I said. 'Imagine what it'd be like being lost out there tonight—the poor guy!' It was a chilling thought.

## DAY 57: Is there no escape?

We woke at 7 am, 8 am and 9 am—lying in our sleeping bags listening to the wind buffeting the tent—waiting for 10 am when we could call Willie to find out if we're being picked up today or not. We've organised to have a blood sample taken as soon as we get back to Cambridge Bay to compare with the one we took before we left Sydney to investigate any changes in our bodies, but frustratingly we need to fast for twelve hours before the test—and that means no breakfast, just in case today is the day!

At 10 am I called Willie. 'Yes, we found him,' I could hear the relief in Willie's tired voice, 'but we're now picking up all the walkers who were out searching. Give me a call about 3 pm and we should be able to send a plane out your way ...'

We didn't get out of the tent very much today, except occasionally to pee. Even this was a nightmare; we'd rug up, unzip and climb into the vestibule, zipping up the inner tent behind us and crouch there in purgatory for a few seconds to muster the courage to rip open the outer tent and dash outside. It's increasingly cold and windy—drifts of windblown snow are starting to pile up behind everything, the wind now 35 kilometres per hour. At 3 pm I called Adlair Aviation back, and was informed that Willie was busy flying until 8 pm tonight. I explained in a little voice that he was going to be picking us up, and at this we were told that Willie was due back between flights soon, and would get some information for us.

We waited in our sleeping bags for another hour and called back. Willie himself answered the phone. 'The weather is not good,' he explained. 'The flights collecting the walkers are taking longer than I wanted. Give me a call 10 am tomorrow, okay?'

'Okay,' I said, and he must have detected the concern in my voice as he added, 'I'm not busy tomorrow, I will definitely be able to get you out tomorrow.' There was a pause. 'If not tomorrow, then Monday.'

'I guess we can have dinner then,' Clark said, trying to put a positive spin on things. The weather really is getting worse out here now—snow is even being driven and compacted inside the vestibule, covering our shoes, cooking gear, bags, guns—everything—in an ever-thickening white layer.

## DAY 58 (25 September 2005): Can you hear something?

Bursts of icy cold wind during the night kept waking us, and we had to continually beat the tent to shake off snow. Opening my vestibule this morning, a giant wall of built-up snow collapsed in on me, into my sleeping bag. Brilliant. Clark's vestibule too is just one big hunk of snow—he literally has to go digging to find things! We lay there willing time to pass, longing to be picked up, give our blood sample, and finally, *finally*, be unleashed upon all the endless treats in the supermarket with our lengthy wish-list. 'So ... hungry ...' Clark groaned comically as I called Willie at the stroke of ten. Apparently, a fuller weather forecast was due in at 11.30 and we should call back then. We slumped back into our sleeping bags, hibernating, trying not to move as any bump of the tent caused all the frost on the inside walls to shed off into our faces and melt onto our sleeping bags. 'Supposing it is all clear at 11.30 and he left at 12,' I ventured, 'then we'd probably still not get to the medical centre until ... about 3 pm!' I groaned. This whole twelve-hour fasting thing was driving us insane. By 3 pm we'd not have eaten for twenty hours.

I wrote and sent out a quick website update about the wolf and the fact that we're still out here, before the laptop battery died. Annoyingly, most of the emails we've been getting over the last few days seem to think we're safe and sound back in civilisation already. 'I bet it feels great to be surrounded by endless food again, boys!?'

The minutes oozed past, and at 11.30 I called the hangar. Willie's warm voice answered. 'We'll leave at about 12 and so keep an eye out for us about 1 pm.'

'So you'll be here at one?' I repeated, my heartbeat quickening.

'Yes, we'll be at your place at one. See you soon!' From behind the video camera, Clark started bouncing around with excitement and turned the camera on himself. 'We're gonna get picked up!!'

'Go go go!!' I shouted, piling on my warm clothes and climbing from the tent. 'Things to do, people to see!' In a flurry of activity, we repositioned the tent away from the runway, trampled down all the snow drifts around camp and sat expectantly on our PACs at ten minutes to one, waiting, watching and listening. As we chatted excitedly, the weather deteriorated around us, visibility dropped and snow began to cascade out of the air. One o'clock came and went, and still there was no sign of Willie. Our chatter petered out and stopped. 'I guess he can't land in this anyway,' I mumbled.

'Even if he could find us,' Clark added. Visibility was shocking. 'He's probably turned back. I guess we just give him a call back at the hangar at about two?'

I suddenly cocked my head. 'Can you hear something?' We both listened hard. The faint but unmistakable hum of an engine was just discernible above the wind. 'It's a plane!' I shouted, jumping up. 'Where is it?' It grew louder and louder, and then suddenly I spotted it.

'There!' I pointed, at once taken aback by how poor the visibility actually was. The plane was perhaps 800 metres from us, and only just visible as a ghostly outline.

We watched, full of adrenalin, as the plane flew high over us, and appeared to continue into the distance. 'I … I wonder if they saw us,' I mumbled. My heart gave a leap as we saw the plane bank and, as it vanished amongst the low cloud, heard it hum back somewhere well to the side of us. Gradually the noise of its engines faded out altogether.

'It's gone?!' Clark's expression would have done credit to a tragic mask.

'He must have decided it was too dangerous,' I said dejectedly, struggling to cope with the fact that we'd skipped breakfast and lunch for no apparent reason. Just as our spirits started to freefall, I heard the engines hum again, louder. As we stared blindly into the white nothing, the outline of Willie's Twin Otter aircraft again materialised, much lower this time, heading right for us! The hum rose to a deafening roar as he passed right above us, and as we waved frantically, the plane banked sharply around and did a second pass. 'He's seen us! He's seen us!' I shouted, unable to contain my excitement.

Four more times he flew past, each time getting lower and lower, presumably sussing out our 'runway'. On his fifth pass, he swung in very low indeed, and opened up the flaps.

'This is it!' I shouted, and the two of us watched in absolute awe as right beside us, Willie dropped the plane heavily onto our snow-covered esker where it began bucking and galloping violently across the lumpy tussocks. Instantly Willie slammed the pitch of the propellers into reverse and the roar of the engines filled the whole world—and the plane, basically, stopped.

'That was ridiculous!' Clark burst out. 'He barely used 50 metres of our runway!' We watched impatiently as he taxied back to the 'start' of our 'runway', the plane lurching and swaying alarmingly as it bounced over various lumps and ditches. At last, he throttled back and cut one engine. The cockpit window slid open, and out popped a weathered, grandfatherly face wearing little round purple glasses, a huge scarf and an orange beanie with a black pom-pom on top. Willie waved us over.

It seemed to take forever to walk over, and I didn't know if I should walk or run. Willie's co-pilot, Scott, had climbed out of the plane and was waiting for us. I didn't know if they'd be happy to see us, or cross with our landing site. I suddenly felt awkward in so many ways, unsure of so many things. I didn't think it'd be like this—but over the last few months Clark and I have gotten to know each other so well that we are perpetually on the same wavelength, I have gotten used to knowing exactly what he is thinking, and now suddenly, here were two other people I'd never met—unknowns, abruptly shattering our introverted little sphere. I held out my hand—way too early, I realised—kept walking and eventually gripped Scott's hand and we shook heartily. He was smiling. 'G'day!' Beside me, Clark shook Willie's hand and it was done—we were now back in the embrace of the outside world.

We bundled the tent away, unscrewed the wheels off the PACs and loaded everything into the cavernous side of the plane. At last we climbed in, clambered over all the gear and wedged ourselves into the two little passenger seats left for us in the cargo hold. Willie taxied the plane around for a while—judging the terrain—while Clark and I hurriedly buckled up and reached for something to brace against, the whole plane bucking violently like a rodeo bull on amphetamines as it rolled, surged, wobbled and lurched over the frozen tussocks.

I leant forward and tapped the co-pilot on the shoulder. 'How's it seem?' I enquired.

He grinned, and in true Nunavut style, said, 'Oh, it'll be okay … I think.'

I hadn't heard this new ending to the expression before, but before I had time to become properly concerned, Willie looked back and said, 'Okay, boys … hang on!' With that, he flung open the throttle and the engines again roared. The plane briefly galloped along the esker, accelerating hard, the tussocks literally exploding into the wheels with so much force I was sure they were going to break off and we'd all plough into the ground at any moment. Just as the horrific vibrating and banging reached a crescendo, Willie pulled back and we pitched up into the air. It was an amazingly short take-off, and gradually relaxing my white knuckles, I was again able to breathe.

Staring out of the window at the endless frozen white expanse passing beneath us, I suddenly got a true sense of just how isolated we have been for the last 58 days. From up here, we'd have just been two tiny specks slowly traipsing across the barrens.

Willie orchestrated a perfect landing into a much colder-looking Cambridge Bay than we'd left, and we unloaded everything into his hangar. At last it was done, and Willie pulled down the giant roller door, sealing out the swirling wind and snow. The effect was amazing. The wind—that has been constantly eroding us for weeks—suddenly just stopped. It became eerily quiet, my ears ringing oddly in the stillness, and then, gradually, the most wonderful feeling began penetrating our jackets and pants—warmth! Clark and I caught each other's eye at the same moment, and we silently shared this heavenly experience that we had all but forgotten. 'Look!' I grinned in ecstasy, pointing down at my shoes where lumps of ice had broken away, and a growing puddle was forming as my hiking boots—which had essentially been frozen hunks of rigid ice for weeks—suddenly began to soften and thaw. I could even flex my toes. I ripped off my beanie for the first time in days, and rubbed my hand through my messy, tangled hair, feeling the joy of circulating warm, dry air.

We couldn't stop smiling at just being warm. In fact, we soon started to overheat, and stripped off to our thermals, while around us, Willie and some of his crew, all wearing full arctic jackets, examined our PACs.

'You are very acclimatised to ze cold!' Willie nodded at us approvingly, adding, 'You must have seen some amazing things. Sit with me and have a coffee?' We explained that we'd love to but had to get our blood samples taken before we were allowed to enjoy any food. 'You haven't eaten in 21 hours?' Horrified, Willie kindly offered to drive us straight to the medical centre, and we piled in.

Looking out the window, Clark and I both hurriedly braced ourselves against the seats in front, shooting each other furtive, uncertain glances as the world tore past us at an alarming speed. It wasn't that Willie was a maniac driver by any means—he was as slow as any grandad—but not having travelled faster than walking pace in months, it seemed horrifyingly fast to us.

At the medical centre, we had our blood samples taken by a nurse who absent-mindedly bent the needles around in our arms as though they were joysticks while asking us all about the trip. At last, cradling our punctured arms, we escaped outside into the cold, blustery street, free men, back in 'civilisation'—if you can call Cambridge Bay civilisation, that is!

'To the supermarket!' Clark announced, broad grins spreading over both our faces as we hurried over. Bursting into The Northern, we headed straight for the confectionery aisle, eyes widening and saliva forming in anticipation as we scooped up Snickers chocolate bars, chocolate milk, a packet of biscuits and chips each (identical purchases) paid for them and sat outside in the snow.

'Wait,' I said. 'We need a photo!' Anyone else in such a situation would have hit me, but Clark only laughed, and held up his first piece of unrationed food in over two months while I took the shot. He was almost crying he was so happy. We congratulated each other, and ceremoniously bit into a choc-chip biscuit at the same instant. The taste—a *new* taste—was every bit as good as we'd been imagining for the last eight weeks.

As we hurried into the hangar to pack up all our gear, Willie appeared, instantly dissipating our stress with his warm, kind-grandfatherly manner, wheeling two chairs towards us. 'Come and have a coffee, boys ... sit down.' Having already heard from many locals that Willie was unquestionably a living legend—a pioneer aviator from back in the 1950s and now 73 years old and still flying essential air ambulance services for much of the Canadian Arctic— we were eager for a chat.

'Zat was one of ze most difficult landings I've ever had to do in 49 years of flying,' he announced. Apparently, the wind was blowing almost perpendicular to the landing site, there was 'a very low cloud ceiling' (meaning he was basically flying inside a cloud the whole time), and it was raining freezing drizzle that obscured his windscreen, making it impossible to tell how far off the ground he was. 'Zat is why I had to make so many passes … little lower each time until I found the ground.'

We raised our eyebrows, impressed. 'Ze only reason I decided to land,' Willie smiled kindly at us, 'was zat you just looked so sad down zere!'

I asked about the tundra tyres on the plane, commenting that we'd been told the nearest tundra-equipped plane was way up in Resolute. 'Oh zey are not tundra tyres,' he gestured, smiling, 'zey are only medium tyres … It's all we have. But zey are okay.'

Suitably humbled, we started explaining about our trip. Willie took great interest in our gear, and especially the PACs. 'Zese are very good,' he said, nodding appreciatively. 'You are not crazy like I thought.' The more he heard about our expedition, the more impressed he became. 'You were out there alone for 58 days?!' We nodded, a little embarrassed, as he turned and announced to the rest of the crew in the hangar. 'Zese two are *real* men! Unlike you— you boys wouldn't survive one day out where zey have been!'

Everyone we passed on our way back through town seemed to recognise us, and as we passed Colin's house—the-ex-dog-team driver we'd met before leaving—he excitedly ushered us inside. 'I've got something to show you boys,' he said. 'Wait here …' He returned moments later carrying the most gorgeous, fluffy puppy we'd ever seen. 'He's going to lead my dog team.'

We stared at him, 'You're starting a new dog team?!'

'Yep!' He grinned. 'I've wanted to for years—I thought maybe I was too old—but you boys inspired me with your crazy trip!' Pride and excitement twinkled in his eyes, and a tremendously rewarding feeling washed over me.

After enjoying the bliss of our first shower in 58 days and devouring a wonderful roast meal at a friend's place, we ended up celebrating our first night back in 'civilisation' with some cheerful travellers at the local lodge. However, after politely declining another vodka and watching those around us, intoxicated, spill their own, I started feeling increasingly alienated—repulsed even—by my surroundings, and I could see Clark too was suffering. The room was hot, dry and seemed incredibly stuffy. In the corner, the TV was on, blaring some tacky game show. There was so much noise inside the building and out, and the very air—warm and thick with the scent of air fresheners—felt sticky and claustrophobic. Surrounded by raucous merriment, Clark and I just stared at each other. I will never forget the look that passed between us: a turmoil of regret, disappointment, and—being honest—disgust. But also such pained confusion. We were finally back in the real world; wasn't this what we had been dreaming of for so long? Why weren't we overjoyed? We weren't even happy.

'Get me back out to the tundra, Clark,' I said quietly. 'I don't want to be here.'

PART THREE

# THE CALL
# OF THE WILD

# BACK FROM THE ARCTIC

Back home in Sydney, among the joys of unrationed food, hot showers, sleep-ins and, above all, the radiant warmth of the summer sun, I floated on a mental high for days. Media engagements kept us busy: interviews, presentations, articles and lectures. A public lecture organised by Australian Geographic sold out, and in a desperate bid to start climbing out of substantial Arctic debt, Clark and I ran a profitable second lecture a week later.

The biggest thing I'd been looking forward to was simply having time on my hands—time to relax, to do nothing, and to catch up with friends. However, as it turned out, diving back into the social scene wasn't as seamless as I'd hoped. At parties and social catch-ups, I found it hard to hold a conversation with my old friends, and they with me.

'So, um … how was the Arctic?'

I didn't even know how to begin to answer such a question. 'Yeah, it was … amazing!' I'd try to sustain the conversation over a few more obvious questions—'Was it … cold?'—and then, unable to convey the magnitude of the experience, I'd falter and the topic would awkwardly shift. Clark and I had experienced *so much* out there—learned *so many things* about life and the things that really matter, we'd had so much time to reflect and ponder life goals that trying now to blend in with conversations about who should be evicted from the next reality TV episode, or what the latest computer playstation game was like, just left me feeling false, disconnected and alienated.

Like an aquarium fish briefly released into the ocean, I now felt increasingly as though I'd been plopped back into the tank, where my revelations of freedom only briefly struck a distant chord with a handful of my fellow fish. We had gone out looking for 'adventure', but in the process we'd discovered a whole lot more, as if suddenly life's potential and purpose had fallen into place. And so, to my dismay, part of me now no longer felt satisfied or at home. With my nose pressed up against the metaphorical sides of the fish tank, I fretted over why it was that no one else seemed to even notice the glass.

The changes we went through were not only psychological. Some people saw it in our faces. 'Man, your eyes look different, older or … *something*.' Others pinned it down to us both having 'squarer jaws', and looking at photos taken before we left, they were correct; perhaps it was from literally gritting our teeth for hours on end as we hauled? The most profound change that we both experienced was a new appreciation of, and outlook on, life's challenges. Over the previous year, Clark and I had had to overcome so many seemingly impossible hurdles and setbacks that we subconsciously developed a very simple, positive and objective attitude towards them. I tried to summarise it in a quote for Australian Geographic: 'Break problems down into smaller parts, and then fix what can be fixed, abandon what cannot, both mental and physical.' And I think that's the crux of it. Applying this philosophy to life's patchwork of little 'problems' back home, Clark and I found that daily troubles just seemed to flatten out against the bigger picture. 'You're always so calm about everything,' we often heard, and we really felt it, too.

As I walked back into my ex-workplace, Siemens, to thank my boss for letting me finish my work placement early those few months ago, the receptionist pulled me aside. She, too, had followed our progress. 'What does it feel like?' she probed. 'You must feel like you could do almost anything now!'

I laughed and jokingly reminded her that we didn't make it to the far side, but, inside, her comment really struck a chord. That was exactly what I felt; not openly or arrogantly so, but I suddenly realised that I now had complete confidence in myself, and believed that if I really wanted to do something, anything, I just had to work towards it. Life was mine to steer, and my opportunities were only limited by my imagination. Except, unfortunately, for the next few months, during which I was sworn to endure my fourth and final work placement for my university scholarship, at Sydney Water's North Head Sewage Treatment Plant.

Boy, was that a reality check. When I was on the expedition, the only thing I could be certain of as I lay down my head to sleep each night was that, the next day, I'd likely see and do things that few, if any, had ever seen or done before. It was tremendously motivating. Now back at home and working nine to five, a little bit of me died inside every night as I closed my eyes on yet another utterly predictable day. Waking at the same time every morning, I'd get dressed into the same blue uniform and wait for the same bus surrounded by the same crowd of office workers. Although to be honest, after getting used to the sickeningly sweet, all-pervasive smell of the sewage treatment plant's chemical masking agent—presumably hiding a much worse smell beneath—the work I was given at the plant was actually quite interesting, and kept me busy.

For several months, life revolved primarily around post-expedition work, and I met with Clark most weekends. Discovery Channel pulled out of the documentary deal, citing a 'change of management and focus' which we were secretly quite relieved about, as from our earlier insight into the kind of documentary they wanted to make, we knew it was one we did not want to appear in. We spent time editing together our video highlights in a bid to entice production funding, but in the end it seemed that, as neither of us died tragically en route or even had a mental breakdown, our story just didn't have enough drama in it for TV. *What's wrong with a success story for once?* we kept wondering, an example of an inspiring adventure that didn't end in disaster? 'It'll be okay,' Clark said with a grin, 'we'll just make the doco ourselves, enter it into film festivals and go from there.'

It was true; everyone who had heard about our expedition loved it, our sponsors were thrilled with the exposure they had received, and all in all our expedition was heralded as a success. No one, we were relieved to discover, even hinted that we'd failed by not reaching that far side. Except for being in about $15,000 debt between us, we couldn't have been happier with the outcome of the trip; however, as time ticked past, slowly but surely we began sliding down that slippery slope back towards normality. On Christmas Day I called Willie Laserich, our bush pilot hero, to wish him well and he, like everyone else, asked the recurring question which kept me afloat in the drowning sea of monotony: 'Where's the next adventure?'

'No, let's go somewhere warm!' Clark rebutted over coffee at my suggestion of returning to Victoria Island to finish the job, and I had to admit he had a point. We also didn't want to get pigeonholed as just 'Arctic' explorers. 'A desert? Or maybe a jungle?' We had chatted to most of our previous sponsors about the idea of a 'next trip' and were blown away by their almost unconditional support. The CEO of Air Canada basically handed us a map of their flight routes at a lavish Christmas party we spoke at and said, 'Just let us know …' Gore-Tex said their fastest growing market was in China, and hinted that if we could come up with a cool trip over there somewhere, 'funding wouldn't be an issue'. The world, it seemed, was our oyster.

Scrolling excitedly around and zooming in on worldwide satellite imagery just released by Google Earth, we soon came up with countless amazing adventure destinations. 'Let's sit down and define what we want from a perfect adventure,' I said, pulling out a sheet of paper. After much umming and ahhing, we essentially developed a mission statement for our philosophy on adventuring:

> *Defining the true spirit of adventure is difficult, but we feel it important that our journeys be unique and innovative. We are not inspired by simply trying to break or better records; to us, that's a competition, not an adventure. Adventure should be about trying something new and embracing the unknown—finding yourself on the very edge of what is possible physically, mentally and technologically.*
>
> *We don't set out to try and 'conquer' the elements, but instead experience them and endure them when we must. Outside your comfort zone, existence becomes both wonderfully simple and brutally honest. It's about living life, not glory.*
>
> *Safety is always our number one priority. Risks are inherent in all adventures and certainly no adventure is worth dying for, but through meticulous planning and preparation we focus on reducing these risks down to a level we feel comfortable with. In today's increasingly secure and almost numbingly comfortable lifestyle, to a certain extent a little responsible risk-taking and occasionally 'doing it tough' enables one to truly feel alive.*

In this light, we started culling back our options. We figured our location had to be remote, else if we passed any villages then various absurd conundrums cropped up: Do we stop at these communities and 'experience the culture'? No—while no doubt very interesting, such 'stopping along the way' trips were more 'personal journeys' than full-on expeditions. Do we then travel around and avoid any towns? No—that quickly becomes pretty stupid; tediously winding around perfectly good accommodation and supplies, while pretending we're somehow achieving something by doing it 'the hard way'.

We mulled over the atlas for weeks. 'If it's going to be unsupported and months long,' I pondered aloud, 'we'll be taking a hell of a lot of gear with us. We can't just hike with a backpack. So it's got to be either a raft/kayak trip, or another hauling trip.' Clark agreed, and for several days we admired some of Russia's great river systems in detail before deciding they were either too long to do 'start to finish', or passed through too many communities.

'Well, we're already known as "those crazy guys who build crazy carts",' I grinned. 'It could be our little niche.' Considering this, Clark eventually nodded.

Some kind of sled/cart/crazy new vehicle trip it was. But where? We needed a wilderness, diverse in wildlife and terrain, thus requiring a special cart. 'And it can't be tree-covered,' I added in sudden realisation. 'We can't exactly haul anything through trees!' This quickly erased jungles, leaving us with deserts, high-altitude areas above the tree line, or polar wildernesses.

Deserts we deemed too monotonous, and for several months we planned towards the treeless high Tibetan plateau—we even bought a map—but in the end, there were just too many villages, and we could think of no logical 'route' or 'reason' for travel from A to B. Our destination options were now reduced to polar regions. 'We don't want to do a South Pole trip,' Clark stated firmly. 'It gets done so many times each year it's almost becoming like Mount Everest.' (Few people seem to realise that over 3000 expeditioners have summitted the world's highest mountain.)

'Antarctica as a whole is prohibitively expensive and not *that* diverse, either,' I pointed out.

'We could always develop some new cart or vehicle to traverse the Antarctic continent? Kite? Solar powered?' Clark offered. That idea soon grew stale as well, and we found ourselves turning to the only region of accessible, remote, diverse polar wildernesses around the Arctic Archipelago.

'Well, well, well ...' Clark said with a mock sneer, 'looks like we're going back to Victoria Island after all!'

My heart leapt. 'It'll be great to finish what we started,' I said encouragingly. 'Rather than just trying somewhere else and possibly failing there, too. Let's go back and show Victoria Island that we're not beaten!'

I could see Clark at last warming to the idea. 'It'll make for a great doco,' he said grinning, announcing in a dramatic voice-over tone: '*After two years of licking their wounds ... now it's personal ... and they are returning to dig up the flag ... and finish the dream that began ... almost four years earlier.*'

Both beaming with excitement, we agreed then and there to do it. There simply was no better place on the planet to do an exciting, diverse, wildlife-filled, lengthy, unsupported, remote adventure than good old Victoria Island.

# LET'S FINISH WHAT WE STARTED!

By this stage it was October 2006—we'd been back a year and a lot had already happened. We'd both returned to university—I for my final year. I'd somehow caught the eye of a wonderfully attractive and intelligent Russian woman a year above me, just starting her PhD in Electrical Engineering, and to my amazement, she became my first serious girlfriend. Suffering severe adventure withdrawal, I had convinced my good friend Jasper Timm to return to Tassie with me during the midwinter break of 2006 and do the Overland Track—again. Life was great. I was finally reconnecting with my friends, my uni scholarship and a series of public lectures had almost lifted me from Arctic debt, and at last Clark and I had the 'next adventure' to plan! Opportunities kept surfacing, and I even got an assignment from UK-based magazine *Yachting Monthly* to be 'Crew Leader' and help sail what is apparently the world's most famous yacht—Sir Francis Chichester's *Gipsy Moth IV*—from Sydney up to Mooloolaba in Queensland. We got slammed by one of the worst storms to ravage the New South Wales coast all year, with 5-metre waves breaking into the terribly open cockpit, but it was just awesome to be back in my element of adventure—and being paid for it! I'd already decided that Electrical Engineering wasn't my career path, but being more than halfway through my fifth and final year, I gritted my teeth and kept at it. As with Victoria Island, I figured it's always a good policy to finish what you start.

'So, do we start back at the east coast, or carry on from where we left off?' It was a pretty fundamental choice, and we ultimately decided that there really was no point in retracing our steps. This time we had a much clearer purpose—we were going back for an adventure, not to try and set some record for 'crossing the whole island in one go' and, as Clark so eloquently put it, 'I've seen the first third of the island, and to be quite honest, I'd be happier if I never saw it again.' We'd certainly paid our dues for that portion, and so we decided to fly back to our 2005 end point, ceremoniously dig up the flag we'd conveniently left there, and head onwards. 'In a *totally* redesigned PAC!' I said vehemently.

'So, let's start with what didn't work with PAC-1,' I said, trying not to laugh at Clark's exasperated 'where do I start?' expression.

'Well, let's see …' he began with a smirk. 'It sank into the mud, it broke through the ice and the snow, it couldn't wheel over Death Terrain—'

'Okay, okay,' I cut in, drafting a sketch. 'So we need bigger wheels …'

'And it was a little heavy,' Clark reminded me, 'it leaked, it kept breaking, and converting from wheeled mode to kayak mode was a nightmare.'

Looking at my drawing, an idea started to form. 'If the wheels were big enough,' I pondered, 'they could provide enough buoyancy to float the whole cart, then we could just wheel the cart right into the water and jump on top!'

'Yeah, but it'd be kinda unstable, wouldn't it?' Clark had a point.

'If we could join the two carts together, that'd make it stable, like a giant pontoon, floating on four wheels.'

Another quick sketch led to a brainwave from Clark. 'If the carts were wide enough, we could even set the tent up on top!' he said excitedly. 'Imagine not having to search for a tent site each night, just haul until we can't walk any further, clip the PACs together, and bingo, we've got ourselves a perfectly flat, smooth table to pitch the tent on!'

Another stroke of inspiration: absolute minimalism. 'It wouldn't even need to be waterproof,' I thought aloud, 'the cart could just be a frame with netting slung underneath, and we keep all our gear in giant waterproof bags!'

It was an exciting idea, and one final masterstroke occurred to us simultaneously: 'The whole thing could just bolt together out there—' Clark began, already nodding knowingly as I cut in.

'—just a set of metal tubes! We could even bring the whole PAC with us on the plane from Sydney as check-in luggage!'

'No more shipping and trucking strikes for us!' Clark laughed eccentrically. The entire PAC-2 concept really was revolutionary, and we spent the next few weekends eagerly designing it in more detail.

We sucked every scrap of hindsight for all it was worth, and the overall mantra for PAC-2 was that it had to be simple, lightweight, bulletproof and repairable. Even the joints in the frame would be held together using a rubberised clamp rather than a rigid join, absorbing the peak shock-loads instead of fracturing and snapping like PAC-1's hauling bracket. Well versed in the next step, we were already accumulating all these interesting facts into an ever-growing document, 'The V.I.2 (Victoria Island 2) Expedition Document' which we'd soon use to lure our sponsors on board, but not yet.

By Christmas 2006, I finally finished my Electrical Engineering degree, and was a free man. My results were good: I'd managed to get High Distinctions for the majority of courses over the full five years, and my thesis project—developing a wireless network of satellite-linked camera traps for use in wildlife research—turned out to be the only original project (that is, not just selected from a list) undertaken that year, and earned me top grades. Adding further to my resumé, earlier in the year my school of Electrical Engineering put me forward as their candidate for an annual Engineering Leadership award. I documented the project management and problem-solving skills that I used in our 2005 Arctic expedition, and, up against representatives from every other field of engineering across the university, won the award and cash prize. This final lump sum neatly filled in the last trace of Arctic debt.

Completion of almost seventeen years of formal education brought me to an important crossroad in my life. Having graduated from uni with first-class honours, I had several high-paying job opportunities presented to me—including one to oversee project and logistical management for part of the Royal Australian Air Force—and I had to make a pivotal choice. Around me, all my friends were accepting great jobs at Telstra, Energy Australia, Cochlear—some with amazing starting salaries—yet the idea of getting an office job now horrified me more than ever. The pressure from many people around me, including my dad, was intense. 'Don't just throw it all away,' he said. 'You need a job, even just for a year or so, to build up some capital and then you can go off on your holidays.' And most poignant of all, 'Do you think they'll still be offering you these jobs three years from now, Christopher, when you've been unemployed all that time, just messing about travelling?'

I very nearly caved in, but my mum always quietly stuck up for me. 'I understand what you're doing,' she'd say, sneaking up to my room after I'd stormed off following yet another row with my dad over my apparent short-sightedness. 'I believe you can make adventuring work, somehow.'

Having made my decision to firmly follow my passion, to my overwhelming and eternal relief and gratitude Dad eventually changed his tune. 'Well, if that's what you've decided, Christopher, then I'll support your decision, of course. I think you'll make it work too.' He patted me on the shoulder. 'Just realise that you can't keep doing this forever.'

Driving into the Blue Mountains to speak at a climbing festival in mid April 2007, something was clearly weighing heavily on Clark's mind. 'What's up?' I probed.

He didn't reply for a moment, evidently picking his words. 'Now, this is just an idea,' he soothed pre-emptively, 'but it's something I've been thinking about for a while.' He flicked me a hesitant glance, checking to see if he should proceed. Horrified he was about to suggest that we delay—or worse, cancel—Victoria Island #2, I stared blankly back at him.

'Yes?'

'Well, you know how I'm interested in ocean rowing?'

'Yes,' I repeated, still not liking where this was going.

'Well … I want to enter the Woodvale Challenge, to row across the Indian Ocean, in 2009.' He jumbled the words out and focused on the road ahead, waiting.

'Cool,' I said innocently. 'When in 2009?' Victoria Island was planned for the Northern Hemisphere summer of 2008, that is, May until October, if it took that long.

'Well, you see, that's the catch,' Clark winced as he spoke. 'It starts in April 2009, so I'd have to leave within a few months of returning from Vic Island.'

There was an awkward silence. We both knew a rowing trip like that would take well over a year to plan, train, raise sponsorship, build and kit out the boat, etc. 'You'd basically have to start preparing *now*,' I mumbled. The fact that I knew he knew this made me angry inside—was he committed to Vic Island or not? How convenient that he was driving, I thought—he had an excuse not to even look at me while breaking news of his expedition infidelity.

'Yes, I know,' Clark said heavily. 'That's why I needed to ask you now if it was okay or not.' He paused, and then reading my silence correctly, hastily cleared things up. 'I'm still 100 per cent behind Vic Island, don't worry about that—this would just be … on the side. I'll delegate most of the prep to my housemate Ryan, who wants to go with me.'

I shrugged grumpily. 'Well, okay. I can't tell you what to do. I personally think two expeditions might be biting off a little more than can be chewed, but I guess we're used to that. Sleep's overrated anyway, right?'

By now Clark, too, had scored himself an amazing girlfriend, Bea, who was studying the same degree as he was, and he'd also become a member of the Explorers Club. I had started my second business, Expedition Facilities at <www.ExFac.com>, an automated online hub designed to help foster the spirit of adventure. It enables expeditioners to access a simple website that sends email news updates to subscribers, includes Google Earth tracking capabilities for others to follow their progress, and so on. A few months later, in July of that year, for want of something better to do, my girlfriend and I did the Overland Track, in—you guessed it—midwinter. This almost annual pilgrimage had become for me an exciting little reminder of snow, ice and hardship that I applied like a nicotine patch to get me through each year. All too soon, however, the mounting pressure of Victoria Island forced us once again to withdraw from the world around us and seriously focus on the expedition.

Finding large, lightweight wheels proved to be the sticking point. I spent weeks researching every possible tyre from ATV (all-terrain vehicle) wheels and low PSI (pounds per square inch, i.e. low pressure) golf cart wheels, through to the elusive 'tundra tyres' designed for light aircraft. None of them fitted the bill; they were all just too heavy.

'What about tractor inner tubes?' Max Riseley, a family friend and inspirational engineer, suggested. 'You'll have to build your own rims,' he said, 'and make them from something light, like fibreglass composite. I'll fax you a sketch of what I have in mind.'

It was a great idea, and after downloading the complete range of tractor inner tube specifications online and running size, weight and buoyancy calculations on them all, I found one that would be ideal. My local tyre centre ordered it in, and within a week, Clark and I hurried inside the garage, turned on the compressor and watched our PAC-2 wheel inflate. Standing almost 1.5 metres high, and with about 37 centimetres tube diameter, it only weighed 6.5 kilograms and could provide almost 500 kilograms of buoyancy per tube (before it would sink entirely)! 'This is great!' I laughed, overjoyed to have finally found such a perfect solution. 'And if we bring a spare,' I grinned sillily, 'we could blow it up in the afternoons and play in the lakes!'

Armed with sizes and dimensions to work with, we wasted no time in finalising the cart design. Having decided to do all the engineering myself this time rather than drag my dad into it, I set to work reading entry-level mechanical engineering textbooks, learning all about the 'yield strength' of different metals and the 'section modulus' of different cross-sectional shapes of extruded tubing, and how they'd all cope when loaded up, supported in the middle on an axle, and bounced across the tundra.

It became surprisingly complicated. It's easy enough to design it *just* strongly enough (and therefore as light as possible) such that it wouldn't quite buckle and break rolling across smooth ground, but as soon as you start factoring in bumps and wheeling it off little ledges and so on, the dynamic forces skyrocket. What 'factor of safety' should I build in? It was a constant balance between being too heavy, or dangerously weak. My dad was always for making it heavier and stronger, but with the immovable weight of PAC-1 still crushingly fresh in my mind, I was adamant about shaving off every gram I thought we could get away with. In short, it was a gamble.

Things got even more involved when I turned my focus to designing the ball-bearing wheel hubs that had to slide into the axles. I discovered that the grease inside ball bearings alone—the highest quality ones around, specially imported from Germany—would have frozen virtually solid in the Arctic! I had to have the bearings carefully opened and re-packed with lower operating temperature oil. The axles themselves I designed from extra high strength aluminium 6063-T6, which had to be specially ordered.

Meanwhile, Clark's rowing preparations were gaining pace. As neither he nor his rowing buddy, Ryan Storey, had ever been at sea before, they both enrolled in full-on Yachtmaster sailing qualification courses run by a friend of ours. Learning celestial navigation and meteorology sounded like far too much fun to miss out on, and I also attended the classes. Having gained our Yachtmaster shore-based tickets, we all then progressed to Coastal Skipper level. Down in Tassie a few weeks later, a friend, David Pryce, upon hearing that Clark and Ryan had never been to sea before and were about to try to row across an ocean, laughed heartily and said, 'Well, we'd better get you both some ocean experience then! Do you want to help us sail *Blizzard* over to Chile?'

It's not every day that you get asked if you'd like to sail a 66-foot (20-metre) aluminium expedition schooner from Tasmania almost halfway around the world, across the infamous Southern Ocean—via several sub-Antarctic islands—all the way to Patagonia. 'It should take about a month and a half—we leave in October.' Dave looked at me. 'You can come too if you want, Chris.' Despite mounting Victoria Island pressures, this wasn't something I was about to pass up.

In the months before our sailing voyage, we fixed our attention on another major unknown—what *rims* would we use for our tractor inner tube wheels? Clearly we couldn't use a standard tractor rim, and following Max's idea, we met up with a local successful engineering firm, EMP Composites, for some advice. The owner, David Lyons, took a keen interest in the project, and agreed that, yes, a composite rim would be the best solution. To allay my fears that essentially a sandwich of foam between two layers of fancy fibreglass could be anything like strong enough, he passed me a sample, and a hammer, and asked me to give it my best shot. I couldn't even dent it. Amused at our amazement, he flung around some more expensive-sounding terms like 'carbon fibre Kevlar composite laminates' and wrapped up the meeting with the words, 'I'd actually like to take this on as a little EMP-sponsored project, if you're willing?' We left him in no doubt that we were, indeed, very willing.

Having planned our new route, calculated a better meal system (eliminating the dreaded 'rice-only dinner'), and added all this and more into our epic sponsorship proposal document, we hurriedly despatched it firstly to all our previous sponsors, almost all of whom replied with a resounding 'Yes!' On a massive mental high, we packed our bags, flew to Hobart, helped provision the yacht, and set sail for the other side of the world.

There's something quite unforgettable about standing precariously on the stern of a yacht, at night, in howling winds laced with snow, shackled on and gripping the steering wheel in front of you with sopping, freezing gloves, and suddenly feeling the whole stern of the yacht rise up into the air. Bracing but unable to look back, you can hear the huge wave rolling in from behind as the yacht surges forward, accelerating, and then, amid a deafening roar of crumbling white water, you can feel the yacht begin to surf. Now perched at the helm of a 66-foot rocket ship, hurtling into the darkness at 22 knots (41 kilometres per hour), every inch of your body is straining to sense and pre-emptively correct the slightest wobble in this unbalanced missile's track, knowing full well that if you allow her to turn even the slightest amount the bow will dig in, and the almighty power of the wave pushing from astern will spin the yacht side-on, and then roll her—possibly right over—with potentially fatal consequences.

Sailing the Southern Ocean was a steep learning curve for me, and I can only imagine even more so for Clark and Ryan. Hand-steering all 6000-plus miles (10,000-plus kilometres), we blearily staggered our way through a rotational watch system, and even managed to navigate the last 1600-odd kilometres using celestial navigation. It was an exhausting eye-opener, but a wonderful experience. We were pretty lucky with the weather, only getting caught in a few 50–55 knot (100 kilometres per hour) pockets of wind, and there were even periods of surreal calm, where we watched snowflakes falling silently into the ocean around us. Wandering albatrosses circled us in memorisingly graceful arcs, the tips of their 3-metre wingspans seeming to all but touch the water as they rode the unseen pressure waves. The sub-Antarctic islands teemed with wildlife like I've never seen—we pretty much had to ward off sea lions as we stepped ashore, and huge Southern Right whales rubbed themselves against our inflatable dingy.

By the time we sailed into mobile phone reception at the quaint Chilean fishing village of Puerto Montt 39 days later, my wonderful Russian girlfriend, with whom I'd shared a blissful relationship for over a year, had left me. The parting gift was my $1600 mobile phone bill as I repeatedly called her via global roaming, begging some form of explanation, which she would not give. It was a painful blow at the time, and a poignant reminder that, as my dad had said, 'You can't keep doing this forever, Christopher.' I feared perhaps she'd glimpsed a future in which she was repeatedly left at home or work while I went off travelling. My adventurous lifestyle was what had helped lure her in the first place, I am sure, but it was truly a double-edged sword. Either I needed to find a girl who was not in the least bit outdoorsy and thus content to stay behind, or one who could come with me and share my crazy adventures—if such a girl existed. Right now, though, I sadly had no time for such things, and after a few short days in Chile we flew safely back to Sydney.

Back at home, an enormous pile of letters and my overflowing email inbox took me the best part of three days to sift through. There was a lot to digest, including the devastating news that my Arctic hero— our legendary bush pilot, Willie Laserich—had sadly passed away in hospital following heart surgery. Not only had the world lost a truly great man and we a true friend, we'd also lost our way of getting back out to our start point.

EMP had finished the mould for our wheel rims, and we hurried over to watch the first rim being made. Layer upon layer of Kevlar and carbon fibre was painstakingly laid across the mould, sealed under a sheet of plastic with a vacuum pipe sticking out of it, which then sucked out all the air and drew in the epoxy resin. Once it cured overnight, we just popped it off the mould, trimmed and sanded the edges (desperately trying not to let the prickly fibreglass dust settle on us) and then fitted the wonderfully light and strong rims onto our axle hub ready for testing. 'Well, that's how it's done, boys!' EMP owner David said proudly. 'Now you can make the rest yourselves, if you like.' We needed to construct a total of eight half-rims for the trip, plus some extra ones for testing. It was going to be a long, itchy process.

Over the next month, we divided the daylight hours between PAC-2 frame building in the garage at home, and rim construction at EMP. Hacksawing, grinding, welding, bleeding, filing, circular-sawing, sanding, bending, cutting and pop-riveting ... by 5 pm each day, when we'd call it quits to give our neighbours some peace, we both looked like dirty (but happy) little chimney sweeps. Progress was good, and we were feeling increasingly confident in our PAC-2s. We were going to great lengths to lighten everything, including shortening all the bolts, and even drilling big holes out of whatever we could—Swiss cheese style.

Late one December night—with about six months to go—we finally decided to start training. Heaving the old truck tyre into the back of Clark's car, we drove down to a deserted Palm Beach, shackled up and took turns hauling. It was hard, but not as hard as we'd remembered when we trained in 2005. Determined to be in top physical form, we tyre-dragged most evenings around midnight for an hour or more, and we could really feel our strength build. What started out as swapping every hundred metres with the other person walking beside offering encouragement, soon grew into one of us hauling the entire length of the beach (2.3 kilometres) while the other ran three lengths. Conveniently, both tortures took almost exactly the same time, thus spurring each of us on into a continual race. One hauling, one sprinting to the finish line, we'd then swap again, and again, until we were so exhausted we struggled to get the tyre back to the car. Pretty soon, however, we'd even done away with the car, and dragged it all the way from home to the beach and back again afterwards, training for as much as three hours a night.

With four half-rims finally built, we assembled our first complete PAC-2 in early January 2008 and stood back to admire our handiwork. 'It's bigger than I thought,' Clark mumbled.

Wider than our driveway and longer than a car, it was certainly a sight to behold. Eager to test it out, we loaded it up with 100 kilograms of water containers and I shackled up and took the first few hesitant steps. Disappointingly, it was actually rather hard to pull. Although the enormous tractor inner tube wheels gave a soft, spongy kind of suspension which let it roll up and over obstacles that would've stopped our first PACs in their tracks, the hysteresis losses—that is, the energy lost through flexing and distorting the rubber—as we wheeled these squashy, essentially 'flat' tyres, was a little daunting. Trying to pump them up any further was useless, as they simply expanded instead of gaining pressure.

To firm up the tyres a little and to add some extra protection for PAC-2's thin balloon-like wheels, we proposed a fabric tyre cover and set to work acquiring samples of every kind of fabric we could get our hands on, testing how hard-wearing and durable each was. Various patches of sailcloth and other materials quickly became frayed and worn when subjected to vigorous scrubbing. Then I tested some 100 per cent pure Kevlar—the stuff they use in bulletproof vests—and let me tell you, it lived up to its reputation. Ordering 18 metres of ballistic-grade Kevlar fabric and a 3-kilometre spool of Kevlar thread to sew it with, we dug out my parents' old Singer sewing machine and learned how to sew in the spare room. Once completed, our first set of silky, golden wheel covers looked spectacular. Slipping them over the tyres and pulling the spectra drawstrings firmly on each side tightened them against the tube, enabling us to pump the wheels up to much higher pressures, avoiding that sluggish 'flat-tyre' feeling when hauling.

The sharpest, nastiest rocky area we could think of for testing was the Avalon Beach rock platform, exposed at low tide. Every head turned as we wheeled our contraption past the public pool, and I saw one little kid tug her grandfather's arm and whisper, 'What's that, Pa?' to which he hesitantly replied 'I have absolutely no idea … ' This time we loaded it with 150 kilograms and again I leant forwards into the harness. Obediently, the PAC-2 rolled forwards, with amazingly little effort! We ground it past, into and over as many savage boulders, rock edges and spiky-shell-covered ditches as we could find, and then stopped to assess the damage … and to our genuine amazement, it hardly had a scratch on it! With a bit of momentum, the PAC-2 seemed to just roll effortlessly along behind us, irrespective of sizeable boulders in its path.

'Bring it on, Victoria Island!' Clark shouted in euphoria. 'We're ready for you, *Death Terrain*!'

'Shall we see if it floats, guv?' he grinned. For our final check we ceremoniously rolled it into the local ocean pool while onlookers crowded around, perplexed. Someone eventually summoned the courage to ask what it was all about, and an elderly man shuffled up to Clark, and asked, 'How long will it take?'

'Oh, about three to four months ...' Clark began, but seeing the look of horror in his face added, 'Well, we're hoping less than 100 days.'

Shaking his head, the old man said, 'No, no, I mean how long will this *test* take? I want to go for a swim.'

Bobbing merrily around like a cork, the PAC-2's wheels barely even sank into the water at all. 'Tick PAC-2 floats!' I shouted.

After a day's exciting retail therapy buying all our amazing outdoor gear at one of our major sponsors, Paddy Pallin, the next thing we needed to do was to cold-test all our electrical gear. The operating temperature of our GPS, satellite phones, cameras, ASUS 'Eee PC' laptops and video cameras were all only rated down to 0 degrees Celsius. Unfortunately, the average household freezer only gets down to about minus 18, which just wasn't cold enough. But thankfully Clark finally located a giant warehouse freezer the size of a soccer field which went down to minus 40 degrees, allowing us to test all our equipment, including our PACS, in real Arctic temperatures.

It was potentially a very expensive morning's entertainment, loading tens of thousands of dollars' worth of brand-new high-end electronics into the huge freezer, and standing around shivering as we watched the thermometer fall. Frost was now forming on my beard—even sticking my eyelashes together— and still the laptop, the video camera, our redesigned bear alarm and everything else soldiered onwards down to minus 30 degrees

Celsius. The LCD screens became a little sluggish as the 'liquid' in them turned viscous, but all devices—amazingly—still worked at minus 38 degrees, the coldest we got. 'All right, I'm done,' said Clark, shivering. 'Let's get outta here.'

On our way out, one of the operators pulled us aside, shook his head and said, 'Guys, I've worked here in the cold for years, I know what it's like. So, why the f*&k you boys'd want to go there for the *fun* of it—you must be crazy, I reckon.'

As the weeks rushed by, our To-Do list shortened and our sponsor list grew. Due in part to some lucky shots I took last expedition, Canon surprised us by agreeing to provide some amazing camera gear, and ASUS, the makers of the brilliant little Eee PC netbook computers that we'd written rave reviews about on our website after successfully freezer-testing them, jumped on board as major sponsors of the expedition. The jewel in our sponsorship crown—the naming rights—was snaffled up by ever-expanding and user-friendly internet service provider iiNet, and complete with an integrated educational program linking every facet of our expedition into the Australian school curriculum, the iiNet 1000 Hour Day Expedition moved into its final stages of preparation.

Early in May, I was surprised to receive a phone call at 3 am. 'Mr Bray, I'm from the credit card fraud squad. I'm sorry to call you at this hour … are you in Australia at the moment?' Blinking stupidly at my watch, I assured the female caller that I was. 'Because someone has just used your credit card to buy about $2000 worth of,' she paused, 'of what looks like … *groceries*, over in Canada.'

My alarm gave way to amusement. 'Oh, right, yes!' I said, grinning, 'I guess my shopping order has gone through; thanks!' A day earlier I'd ordered all our food for the expedition, including 25 kilograms of chocolate, 20 kilograms of cashews, 10 kilograms of peanut butter, 400 burrito tortilla flatbreads, 200 freeze-dried meals, 19 kilograms of milk powder, 17 kilograms of couscous, 5 kilograms of butter and 5 kilograms of lard. All up, approximately 100 kilograms of food each, for 100 days, which should provide enough energy to haul and keep our bodies warm for the duration of the trip, while being as lightweight as possible.

I'd totally redesigned our website, building in forum-style interactivity that we could manage from out on the island, organised competitions to activate at particular stages of the expedition, and even a live tracking system, which would update our position every few minutes and display it on an embedded satellite map. We paid for a friend in Cambridge Bay to buy two brand-new, lightweight shotguns, bullets and bear spray and have it all there waiting for us. Having completed both PAC-2s, we took them for a weekend's test run out along an abandoned 4WD track in the Blue Mountains, and they exceeded our highest expectations. Noting down just a few minor modifications needed, we began at last to feel that we were getting on top of things. This time, we would be ready.

The final month of madness was bizarre to say the least. Clark stabbed me, we got more sponsorship, and had a doctor advise us to sample some serious drugs. All in a day's work for Chris and Clark.

But back to the part where Clark stabbed me: one of the big things still to do on our list was to sort out our expedition first-aid kit. Having just done our Remote Area First Aid courses, we were both psyched to put together an awesome first-aid kit, and after compiling a list, Clark was personally ushered around his local Mega Save Chemist by the pharmacist, gradually filling up two huge plastic bags with painkillers, bandages, and antibiotic, anti-nausea, anti-inflammatory and anti-everything-else tablets. Happily, we'd had no cause to use our abdominal pad dressing on our 2005 expedition, and so we didn't need to buy a new one of those.

Despite probably being able to open our own bulk-buy chemist with the quantity of drugs Clark brought home, we still felt a bit underprepared in the painkiller department, and I called up my local doctor, Peter, and told him so. He invited us around to the surgery, where he stayed back after hours and explained our options. Rather than our carrying morphine, which apparently is a nightmare to travel through Customs with, he suggested a relatively new drug called Tramadol, which comes in both tablet and intramuscular injection form, and, after explaining the dosages, he placed a pile of both varieties in our hands, along with a handful of syringes and medi-swabs.

We both wanted to have our flu vaccine that day too, because being less than a month away from leaving and feeling very run-down, we knew that every possible illness and injury on earth would now try to inflict itself upon us. Peter agreed, and proceeded to inject Clark with the vaccination and then turned to me.

'I—I was wondering ...' I began, while a little voice inside tried to shut me up, 'if maybe Clark could give me my flu shot, as practice, under your supervision?' Clark looked almost as shocked as I was.

'Well, yes, actually,' Peter said. 'I think that would be a great idea.'

A mischievous smile spread across Clark's face as he ceremoniously snapped the cover off the syringe, and levelled it at the freshly medi-swabbed deltoid muscle on my arm. 'So I just stab it in? Yeah?'

Peter laughed. I died a little inside. 'Well, not so much "stab", as just, you know, "move inwards".'

I braced myself and Clark 'moved inwards'. The tip of the needle lodged firmly into my skin and stopped.

'Wow, it's harder to poke through than I thought,' Clark commented.

'Yes, erm ... just keep ... moving inwards,' Peter urged again, and the needle slipped through the skin and slid effortlessly up to the hilt into my muscle.

'And now I just squeeze it all in?' The whole process actually only took about two seconds, and despite my trepidation was utterly painless. Clark did a first-rate job.

Wishing us well, Peter refused to accept payment, and said, 'Now, I'd advise that tonight sometime you both have one of the Tramadol tablets, just to check that you don't have any abnormal reactions to the drug.'

Our Tramadol party went off without a hitch. In fact, neither of us noticed anything at all. Bit of an anticlimax, really, after the day's excitement, but at least we went to bed safe in the knowledge that if the house fell on top of us while we slept, we wouldn't feel a thing.

The final weeks became a blur of last-minute tasks such as presenting sponsor and school talks, cramming about 9000 songs and audio books onto our iPods, throwing a fancy 'send-off' party at Ryan's Bar in the heart of Sydney, being filmed by Discovery Channel Canada for an 'Australian Special', and even writing a will and organising our crisis management team, including briefing a friend who would face the media in a worst-case scenario—thus helping to shield our families. There was a series of media events to attend, including several Australia-wide TV news interviews and an appearance on Channel Seven's nationally broadcast *Sunrise* breakfast program with 'Kochie and Mel' the day before departure, which boosted the number of our followers online considerably. Hurrying out of their studio and wiping off all the obligatory makeup, we dashed to ASUS's launch of their latest Eee PC, which they actually marketed around our expedition—the promotional posters showing us taking their lightweight, shockproof little netbooks into the Arctic.

The final hours ticked quickly away on our fancy solar-powered Citizen Eco-drive watches (yet another major sponsor), and before we knew it, our last day in Australia had gone.

'Do you have any bags to check in, sir?' Shifting uneasily in front of the Air Canada desk at the airport, I nodded innocently. The check-in operator smiled politely, 'How many bags?'

I looked at her hopefully, 'Doesn't it say something about some … erm … excess baggage on my booking details?'

As she scrolled down her computer screen, her eyes lit up. 'Yes, it says here … "Please waive excess baggage charges"… ?' She looked quizzically at me and recognition dawned, 'You're one of the Arctic explorers! I was told you'd have a few extra pieces of luggage. How many did you say you have?'

Behind me, Clark wheeled forward a tottering pile of bags on a trolley. 'Wow, that … that's quite a bit of luggage!' the operator stammered.

'Um,' I gulped awkwardly, 'there's still three more trolleys.' And, sighting Clark now heaving some other objects over, I added, 'And some things that didn't fit on the trolley.' We had dismantled both PAC-2s into a total of four bubble-wrapped packages, including the eight half-rims neatly stacked inside each other, and the giant carbon-fibre hardtops for each cart that concertinaed away into something resembling a large suitcase. Bags 5, 6, 7 and 8 were all large yellow 49-litre submersible Ortlieb duffle bags, and alarmingly, so too were bags 9, 10, 11, 12, 13, 14, 15, 16, 17 and 18—all stuffed full of, amusingly, still more bags folded up, and other expedition gear weighing a total of 290 kilograms.

'Thanks very much!' Clark said with a grin, placing the last bag on the conveyor belt. Most of the airport paused to watch the giant yellow caterpillar of identical bags snaking off into the distance.

'Good luck on your trip, boys,' she said kindly, handing us our boarding passes, each one bristling with so many baggage receipts that it resembled an origami hedgehog.

A pleasant fourteen-hour flight landed us in Vancouver, where we spent a few days madly shopping for obscure things like ice screws and meeting up with friends as well as Clark's dad, who happened to be in town for work.

One night, after another evening spent trying to fatten ourselves up with 1-kilogram steak meals and double desserts, we collapsed on our beds and checked our emails. Clark suddenly drew in his breath and I looked over as he stared at the screen. 'What's up?'

Still staring at his Eee PC, he said that one of his mates back at home had just broken up with his long-term girlfriend. When I asked why, Clark turned to look at me with an inscrutable expression upon his face.

'Apparently, she told him that she wants to be with you!? What's going on, Chris?'

Caught totally by surprise, I just stood there, stunned. For a fraction of a second I was overjoyed—Jess was an absolutely amazing girl, beautiful, bubbly and brimful of ideas—whom I'd met almost half a year earlier during a caving trip she'd organised with some of Clark's mates. As we shared a few passions such as photography and importantly the outdoors (she was an outdoors wilderness guide), we'd kept in touch and chatted a few times at other social gatherings. Admittedly, we had met up briefly for the occasional short kayak or bike ride, but all with the prior knowledge of her man—and that was it. On her last visit, perhaps a week before we left, I had half fancied that there was 'something different in the air' between us, but I couldn't be sure, and I had pushed those thoughts out of my head as absurd. Now here I was—days before embarking on probably the most testing team-dynamic trial of my life where Clark and I had to be able to trust and rely on each other utterly—standing potentially accused of cheating on one of his best friends.

'We should probably talk about it now, whatever it is,' Clark suggested uncomfortably, 'else there'll end up being unspoken tension between us for the rest of the trip.' It was awkward, to say the least, but he was certainly right. Although innocent of what his mates accused me of, I still felt horribly guilty, and worst of all, felt terrible for Clark, caught painfully in the middle, having brought me into his group of friends in the first place. After explaining my side of the story, to his credit—and my relief—Clark agreed that it wasn't exactly 'my fault', and rationalised that we should just set the matter aside until we got home.

However, flying north the next day, I felt the dilemma continued to hang ominously over our heads. Sensing this, Clark backed me up as we boarded our last plane. 'It'll be okay, guv, it's just rather unfortunate timing, that's all. It'll sort itself out when we get back.'

Idly flicking my boarding pass, I noticed a little green sticker. 'Landing subject to weather,' it read. A welcome distraction. I asked the flight attendant about it. 'Oh, that just means that we might not be able to land on Victoria Island today; this time of year the weather's pretty bad.'

'And if we can't?' I enquired, intrigued.

'Well, the plane will just ... land somewhere else.'

Of course it would. Grinning, I felt the pioneering excitement of the North seeping back into my veins.

# OUR HOME AWAY FROM HOME

Victoria Island! As the flight attendant opened the door, the cold Arctic wind boisterously elbowed its way inside the cabin, bringing with it a swirling confetti of snow to welcome our arrival. Walking down the stairs onto the icy runway, and traipsing through a carpet of snow to the terminal, we were both struck with a feeling of being home. Though the cold air took our unacclimatised breaths away and the brilliant white glare made us squint, around us were the sights and sounds we had both become so attached to in 2005. The honking of geese returning for the summer, the uniquely flat, lake-strewn landscape, and the unforgettable charm of the Cambridge Bay township in the distance.

No sooner had we sheltered inside the airport when our friend Wilf greeted us heartily, helping to carry our endless parade of bright yellow bags out to his truck. As he held the door open for me, I hurried to catch up. 'There's no hurry,' he chuckled. 'You're in the North now, there's no hurrying up here. Take your time, aye.'

He was right, I had forgotten the timelessness of the Arctic. Drawing a deep breath and exhaling, I felt all the pent-up stress we'd both become accustomed to during the previous year or so exhale with it. Five minutes later at his house, Wilf showed us our room, a fridge full of VB (Australian beer he'd had flown up especially), threw us the keys to his house and to a truck that he'd just dug out of a snow bank the week before for us, and told us that dinner—a barbecue of bacon-wrapped steaks—would be ready in just a few hours. I didn't think anyone on the island even knew what day we were coming, yet Wilf had already organised everything, and around town, familiar faces lit up when they saw us, and even strangers smiled and waved, asking if we were 'the two Ossies'.

No sooner had we walked into Willie's old Adlair Aviation hangar when his son René turned up in the Learjet, having just done another medivac. After helping him push the million-dollar plane back into the hangar, we had a good ol' yarn. Like father, like son, René sat back in his chair, offered us a coffee and swapped stories while providing us with invaluable tips and advice. Unable to perform off-strip landings for a time, he couldn't fly us to our start point, and instead suggested we wait around and try to tee up a side charter with a mining company that frequented flights into Cambridge Bay.

Downing the dregs of his coffee, René flicked us a key to the hangar. 'Well, if we can't fly you out, we can at least give you our hangar as a base.' As he stood up, the door creaked open and an absolutely enormous dog strode in and walked towards us. 'Solomon!' It was René's arctic wolf/malamute cross, without comparison the most incredible dog I've ever seen. After investigating each of our eighteen bags, he curled up, head on his massive paws, and watched us slowly assemble the first PAC.

We spent the next few days and nights almost perpetually at the hangar, sometimes until 5 am, finishing the PACs, organising our gear, weighing our food into ration packs, and wiring up electronics, including the GMN XTracker that pinged our position back to our website map every few minutes.

'Pizza?'

'Oh, thanks René! I needed that.' I wonder how many people have Learjet-delivered pizza at 4 am, from a town a thousand kilometres away? Just one of the perks of operating out of a medivac hangar.

Next we picked up our two brand-new 12-gauge pump-action shotguns from a guy who generously bought them for us months ago back on the mainland, along with our bear-spray cans, flares, bear-banger pyrotechnics, ammo and trigger locks. Despite feeling a little black-market, it was actually all 100 per cent legal—I had filled in the paperwork over a year ago—and so we just walked into his house, gave him a fistful of money to pay for all the shopping, and walked out with enough weapons to start a small war. Ironically, the lovely old chap who did all this for us was the local Anglican minister. What a town!

Back at the hangar we asked René where we could go to test the shotgun. 'Here's fine,' he said, and with that, he reached for a bullet, sawed the front off with his pocket knife and removed the projectile, loaded the now empty bullet into the shotgun, pointed it at the side of the hangar and fired.

BANG! It was louder than any of us could have imagined, and even René swore in surprise. 'It works,' he said, handing the shotgun back to me with a grin.

Eventually everything was all sorted, and our fully loaded PACs weighed in at 249 kilograms each, almost a whole kilogram lighter than our last attempt. However, this time we were carrying enough supplies for 100 days—almost twice the duration of our 2005 attempt—and after successfully test-wheeling our loaded PACs on the snow-covered tundra nearby, we started feeling increasingly confident that this time, we were ready. All we needed was a plane to take us out there.

In between learning how to kite-ski with our old friend Brent, driving snow mobiles and eating wonderful caribou dinners, whenever I spotted a Twin Otter plane land at the airport, I'd hurry over and ask the pilots as they refuelled if they could do a side charter and drop us off, but again and again I was knocked back. They had either already flown their maximum allowed hours that day, or were in a hurry to head back to the mainland for their next job. As the days drifted on, patches of the snow cover around town started to melt away. In the days before we left Australia, the temperature in Cambridge Bay had been around minus 25 degrees Celsius, but since then it had rocketed up. 'Yeah, when the temperature rises, it rises fast ...' Wilf nodded. No one else seemed very surprised at the early thaw, but with midday temperatures already sneaking above zero and the midnight sun no longer setting, I was getting worried. We had expected several weeks of nice solid ice and snow to haul over before our world turned to a giant slushy mess.

It was starting to become a bit of a joke, and recognising us, the various pilots would just shake their head or give us the thumbs down signal before we'd even legged it halfway across the airport to ask for a charter. But on 29 May, having been in

Cambridge Bay for nine days, we got some news from René. 'One of the pilots was just in here looking for you,' he said excitedly, 'they're doing a quick run back to the mainland, but after that they said they have just enough time to get back here and drop you guys out there. Better get your stuff together!'

PART FOUR
# BACK TO
# THE ISLAND

# DAY 1 (30 May 2008): Finding the flag

As we flew the 200-odd kilometres north of Cambridge Bay towards our 2005 end point, to our relief, the world beneath us turned from patches of melting snow into a smothering of pure white. Crammed in amongst the rest of our gear in the back of the Twin Otter, we both peered excitedly out the window, watching the plane's shadow flit across the silent blanket of snow. The pilot veered towards a group of dark objects—a herd of muskox—which predictably whirled into their defensive circle formation as we droned overhead, and we even spotted an arctic wolf gliding swiftly across the barren white landscape. We couldn't wait to get out there.

Our pilot was unsure whether to land on the esker or the frozen lake, but after multiple passes, he opted for a section of the lake where he figured the snow didn't look too deep, and with a 'Let's give it a go', swung in for a very committed approach. Clark and I braced hard as the plane's wheels began slamming into the crests of snow. Throwing the pitch of the props into reverse, the pilot, co-pilot and both of us stared transfixed at the large embankment wall surrounding the lake as it rushed towards us. We came to a heart-pounding stop right in front of it, and all leapt out onto the windswept, snap-frozen lake. 'It's a bit colder out here, boys!' the pilot said, and grinning we nodded—with everything still well frozen, it looked perfect for hauling.

We unloaded all the gear, and before we knew it, in a swirl of snowy prop-wash, the plane had galloped along the frozen lake and veered upwards—just clearing the embankment at the far end—and quickly vanished into the distance.

Surrounded by what we hope is everything we'll need to get from here to the other side of the island within the next 100 days, we set to work assembling our PACs, powering up our website tracking system, and eventually turned on our own GPS. 'So, back where we were three years ago!' Clark announced. 'Almost, anyway.' He frowned. 'Dammit. It says the start—where we left the flag—is about 4 kilometres back that way!'

'Let's do it!' We both shouted, brimful of boyish excitement. 'I can't believe this is finally happening!' Shackling up and tentatively leaning into my fully laden harness for the first time on snow, to my euphoric delight, my PAC rolled obediently forward! It actually gained momentum and I could almost walk *normally* with it. Clark too had coaxed his PAC into a decent stroll. 'That's *amazing*!' he laughed, absolutely beaming.

Less than a minute later, however, we hit our first incline. As we tried to climb out of the lake basin, our smiles and laughter gave way to contorted grimaces and panting gasps so deep that the metallic taste of blood soon permeated my lungs. Starting to feel a little dizzy and nauseous, I felt my body was screaming out for me to pause. I started to slow and nervously shot a worried look over at Clark. Catching each other's desperate glances, we simultaneously summoned the testosterone to continue forcing ourselves onwards and upwards, determined to avoid the psychological blow of not even making it up our first hill.

We made it to the ridge. Just. 'They … work!' I puffed.

'You know what?' Clark managed, 'I think we … might just get to the … far side this time!' Ironically, we both knew the other was only pretending to be so upbeat—but already well-versed in the powers of positive thinking, we allowed ourselves to be buoyed by each other's false optimism.

After about an hour's sweating and groaning we passed the furthest point we'd hauled to in 2005 and unceremoniously ditched our carts there while we went in search of the flag unencumbered. Wearily clambering through the snow, our legs really started to ache—totally unaccustomed to the motion of staggering through snow crusts that always give way at the most awkward moment for each step. The temperature dropped to minus 4.3 degrees Celsius as we floundered up the side of our unnamed hill, and there—to our great joy—we spied the aluminium bear alarm pole that we'd sealed the Australian Geographic flag inside.

The stone cairn we'd built to hold it proudly upright had long since collapsed, presumably from the action of wind and snow, but there it was, lying in a sorry state of decay, our bright-red duct tape now faded to a flaky white gauze-like wrapping. 'It's amazing to think that we were the last people here, all those years ago,' I murmured, cutting through the tape with our Leatherman and pulling out the plastic bag containing the flag and our little handwritten note. It's hard to describe what it was like holding it again: when we left it, we had no intention of ever coming back for it, or ever being in this amazing place again—yet here we were.

I set up the camera, and, posing for a shot ceremoniously holding the flag, we then watched in horror as the tripod keeled over in a sudden gust of wind, smashing my brand new $7000 Canon EOS 1D Mark III digital SLR into the nearest rock. Amazingly, it survived. After anxiously posing for a second shot, we carefully tucked the flag away and traipsed back to our PACs.

It was already late in the day when we returned. We smoothly latched the two PACs together, set up our tents neatly on top and zipped them together with our custom-made linking fabric tunnel forming a sheltered foyer between the two, where Clark prepared a hearty dinner.

Everything is unfolding flawlessly—we really couldn't be happier. Our only concern is that there seems to be a lot of mud around here, not all of which is totally frozen, and so with temperatures now rising overall, we've decided to travel at 'night' from now on, when the sun swoops through the lowest and coldest part of its perpetual 24-hour orbit around us, to help ensure the snow and mud have the strongest possible frozen crust on top. It won't last forever, though. Each 'midnight' the sun passes higher and higher above the horizon, and soon even these coldest hours will eventually rise above freezing, and when it does, there'll be no stopping the terrain around us thawing into a sloppy nightmare! The race is on to get to some firmer ground before it all melts around us.

## DAY 2: First day of hauling

After deliberately sleeping through most of the day, we woke at eight in the evening ready for our first day ('night') of full-on hauling. As I was wedging my feet into my frozen Scarpa boots, I happened to glance over to meet the unblinking stare of a pure white arctic wolf about 75 metres away, just looking at us. By the time I'd swapped to my epic 400-millimetre lens and Clark had emerged with the video camera, it had vanished as silently as it had arrived. We tentatively walked over to where it had been and spotted it loping gracefully across the snow, pausing every twenty or so paces to turn back and stare in evident wonder.

We hauled for nine hours today, and it was a hard, hard slog. Both of us grew incredibly weary in the sessions between our breaks, and as I admitted into the video camera that I held shakily in front of me: 'All I want to do is fall to my knees, vomit into the snow, close my eyes and go to sleep.' We did actually collapse many times, but usually only because the snow crust gave way unexpectedly, and when we did, it took some time to muster the willpower to stand and continue. The physical exertion certainly rivals 2005 levels and we're often near horizontal in our harnesses, slowly forcing the muscles in each leg to straighten and piston us forward, but unlike in 2005, we have actually made progress. We simply turned our iPods up a little louder, and kept telling each other that being the first day of hauling, our PACs would get lighter, we would get fitter, and also better at picking the most efficient route forward.

As we hauled, the temperature hovered around minus 5.2 degrees Celsius (minus 18 with windchill) which kept much of the ground solid, except for the odd soft region of snow into which we sank. Encouragingly, though, while we ourselves then flailed pathetically around in knee-deep snow, behind us the enormous wheels of our PACs—though loaded with 249 kilograms—barely sank enough to leave an imprint. They are fantastic.

Several of the steeper inclines today required us both hauling and pushing together to grunt each PAC up separately, which—although annoying—worked well. This part of Victoria Island is surprisingly hilly, which makes route selection critical. All too often today we had to down carts and walk ahead to suss out the best way forward,which wasted a lot of time and energy, but I'm sure we'll get better at reading the terrain. It's all just so foreign to us at the moment and we're learning by trial and (a lot of) error.

Just as we promised ourselves we would, we made sure that despite the pressure to haul, during each nut break we spared the time to walk over and explore the nearest interesting feature. After all, as we realised in 2005, that's what a trip like this is about in the end. We feel far more comfortable with ourselves this time around.

Eventually when we could haul no further, we decided to call it a day. Again we effortlessly linked the PACs together and (very smugly) set up the tent within about five minutes and climbed inside. It's fantastic how well our systems are working! During the day we leave our Thermarest mattresses and sleeping bags inside the tent with the arching tent-poles still set up but all just folded flat and loosely strapped down underneath the solar panels. To set up camp, all we need to do is stretch out the little hooks we've sewn into the four corners of the tent and clip them into four pre-drilled holes in the PAC frame, and bingo—the tent stands up like a pop-up book, welcoming us inside!

Compared to the soul-destroying 1.3 kilometres we managed on Day 1 three years ago, we are absolutely stoked that today we've stumbled a grand total of 7.1 kilometres 'as the crow flies' and just over 8.5 kilometres 'as the PAC rolls' (measured by a fancy bike computer fitted to our PACs). Considering that if we divide the 700-kilometre distance ahead by our 100 days of food, we really only need to cover 7 kilometres each day, we've already—on Day 1—exceeded our quota!

It is quite surprising how quickly we've both just slipped back into expedition mindset. Sure, it's still impossibly hard work out here, but unlike the start of the 2005 trip, we don't feel so desperately out of our depth—in fact, I almost feel like I'm back in my element, free again in my world, and I'm absolutely loving it! It's the same joy I discovered way back on my first hike—I love how usually insignificant things, like sipping cold water or lying down to straighten my back, all feel so good out here that they make me smile.

## DAY 3 (1 June 2008): Tough, but good going

A record of 9.25 kilometres today! Disconcertingly, though, the melting snow crust seems increasingly unwilling to support us, and every step or two we're now breaking through, which saps a lot of energy. The complete inability to judge depth, scale, size and distance out here in a world with no reference points continues to amaze us, as it did last time. Some eskers look like they go on for miles, yet take three steps and suddenly a huge void appears, requiring us to descend into a snow-filled valley and tediously struggle back up the other side, one PAC at a time.

We both have painful bruises on our hips from leaning so forcefully into our harnesses, but despite the hardships, it's a breathtakingly beautiful place. The perpetually low-angle sunlight casts the pastel pinks and purples of sunrise across the snow out here for hours. Every nut break reveals new discoveries: giant wolf prints to marvel at, a plethora of lemming jawbones to count, and the neverending question—'Is that white thing on the skyline moving or not?' With so many elements to take in wherever we look, it feels like we've reached a state of heightened awareness and—as I always do on such expeditions—I'm already feeling so much more alive.

## DAY 4: Our old friend Death Terrain!

Waking just as the local 'day' was drawing to a close, we watched in awe as the thermometer plummeted from a balmy 3 degrees down to a chilly minus 6 within the space of 45 minutes.

We're getting more efficient at our systems, and were out of the tent and hauling by 9.30 pm today, which was great. Although the map said we were apparently following an esker all day, it lied—as usual—and we found ourselves plunging in and out of every conceivable type of terrain, ranging from the odd stretch of wonderfully frozen gravel esker, through long expanses of solid, ice-covered snow, plenty of softer regions where we sank up to our knees, and, yes, good old Death Terrain.

As we stared out over the vicious concoction of random shards of ice-shattered rock—each one carefully aligned to cause maximum puncture-damage—the deep psychological gashes inflicted upon us by this terrain in 2005 suddenly reopened. Tentatively hauling my PAC forward until its balloon tyres pressed dangerously against the first limestone dagger, I held my breath. 'Moment of truth!' Clark shouted, and expecting nothing but the burst of escaping air, I threw myself forward in my harness, stepping awkwardly out across the jagged minefield. Behind me I could hear the huge tyres resonating with the sound of grinding rock fragments snapping and pinging out sideways as the PAC lurched and sprang from one stone knife edge to another. Miraculously, though, not only did the tyres stay inflated, but close examination of our Kevlar wheel covers afterwards revealed they still seemed as good as new. 'Well, what do you know!' I said, impressed. 'Genuinely bulletproof!'

As we pressed onwards, the temperature descended to a new record low of minus 9 degrees, covering our PACs and solar panels in a thick icy coating which we had to keep wiping off in a bid to harvest any available sunlight. My nose feels a little burnt, but I'm thinking that's more likely to be from the wind than the ghostly outline of the sun that we spotted intermittently sliding around behind an ever-thickening veil of cloud.

The wind was so bitterly cold during lunch today that the whole experience was actually quite traumatising. If we dared stand still to prepare our food, we quickly froze to the bone, but shuffling around there was absolutely nowhere to hide from it either; the deathly cold was omnipresent.

Stopping for a nut break around 'mid afternoon' (Chris and Clark time), I happened to park my PAC side-on to the wind, and crouching down in the lee of one of its huge carbon fibre and Kevlar wheel rims, made a wonderful discovery. Not only did they act as a great wind break, but their conical shape actually seemed to reflect and focus what little warmth the sun offered, literally warming the space in front!

'Clark!' I waved him excitedly over from the trance-like circular track he was shuffling around, and we spent the remainder of the break huddled together, basically doing our best to climb inside the wheel rim. Desperate times.

I have noticed that Clark and I have very different hauling techniques. Clark has the slow and steady approach, while I have been progressing in a series of short, high-octane bursts, lasting only a minute or so, which would soon find me hanging in my harness catching my breath, only just ready to take off again as Clark drew level. It has been working okay—overall we both progress at the same speed and thankfully neither has to wait for the other—but I have to admit that by the end of each day I'm feeling increasingly shattered. Waking randomly during the last few nights, the first feeling that has been flooding my mind is dread—dread that it's time to get up and face it all over again. Already empty, I was really starting to struggle inwardly with the thought of having to maintain my level of energy for the next three months …

Today, however, I tried Clark's tortoise technique, and it works a treat! Despite having punched out a new record of 9.87 kilometres as the crow flies (10.25 kilometres as the PAC rolls), I'm actually feeling good this evening! It's a huge relief for me, a real load off my mind, and while chowing down on our new favourite meal— dehydrated Mexican Chicken from Back Country Cuisine—our optimism and morale has never been higher. As Clark commented, 'I'm not even worried that we've run out of esker.' (Even the map finally admits this.) 'I guess tomorrow we'll just head in the vague direction of Hadley Bay?' It's still a good 90 kilometres away, and there's a tangle of several large lakes in the way, too, which we're hoping will still be frozen, else I'm not quite sure what we'll do.

## DAY 5: Hello frozen lakes!

The flap-flap-flapping of the tent shaking violently in the wind, the drifts of snow building up actually *inside* our tent vestibule, and the streams of spindrift snaking across the frozen ground all accentuated the already unappealing weather this morning. Daunted by the unknown terrain lying in wait now that our esker had ended, somehow we made packing up camp a somewhat more drawn-out procedure than was strictly necessary. Eventually we got our act together, used our GPS to orientate ourselves, and headed off in what we hoped was the direction of the first big lake straddling our path to Hadley Bay.

In the white mirage ahead I spotted a pile of black dots which I assumed to be distant muskox but Clark soon corrected me, pointing out that they were in fact geese, quite close at hand. Hauling onwards for some time in quiet contemplation, it eventually struck me that these geese didn't seem to be getting any closer, and this, combined with the fact that they weren't moving, convinced us both they were rocks. As we drew nearer—still with no idea if they were small rocks up close or big boulders in the distance—they suddenly stood up, grew horns and became muskox.

We hauled as close as we dared and—shivering convulsively in the cold—got some fantastic photos and footage of these shaggy, ice-age beasts standing firm, enduring the merciless, bitter wind, their faces encrusted with ice and snow, framed all around by swirling white.

Further on we at last reached our first serious lake, and *oh my* was it good to haul on! Sure, snow covered the lake ice in a layer of sometimes deceptively deep powder, but underneath it was flat and hard. For once we were able to march solidly, and without having to continually stop to determine the best route—or help each other double-haul up hills—we clocked up some fantastic kilometres. Visually too it was astounding. Wherever I looked it was just white—everywhere. There was literally no change as my eyes travelled from the snow underfoot, up past where the horizon must have been, all the way to the white sky directly overhead; all was the same dull, depthless white. Tuning out with the assistance of my iPod, it felt every bit like I was suspended in the middle of a giant white void, with streams of snow curling and swirling around my partly obscured feet, and ahead, Clark's PAC seemed to float weirdly in space.

An arctic fox flitted across what looked like the sky in front of us, carrying a large goose egg in its mouth. I don't think the geese have started nesting yet as it's still too cold, so it was likely an egg the fox stashed in the ground last autumn to last it through the winter. It's amazing how they manage to find the same spot again months later, even when it's covered by snow, and here we are, veering continually off course and almost doing circles merely trying to get across the lake.

We've brought almost exactly 100 kilograms of food each for this 100-day trip, so our carts are getting about 1 kilogram lighter every day, except for my cart, which is becoming increasingly weighed down by all the lemming jawbones I obsessively collected yesterday (for want of something better to do during nut breaks), and the rubbish bag, and the fact that for convenience we actually group all the food for the current ten-day session (we've invented the ten-day week out here) into one bag that Clark carries. So in actual fact, my PAC is getting *heavier* (damn lemmings), while Clark's is getting *lighter* by 2 kilograms of food every day. Of course it will even out in just five more days when I ceremoniously get to offload my next ten days' worth of food—10 whole kilograms—into Clark's 'week bag'. I can't wait.

To our great delight, we cracked 10 kilometres as the crow flies today! Frozen lakes are an absolute dream to haul over, and poring over the map, we're pretty excited about the possibility of linking up with a few more big ones up ahead. Today was a great day, and we're in the highest of spirits. To top it all off, we got a wonderful swag of emails full of support from our website, including a particularly charismatic one from some guy called Ray in South Africa, who wrote, 'Hey guys, behind you all the way!! Give it horns!'

## DAY 6: Doomed to fail

Over the last five days we've been slowly but surely building up our confidence—confidence in ourselves physically and mentally, confidence in our systems and procedures, and confidence in our PACs. This morning, one of these took a huge and devastating hit.

The 'morning' started brilliantly—the sun was even dazzling enough to warrant rubbing sun cream on my nose—and getting ready to set off, things felt like they couldn't be any better. As Clark shackled up, I casually inspected the Kevlar cover of my right PAC wheel: a little nick here, a loose thread there—and then I spotted a gaping split 7 centimetres long! The complete shock and horror of this discovery momentarily paralysed me, and then, as the flood of ramifications started to spill into my numb mind, I shouted hoarsely for Clark.

Closer inspection revealed that my entire Kevlar cover was actually criss-crossed with wear lines, and this gash was merely the first one to actually wear right through and spring open. There are countless others that—given another hour? day? week?—will certainly also split. We made these covers double-thickness, and thankfully the spilt is only in the surface layer, but the inside layer is merely an inlaid strip glued in place, and is in no way able to constrain the tyre pressure. So if (or, more realistically, *when*) this split opens enough, the pressure of the balloon tyre will rip it right across from one side to the other, and unfortunately then there'll be nothing restraining the tube's pressure and it'll simply slide the inside layer of Kevlar apart—just like you'd unscroll a newspaper—and that'll be it. No more wheel cover. The same wear is happening on my left tyre, and to a much lesser degree on both of Clark's tyres.

Of course, we have spare patches of Kevlar for any splits or tears—perhaps enough for four or five big ones—but not for the

TOP: Engineers at EMP Composites help out with wheel rim design ideas.
LEFT: Clark laying carefully cut sheets of carbon fibre onto the wheel rim mould.

THIS PAGE, CLOCKWISE FROM TOP LEFT: Vacuum-infusing the wheel rims with epoxy resin; Clark finishing off the carbon fibre hardtop for the PAC-2s; Learning to sew Kevlar wheel covers with my parents' old Singer sewing machine; Our eight half-rims and carbon fibre hardtops all finished—thanks, EMP!; Admiring the first completed wheel with bulletproof cover; Lifting the first wheel rim out of the mould. OPPOSITE PAGE, CLOCKWISE FROM TOP LEFT: Chris proudly showing off the first completed Kevlar wheel cover; Superman holds up the first completed wheel axle pair; Chris machining up parts for the axle hub on the lathe at home; Assembling the axle hub with bearings, et cetera; Clark deposits our 'excess baggage' at the Air Canada check-in counter; Up to three hours of serious training each night—dragging a truck tyre along the beach; National TV news crew filming the PAC-2 testing on the beach.

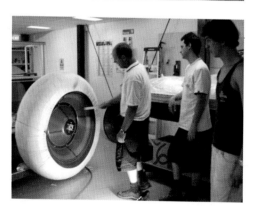

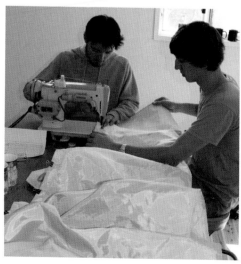

TOP: Unloading the plane on a frozen lake. LEFT: Clark wedging in strips of food packaging to prevent the rim chafing the rubber inner tube. OPPOSITE PAGE, CLOCKWISE FROM TOP LEFT: Our favourite dinner, dehydrated Mexican Chicken—saved only for special days; My view when hauling in a whiteout—it looked as if Clark was hovering in space; Crazy weather—me double-hauling the PACs joined together; Hard going. The large wheels do a good job at not sinking into the snow—can't say the same for us, though!

OPPOSITE PAGE:
A 'second' sun rises—
the rare solar-dog
phenomenon occurs
when ice crystals in
the sky refract the light.
THIS PAGE, FROM TOP:
Clark cooking dinner in
the 'foyer' between our
tents—note the drying
socks; Route planning,
having surprisingly
reached Hadley Bay, but
how much further can
we make it?; The aptly
named Death Terrain—we
were plagued by endless
expanses of razor-sharp,
ice-shattered limestone.

OPPOSITE PAGE, TOP: Desperate times–converting our PACs to The Nugget by stripping off all unnecessary weight. OPPOSITE PAGE, BOTTOM: Disaster: rolling downhill, The Nugget's rear axle buckles–surely the expedition doesn't end here? THIS PAGE, CLOCKWISE FROM TOP LEFT: Chris checking emails and updating the website in the tent each evening; Clark cuts off the bent part of the axle using a 3 cm fragment of hacksaw blade; We caught three giant lake trout, each over half a metre long, in just five casts.

OPPOSITE PAGE: Clark's 24th birthday surprise party—with balloons, laptop music, mini bottle of vodka and dried char! TOP: Over 1 km from land, Clark hauls the floating Nugget across a large but strangely shallow lake. BOTTOM: Arctic caribou (reindeer) shedding its winter coat.

LEFT: For two weeks the air became thick with mosquitoes—we had to breathe through gritted teeth to prevent choking on them. BELOW: Rafting down the Kuujjua River in HMAS *Nuggct*. OPPOSITE PAGE: Clark trying not to break his legs while hauling The Nugget over Victoria Island–style 'gravel' (endless boulder fields).

OPPOSITE PAGE, TOP: Stranded on the far side for days awaiting pickup, we had several encounters with polar bears. OPPOSITE PAGE, BOTTOM: Horrible terrain—Clark struggles to restrain The Nugget from careering down the hillside. RIGHT: Walking on thin ice—hauling the PACs across what was left of the frozen pancake of ice on some of the larger lakes rather than face the horrors of the terrain ashore. BELOW: So much for 'bulletproof' Kevlar wheel covers.

TOP: Zombies: desperate, weary hauling machines—we MUST get there! BOTTOM: We've done it! Exulting at the most westerly tip of Victoria Island, after a total of 128 days! Now we play the waiting game—the man who was to pick us up has been thrown in prison.

multitude that seem already to be spawning. It's pretty damning news on Day 6, and we are both utterly and completely crushed.

The immediate problem we face is obvious—how do we stop it getting any worse? The answer is far from clear. Considering most of our terrain so far has been simple snow, it can't have caused much wear and tear. Our original pair of prototype covers (which we've brought with us as spares) were only made from a single layer of lighter grade Kevlar, and they survived days of deliberately savage wear in the mountains and emerged in as-new condition. How can a few days of snow hauling have brought these extra-durable covers to their knees? Is it the cold? Does Kevlar become so brittle in the cold that the gradual flexing back and forth as we roll along has simply split the fibres? The freeze and flex tests I did in the freezer at home didn't seem to show any sign of this, but … what else could it be?

We could try and haul by day instead of night, when the temperature is usually above zero, but that means the ground will be a sloppy melted mess and near impossible to stagger through—but perhaps this is what we need to do? Or—thinking longer term— perhaps we really ought to just camp out here until it's significantly warmer in a few weeks, rather than potentially risk the whole expedition by daring to roll any further now? But the problem might not be temperature-related anyway, so we can't just wait around on that chance.

Viewed objectively, the most likely eventuality is that both my tyre covers will fail. I'll then replace them with our two old, thin prototype covers, which will also surely fail even faster than these, by which time a similar fate will likely have befallen Clark's covers. Then we will be faced with a real challenge. Without wheels we can neither float nor roll.

We decided to measure the size of the split and start hauling regardless; there really is nothing else we can do. It was a terribly bleak day today, and we both felt empty and frustratingly helpless. To make matters worse, the sun withdrew behind an ominous churning blanket of low black cloud, and the wind steadily increased, freezing us to the core. Wearing our Gore-Tex Pro Shell Primaloft jackets (our extra-warm 'stand-around' jackets) as we hauled, the spindrift started streaming across the snow-clad ground, and the wind bit so hard into the slit of exposed skin around the sides of our masks that we had to haul with our faces awkwardly turned away from it, grimacing. The mouth vents in our balaclavas even froze over and attached themselves to our increasing facial hair. What's the point? I kept asking myself, over and over. We're obviously not going to make it anymore. Why put ourselves through any more of this hell? We're clearly going to have to abort in a few weeks anyway. What a complete waste of three years of planning. We've failed two attempts now. No one will back us for a third, and I don't have the energy to start it all again, anyway. What a disaster.

Pausing for lunch we pulled both PACs alongside each other with about a 50-centimetre gap between them, unharnessed and both squished inside the wind break formed between the two tyres. It was pure heaven wedged in there; even the sound of the wind ceased. 'We may as well enjoy the tyres while we still have them,' I snorted, and Clark managed a dry laugh.

In that moment—huddled dejectedly between our failing wheels, with our backs being blasted by 40 kilometres per hour wind-blown snow—we were broken men. I could see it in Clark, and I knew it was written all over me. There is no avoiding reality out here—things are what they are—and I guess that's one of the great things about trips like this. 'Life becomes both brutally honest and wonderfully simple.' I could hear my own words. 'Just fix what can be fixed, and abandon what cannot, both mental and physical.'

Clark too must have been reaching his own epiphany, and mumbled, 'We can't fix them, but they're not broken yet so who knows how far we'll get.'

Nodding, I agreed. 'Maybe the tyres will last even without the covers for a bit,' I suggested hopefully, 'and when we run out of puncture repair patches, maybe we can roll along on just the rims?' Our mood lifted with every passing second.

'Yeah, we'll just see what happens—let's do our best to get to Hadley Bay anyway!' Clark said as we both stood up. 'We'll give it horns!'

We both really rallied this afternoon, and although the success of the expedition now looks unlikely, morale is actually higher in the tent tonight than it's been all trip—a real testimony to what positive attitudes can do for a team. How could we not be grinning, though—Clark did just accidently set off the tripwire alarm while heading out to the toilet. Good times. As renowned Australian adventurer Tim Cope once said, 'Adventure only really starts when all your carefully laid plans go to ruins.' Our adventure, it seems, is only just starting.

## DAY 7: Melting already?

Evidently it snowed rather a good deal while we slept. So much so, in fact, that Clark had to engage in open-cut mining operations in search of the solar panels he'd placed on the ground to collect sunlight overnight. Great drifts of white had formed into beautifully long comet tails behind anything and everything.

The temperature, instead of dropping to a healthy minus 6 or minus 7 degrees to firm up the snow underfoot, languished around minus 1 to minus 1.5 all day today. Frustratingly, although technically a degree or so below zero, all the water up in these 'ere parts must be used to the cold, and doesn't seem to actually freeze until somewhat colder temperatures—so all the wind-blown snow and freezing drizzle collecting on our jackets, pants, tent and everying else just melts. It's our first taste of being damp, and makes us feel even colder. The wind didn't let up all day either, and the net effect was a rather draining day.

The various lakes we crossed were themselves thankfully still frozen solid; however, the surface layers of old melting snow and recent powder rarely supported our weight, and every few steps—without warning—our feet would break through into a well of slush. Adding insult to injury, the moment our feet became twisted down one of these wells, the PAC's momentum shoved us bodily forward, over onto our hands and knees. The funny thing is, though, how much of a lottery the whole thing is: Clark might be hauling right beside me on apparently firm snow, and then for no reason I'll plunge through while Clark suppresses a laugh and keeps hauling until he breaks through. Scrunch, scrunch, collapse, scrunch, collapse, collapse, collapse. The worst is when, in falling over, our gloved hands plunge through into their own Slurpie-like well, flooding with icy water. So it's been a hard day, but it's all part of the fun, and we're in good spirits. The tear in my Kevlar cover doesn't seem to have widened too much further today—perhaps 5 millimetres—and one other wear-line seems to be opening, but only a little. Perhaps this warmer weather has helped slow its degradation after all?

We're camped in the middle of Zeta Lake at the moment, and depending on the temperature when we wake up tomorrow, we might be marooned out here surrounded by a sea of slush, or alternatively, we may be able to haul briskly onwards to Hadley Bay. Despite soggy conditions we made 8 kilometres as the PAC rolls today (7.62 kilometres direct by GPS), so we're more than happy with that. We've now also crossed the 71 degree N line of latitude, and crossed the 106 degree W line of longitude. You'd be surprised the number of little things we can find out here to celebrate with a little extra chocolate ration.

## DAY 8: Duck-footed sled dogs

This morning we decided to pump up all four tyres to a slightly higher pressure, the idea being that the tyre will then flex and deform less as it rolls, therefore hopefully reducing the flexing fatigue that seems to be the most likely cause of the tear. Clark's tyres were already slightly tighter than mine, which perhaps explains why his are in better condition. Only time will tell. In the meantime though, I just hope that the increased pressure won't further rip the existing tear in my tyre cover.

The snow around camp seemed surprisingly pretty firm and we set off (albeit rather late, after the morning's tyre pumping), but we soon found that it was actually much slushier just outside camp. In fact, the lake's snow cover became so slushy that we very quickly smeared to a complete halt, our feet churning uselessly in the sloppy mess beneath us as even the wheels started to sink in. With a few tricks still up our sleeve, we dramatically produced our Yowie snowshoes—awesome little strap-on, semi-flexible snowshoes with spikes on the soles—and continued hauling. They worked a charm, but only for a few more iPod songs, after which the snow became too slushy even for Yowies, and we just stood there panting, like exhausted ducks with our huge snowshoe feet, totally beaten. We literally couldn't move our PACs at all—we were hopelessly stranded in the middle of a giant melting icecap. 'Bummer,' I muttered, casting around for ideas. 'What now?'

Clark proposed joining the PACs together (as we do each night) and he tried hauling from the front, while I pushed from behind. This only worked until I caught up to Clark's sloppy wake, whereupon all my traction was lost. 'Maybe if we both haul from the front?' Clark suggested, 'Like a dog team.' I had my doubts—and also my concerns for what these loads would do to our PACs—but desperate times call for desperate measures and we rigged up a 'double-haul' system, one harness tied in front of the other, both attached back to the same towing points.

'Okay: One … Two … THREE!' I called and we both flung ourselves into the harness, and to our delight, the whole ungainly 500-kilogram, 8-metre contraption began to scrunch its way through the snow behind us! It was intolerably slow progress, but it was progress nonetheless, and we spent the rest of the day inching our way across the giant Slushie that is Zeta Lake. We felt like a cross between sled dogs and the old-school heroic explorers like Shackleton, hauling their enormous wooden boats arduously across the snow. At least having four fixed wheels made the vehicle tend to self-track in a relatively straight line—which is something we have yet to master individually in this featureless white void. The teamwork aspect of double-hauling worked well, too: when travelling individually we've been free to pause and catch our breath whenever the need struck, but together, the fact that the other hadn't stopped urged us both on. The effect was a series of epically long marches that dragged on forever, until eventually a particularly slushy patch would suck us to a halt, and being literally unable to pull free, we'd both hang weakly in the harness. Only then—safe in the realisation that neither of us was still hauling—could we dare declare a nut break.

It was during one such nut break when Clark, inspecting the tyres, spotted that our excessively pumped-up inner tubes are actually starting to wear through against the edges of the rim itself! With the rubber inner tubes being less than 2 millimetres thick, the fact we can actually see a groove worn into them around the entire circumference is pretty frightening. It's a cruel world—if we don't pump them up tightly, the Kevlar covers flex and wear—but if we do, the inner tubes themselves wear away and will surely split, something that our puncture repair kits simply won't be able to handle. What to do?

'Well, we can either do nothing,' I rationalised aloud, 'in which case I'd say they'll burst by the end of the day, or we can let them back down again.' Deciding we'd rather have torn covers than no tyres at all, we undid the morning's pumping and continued on our way—looking very much like two exhausted, duck-footed fools wearily dragging a giant campervan. We pushed on an hour or so past our usual chuck-hiking-poles-down time, urged on by the knowledge that the snow is only going to get softer in the coming days, and we need to get across these frozen lakes to reach Hadley Bay—if we get that far.

We managed 5.36 kilometres today, and have crossed the lake itself. We're now parked in a little alcove side lake, and tomorrow, we shall see … It seems pretty likely we'll wake to find ourselves marooned in a sea of total slush, or worse still, floating around on a liquid lake, locked in by hunks of ice. I secretly love that each night we go to sleep with no idea what tomorrow will bring. The only scary thing is that the snow here is too slushy to set our bear alarm.

## DAY 9: Slow progress

We both agree that today was the hardest slog yet. We made 6.08 kilometres by the GPS in a direct line, but there was nothing direct about today's route. It was also our longest ever day of hauling—over ten hours—and the cruel weather ensured that this didn't include lengthy nut breaks.

The snow is increasingly sloppy, and we spent most of the day with the PACs joined, double-hauling dog-team style, scrunching and splashing our way along. With nothing to aim for in this white nothingness, all I could do to vaguely maintain course at the front of the dog team was attempt to keep the wind biting into my face at the same angle. From behind, Clark could see me veering left or right relative to his wanderings and would bang the appropriate harness rope in correction, but even still, it was hopeless. Checking the GPS we'd often find ourselves travelling almost 45 degrees off course. The furrows pressed into the snow by our wheels are now so deep that turning this rigid contraption is basically impossible—a cruise liner would have a tighter turning circle. It is actually easier now to untie ourselves, walk around, separate the PACs and realign them individually, then reconnect them in the new direction, shackle ourselves back up, and keep going.

Just as we climbed wearily into the tent at the end of our depressingly overcast, cold and windy 'day' (local night), as usual the wind eased and the weather started to fine up as the sun climbed higher in the sky, burning away the cloud. Despite the problems it will bring, I am secretly looking forward to when local night temperatures rise above zero, removing any point in us continuing to haul through the miserable 'night time' weather. The world we haul through is dead and totally uninviting, yet frustratingly, whenever we peep out of our tent when we should be asleep, the world is bathed in wondrous sunshine and there's often even a caribou or two around. Relentlessly teased by these visions, we've both started to become besotted by this balmy image of what the daytime Arctic must be like—sun perpetually beaming down, great lines of caribou streaming past, arctic foxes flitting around the butterflies, baby lambs bleating and frolicking in the flowerbeds as puffy cotton-wool clouds drift merrily across the rainbowed heavens. Well, maybe we're in for a reality check, but right now, I have to say, night hauling sucks.

Connecting briefly to the internet via our Iridium satellite phone before bed, I uploaded our daily news piece and photo to our website. Checking our emails, we received some exciting news—CASARA (which I'm guessing stands for something like Canadian Air Search And Rescue ... Aardvark) wrote to say that they 'May utilise us as Targets'—in the next day or so for a bit of 'spotter training' for their Hercules aircraft team! Awesome!

In the meantime, the race against time continues—tomorrow we'll try to cross the next big lake and then follow the linked series of lakes and rivers north towards Hadley Bay before they dissolve away from under us. Unfortunately, the reality is that Hadley is still probably another ten days away at best, and so we're unlikely to get there before the world melts and we start puncturing our weakening tyres on whatever's beneath.

## DAY 10: The sun!

Today was—minus the frolicking lambs and butterflies—almost exactly the dreamy Arctic summer's day we have been imagining.

We woke a little late, but in our defence decided that today we'd shift the official Chris & Clark Time Zone forward two hours, getting up at 9.30 pm local time and hauling through until 8.30 am. Not only would this mean we'd actually get up on time, but we also hoped this might enable the snow to be a bit crisper by the time we started hauling, and perhaps enable us to enjoy some of the 'daytime' sun towards the end of our day.

Well as it turned out, the entire day's weather was bliss. The dazzling sun swept around the clear blue sky, topping up our solar panels and warming our spirits despite the temperature falling to a crisp minus 6 degrees, which kept the snow underfoot relatively firm.

We double-hauled with snowshoes all day, and although we did break through occasionally—our snowshoes sloshing up great spadefuls of water which congealed our boots and pants into one solid hunk of ice—for most of the day, the lake surface was perfect: an endless flat expanse of windswept snow and ice, whisked into mini sastrugi (ridges formed by the action of wind) as if the waves on the lake had been snap-frozen in time, featuring peaks, troughs and even curling crests. With every snow crystal on the ground shimmering and glinting like a carpet of diamonds in the sun, our mood today could not have been better.

Being Day 10 has its own rewards—almost all our food rations are portioned out into ten-day packages so that we can't eat too far ahead of ourselves, and this means that today we got to finish whatever's left in each bag. So when it was time for our first nut break, instead of the usual precise handful, we poured the remaining glut of cashew nuts onto our PAC's carbon fibre hardtop and split the spoils between us—almost twice the usual amount!

We managed a welcoming 9.05-kilometre GPS direct distance today, and we're almost across the last of the big lakes. It's looking more likely that we may reach our goal of Hadley Bay after all. With our wheel covers deteriorating the way they are, though, I think we have both now let go of the idea of the far side of the island. Hadley Bay is about as much as we can realistically hope for, and that would be fantastic. Currently we're waiting for our saucepan of snow and ice to melt so we can boil some water for dinner. We're both starting to get seriously hungry already these past few days. I actually spent most of today thinking about a café I'd like to open, and wondering if we should have shot a ptarmigan that visited us around lunchtime.

# DAY 11: Billycarts and fogbows

Despite keeping a keen ear out for approaching Hercules spotter planes all night, we neither saw nor heard anything. Actually, we did hear a jet roaring past and eagerly peeped out through the tent, only to realise it was just a passenger plane, so high in the infinitely blue sky that it was scarcely more than a silver dot scratching a thin white scar behind it. It's strange how loud everything sounds out here without background noise; even our footsteps are sometimes so noisy—rasping against the snow—that it's hard to endure. Anyway, no Herc visit—perhaps they couldn't find us, but I prefer to believe that they just decided to practise on some target closer to home.

Like yesterday, today too started out with brilliant sunshine, and inside our tent felt almost like a greenhouse—it was heaven. However, while we slept, the gloriously warm weather had seriously deteriorated the snow, and we toiled hopelessly for the first 300 metres, each footstep plunging through into ponds of water, trapping our snowshoes and twisting our ankles. Things looked very grim indeed, and after more than an hour of pushing ourselves to breaking point, we'd made almost no progress—we could still see our campsite just behind us. Hauling our PACs individually proved just as useless, but in a rare stroke of luck, we happened onto a region of firmer snow, and managed to tentatively double-haul across the remainder of the lake. Cresting the rise out of the lake, we eventually stood on what our map promised to be the start of a series of downhill rivers and lakes leading all the way to Hadley Bay.

After lunch at 4 am (perfectly normal) we began our descent, double-hauling down quite a steep little slope. I suddenly felt my hauling trace slacken, and looking back, saw the PAC actually rolling slowly forward of its own volition! Both thinking exactly the same thing, we looked at each other and grinned. Like a bob-sled team we each hurried around behind a wheel and, pushing, built momentum and then sprang aboard as our giant 8-metre billycart trundled on down the hill. It wasn't exactly high performance, but the huge thrill of gaining distance while doing absolutely no work took a long while to wear off.

As we reached the first of the linked lakes, a heavy mist rolled over and visibility dropped to about 30 metres, which again made holding a straight course rather hard, until a rainbow (fogbow?) conveniently appeared in the mist ahead, guiding us onwards. For the first time in a few days we split our PACs in two again, and hauled the last few mini lakes independently.

Pausing for a nut break on an island protruding through the frozen mantle, Clark made an important discovery—the jawbone of a rather large fish, presumably an arctic char! It's the first evidence that despite the complete failure of our 2005 arctic fishing trip, there are actually fish out here. In completely unfounded anticipation, we've already started hoarding the salt that collects at the bottom of our nut bags to sprinkle over all the fish we'll catch when the lakes start to melt.

All up, we stumbled to a halt after 10.25 kilometres as the PAC rolls today, and 10.03 kilometres direct by the GPS. That's our second-best distance so far!

## DAY 12: Rubbish recycling

Before going to sleep last night, we made the unpleasant discovery that—despite lowering the tyre pressure—our wheel rims have continued to chafe further into the thin rubber walls of our inner tube tyres. Some places look so deeply worn that I'm very surprised it hasn't already cut right through. So we decided that first thing this morning we'd do whatever we possibly could to pad or smooth the rim edges before going anywhere.

While formulating this plan of action last 'night', the sun was shining and the prospect of standing around this morning lining the edges of the rims with smooth duct tape sounded tolerable—guiltily lethargic even. Typically, however, Victoria Island had other plans for us, and by the time we woke, the temperature had plunged to minus 8 degrees Celsius, and the increasing windchill reduced it further to a painful minus 15. Snow set in too, and the accumulating spindrift completely buried anything we set down even briefly on the ground. Great. Just the day to stand around without gloves on doing fiddly work. Still, it needed doing, and it was the kind of preventative maintenance we couldn't afford to delay.

It was excruciatingly cold work, but looking on the positive side, inclement conditions are perfect for encouraging efficiency. So without further ado, we quickly unloaded both carts, deflated each tyre in turn and started lining the sharp rim edges with our roll of silver duct tape—only to discover after finishing rim #1 that we'd run out of tape. A quick mental calculation revealed we'd actually need almost 24 metres of tape just to go around both sides of each rim, once. Yikes. 'What else can we use?' Clark blurted out, frantically shuffling on the spot to keep warm, his hands shoved under his armpits.

I looked wildly around for inspiration. 'The labels on our dry-bags!' I shouted, 'They're all duct tape!'

We hastily peeled off the 20-centimetre strips labelling each of our sixteen identical giant yellow drybags, and having soon used all that up too, wondered what we could use next. We stood there in the cold, our minds slowly ticking over impractical ideas as the numbness advanced. We started hobbling laps around our PACs just to get some circulation and life-indicating pain back into our toes, and then, eureka! I had an idea. What's like duct tape, that we have lots of? 'Empty freeze-dried food packages!'

It was a long shot, but it worked. We half-pitched the tent and wiggled our torsos inside to escape the wind and lay there—Leatherman in hand—slowly slicing our licked-clean foil packages from the last eleven freeze-dried dinners into duct tape width strips. Wedging these between the inner tube and the edge of the rim, they were squashed firmly in place and formed a perfect shield against the sharp edges. I knew there was a reason I was carrying all our rubbish with us.

By the time we'd gotten under way the wind had died down, and the sun had burnt away the veil of clouds—once again we found ourselves hauling through that sparkling world of happiness, on perfectly frozen ground, loving life. Then, just as we were really starting to enjoy the sun, something odd happened. Another sun started to come up. What started as a sunrise-like glow on the skyline soon burgeoned into a full-on ball of bright light rising from the clear blue horizon a good 30 degrees or so below the real sun. Strange patches of light and even inverted rainbows formed above and to each side of the original sun. Caused by ice crystals in the sky refracting the sunlight, I've read about these 'sun dogs' before but never seen one—it was spectacular.

Slightly blind from staring at all the suns, we hauled onwards. As we approached the far side of yet another lake, I kept squinting at the horizon ahead, blinking, trying to confirm what I thought I was looking at, before I finally stopped and called to Clark, pointing. 'Is that a … a house?!' Hauling excitedly towards it, it turned out to be an abandoned (at least for the season) metal frame over which a canvas cover could be thrown to form a small tent-frame cabin for the summer. Except for an old fuel drum, dinged and discarded, there was nothing else around, and after our nut ration ran out, we hauled onwards a little further before calling it a day. We didn't get very far (2.9 km), but at least we still have four wheels, and with a bit of luck, our repairs may hold until we get to Hadley. We haven't really discussed what we'll do if we get that far—it'll be a lot cheaper to get a seaplane out of Hadley Bay than to charter a Twin Otter to wherever our wheels finally die—if indeed we're lucky enough for that to happen somewhere near where a plane can actually land at all.

## DAY 13: One giant Slushie

According to one of our website comments last night, yesterday's tent frame belongs to the seaplane pilot Fred Hamilton, who flew Clark and me out to our start point in 2005. Apparently these lakes between here and Hadley Bay are teeming with big lake trout, and if we dangle a lure into any open 'leads' or cracks in the ice, these hearty meals will attach themselves to the end of the line! For now though, beneath the slurry we've been hauling through, the surfaces of the lakes themselves are still well and truly frozen. I can't wait. Now that we are in full-swing hauling each day, we are constantly hungry. Our days revolve around food: the motivation to wake is breakfast, we haul between nut breaks purely to reach them, and come mid afternoon, we start daydreaming about clambering inside the tent to rest our aching joints and muscles, wrap our frozen hands around a warm drink, and eat dinner. A fish or twenty certainly would not go astray.

Rather than having to wait around for ice in a saucepan to melt, these days we can simply scoop water from wells trampled in the snow, and so our breakfast porridge was ready in record time this morning, and we set off bright and early.

Although only one sun hung innocently above us in the sky, I have a sneaking suspicion that there might have been six or seven of them out blazing while we slept, because overnight it seems the whole world has melted into one giant Slushie. By the time we started hauling, the temperature dropped and lingered around minus 2 degrees—just enough to weakly clad the ocean of slurry with a deceptively thin layer of ice—and progress was torturously slow.

We teamed up and double-hauled for as long as we could, but whoever was playing lead dog couldn't help but collapse the snow crust on his way through, leaving dog #2 sloshing around helplessly in his swampy wake. So although it was infinitely harder, we were forced to separate into two individual PACs and fight it out ourselves. Virtually every step we took simply chewed away another chunk of would-be ground in front of us, dropping it into the ice bath now overflowing inside our boots, while behind us the PAC wheels hunkered ever deeper into their parallel blue-water troughs. Once bogged like this, it was impossible to free the PAC on our own, and it seemed we were perpetually walking over to help un-bog each other, only to walk back, haul twenty paces and have to call out ourselves. 'Now me! Sorry, guv!'

The only chance to cross these particularly slushy, lighter blue regions seems to be speed. We try to scurry across, treading as lightly as possible with our snowshoes, passing some of our weight forward through our outstretched hiking poles in our mad dash—but inevitably, we usually only get about halfway before we feel the ground turn elastic underneath us, sag and then utterly collapse. 'NOOOooo! Dammit!' Desperately trying to clamber out before losing momentum, our wildly splashing duck feet kick water right up our backs, where of course it freezes solid while we wait, beaten, for help to arrive.

Still, such is life, and we are now finally back in the tent, utterly exhausted but warm, and about to enjoy a lovely freeze-dried dinner of Honey Soy Chicken, prefixed by an appetiser of hot chocolate, and followed by a dessert of couscous and a vanilla protein drink. Clasping my hot mug, all I can hear is the flapping of our tent, and the faint hum of the wind vibrating our polar bear tripwire alarm.

## DAY 14: Two weeks in

We woke to the unmistakable scream of our bear alarm. Yelling at each other between our tents we panicked to unzip our sleeping bags and poke our heads out either end to check if there was a huge white bear lumbering towards us or not. There wasn't. Clark caught a glance of a seagull just as it disentangled itself from the tripwire and flew away. It took a long time for the adrenalin to settle enough to sleep, but no sooner had we drifted off when the alarm went off again; this time the tripod support had fallen over because the snow it was standing on had simply melted away.

Morning came all too soon and we set off, already drained from yesterday's over-exertion. As we splashed wearily around in 30-centimetre-deep water for over an hour, straining feebly left and right, and then trying left again, we felt our strength ebbing away. After a few uncontrolled verbal outbursts brought on by stabbing pains in our knees, we finally staggered into an upright position, regained composure and turned to look at each other. It was pointless and we knew it—the race against time had been lost.

'Where's the closest shore?' I asked, peering ahead, but knowing full well the answer lay behind me. Dejectedly, we separated our PACs, bullied them with an effort to turn 180 degrees, and—with our tails between our legs—took it in turns smearing them one at a time all the way back along their wheel ruts to our campsite, and then onwards to the shore behind that. Gazing out over the lake as we sat licking our psychological wounds, we could see it was now interspersed with patches of blue-grey meltwater lurking beneath the surface. It seems our days of hauling across frozen lakes are over.

Our problems, however, were far from over. The ground upon which we stood was itself a sloppy concoction of ponds, mossy tussocks and trenches. After less than two minutes of attempting to haul over this new variety of soggy hell, we again found ourselves un-harnessed and looking at each other, scowling vehemently at the impossibility of it all. 'Maybe double-hauling will work here too?' I suggested. 'Let's link them up.'

To our delight, we found that joined again as one enormous slug, the vehicle straddles the ups and downs with surprising ease, and the slight elasticity in our harness rope is just enough to smooth the lurching into one continual, sustainable motion. And—music to our battered ears—rather than the grating scrunching of ice, walking over this new marshy terrain is blissfully silent.

Over a very late lunch we reassessed our route to Hadley Bay to now avoid lakes at all costs. By the time we got under way it was almost dinner time, but we managed a cracking pace and squeezed out a total of 3.81 kilometres today, mostly during the final hour. It might not sound far, but after languishing a mere 100 metres from camp for most of the day, we are elated. Having cracked the secret to hauling over this ground, we'll attack the kilometres ahead with renewed vigour tomorrow morning.

## DAY 15: Our first river crossing

Last night was a scorcher! By the time we'd finished dinner and sent the website update, the baking sun had heated our tents into saunas. I opened my tent vestibule to try and tempt in a refreshing breeze, but the world outside was oppressively still and silent. Ridiculously for two people who only hours ago had to smash great hunks of ice from their shoes before then having to literally prise their frozen shoelaces apart using Leatherman pliers, we now sweltered on top of our sleeping bags, unable to sleep. Stripped down to our Skins half-tights, we just lay there while the orange walls of our tent irradiated us from above. Deliriously, I imagined sitting at a beachside café in Sydney, sipping a refreshing iced coffee—and then, on the spur of the moment, decided to make one.

'Iced coffee, guv?' We simply mixed up some water, instant coffee, milk powder and sugar, and lazily reached down to the ground and scooped up two mugfuls of perfectly granulated icy snow and poured the flavouring over the top. It was *perfect*. Crisis averted, we both fell asleep just as a slight breeze stole inside at last.

We awoke this morning full of energy to throw ourselves into our harnesses and make the most of the day. We got under way fast, and hauling dog-team style we managed a sustained, strong march: one foot in front of the other, for 30-minute intervals. We'd then take a swig of water, pop a piece of chocolate in our mouth, and get right back into it. Two weeks in, we're feeling stronger and fitter now—my lungs feel like they have expanded to twice their old size, and my resting heart rate has dropped from around 55 to 39 beats per minute. For once, visibility was great today, allowing us to pick a point on the horizon, press 'play' on our amazingly engrossing Harry Potter audiobooks on our iPods, and completely tune out. The half-hour intervals slipped past without us even noticing them, and despite some modest hills and sections where we sank beyond our knees into slushy snow, we plodded ever onwards.

Our march across the tundra ended abruptly after lunch when the first flowing stream we've seen cut across our path. It was quite exciting, and evidently all the local birdlife thought so too: the whole area was crowded with geese and other birds, all admiring the chasm it had melted through the snow. It took us over an hour to individually struggle each PAC across and wade them up the deep snow embankment on the far side, but we managed eventually. As the GPS ticked over the 11-kilometre mark (a new record) we wearily climbed inside our portable un-motorhome and went to sleep, parked—for the first time—on soft, mossy, melted tundra.

## DAY 16: Brunch at High Arctic Lodge

Progress was rather slow this morning through some deep patches of snow between sections of wet tundra. Without warning sometimes we'd plunge up to our thighs in snow, and, unable to climb out without sinking back down, progress then became akin to climbing an endless flight of steep stairs, towing a small car behind us.

Recharged by nut breaks, each hauling session typically starts with us taking our respective positions in our dog-team harness, me calling 'Ready?' from the front, and after receiving Clark's 'Yep, ready!' confirmation, we then fling ourselves forwards with a hearty ox-like lunge—necessary to overcome the cart's tremendous inertia—and grind our way forwards. Usually this technique works well, except on two amusing occasions today, when Clark forgot to actually clip his harness into the rope trace. The result was much like that game of trust we've all played as kids where you let yourself gradually fall backwards trusting implicitly that your mate will catch you, except that there is nothing gradual about the way we lean forward into our harness, and I didn't so much 'catch' Clark, as feel him crumple headlong into my back. Hilarious. We both almost died laughing, but mostly because we were remembering an even more stupendous scene that occurred yesterday. We were bogged in a particularly soft section of snow, and having kicked solid foot pockets to brace our feet against, we were both giving it absolutely everything we had, grunting with the superhuman effort of trying to straighten our legs while straining almost horizontally in our harness when suddenly POW! POW! Both cords to my harness snapped in quick succession, and I quite literally launched myself spectacularly across the snow for perhaps 8 metres, arms churning windmill-style in the air as I desperately fought all the way along my runway to regain my balance and not face-plant into the sloppy snow.

Over a hill today we caught sight of a cabin—Fred Hamilton's 'High Arctic Lodge'—a summer fishing retreat that he flies keen anglers out to by seaplane. As the lakes are still frozen and the hut is partly embedded in a bank of snow, Fred's first customers won't be around for another month, but he'd kindly emailed us to say if we needed anything, to help ourselves.

Toiling slowly towards the little red shack, my mind was working overtime, inwardly debating whether or not we should allow ourselves to accept Fred's offer and gorge ourselves on his supplies. We are both gnawingly hungry, but the big challenge of this expedition is to do it unsupported. If we caved in and ate his food, we might just as well pay for air drops every second week and do away with the PACs, making the whole trip quite easy. 'I must stay strong!' I kept telling myself, 'I must stay strong!'

The hut took forever to get any closer but at last we were standing in front of the door, which was nailed closed with a protective fabric cover to keep snow from being driven inside during the long, dark winter. The 'key' was nothing short of a hammer, which was of course wedged under the doormat. Perfect. We creaked out the nails, pulled open the door, and walked inside.

As our eyes adjusted to the dark, we saw we were surrounded by everything you could ever want if you were living out here for a few weeks, cooking fish, and sleeping in warm comfort. Although only tiny, this little cabin in the middle of absolutely nowhere would be a lovely spot to enjoy in the summer. Gazing longingly at all the jars of honey, packets of jam, sugar and even sweets teasing us from every shelf, I found my stomach starting to grumble hungrily, and I caught a look from Clark that showed he too was teetering on the brink of temptation. 'Let's have lunch!' he announced, and in response to my half-surprised, half-excited expression, hastened to clarify. 'Our *normal* lunch, I mean, let's eat it early, now, to stop us eating any of this!' Laughing at what I'd thought he was suggesting, we hurried back to our PACs and returned with the usual ration of peanut butter and butter on tortilla flatbreads, and our thermos of coffee. We sat and ate inside Fred's hut out of the wind, trying not to stare at all the wondrous flavours of food stacked around us, and, after taking a few quick photos, nailed the door back how it was and shackled up to our PACs. 'I could so easily have eaten everything in there,' Clark admitted as we toiled away, 'I'm kinda proud we didn't, though.'

We are camped only a stone's throw away from Hadley Bay tonight, and if we're lucky, we might get there the day after tomorrow, which will be a fantastic milestone! Fingers crossed. After Hadley Bay though, we're still not sure quite what to do. I think we've halted the wheel rims chafing the tyres, but the Kevlar covers are really starting to fail on us. Paddling across lakes or floating down rivers might soon be the only thing we can do without puncturing our tyres, so instead of our planned north-westerly route, we're considering heading directly west after Hadley, in a desperate (and rather unlikely) bid to reach the headwaters of the Kuujjua river some 100-plus kilometres away. Rafting down this would help carry us a good deal westward (although southerly as well, but that's fine).

The thing is, we are not sure what the river will be like at all. Is it dangerous? What if there are major rapids, waterfalls, or even canyons with deathtraps lurking at their ends? We don't even know if there'll still be any meltwater left flowing in it either, when and if we reach it—and we both admit that's a rather unlikely 'if'.

Still, those are problems for the future. Victoria Island has certainly taught us to live in the present, as who knows what might happen tomorrow.

## DAY 17: Wet socks and repairs

We awoke to a beautifully quiet morning—not even a breath of wind to rustle the tent. With all the snow around now completely sloppy, there's no noticeable 'crisping-up' effect during the colder nights at all, and so we've begun deliberately shifting the Chris & Clark Time Zone forward an hour or so each morning for the past few days. This is easily achieved, as all we have to do is ignore our alarms and sleep in for a while, which we seem to be doing of our own accord anyway. The only down side is of course that we have to haul for an extra hour or so into the evenings. We're now waking at 10.30 pm and quitting around 10 am Cambridge Bay time. Pretty soon we'll be merrily hauling during genuine 'daytime'—we can't wait!

After our usual delicious brekky of oats and coffee, we packed up and got stuck into some preventative maintenance on both our PACs—beefing up the front spacers which have started to fatigue and split, likely from the excessive loads of double-hauling. The repair consisted of drilling sixteen holes with an awkward hand-drill (that itself first needed fixing), then pop-riveting on two pieces of angle (which we first had to make from cutting and banging a flat strip of aluminium), and undoing and re-doing various awkward-to-reach bolts. The whole operation took much longer than anticipated, and it was almost lunchtime before we finished the repair on my PAC. Frustrated, worn out and irritable, it didn't take much to convince each other that it really was best not to fix the other PAC today, but instead wait to see how this repair goes.

The highlight of our short day's hauling was crossing a fairly major creek flanked again by deep snow. Rolling down into the semi-frozen waterway was the easy bit, but getting our PACs up the other side developed into an epic tug-o'-war between us on the far bank hanging onto a long rope, and the conjoined PAC sitting stubbornly midstream with hunks of drifting ice starting to build up against its side. As we strained and slipped all over the place in the snow, a stalemate was reached and as I angrily sloshed back down to the PAC and started to push it from behind, I felt icy water rush down inside my boots. An outburst of rage surged within me, but as I knew Clark's boots were already swimming, I managed to bottle it up inside.

Meanwhile, Clark slipped for the umpteenth time in the soupy snow, twisting his already painful and swollen foot as he tried to haul the PAC up. 'F#%K OFF SNOW! We have no use for you anymore!' Clark shouted, adding with a chuckle, 'Bring on global warming, I say!' Right now, this snow is a nightmare, and just makes our days hell. We can't wait for the sun to melt it all away.

Sitting on our respective verandahs this evening (the section of our hardtops that extends out in front of our tents)—having come a pathetic 4.1 kilometres—we both gratefully pulled off our hiking boots with a sucking, slurping noise, and wrung bucketloads of repulsive grey water from our two layers of Icebreaker socks. We must *really* stink by now, but thankfully as we both do, neither of us can smell it.

Despite the world turning slushy, it's a pretty special time of year to be here. All around us as the snow melts revealing the tundra beneath, everything is suddenly bursting into life. Plants are vigorously growing and flowering and attracting huge Vs of geese and other birds streaming up here to mate and nest, which in turn has brought out the foxes and so on. The warmth seeping into the ground has lured the lemmings out of hibernation, and suddenly they too are everywhere, darting from hidden burrow to hidden burrow, or peeping up to goggle at us as we haul past. Tiny black spiders—no more than 3 millimetres across—clamber over individual snow crystals, and hundreds of insects are starting to whirl noisily in the sky. Huge bumblebees and flies zip hurriedly around as feathers and seeds waft past on the gentle breeze. The air is thick with scent and bird calls. We feel pretty lucky to be out here surrounded by all this. We're just a little apprehensive about how long we have left before the infamous hordes of mosquitoes will arrive. It can't be long.

## DAY 18: Beneath the snow

We woke to find little streams of meltwater snaking right underneath our PACs, and with the temperature languishing around 0 degrees as we set off, we squelched our way through an increasing number of the same quicksand mud pits that traumatised us so deeply in 2005.

The most exciting part of the day was when we met the river that eventually empties into Hadley Bay. Flowing in quite a canyon here, it was a sight to behold—free-flowing water rippled across the bottom of the ravine, reflecting greens, blues, browns and yellows up against the snow-clad cliff face on either side. Pairs of geese loyally followed each other around, and looking up for the source of a shrill, screeching cry, we met the watchful gaze of a hawk suspended motionless above us.

'I wish that thing would shut up,' Clark frowned as it unleashed another piercing cry. 'It's just alerted our presence to every polar bear for miles around!' Hadley Bay is apparently an important breeding area for polar bears, and the closer we get, the more likely we are to encounter one. Already many of the rocks around us are starting to look suspiciously like bears.

The squelchy moss-terrain is starting to give way to crumpled rock the closer we get to the coast and, unable to cross the river there, we soon found ourselves traversing fields of Death Terrain as bad as any we've seen.

'Watch out—go left! Left! Left! STOP!!!' We both looked back in horror as a particularly vicious 30-centimetre shard of rock passed directly under the front tyre, tilting the entire PAC as it rolled onto it and came to rest suspended on the point, pushing into the tyre like a pen thrust into a balloon.

'Get it off!' we shouted at each other, as I ran back to help take some weight while Clark hauled forwards. That was close. Now with the rock trapped between the front and rear tyre, we had to separate the two PACs. 'Going solo's the only way we can steer around the worst ones anyway,' I said, shackling up.

Hauling gingerly over this sea of knives, it wasn't long before we were peering desperately around for the sanctuary of the nice soft slushy melting snow that we have spent all week wishing would go away. There was no escape. Pausing to assess the damage over a nut break, I found one of my wheel covers even had a tear right through the inside layer of Kevlar, exposing the bare rubber of the inner tube underneath! How it didn't puncture the tyre I have no idea. We deflated the tyre enough to slip in a small piece of spare Kevlar cloth to cover the wound, reinflated the tyre and cringed our way onwards.

There was some comic relief at the end of the day, however. When we checked our email, there was one from my dad—sent yesterday, just after the frustrating river crossing. Apparently, he'd 'noticed' via the satellite tracking that we'd spent a good 30 minutes midstream, and had started to become worried, until he saw us move across to the far bank, where he 'noticed' another delay, at which point it all made sense to him—the first delay was probably us catching a fish, and the second delay was us eating it! Not only was this beautiful idea so far removed from the traumatic reality that we couldn't help crying with laughter, but it was amazing to think that he'd literally been watching us. It's as though our website updates—complete with daily photos, temperature information, and a live tracking feed—have literally turned this remote Arctic expedition into a spectator sport.

## DAY 19: The last little bit to Hadley Bay

Today's 'last little bit to Hadley' wasn't anything like as easy as we'd anticipated—it took all day, and it was only the promise of our favourite dehydrated dinner that we've been saving that got us here.

The day started, as usual, one hour later than yesterday and we headed north, beside the river and watching for an opportunity to cross it. Eventually we found a stretch where the vertical canyon walls flared out a little into merely steep snowy slopes topped by a fortress of boulders, and where the width of the river narrowed to perhaps 15 metres. We lowered each PAC individually down the precarious slope into the river valley and waded into the freezing water as hunks of ice bobbed past. It turned out the river was rushing over a slippery ice bottom, and, while we struggled to gain any purchase with our wetsuit booties, midstream the PACs actually floated, almost sweeping us away.

During a nut break on the far side we wandered over to investigate the first stone tent ring we've found this trip. Smothered in millennia-old orange lichen, these boulders formed one of the most rectangular perimeters for ancient skin tents we've seen yet.

The second river crossing today was even less predictable, pretending to be far narrower and shallower than it really was, and we both ended up flooding our boots, which had only just started to dry out from our last river catastrophe two days ago. Adding to the ambience, snow started to fall in force, and visibility closed in. The terrain on the west side of the river was completely different—much flatter—a sea of dirt and pebbles across which thousands of pretty purple flowers grew, each only 5 millimetres across, hugging close to the tundra. We've started to see animals again too, herds of muskox dot our view forward, and one pair of evidently feisty, testosterone-charged bulls actually engaged in a battle for supremacy right in front of us. Facing each other and then thunderously charging headlong, they'd simultaneously lower their enormous horn-clamped skulls at the last moment, just before slamming together with a sickening jolt that stopped both mighty beasts dead in their tracks. With the echoing thunderclap of their collision still reverberating around us, they'd repeat the ritual, doubtless losing countless brain cells each time, until one seemed to lose interest—or perhaps couldn't remember what he was doing anymore—and wandered off.

Despite this northern coast of Victoria Island being permanently locked in by sea ice, it was fascinating to see lumps of gnarled, weatherbeaten knots of wood and other flotsam that must have ridden the frozen Arctic Ocean perhaps for years. Without any trees on Victoria Island, they certainly couldn't have come from anywhere around here. Disappointingly, amongst this natural flotsam we also hauled past the odd bit of pollution: cigarette lighters, bits of plastic and so on. It's quite upsetting to see rubbish way up here near the ends of the earth, and so we've been picking up the lighter pieces as we toil past. I guess that people who dump rubbish at sea must think it will just get swallowed up by the vastness of the deep. Clearly, it doesn't.

We couldn't stay annoyed for long, however, as—cresting the last little rise—we found ourselves overlooking a spectacularly crumpled expanse of blue sea ice: Hadley Bay!

We made it! We've just set up camp on the south-western corner of the bay, and the campsite is perfect. Perfect weather, perfect terrain, perfect view and perfect food—Mexican Chicken tonight! We are genuinely thrilled (and even a little surprised) to be here at last—the biggest milestone of our trip yet—a point you can spot on any map of the world.

## DAY 20: Back to sleep?

Just as we went to bed last night, the gorgeous summery weather did a total backflip. The wind blew up from nowhere, grabbing the tent and shaking it like a terrier, while dark clouds swept in, unleashing an odd mixture of rain, snow, sleet and hail that pummelled and splattered loudly against the shuddering sides of the tent. Inside, we tried to get some sleep despite the din, but it was impossible. Tossing and turning, I fought hard with the desire to use ear plugs, but terrified I wouldn't hear the bear alarm go off, I resisted. At last, after several frustrating hours, we both managed to pass out.

Morning, when it arrived, was even less pleasant. It was as if

God was dipping his fingers into a giant Slushie, then flicking his hand at us, flinging teaspoon-sized splats of icy slurry down upon us. The walls of my tent bowed in oppressively against me from the force of the wind, and water had somehow wicked through too, almost pooling around my sleeping bag.

As Clark cooked up the usual hearty breakfast, strangely neither of us mentioned anything about setting off. We both avoided the subject entirely, and returned to our respective tents to eat brekky, sip coffee, listen to our iPods and generally pretend we were somewhere else. Time ticked on, the weather continued to pour hate down upon us, and eventually I poked my head through to Clark's tent and ventured, 'So, I guess it must be about nut break time, then?' We enjoyed it from the comfort of our sleeping bags, followed soon after by delving into our chocolate ration for the day. The weather gradually started to ease, and for a few brief blissful hours, we did actually relax. It was heaven. We still can't believe we made it this far.

After lunch we did a session of serious route planning for the weeks ahead, up onto the plateau towards the Kuujjua River, and when we could stand the guilt no longer, we packed up camp. Clark downed a few painkillers and anti-inflammatories for his foot, which has been causing him some grief these last few days after spraining it, and we set off in high spirits, hauling around a corner and directly into the most vicious region of Death Terrain we've ever seen.

It was similar to the 'original style' expanse of jagged ice-shattered limestone, but here, *every single piece* was razor sharp and protruded lethally upwards 30 centimetres or more. There was no other way but forward, and so with our hearts in our mouths we crunched our way along, trying hopelessly to guide our unsteerable four-wheeled beast around the worst of the daggers, flinching at all the terrible cracking, popping, grinding, splintering and snapping noises as the tyres rolled over it all. Without exaggerating, every instant we expected to hear the dreaded 'PSSSSsssssssss' of our first ever puncture.

But somehow—amazingly—we got through it. We did sustain several more major tears in both layers of Kevlar—through which the inner tubes have started to bulge—but to our complete bewilderment, no punctures.

After the Death Terrain subsided into a gravelly swamp, we could at last breathe easier and admire the magnificent scenery as we hauled alongside the frozen ocean. Patches of turquoise-blue meltwater wound their way around the jumble of pure white pack ice and the occasional larger berg—the hearts of which glowed a brilliant electric blue. It's perfect polar bear environment and we watched every chunk of ice nervously as we passed, half expecting it to spring to life. It's rather scary, actually, constantly being aware that we could be being hunted—stalked by the world's largest land carnivore—every time we turn our backs.

We racked up 3.85 kilometres as the PAC rolls this afternoon (3.6 by GPS), before we suddenly ran out of steam. Not bad, really, for half a day. About 600 metres away, the mouth of a large river is spilling deeply out into the pack ice—but we'll deal with crossing that in the clarity of morning. For now, though, we're enjoying chowing down on a tasty packet of Chicken Tikka Masala, while peeping out at the view over Hadley Bay, watching a big black seal lazing on the ice, watching us.

## DAY 21: Grumble

Today was an absolute nightmare. It started out serenely enough, hauling towards the large river we stopped just short of yesterday, and luck, it seemed, was on our side. Drawing closer, we realised that instead of having to haul kilometres upstream to look for somewhere vaguely crossable, we could perhaps just cross the sea ice in front of us. Empowered by this novel idea, we each donned drysuit and life jacket, slung a shotgun over our shoulder, wedged a bear-banger pen flare in our pocket and took our first tentative steps onto the ice.

We walked out further, our confidence rising. 'This is totally do-able!' I shouted. 'And it'll make for great photos too!' It looked spectacular, winding in and around brilliant blue puddles, past towering jumbles of ice with seals slipping silently into the water around us as we passed. We hobbled back, unlinked our PACs, pointed them in the right direction, joined them together again, and hauled boldly out onto the ice, our eyes flicking nervously left and right, searching for polar bears.

Right on cue, the sun came out, the wind ceased, and the pools of water formed perfect mirrors. We paused long enough for a few spectacular photos and video grabs, and then hauled onwards to the far side of the bay. It was magic. We saved ourselves several kilometres—perhaps even three or four—and enjoyed every minute of it.

Unfortunately, that was where our luck ran out.

Having clambered ashore, another stroke of personal genius suggested we could cut a further 5 kilometres off our route by attempting to cut *over* the mountain in front of us, rather than haul all the way around following the shore. Feeling pretty gung ho from our last success, we nodded in agreement. 'Yep. Let's do it!'

Trying to haul up the side of that hill nearly killed us. With the enormous weight of the double PAC constantly threatening to roll back down the mountain and drag us unceremoniously to our deaths, we doggedly fought our way upwards for two unrelenting kilometres. Slipping over awkwardly on ice, we were constantly forced onto our hands and knees for grip, sloshing through snow, squelching boot-deep in mud, and splashing and thrashing through small ponds. Every time we paused to quell the urge to vomit, we could feel the PAC shifting and starting to slip, so we'd desperately struggle onwards.

Our hard, positive veneer of optimism was wearing rather thin after a few particularly nasty slip-ups, when suddenly—about halfway up—we came upon what was clearly the birthplace of all Death Terrain. A wall of mangled rock rose out of the earth, all pre-shattered it seemed; stacked up and then just spilling out into such a malicious field of death that it seemed hard to attribute such precisely fashioned hatred to mere chance. We gaped at it. The rest of the hill—the remaining two kilometres—was apparently composed of this stuff. It wasn't even remotely possible. We turned to each side: more Death Terrain. As one, we slowly looked back down the hill, down our smeared wheel trails all the way to the pack ice below, and bit our tongues in an effort to remain calm.

We bitterly lowered the PAC halfway down, and then—spying a string of muddy swamps amidst the Death Terrain to the left— decided to try and follow them around the mountain instead. At least the mud offered respite for our wheels, though not for our rising frustration. We linked these mud pits like a dot-to-dot, trying to avoid the worst of the Death Terrain in between, but there was too much of it. Joggling over it, I was continually pausing to try and kick down, break off, or dig out particularly savage lances before the PAC inevitably reached them, but more often than not this was only a token gesture, as there were lances everywhere.

It's not that stumbling over rickety Death Terrain bothers us in itself, or that our boots overflowing with water, grit and ice affects us so badly, or that having pungent mud over everything including our nut breaks is intolerable—even the aches, pains and cuts all over us are manageable—but there is one thing we can't ignore. The fact is, we're scared our Kevlar wheel covers simply can't last much longer. Any more Death Terrain like this is certain suicide for them, which, so early in the expedition, will spell disaster. The tears are already snagging on the jagged rocks and spreading by the hour. Crushingly, we have been lured well beyond where our mud dot-to-dot ended, and to our dismay, there is now Death Terrain not only in front and behind us, but above and below us too. We are marooned in a world of sloppy mud, rimmed by horrific Death Terrain we dare not cross, with no real way out. We can now see the black inner tubes bulging through recently slashed tears on several sections of our wheel covers, and the rubber looks terribly scratched and abraded.

On a brighter note, it just started pouring with rain, so at least our socks that we hung out to dry on the tent ropes outside will be getting … a wash? We're really scraping the bottom of the barrel of optimism out here now, and feeling pretty low. I'm sure after a good night's sleep things will seem brighter, though, providing the stove doesn't burn down both tents while we cook dinner. Really, it wouldn't surprise me.

## DAY 22: Shredded Kevlar and battered spirits

Today was just one of those days. Having burnt almost all our anger and frustration yesterday, we spilt the rest today within the first hour of hauling. From that moment on, we merely toiled onwards, slowly, methodically, mechanically—broken men—accepting each punishment as it was dealt out to us, and then slowly standing up and falling silently back into the line of the harness. We were beyond caring, our boots overflowing, our gloves saturated and icy water wicking right up our sleeves into, it seemed, our spirits.

Even the soggy snow now hides Death Terrain underneath—nowhere is safe. Stopping eventually for a nut break and to lick our wounds, we reassessed the rapidly deteriorating wheel covers. There were a total of four major tears now, right through both layers, and plenty of other slashes gaped openly through the first layer, some up to 30 centimetres wide. Standing in deep slush, we deflated each wheel in turn, slid in our ever diminishing reserves of spare Kevlar fabric, and pumped them back up. Just as we morosely headed off, the front spacer bar of the PAC—the thing we repaired only a few days ago—snapped again, this time completely in half. We cursed at it, but being in no place to attempt a repair, stumbled onwards into what looked innocently like a snow-clad field. It wasn't.

Here's a fairly accurate analogy: picture a large ice hockey rink with several fire-hoses sluicing water across it, then randomly scatter it with suitcase-sized ice boulders, and fill the whole rink with just enough frosty slush to cover it. After dusting the surface with powder snow to hide everything, strap some garbage bin lids to your feet to simulate snowshoes, tie yourself via a long rope to a small beach buggy car, and then try to drag it around and around the ice rink, for hours. That's how it was today, except that it was also raining and foggy, so we couldn't even see where we were going, or if this hell was going to end. Constantly slipping and falling awkwardly into pools of water, the PAC would often strike against unseen boulders, absorbing our hauling energy for a while and then springing backwards, yanking our waist straps so violently that we practically jack-knifed down into the slush. Progress was a series of five small lollipop steps forwards, followed by perhaps two steps sliding backwards, if we were lucky enough to remain upright. To add insult to injury, this entire time we were hauling beside solid, dry ground, but, being Death Terrain, we dared not use it.

Despite the miserable conditions today, we did have one comforting thought. Traipsing through the endless ice rink, I suddenly stopped and turned to Clark. 'Imagine if this was 2005, and we had to pitch our *tent* down somewhere on this.' We instantly felt better.

Although the PAC-o-meter (the modified bike computer) shows we hauled a whopping 6.74 kilometres today, the harsh reality of the

GPS revealed that most of that distance must have been zigzagging around, because in a straight line we've only come a depressing 3.79 kilometres. Looking to the future, though, tomorrow is my 25th birthday! As far as I can recall, birthdays are always happy, fun, warm days, filled with presents, laughter, copious amounts of good food and general all-round merriment. So I am very much looking forward to all this tomorrow.

## DAY 23–24: My 25th birthday!

After the trauma of yesterday, fate had one last nail to drive into us just before bed. Doing our usual email check, we received one informing us that the chap who was going to pick us up from the far side of the island by boat had actually just been thrown in jail. This leaves us with no end-point pickup, as our backup option—a mining exploration camp (we were going to detour one of their weekly resupply planes)—has unexpectedly decided to shorten their season and will have already gone home by the time we need the pickup. Brilliant. We went to sleep feeling rather downtrodden indeed, and rain lashed the sides of our tent harder than ever.

Then, inexplicably this morning, we awoke to a totally different world. Peeping out of the silent tent, we noticed that the thin clouds in the sky looked almost summery. The wind had completely died down, the rain had vanished, and we could see for miles. There were even some caribou wandering around in patches of *sunlight* on the distant hills! We could not believe it. 'Happy birthday, guv!' Clark beamed. 'I called in a few favours with the weather gods.'

Our spirits skyrocketed. This expedition is such an emotional rollercoaster. 'And guess what?' Clark added, trying hard to bridle his excitement. 'I think …' He paused for a mental calculation. 'Yep, I think we've finally come full-circle with our time-zone shifting. Not only it is actually morning for once and we'll be hauling during the day, but because of all those 25-hour days, we've actually been out here for an extra 24 hours now—so today is not Day 23, it's Day 24!'

My eyes lit up as realisation dawned. 'We've got an extra day's worth of food we haven't eaten!' Clark passed me a double helping of oats—with twice the sugar and butter—and the coffee was twice as creamy and strong. It was the best breakfast either of us can remember in a long, long time, and I literally can't think of a better birthday gift.

After this leisurely brekky, feeling for once almost 'full', we packed up and clipped into our harnesses. Just as we did so, the sun burst through the clouds, flooding our world with the warmth and cheer that yesterday seemed so impossibly far away. We hailed the sun gods, Clark sang 'Happy Birthday', and we headed off, downhill.

Bliss. The kilometre or two of gently sloping downhill was mostly snow-clad, except for where the tops of Death Terrain rocks poked through in an attempt to rain on our parade. We saw them coming and arced left and right around the worst of them, jeering at them until we came to a stop in front of a stream.

We kicked down the snowy banks to form a boat ramp, and pushed the combined PAC into the middle of the stream, forming a bridge neatly across to the other side. We then simply scrambled on, over, and off onto the other side—perfectly dry—and kept hauling. It was perfect. The next stream crossing was rather more formidable but with the final 100-metre approach being steep enough to billycart-ride, we couldn't resist, and ended up careering into the water with a triumphant yell at 10 kilometres per hour (according to the PAC-o-meter). Stranded midstream, we tried to re-enact our success of bridging the first stream, only to find the current far too strong, and our cart simply swung downstream and took off, merrily bobbing along as we frantically hobbled after it. We got it sorted eventually and, despite wet boots, ate our double nut break still brimming with cheer.

After a double lunch, the next river crossing was not exactly a textbook performance either, and we emerged some five minutes after plunging in, wet and wide-eyed, but chuffed to have discovered that our carts actually float really well in deep water, even with us clinging on top like half-drowned rats. The sun was still pouring happiness into our day as we began our final uphill slog. It was stupendously difficult, and we ended up sinking into a sucking slurry of quicksand. The more we struggled, the further in we sank. We unclipped and tried to walk away, but we could barely even extract ourselves from the shin-deep mud—I almost lost my boots in the process. Somehow we managed to separate the carts, and—groaning with the effort—got one PAC to start rolling. Adrenalin kicked in and we went for it, giving it everything we had to keep up momentum. By the time we got it to the top, we were shaking, dizzy, and our breaths were coming in ragged pants. 'All right,' I gasped, turning back down the hill, 'now the other one ...'

And at last here we are, camped with commanding views of the surrounding landscape, and the sun is still shining! Being the Summer Solstice—the 'longest day' in the Northern Hemisphere (all that means here is that the sun reaches its highest point in the sky, and will continue its 24-hour spiral back lower and lower from now on)—we can actually feel its warmth. This sure beats having my birthday in Australia, where it's the Winter Solstice—the shortest day of the year! We just enjoyed the dehydrated meal of my choice: you guessed it—Mexican Chicken. It was the most appreciated birthday dinner ever eaten.

Munching away, we gazed at our wheels. 'They look a bit like Frankenstein's monster,' Clark mused. It's true, like a badly bandaged ogre, the slashes are now so broad that some have pretty much split from side to side, others gape lengthwise. Great A4-sheet-sized flaps of Kevlar are hanging off, and unsightly tumour-like bulges of inner tube are starting to push through. But that's the way it goes out here, and nothing—not even this—could dent our perfect day.

## DAY 25: Transformers!

Our goal is currently just to try and reach the Kuujjua River. While it still feels unlikely, if we *can* get there, we might then be able to raft down it for about 100 kilometres, which would then leave about 250 kilometres to the far side of the island. The way things are going, though, the only way this will be even remotely possible is for us to somehow coax our wheels to survive at least until we reach the river—because rafting requires our inner tube tyres to be full of air. After the river, who knows? We can't realistically see our tyre covers lasting even *to* the river. Afterwards, perhaps we can try to travel Indian style, simply carrying what we can for the last epic stretch? Maybe we could relay piles of gear in stages, slinging as many bags as we can lift between us, hanging them underneath two long sticks (probably our two axles) which we could tie to our harnesses, linking us like a train? As we eat through our food, perhaps towards the end we'll be able to carry all our gear in one go each day. If we are more than lucky, perhaps we might after all stumble to the far side of the island in 75 days' time, with nothing more than what we can carry on our backs. The wheels will be long gone.

For now, though, it all critically hinges on us getting to the Kuujjua with our tyres. The two biggest killers of our Kevlar are Death Terrain, and the huge weight on the tyres. To combat the Death Terrain we will pick our route extra carefully using Google Earth images, and have promised ourselves that we won't hesitate to go well out of our way to haul right around whole regions if needs be. When we do have to cross it, we'll unload most of the weight from the cart and carry that across by hand. Now, the other factor is the enormous weight we are carrying—if there was any way we could shed some kilos we'd get there faster, doing less damage to the tyres at the same time. So we did something radical this morning: we transformed our epic 8-metre double PAC into a single super buggy—a little four-wheeled nugget—a robust, double-hauling machine, with crappy wheels.

With a single hacksaw blade we amputated the front 2 metres from both PACs. We also set aside one tent, our ice hatchet, spare axle, half of our carbon fibre hardtop which we cut off, and various other items that we have decided we can survive without. This likely adds up to between 25 and 30 kilograms of weight saved. We have bundled it up into a tidy package, and placed it on top of our cart for now, but tomorrow, we'll leave it beside a large lake on the way, where we can get it collected by seaplane in the future.

This transformation was a rather big and committing decision, and although we're now both horribly cramped together inside what is basically a one-man tent along with all our electronics, we do at least have the 'comfort' of knowing that we really are doing everything we possibly can to maximise our chances. We spent all day transforming our PACs into 'The Nugget', and patching the Kevlar covers as best we can. Tomorrow, we're going to 'give it horns' and aim to reach the Kuujjua by Clark's birthday in exactly two weeks' time—Day 39. Any later than that and the river (which is mostly fed by snow melt) will likely start to run dry. It's always such a race out here—but we love a challenge. It's ON!

# DAY 26: Onwards!

We set off, onwards and upwards, starting the climb towards the plateau that forms the western half of the island, towing our newly modified and truncated PAC, 'The Nugget', with a sense of optimism. Despite still carrying the package of excess weight to deposit beside the lake, the new hauling setup and PAC layout felt really good. Traipsing through an endless sea of mud that would have stopped us dead in our tracks with PAC-1 in 2005, we're finding ourselves able to force a tedious but sustainable march. It's so muddy that our huge wheels are actually pushing small bow waves of muck in front, making hauling a real effort. Three kilometres later we finally made it to the lake, and very happily offloaded the package. We took the GPS position, had a nut break and marched onwards—feeling physically and psychologically much lighter.

We had to pause multiple times today to perform emergency care on our Kevlar covers, which are quite a sight to behold these days. The longitudinal tears around the tyres are spreading like the plague—linking up with others—and the pressure underneath is bloating the inner tubes to form huge bulges that make 'rolling' quite laughable.

It was looking like the whole thing was about to fall apart, when I suddenly had an idea. Tightening a loop of spare webbing around the Kevlar cover—from one side, over the top wearing surface, and back underneath against the rubber—really helps hold it all together. It's worked a treat, and we've put six of these bandages on now. Not only do they stop the Kevlar tears from gaping open and exposing the rubber, but they also hold in the tumour-like bulges, preventing the covers from splitting any further. We're very happy with this expedient, and so long as we don't run out of spare string and webbing, we can hold the tyres together for a while longer … we hope.

Having pondered long and hard about the root of all our Kevlar troubles, I've finally come up with a theory as to why they split so early. I think perhaps one of the only things that can easily abrade Kevlar is … Kevlar! Those single-layer prototype covers worked a treat, and so we mistakenly assumed that doubling up and making the 'real' ones from two layers would make them twice as strong. Wrong! It looks like each crease or rumple on the inner layer has created a little raised strip that has rubbed against the outer layer, wearing away upon itself until it quickly split open. How ironic. We live and learn. Every day out here we're learning, mostly about how to deal with problems—physically as well as psychologically!

The weather was beautiful today and it honestly felt like summer with the temperature soaring to a record 16 degrees Celsius. Beneath bright blue skies, we even put sun cream on, got out our Dirty Dog sunnies and rolled up our sleeves. I'd forgotten just how good warmth feels—luxurious, dry, glowing warmth. It feels so different from the sweaty heat brought on by exhausting exercise.

Towards the end of the day, we both abruptly ran out of energy, staring dejectedly up a slope looming in front of us. It's always great to end our day on a high, literally, and so we had a bite of chocolate and gave it one last slog to the top. We're glad we did—the ground up here isn't even that muddy, and the view is very encouraging: it looks like smooth rolling tundra—for the next stretch, anyway. With all the snow melt going on, it's quite an amazing landscape. Whole hillsides are awash with cascading sheets of water—the surface grass and tundra literally submerged—and in all directions the air is full of the sound of flowing water.

## DAY 27: More of this, please

We didn't see a single bit of Death Terrain all day, and our hopes are rising that we may have seen the last of it for a while—the ground has changed to a rolling expanse of grassy swampland. Sure, it has mud and is largely underwater in places, but it's not bad at all. 'This has to be the best terrain we've hauled over yet!' Clark called out as we set off. It certainly is. A steady march between well-earned nut breaks, and the kilometres just started to tick themselves off.

There's a lot of shattered eggshells lying underwater on the tundra, and every so often tiny little birds—obviously fresh to this world—erupt from the grass and scamper hysterically across in front of us, evidently yet to learn that flying requires both getting airborne as well as flapping your wings frantically, and no amount of running, squeaking and falling over can replace the former. To our immense delight, we racked up 9.3 kilometres (GPS) today, despite three river crossings, weaving around a few lakes, and a few tyre repairs! And, better still, it looks like more of the same tomorrow!

## DAY 28: It's a record!

Today we smashed our daily distance record! We hauled a whopping 12.22 kilometres as the PAC rolls (11.23 by GPS, also a record), pushing well beyond our limits after promising ourselves the reward of a second dinner if the record fell. We are actually so buggered that as we staggered dizzily around setting up camp, we felt a little delusional. Our minds were drifting in and out of focusing on whatever we were doing, and I experienced the rather odd sensation of reaching out for part of the bear alarm we were setting up, only to have my fingers close around empty space. I missed the handle by several centimetres, despite looking right at it.

Tomorrow we'll have to deal with a rather imposing set of mountains looming up ahead, and we're also a bit nervous about a particularly wide river crossing. Still, we'll—um, cross that bridge when we come to it. (Wouldn't that be nice!)

## DAY 29: Tent-bound

Shattered from yesterday's epic effort, the thought of looming mountains and a giant river crossing was all too much for us this morning, and we stayed inside the tent all day. We periodically peeped hopefully out through the vestibule to check if we'd been teleported to another place—somewhere sunny, warm, windless, dry and inviting—but depressingly, we were always greeted by the same horrendous view.

The weather has just been unbelievable. The tent relentlessly tried to thrash itself into ribbons around us, the sides bowed in against us, and bullets of rain pelted seemingly from all sides at once. Trickles of water have also started running down the inside of the tent, simply because the sheer volume of people and gear we have crammed in here is pressing the inner tent skin against the outer, wicking the drops through. Constantly ready to leap out and start hauling the moment the weather improved, as we waited it only got worse: the wind rose to 40 kilometres per hour and the temperature dropped to minus 5 degrees Celsius with windchill. Occasionally we dashed outside to try and break the world record for speed toileting as great curtains of icy rain swept over us, and returning dripping wet—like drowned lemmings—we scurried back into the depths of our damp sleeping bags to try to regain body warmth and composure. While our bodies are loving the chance to revitalise, we're thoroughly sick of being stuck in here. Irrespective of the weather tomorrow, we've decided to face it.

Clark has just pointed out that the wind's swung around 180 degrees, so I guess the weather system is passing through. Tomorrow we'll have been out here for a month. That sounds a lengthy period, until we remember that we could well be out here for anything up to a third of a year.

## DAY 30: Disaster!

The atrocious weather finally relented as morning arrived. We poked our heads outside and marvelled at a patch of blue-ish sky on the horizon gradually drawing nearer, and by the time we'd shackled into our harness, the sun had come out. What a difference the sun makes to a day out here.

We racked up 3 kilometres in no time at all, and arrived at the river. Placing the paddles on the deck we rolled The Nugget down the bank and into the water, pushed out to floating depth and hopped aboard. It was fantastic. We were merrily carried downstream as crystal-clear, convoluted shapes of ice rose and fell around us. Holding a camera aloft lashed to the end of my hiking pole, we got some cool action shots, and then paddled to the far bank. The wheels touched the bottom and we simply leapt out and hauled The Nugget up the far bank. 'Well, that bodes well for the Kuujjua, hey!' I said, grinning. 'What an awesome raft!'

Having climbed steadily for the last few days, we're now surrounded by quite steep hills with the promise of the relatively flat top of the plateau still several days away. It's not so bad, though, as the terrain at the moment is dry compacted dirt, and is a real pleasure to haul over.

With about ten minutes left before lunch, we crested a low ridge and looked down into the next small valley which ended in another perfectly graded slope up into the rest of the plateau. Some white caribou grazed calmly nearby, and a muskox shifted its bulk lazily across to chew a patch of tundra on the hill opposite. We started hauling down into this little valley, and joyously noticed The Nugget starting to roll gradually of its own accord behind us.

'Billycart ride!' Clark shouted, and both beaming with happiness, we hopped on as it trundled down the slope towards the soft, swampy looking bottom. We were filming at the time.

'Woohooo!! I wish the whole island was downhill!' I laughed. 'Oh—oh no! NO!' It was then that disaster struck.

Suddenly, something happened to the back left wheel. The Nugget bounced to a premature, lopsided, grinding halt as we sprang from either side, turning around to see what had happened. As I turned, I suspected that we must have finally run out of luck and got our first puncture, but as my eyes met the devastation in front of us, clearly it was no puncture. The entire wheel was lying over, twisted out almost horizontally. The camera was still rolling and Clark pointed it at me, a look of horror on his face.

'Well,' I began, stalling for time as I tried to think what must have broken, 'it looks like we've struck a rather bad problem ...' Either the axle had broken, or—worse—the wheel hub with the bearings and all had torn itself right out of the centre of the rim. With a sickening feeling of dread, I peered underneath the wreckage, and stared numbly at what I had hoped never to see. The end section of what used to be our axle was now a mangled, torn, twisted mess of aluminium, with the wheel hub bent out almost at right angles.

In the space of about fifteen seconds—as if someone had just pulled a plug—all the warm, enthusiastic, optimistic vibes that had been buoying us along totally drained away, and we stood there in the muddy ground, completely deflated and in shock. 'It feels like we've just been in a car accident,' Clark mused weakly, staring unblinkingly at the wreckage. With absolutely no idea what to do—or even if there was anything we *could* do—we simply collected our lunch things and wandered silently over to a wind-sheltered embankment and huddled together, shaking our heads.

As the enormity of the problem began to sink in, we came up with a few ideas for how we could perhaps salvage the situation.

Unfortunately all our ideas were horribly drastic, would take well over a day to implement, and would seriously reduce our chances of making it down the Kuujjua, let alone to the far side.

Then we had another idea. It would be a daunting repair—especially with the tools we have—but it was our best shot. We swallowed the last of our peanut butter wrap and set to work. What followed was just over ten hours of intensive surgery in the mud.

Basically what we decided to do was cut off the mangled end of the axle, and unbolt and slide the wheel hub back into the shortened axle. Unfortunately we knew there was more to the operation than that. As our cart is essentially two parallel load arms, a set distance apart—between which we sling our bags in netting, and on top of which neatly fits our carbon fibre hardtop panels—of course the shortened axle would no longer fit underneath. Somehow, we had to make the entire cart (both PACs), narrower.

So we got out our already snapped fragment of hacksaw blade, and took it in turns to subject ourselves to the hand-cramping torture of cutting through a total of about 75 centimetres of aluminium, with about 3 centimetres of hacksaw blade. We cut the mangled end off the damaged axle, and then cut the same amount off the good axle, discovering in the process that it too had buckled slightly. The PAC also has two 'end spacers' (100 x 50 millimetre angle) holding the load arms apart in the middle. Conveniently, one of these was already broken, so Clark then merrily cut the other in half over the course of perhaps two gruelling hours, and we then overlapped them by a few inches and pop-riveted them back together again. I turned my weapon of choice—our Leatherman Multitool—to our carbon fibre hardtops, which of course were now too wide to fit back between the wheels on our trimmed-down frame. Rather than make our tent floor area any smaller than it already is, I just ruthlessly hacked out sections on each side to accommodate the wheels. Annoyingly, before we could even start any of this, we had to first unload absolutely everything from the carts, and even untie the bag netting—right back to square one—in the mud. It was a nightmare, and an extreme test of patience, restraint, and self-control.

Thankfully, at least the weather was kind, but as hacksaw blade fragments snapped even shorter, and the tally of cuts and slices on our hands multiplied, and blood started mixing with the sweat and mud covering everything, the tears—we both admitted—were at times only just held back by a bitter, angry determination, and each other's well-practised veneer of optimism. It took over ten hours of non-stop PAC building just to get it back together in a form where we could pitch the tent on top so we could get some sleep, well after midnight.

All I can say is that I'm glad this didn't happen yesterday, in the pouring rain.

## DAY 31: Resurrection

'I reckon it was the bulging, non-round wheels that did it,' I confided to Clark when he woke. I was feeling a little guilty that my engineering calculations on the axle had failed. 'It should easily have been able to handle the weight, but I guess with our grossly lopsided wheels, the whole thing was bouncing up and down, and those dynamic loads …'

'It's okay, guv!' Clark laughed. 'It's not your fault—it was just … Victoria Island doing what she does best, trying to stop us getting to her far side.'

It rained this morning as we finished off the repairs, re-strung the netting and re-loaded everything. It turns out that the good end of the mangled axle was also bent, but, unable to narrow the cart any further, we'll just have to cope with our back right wheel leaning out at a bit of an angle.

It was 3 pm when we finally finished shifting the bag weights around and stood back to admire our sleek new aerodynamically narrow Nugget. We collected all the metal off-cuts, picked up all the little shards of carbon fibre (well, those that haven't embedded themselves into our skin, itching like fire), and set off through the rain towards the first of the big hills—anxious to leave Ground Zero of yesterday's calamity behind, along with its depressing thoughts of failure.

We have just set up camp in what has to be one of the most beautiful campsites we've seen so far. Just 20 metres away is a lake, frozen over except for its vibrant blue perimeter of clear water, from which Clark just scooped enough water for dinner and breakfast. The terrain is now wonderfully firm—a pebbly tundra that could almost be a farmer's well kept meadow. It looks, as Clark pointed out, exactly like that default Windows XP desktop background of rolling hills against a summery blue sky.

All our clothes are finally starting to dry, and the bits of mud caked all over us, our clothes and our cart are starting to desiccate and break off as powder. For dinner tonight we are enjoying our favourite Mexican Chicken and, very best of all, we still have a functioning cart with four wheels and room on top for our tent, and we just got the cart up some killer hills. We are in top spirits, and riding the high that comes from having foiled yet another of Victoria Island's attempts to ruin our plans.

## DAY 32: Into the hills

Only partly full of brekky, we set off on our first solid day of mountain hauling, determined to make a dint into the kilometres separating us from the Kuujjua River. It's slow going around here as we can no longer just pick a point on the distant horizon and march towards it. With so many hills, ditches, rivers, sections too steep to haul up or too steep to descend, too muddy or too wet or too rocky or too lumpy to negotiate, and all of it hidden behind the present hill anyway, progress is a jolting stop-start affair. Typically, we pick a route up the hill that is immediately before us, grunting our way to the top, and there we pore over our maps and even the GPS sometimes, to try to decide the most efficient way down and up the next. It's a compromise between not going too far out of our way, and not giving up hard-earned altitude by going directly down into a valley only then to have to fight back up the other side. Annoyingly, going downhill is quite an effort now, too. Gone are the innocent, carefree days where we'd just hop on top and billycart-ride down. It seems grossly unfair, though, that we have to expend energy not only going up hills, but down them too!

For smaller descents—perhaps up to 5 metres long—we usually just try and outrun the cart because it takes so much time to unharness, walk around to the back, and so on, and every delay adds up out here with so many hills. This technique works well, until the ground turns into concealed mud, and our continuing to outrun the freight train hot on our heels suddenly isn't an option. After some painful trial and error, it seems the most humane way to stop the cart is for both of us to dive off to one side and let the huge tyre grab and wrap around Clark's hauling rope, dragging it—and sometimes Clark—under the wheel, which then eventually stops. The wheels are big and soft so there's no physical scarring, only psychological.

The climax of our day came after easing The Nugget down a ludicrously deep valley and then having to haul back up what was, by Victoria Island standards, the side of Mount Everest. No explanation can do it justice—it was the hardest prolonged outpouring of energy either of us have ever done. We were on our hands and knees for most of it, frantically scrabbling for purchase—groping in the mud for rocks to hold as The Nugget kept starting to slide inexorably back down the near-45-degree slope. It was genuinely frightening at times, our overpants filling with mud and rocks forced up from the bottom as we were dragged helplessly backwards on our chests, clawing for support as The Nugget tried to gain speed. It took over an hour, and for the first time ever, Clark actually opposed my suggestion that we should try and set up a photo. It was that scary.

When we collapsed on the ground at the top, we baulked at the view down into the next enormous valley where a horribly similar snow- and mud-clad wall leered across at us, waiting. But that's for tomorrow. We live in day-tight compartments out here; the enormity of the bigger picture is just too much to deal with.

## DAY 33: Missing something?

We managed a spirited 7.68 kilometres today as the PAC rolls, and to our great joy, we finally crossed the last contour line on our topographic map, meaning there can't be any serious hills left between us and the Kuujjua River. More excitingly still, the first little stream that flows into the Kuujjua is a mere 6.4 kilometres away. After we reach that, logic and gravity tell us that it must all be downhill! So unbelievably, we have survived the mountains and got up onto the plateau itself, with one, two, three, yes, four tyres!

This morning's snow-covered mountainside shrank in scale to a mere hillside as we marched defiantly towards it, and then just a fifteen-minute snow slope. I love it when that happens out here— good old zero sense of scale. We clocked up a few more uneventful kilometres, pausing to put another bandage on our ragged tyre covers during our second nut break. Setting off once more, we then headed down a steep valley towards a forked river crossing. Unharnessing and walking around to the back of The Nugget, I began helping ease it down the hill for a second or so, before I suddenly froze.

'Clark! Where's our tent?' We both stared in horror at the vacant place in the middle of the hardtop where our tent lives by day, folded up and tied down inside a blue tarp, with our sleeping bags, Thermarests and other important items all inside it. It wasn't there. As one we turned around and gazed behind us across the endless rolling expanse of nothing. It wasn't anywhere to be seen. The wind has been blowing like stink here today and I guess somehow while hauling, the tent must have undone itself and been blown off onto the ground—somewhere between last night's camp, and where we now stood, rooted to the ground in dismay.

At once we slung shotguns over our shoulders, snatched up the GPS, put in a waypoint marking where we stood so we could find The Nugget again, grabbed a spare set of batteries for the GPS, a satellite phone, EPIRB, camera, video camera—and a square of chocolate—and started walking back the way we'd come, trying hard not to dwell on how incredibly serious this would soon become if we couldn't find our tent package with everything in it.

For once, we appreciated the mud. Our footsteps were not hard to trace, and after passing our nut break #2 spot and still having found no sign of our tent, our minds were racing, and the idiocy of it had well and truly rammed home. How could we not have noticed it was gone? Fools!

The ground was firmer in some places, and without the mud, we soon lost the trail. We kept walking. Over more hills. It all looked so different. 'Which side of this mountain did we go?' Then Clark spotted it—a table-sized blue package—sitting there like an abandoned airdrop. We let out a whoop of relief and sloshed over to it, and began the arduous job of heaving this enormous 'sail' all the way back to The Nugget in the howling wind. Replacing it onto the hardtop, we lashed it down extra securely and promised ourselves that nothing like this would ever happen again. It remains a mystery how it managed to escape, but a bent tent pole implies the wheels must have actually driven right over it when it fell off. Foiled yet again, Victoria Island! Ha ha!

# DAY 34 (1 July 2008): Mud like we've never seen

I'm currently listening to my iPod, sitting on the front of The Nugget, legs swinging idly, wearing nothing but Icebreaker leggings and a pair of warm, dry socks. I'm enjoying the feeling of the glorious warmth of the sun soaking into my rather pale skin. At the other end of the cart, Clark has the vestibule folded right back, transforming the dingy little kitchen into a platform commanding a splendid view down over the Arctic tundra towards the apparently limitless blue horizon. The looking 'down' part is significant—we are at the top of the plateau; from here, we're only about 1 kilometre from the little stream (which is downhill from us), that flows downhill (surprise) into a lake, that flows into a river, that flows into more lakes, which flow in turn into … the Kuujjua River, which flows downhill for over 100 kilometres! Against all odds, it seems we have made it. Our spirits could not be higher. The ground around here is firm, and we even set up the bear alarm in bare feet, the sensation of texture beneath our feet (well, the parts of our feet that aren't numb from being squished in waterlogged boots for the last month) wonderfully welcome. The sun is toasty, the air is still, and the almost complete lack of clouds looks so promising that we have spread all our clothes out on the ground to dry for the first time in days.

The day didn't start out so well though—not by a long shot. We headed off slowly, our feet aching alarmingly from blisters and twisted, sprained muscles no doubt exacerbated by heaving The Nugget up so many hills over the last few days. Clark's feet are especially bad, and after he'd downed some painkillers we hobbled onwards, limping and grimacing.

Within about an hour, our hopes for a productive day came crashing down around us as we rounded a hill, and suddenly found ourselves in a rather nasty region of mud. Our feet swam in the muddy slurry, until, sinking deep enough (almost half a metre down), our boots started skating on a layer of what felt like pure ice, providing absolutely no grip. It was by far the worst mud we have encountered, including the horrors of 2005. We tried everything to reach the drier terrain ahead—both hauling; one pushing, one hauling; both pushing—but it was futile, exhausting, and back-breaking work. The wheels weren't even turning, just smearing and sinking deeper.

We tried and tried for hours as nut break came and went unheeded, and so did lunch. At last, beaten and fed up, we unloaded The Nugget, carrying one heavy bag at a time across the mud to the 'safe zone' and sloshing back for the next. Each step sucked down into the mud so deep that withdrawing almost sucked our boots off, rubbing horribly into our inflamed heels. Even when it was completely unloaded, it took an almighty effort to drag The Nugget out and across the mud, where, after our having gone virtually nowhere in the last two hours, a mosquito—the first we've seen—hovered symbolically in front of my face before I clapped it angrily in my muddy hands.

'Oooh, you shouldn't have done that,' Clark said, grinning. 'He's going to get his friends onto us now! You just wait!' Any day now we're expecting the infamous plague of mozzies to rise from the swampy tundra.

The rest of the day wasn't so bad. We crossed the last two streams in our way with Clark only being completely dragged under the cart's wheel on one of them, when it steamrollered his hiking pole and he couldn't free his hand from the wrist-strap fast enough. Ouch. We even negotiated a few boulder fields today with only the odd spine-chilling, grating reminder of our low ground clearance. Dinner just now was to die for, and we ate it actually standing outside enjoying the view and the weather, and the satisfaction of standing on top of the plateau, at long last.

## DAY 35: Ten miracles

Was Victoria Island actually *kind* to us today? Surely not. But, we can't ignore it—we can't stop grinning—everything went suspiciously in our favour. We woke on time (first miracle), and ate brekky outside enjoying an unheard-of continuation of yesterday's perfect sunny, summer weather (miracle two), and set off towards the creek, downhill. The downhill was just steep enough for The Nugget to hold its own momentum but not accelerate, allowing us to walk freely with almost slack harnesses for much of the way. When we got to the stream, it was the kind that could be crossed without even flooding our boots.

At the crossing we watched, transfixed, as a caribou in the

distance leapt and sprang around as though mad, and then bolted, streaking across the tundra unnaturally fast, pausing only to resume its bizarre dancing, as if it were being driven insane by unseen tormentors. As we hauled on, the terrain changed dramatically, and we found ourselves hauling through the Sahara Desert. Sand, all around. Not the soft sink-in type of sand, but compacted, firm sand designed to be hauled over (miracle three).

With the sun still smiling down upon us, we reached the intersection of the rivers, and in doing so, we crossed the state/territory border, crossing from Canada's Nunavut into their Northwest Territories. If that's not reason enough to celebrate by breaking open a second daily chocolate block ration, I don't know what is. We drew a line in the sand, scribbled NUNAVUT and N.W.T. on their respective sides, and savoured the creamy richness of the melting chocolate, which tasted even better than normal because a) the temperature was now 10 degrees Celsius and below that temperature chocolate starts to lose its taste, and b) we knew we really shouldn't have stolen the extra ration. What a moment. A few puffy, cotton-wool clouds floated around idly as we walked over to the union of the two streams.

With the increased volume of water, the stream picked up its pace, deepened, and snaked off westwards, the sunlight dancing on the gently rippling, sandy bottom. 'I wonder if there are any—' At this moment a tiny fish darted across in front of us, from one shadowy pool to another. Miracle four, and five—the prospect of being able to fish as we cruise down the river is surely worth two normal miracles. Loving life, we enjoyed our nut break, debating excitedly whether we could possibly try and go river-mode from here on. We decided to do it. However, as there was only half an hour left before lunch, I thought of a great delaying tactic: 'Let's go for a swim!'

Clark looked at the patches of snow on the banks, and sensibly decided to abstain, generously offering, 'If you want to, by all means go ahead, and I'll film it.' So I pulled off my extra warm jacket, beanie, thermals and, after explaining to camera that having not had a shower in over a month I was going to take a quick dip, I plunged into the river in my Skins half-tights. 'Quick' dip was certainly the key word, and watching the video replay in slow motion it's quite amazing to see that I managed to bounce right back out of the water and almost run across the surface to shore before my initial splash hit the water. It was invigorating to say the least. Once hypothermia set in and I became immune to the cold, I had a quick rub-down in the stream again and spent the next ten minutes leaping, prancing and running frantically around trying to dry off. My uncanny resemblance to the insane caribou did not go unnoticed by Clark.

We found something else to celebrate during lunch (reaching the river?) and decided we deserved an extra peanut butter wrap each. Bliss. We dug out the drybag with our 'river gear' in it—most importantly our Gore-Tex drysuits, wetsuit booties and cool Neoprene 'glacier gloves', and converted ourselves to water mode, zipping our drysuits closed with a satisfying click. It's an awesome feeling, being in a drysuit: we felt utterly impenetrable as we harnessed up and marched directly into the river.

At first, the river wasn't deep enough to float The Nugget and we simply hauled it along, sloshing our way through knee-deep water until, around a corner, the bottom shelved off and we found ourselves bobbing around like marshmallow men, buoyed by all the air in our drysuits. The Nugget rose off the bottom and together we all drifted westward. That is to say, both Clark and I, as well as all our 400 kilograms-ish of gear, moved westward—toward the far side of the island—without us having to burn a single calorie of energy. Miracle six! We hoisted ourselves on board, got out the paddles, and spent the next fifteen minutes trying all sorts of different configurations and techniques for paddling, punting the bottom, half hopping off when it got shallow, and generally learning how to control and manoeuvre our giant amphibious beast around shallows and bends.

The river was a little too shallow on average, and for the first section the wheels were rolling annoyingly on the bottom almost half the time. However, we laughed triumphantly when we came to our first mini rapid, something that would have forced a kayaker to tediously drag and portage, but we simply hopped out, clipped back into our hauling trace and The Nugget just rolled up out of the water behind us like a giant salamander, over the dry bits, and slipped back into the flow on the far side. Never has our PAC acronym (Paddleable Amphibious Cart) felt more appropriate.

The river spat us out into the first lake, leaving us with a kilometre or so of flat, still water to somehow cross before it flowed onwards again on the far side. We had been secretly dreading this part, fearing we'd have to haul around the convoluted shoreline at wading depth, because actually paddling The Nugget through still water was as yet untried and likely a slow torture. We stayed clipped in and walked boldly out towards the centre of the lake. The icy (literally) water rose to our waists, and then rose no further. We looked around suspiciously but kept hauling, ignoring the inevitable. But it just never got any deeper. We soon found ourselves in the middle of the lake—perhaps a kilometre from shore—still hauling through waist-height water. Miracle seven. When I say 'hauling', The Nugget was just bobbing obediently behind us as we barely tugged the hauling ropes at all. In fact, it made so little difference that we actually took turns hauling, while the other waded around taking photos. We strapped our Citizen watches to our harness so we could just glance down to see the time, and, when we noticed it was nut break, an island popped up out of nowhere just to our side (miracle eight) and we simply waltzed over to it until we grounded, and ate some peanuts.

It was when we got to the far side of the lake that the real fun started. The lake drained into the outflowing river, picking up pace and volume, sucking us into it. We hopped aboard HMAS *Nugget* and directed our efforts towards keeping her facing downstream so that when we did touch the bottom (every minute or so) the wheels would just roll, rather than if we snagged broadside, in which case the wheels would likely be ripped right off and we'd abruptly sink.

We got better at it, and in between, marvelled at how fast the bottom was slipping past beneath us, without our having to lift a finger. It was absurd. I snatched up the GPS: 5 kilometres per hour! We actually laughed aloud. 'Think how far we could go in a single nut break!' Already it was an obsession. 'Let's see how fast we can go if we really paddle hard!' 6.5 kilometres per hour, 7 … 7.6 kilometres per hour!!! Miracle nine. At that speed we could get an entire day's hauling in, even before first nut break. Silently hurtling towards our goal, we slipped and spun-out around corners as confused and curious muskox and caribou watched in awe from the banks.

We just can't believe our luck. Our timing is *perfect*. It looks to me that about 90 per cent of the snow has only recently melted around here, filling the rivers to their maximum depth over the coming days. Miracle ten.

We've pulled up onto the river bank here just as it opens out into another lake, and rolled about 10 metres up onto a patch of dry grassy tundra that's so perfect that it would put any commercial camping ground to shame. We've strung up our bear alarm—and for once its tent pegs slid in effortlessly, sealing a perfect end to a perfect day.

## DAY 36: HMAS *Nugget*

After yesterday's glut of good fortune, we expected the law of averages to kick in today and to cop our fair share of misfortune, and we weren't wrong, although as always, things could have been worse.

After brekky we set about making our PAC, HMAS *Nugget*, seaworthy. We unloaded everything and opened each drybag to check if yesterday's little water frolic had caused any water ingress. Our clothes were all okay. Our oats and milk powder were fine, there was a little water in one of the freeze-dried food bags, but as they're individually wrapped in foil packets that didn't matter.

And then Clark opened up the bag containing our nut rations, and his mortified groan of 'Oh no …' made me cringe inside as I turned to look. He was holding up one of our ten-day ration cliplock bags of 'trail mix' (sultanas, peanuts, cashews, Smarties, almonds, etc.), which was completely awash with water. Well, it was likely 'water' yesterday, but it was now a vile greyish slurry of mashed nuts, decorated by splashes of colour where red, green, yellow, blue or brown Smarties had dissolved. He fished out another ration pack from the drybag. It too, was swimming. And the next. And more. In the end, five of our remaining six ten-day bags of trail mix lay on the tundra with serious to medium water damage, and we crouched in disbelief around them, silently mourning their loss.

Thankfully, our ration packs of cashews and peanuts were unharmed, and everything else was bone dry. We dug out some spare cliplock bags and—as though performing surgery—carefully sliced open the drowned ration packs, and set to work delicately extracting what was salvageable. We were relieved to find that if we turned a blind eye to 'slightly damp' nuts, we managed to recover perhaps as much as 30 per cent of the trail mix. Unfortunately the rest—about 35 days' worth—was now reduced to a sticky pile of rubbery cashews that could be bent back upon themselves without breaking, sultanas that were well on the way to being grapes once more, and silicon-like peanuts and almonds … it all lay there in a stately pile of regret. There was nothing else we could do but tuck in before they went bad.

We gorged ourselves silly. It was, after all, nut break time. Over the course of the day, I think we probably ate about fifteen days' worth of trail mix before our stomachs started to emit warning groans. It was fantastic. We figure that the next ten or so days along the river will involve substantially less energy output compared to hauling, and so we can do without trail-mix breaks for the next few weeks. Anyway, I don't think either of us will be able to face eating trail mix again for at least that long.

Converting HMAS *Nugget* to ultra-water-mode took longer than expected, but our philosophy is to 'do it once and do it properly', rather than do a poor job and regret it later. We deflated the tyres, pulled off what's left of their shredded Kevlar covers and pumped all four inner tubes back up. We've no need for the covers when floating, and as Kevlar degrades in water we'll keep them safe in a drybag for later. We tied on tow points and handles to all four corners of our raft, and even installed a grab-line all the way around the perimeter in case we suddenly find ourselves in the water one day and wishing we weren't. It was already 5 pm by the time she was ready for the high seas, so we only had time to roll her into the water and wade across the small lake in front of us.

We are now camped near to where the river sucks out, ready to give our new river-worthy craft a real test run tomorrow. There's just one more large lake in our way, and then after that, it's the real deal—the big, wide, flowing Kuujjua—for over 100 kilometres. Looks like we might just get there in three days' time—Clark's birthday—as promised!

## DAY 37: Kuujjua, here we come!

Our watch alarm went off at 7.30 am and we fought to maintain some form of conversation with each other to prevent us from slipping back into unconsciousness. With an effort we verbally slapped ourselves around enough to pull free from the clutches of sleep, and sat up to an eerily quiet tent. There was absolutely zero wind, and a quick peek outside revealed the start of yet another perfect sunny day. Brilliant.

The first little section was along the remainder of yesterday's lake, and we found it faster to wade and haul HMAS *Nugget* as she floated in the shallows, taking the opportunity to shuffle a few heavier bags around to level her out onto an even keel. The far side of the lake swept us into a short river-like section leading to another, much larger lake—the last one. This linking river was rather shallow too and we mostly walked beside the cart helping her over mossy shallows, preventing her turning broadside. We've got this technique well refined now, but we really hope the Kuujjua is going to be significantly deeper!

Once spat out into the big lake, we drifted idly around and prepared lunch—once again, peanut butter on flatbreads with a thermos of coffee—and enjoyed what was probably our best lunch break yet. We lay stretched out on the deck of HMAS *Nugget*, spinning slowly in the current and wind—which, amazingly, was pushing us in the right direction! The sun beamed down into the transparent water perhaps 2 metres deep, glinting off the sandy bottom. Gazing dreamily down, I suddenly noticed several dark shadows moving around us. 'They're fish! Huge fish!' I shouted, pointing excitedly. They were lake trout, and big ones.

I set up our fishing rod with a lure and flicked a few hopeful casts, but the lake did not provide. The wind died, and adrift in the body of the lake itself, we were going nowhere fast—even paddling—so we struck out for the shore and resumed hauling along the side. The surface of these bigger, deeper lakes is still partially frozen over with a thin pancake layer of floating ice—too thin to walk on, but impossible to paddle through. Unfortunately this means we can't cut across these lakes, and we're forced instead to wind around their convoluted shoreline. Our polarised Dirty Dog sunnies are awesome at letting us see through the surface glare, and after several monstrously thick fish lazily wafted right past us, I reached back and grabbed the fishing rod again.

For about half an hour, we both simply waded along, hauling through the shallows, while I repeatedly cast the lure. It was lovely, and as Clark said, 'This is something I'd actually do for fun!' It felt like a luxury fishing trip; we didn't even feel HMAS *Nugget* drifting along behind us. Just as I was starting to wonder if these trout even knew what they were supposed to do with lures, a large shadow followed it all the way back towards us. Having wound the lure right in until it hung from the end of my rod—perhaps 2 metres from where I stood in the water—the huge half-metre trout sidled up to it and simply sucked it into his mouth. I struck at the same instant and the lure dug in, but only for about a tenth of a second before he just flicked his head sideways and dislodged it.

Now, normally, after a scare like that, the game's up, and all fish I've ever seen take off in a flash, but this guy just continued to swim lazily around our feet while I basically kept bumping the lure into his nose until he eventually grew bored and slid away. I tried all afternoon, but didn't ever have a second strike. Still, it bodes very well for the upcoming days. Some char or trout would go very well with our couscous!

So here we are, pulled 10 metres up onto the grassy shore, with only about half of this last big lake still to go before the real river starts. That leaves us all of tomorrow to get across, so that the next day—Clark's birthday—we can wake up to our first full day of (hopefully) luxurious river travel.

Checking our emails, we received one particularly interesting one from my dad. He's contacted a biologist about the crazy dancing caribou we reported the other day, and it seems it was likely trying to run away from warble flies. Warble flies are delightful little parasitic flies that lay eggs on the fur of caribou, which then turn into grubs that walk down the hair follicle, chew their way into the leg of the animal, and then spend the summer chewing their way underneath the skin all the way up along the back beside the spinal cord, where they proceed to cut themselves a breathing hole through the skin until they're ready to pupate and turn into a fly and flap out of the unfortunate animal's back to go and find another to lay eggs on. Lovely. I'd be running and jumping too if one of them was chasing me. Disgustingly, these flies can apparently do the same thing to humans.

## DAY 38: Something fishy about this lake

Determined to reach the 'proper start' of the Kuujjua by the end of the day, we performed a textbook wake-up, and got ready in record time. We were just about to slide our PAC into the water and head off, when a big old caribou bull materialised in front of us.

We leapt for the video camera and Canon DSLR and lost all track of time, staring in awe as he gradually ambled closer and closer. He knew we were there, as every now and again if we spoke too loudly or moved too fast he'd lift his head, balancing his impressive pair of antlers high in the air, and regard us with mild interest for a few seconds before lowering his lips back to the lawn to resume mowing. Eventually, after he was joined by two females and we exhausted even these photo opportunities, we snapped out of our trance, remembered our goal for the day, and relaunched HMAS *Nugget*.

We waded onwards, listening to our iPods, fishing, chatting away and generally expending no more energy than one would on a pleasant morning's stroll along a sun-soaked foreshore, beside an ice-strewn lake rimmed by snow-clad hills. The landscape is spectacularly beautiful around here. At last, as we drew nearer to the end of the big lake, our hauling ropes went slack, and for a few irritating seconds HMAS *Nugget* kept bumping into us from behind, until we realised what this meant—flow!

We hopped on, hoping to be whisked along to the last, much smaller lake before the Kuujjua 'proper', but it was disappointingly slow—even slower than hauling—so we hopped back out. 'Please let the Kuujjua have a bit more flow than this!' we begged, for the umpteenth time.

As we drifted into the last little lake, I suddenly spotted a monstrous lake trout lazily finning its way almost right between our legs. I grabbed the fishing rod and put a cast well behind the fish, and began reeling it in. Wham! A different fish struck the lure almost at once, but after a few lethargic splashes it pulled free. Adrenalin kicking in, I re-cast and before I had managed to reel back in more than a metre or so, WHAM, an even bigger strike, and this one stuck!

'I—I've got one!' I shouted in disbelief at Clark, and being only 10 metres from shore I simply walked backwards onto dry land as I reeled the giant in. Clark followed me ashore and we both stared down at the gigantic fish in absolute awe. It was a 63-centimetre monstrosity, and weighed just over 2.5 kilograms! Smiling from ear to ear, we divided the fish up in our minds. 'We'll have half of it tonight on our couscous, and then dry the other half!' (Dried in the traditional Inuit way, which we learned in 2005.) I filleted the fish with my Leatherman, stuck two hiking poles out the back of HMAS *Nugget* and webbed some string between them to form a drying rack. Then—as we'd been taught in 2005—I sliced one of the fillets the traditional Inuit way, and draped it over the string to dry, just as we always dreamed we would. The other fillet I put aside for dinner.

While I finished, Clark got the rod and waded out and had a crack at the whole fishing thing too. On his first ever cast—he hasn't even touched the fishing rod this whole trip—WHAM, a strike. But it got off. He enthusiastically cast again. WHAM—and this one stuck. 'I got another one!' It made awesome footage: me filleting one giant in the foreground as Clark dragged in a second through the shallows behind me. Clark filleted this one—destined entirely for the drying rack—and then I had another cast, and dragged in a third fish. Three huge lake trout, each over half a metre long, and all in the space of about fifteen minutes and a total of five casts. That more than makes up for our lost trail-mix rations!

With the stern of HMAS *Nugget* dangling with nutritious bright orange fillets of fish, we hauled the remaining distance to the end of the lake, to the 'proper start' of the Kuujjua River, as happy as we have ever been.

And here we are—just as promised over a week ago. We are camped on a grassy patch of tundra, at the exact point that the Kuujjua kicks in, on the night before Clark's 24th birthday. We made it! First up on tonight's celebratory dinner menu is a Mexican Chicken dehydrated meal (of course) and a cup of hot chocolate. Clark the sugar-Nazi even decided on the spur of the moment to spare enough sugar for a random mug of coffee after that too! Next item on the menu: pan-seared arctic lake trout with cashew-grain salt (that we've been saving especially), resting upon a bed of couscous flavoured with paprika, chilli and 'miscellaneous spice #1' (we forgot to label some of our spices).

# DAY 39: Clark's 24th birthday

I'll let Clark speak for himself today, it being his birthday and all:

*As I snuck back inside after a quick toilet break at about 3 am, Chris woke with a start beside me—'Happy birthday, guv! Here, have this!' He handed me a small something wrapped in a piece of paper from my notebook with string drawn on it to look like a proper pressie. Perplexed, I unwrapped it. CHOCOLATE! Chris had amazingly saved his last square of yesterday's chocolate ration, which I wasted no time popping in my mouth, savouring the taste, thanking him profusely, then drifting happily back to sleep.*

*Ready for a leisurely day of free kilometres floating down the Kuujjua and eating double rations while lazing on the sunny deck of our houseboat, when it was time to get up we found there wasn't any of the usual regret synonymous with facing a day of hauling. I wasted no time cooking up a storm in the kitchen with double porridge and extra sugar in our coffee. As we sat there sipping, staring at the Kuujjua, a mere 10 metres from our camp, Chris reached over and handed me a birthday card (another piece of paper stolen from my notebook, craftily drawn on to resemble a fancy card) and another small package similar to the piece of chocolate. I grinned widely as I read the card and then unwrapped my pressie. In an instant it all made sense: I had seen Chris busily cutting and shaving bits from a piece of muskox bone for the last two weeks and had no idea what he was doing because he was strangely secretive about it. Anyway, it turns out he has masterfully crafted a miniature replica of our 'Nugget' PAC, complete with matchstick men hauling in dog-team style, all wrapped up and packaged in a matchbox!*

*We wasted no time packing everything away, ready to push the final 10 metres before we could realise our long-awaited dream of floating down the Kuujjua. What happened next can only be described as a typical Victoria Island moment. With a 'One, two, three …. push!' we started rolling the short distance towards the river when suddenly— PSSSSSSsssssss! Chris and I looked at each other in total disbelief as we watched one of the tyres deflate—it had snagged on one of the folded tent poles and punctured itself with two huge holes. We have managed to fight our way to the Kuujjua for the last 39 days without a single puncture—over Death Terrain and all—and now, with only a few steps left, over lawn-like grass, it finally happened! When we finished laughing, we quickly repaired the puncture with our bike repair kit and, grinning, pushed onwards. Being my birthday, and with the sun shining and the river flowing, it would take a lot more than a puncture to dampen our spirits. As we rolled HMAS Nugget into the river, it instantly took off at around 3 kilometres per hour with us on top, and we literally had nothing else to do but sit back and enjoy the view.*

*Chris then busted out with yet another birthday surprise—a balloon! He handed me a bright yellow balloon on a string, with the words 'Happy Birthday' printed on it—very cool. I tied it to the side of the PAC and it floated happily beside us for most of the day.*

*The weather started to look a little grimmer after lunch, and we could see rain pouring from clouds all around us except for the little patch of clear blue sky directly overhead that adoringly followed us for several hours, until that too turned into rain. This of course didn't matter as we were already in our drysuits and it really made no difference to what we were doing, which was nothing. As we sat there happily in the rain, we watched in excitement as our GPS told us we'd travelled 12 kilometres as the crow flies—our new daily distance record—without having done a thing! It was about time for camp, but since it was raining and we were making great progress, we decided to cook dinner aboard HMAS Nugget mid-river. Moroccan Lamb was on the cards tonight—another favourite of ours from Back Country Cuisine—and we just sat there enjoying our meal and watching the kilometres tick past on the GPS: 12.5, 12.6, 13 … all up, we managed to travel 15.1 kilometres as the crow flies, and a spectacular 23.5 km as the PAC floats today—double our previous record!*

*We've just set up camp in preparation for my open house party! I'm pretty sure it's going to be the biggest party for hundreds of kilometres around. We've got the Eee PC set up cranking some music, we've got a tiny 30-millilitre bottle of vodka, a cup of tea each, some chocolate, some dried trout, and Chris has about 30 more balloons that he's just filled the tent with—awesome! This party is going to go off with a bang—quite literally—as Chris is about to set off some fireworks in the form of a bear-banger fired from the shotgun. All in all, this would have to be the best birthday ever.*

# DAY 40: Puncture midstream!

After Clark's birthday party last night, we retired to our tent feeling particularly positive about everything—about the successful day, about the weather, the freshly drying trout, and about the fantastic kilometres that we'd racked up that day. As we lay there, listening to the river gurgling past—coursing endlessly westwards—we couldn't suppress a nagging feeling that we were in some way wasting this free conveyor belt. What started as a ludicrous idea slowly began to take form, and the concept of 24-hour river travel began to sound more and more achievable. 'Imagine that …' we breathed, 'if we set up properly, we wouldn't even need to come ashore for nut breaks, dinner, emails, or even to camp. We'd just stay out there on our houseboat, taking it in shifts to steer the raft all day and all night …' With the river flowing anything from 1.5 to 6 kilometres per hour, the potential kilometres we could rack up in a 24-hour period were simply too astronomical to ignore. 'I reckon we can do it. Let's give it a try anyway!' I said.

We rugged up with several Icebreaker layers, hopped back into our Gore-Tex drysuits, pulled our Thermarest mattresses out from our tent and lay them across the deck, folded everything else away and rolled HMAS *Nugget* back into the flow at about 2 am, full of excitement. Would it work? Was this really possible? It was very cold and quiet, but we couldn't have asked for a more favourable section of river to try it out: wide, deep and relatively slow flowing.

Warmed by a quick coffee prepared onboard, I took the first two-hour shift and Clark stretched out on his Thermarest. Before long he was sound asleep, and I spent a pleasant two hours gently guiding our mobile home around corners, avoiding back-eddies and linking up channels of slightly faster flowing water. My shift passed drama free, and I handed over to Clark, grinning a big, adventurous boyish grin. This was more like it. By morning we were both dog-tired, but sufficiently rested to 'begin' our normal day at 7.30 am, as usual. The awesome thing was, though, that we'd already racked up just over 5 kilometres!

Brekky on the go worked a treat, and as we lay back sipping our coffee in the golden sunlight, we both agreed that houseboating is the only way to travel the Kuujjua. We spent the first hour or so today refining our systems so everything was within easy reach, re-filling our week's bag of supplies from various drybags, drying clothes and doing a few other chores as the day slipped on, and the bottom flew past beneath us. Even on a kayak or a canoe it just wouldn't be the same: on board HMAS *Nugget* we can stretch out, stand up, walk around, cook, get to all our gear and dangle our feet in the water—it's perfect.

As the sun strengthened and the temperatures soared, we gradually stripped off our layers inside our drysuit. The tyres became so hot they were literally painful to touch, but with a gentle breeze blowing, we were absolutely loving it.

As always though, Victoria Island sensed our smugness and lashed out.

We were merrily drifting down the middle of the river when beside me I suddenly heard a horrible noise: 'psssssSSSSSSSS'. It grew louder and louder, and was coming from the wheel right behind me. I whipped around and instantly saw what was happening—a small hole had appeared in the puncture-repair patch we'd put on yesterday, and air was rushing out of the tyre, tearing the hole bigger and bigger even as I reached out towards it. 'TO SHORE! PADDLE!! GO!! GO!!' I shouted, holding my thumb over the burning hot hole, feeling it gradually spread, while my mind raced ahead visualising what was about to happen. If this wheel deflated, HMAS *Nugget* would start to sink around us until this whole side would be underwater, while still being carried downstream. 'We're getting there!' Clark reassured me, as I smeared puncture repair glue around the rubber on all sides of my finger and—hoping against hope—whisked my thumb away and slapped on the biggest repair patch we have. It held. For about ten seconds, and then it too stretched out in the heat and burst its boundaries. 'PSSSSS!!!!'

Somehow, we got to shore just in time, and propping the corner of HMAS *Nugget* up on our Manfrotto tripod, we pulled off the deflated tube and replaced it with one of our two spares. While Clark pumped it up—requiring a mere 1004 pumps from our large stand-up pump—I tried to repair the punctured tube. The tear was now too big for our commercial bike tube patches, so I cut out a large section of bike inner tube rubber we brought, and smeared it with some horrible rubber-to-rubber glue, the packaging for which bore endless warnings about not getting this stuff on your hands, as your body will absorb powerful neurotoxins right through your skin and into your brain. Trying not to breathe, I patched up the tube, folded it away for later and we re-launched HMAS *Nugget*, just as a rain squall closed in, cooling things down nicely. Another crisis averted.

With the rain came wind, and we were blown firmly against the far bank of the river, having to repeatedly punt ourselves off the shallows with our paddle, while the wheels resonated with nerve-racking sounds as they grazed and bumped their way along the bottom. The wind calmed, and as we passed a few more rivers that fed into ours, the Kuujjua became stronger, deeper, and more dependable. We lay back, plugged my iPod into our little Eee PC laptop speakers, and actually relaxed—sipping hot chocolate, listening to some Angus and Julia Stone and even some Pachelbel's 'Canon in D Minor' (a famous piece of irresistibly calming and reflective classical music) as we spun serenely onwards, past the ever more beautiful scenery of the Shaler Mountains. It was a moment we'll never forget.

At one stage, Clark pointed ahead and I rolled over to watch a bull caribou prance down to the bank, stand for a second in the shallows mentally steeling himself for the task ahead, and then stride confidently into the icy water, and swim all the way across the Kuujjua—well out of his depth—as we bore down upon him, cameras blazing. Once out on the far side he shook himself dry, did a few energetic leaps to warm himself up, and then paused to regard us as we passed silently by, the water dripping from his shaggy goatee sparkling in the golden sunlight.

Starting to get a little fancy with our raft, I managed to pump some more air into one of our tyres en route to level out HMAS *Nugget* a little. It feels like such a self-contained houseboat now, we have no need for the shore. The river has burst its banks in a few places, spreading out into bays and fields that are not marked on the map, indicating that through pure luck, we have managed to get here pretty much slap-bang at the time of maximum flow. The mosquito plague has just begun in earnest, and whenever we dare set foot ashore great humming clouds descend upon us. Thankfully we are covered head to toe in our mozzie-proof drysuits, and remaining out in the middle of the river seems to help reduce mosquito numbers.

By 6 pm—our arbitrary end of the day—we'd managed 22.3 kilometres, despite only starting this whole 24-hour rafting adventure in the wee hours of the morning after the party died down. Tomorrow—which just started a few minutes ago—we're really going to see what's possible.

## DAY 41: The wind and the wolves

Today's progress was nothing short of unbelievable, and that's only half the story—it was a day of contrasts, hard work and high adventure on the river. Our 'day' started at 6 pm last night when we reset out daily kilometreage and continued our unstoppable magic carpet ride down the Kuujjua, adjusting to life permanently within a drysuit. The night was cold, but we had extra Icebreaker layers on under our drysuits in preparation, and that kept us warm during the (brilliantly sunny) 'night' (we still have more than two weeks to go before the sun first dips even slightly below the horizon).

I must admit, having not slept properly in several days, we were soon struggling to stay awake, and there was one embarrassing moment when we both suddenly woke to find HMAS *Nugget* docked against the river bank, with a caribou looking at us. We sat bolt upright. 'How long have we been like this?' I asked, looking at Clark, who was evidently about to ask me the same question. We didn't even know who was supposed to be on watch. After this, we decided to administer a steady drip of coffee into our systems, which helped.

As the river widens it's becoming shallower, and invariably we scrunch or bang to a halt every half an hour or so on random shoals. If whoever's on watch spots them early enough, he can usually paddle around them, but if he doesn't, there's nothing for it but to hurriedly shake the other awake, and both instantly plunge into freezing, rushing, knee-deep water to try to push around to avoid collision. 'To the left! Look out!' It's a very rude awakening to find yourself slipping around in an icy river and being shouted at before your eyes have even adjusted to the sunlight!

The wind has been increasing too, and eventually it became impossible for one person to keep HMAS *Nugget* midstream on their own. We really are at the mercy of any real wind other than a following breeze; the windage of our houseboat is such that we simply get blown sideways against the downwind bank. If we're lucky then we'll just grind to a noisy, juddering halt in the shallows, but more often than not we come to a somewhat more abrupt halt with the wheel rim smashing against a submerged rock.

Progress in these conditions is an arduous process requiring we both paddle for all we're worth for perhaps an hour, trying to lift ourselves free from the clutch of the downwind bank. Once back out in the flow, we then have to keep paddling to try and hold our ground against the wind, until eventually, exhausted, we have to give up, and enjoy a brief period of rest while we're blown back again. Leapfrogging along the riverbank in this way, neither of us got a wink of sleep all day.

'Oh, no! Stop!' I suddenly heard Clark shout, and turning, saw him leaping off into the waist-deep water, staring wildly at the bottom. 'I dropped my iPod!'

This was no laughing matter. The iPod is literally what keeps us going out here—especially when hauling—our sanctuary when all around is unbearable. I felt terrible for Clark, and pulled HMAS *Nugget* to the bank and stood silently watching his frantic searching, not sure what to say.

'Got it!' Plunging down, Clark triumphantly held it aloft, dripping. He immediately switched it off, and it's been sitting on deck drying ever since. We're both silently praying it'll still work.

Genuinely large mountains slid into view and towered over us as we snaked past—great raised plateaus with perfectly flat tops, rimmed all around by sheer cliff walls—a real 'Lost World' or 'Land Before Time' kinda place. Soon the wind picked up so stiffly that it formed whitecaps on the river, and we were helplessly pinned against the shore—unable to go anywhere. Deciding to make the most of it, we managed to get about an hour's sleep while it blew over.

Chewing on some now wonderfully dried trout after we woke, the big excitement of the day came as we pushed off and once again fought to paddle back out into the main flow. I spotted two white blobs moving around a big black blob on the far bank, above which flitted several much smaller black dots. Scale, is—as I've said many times—non-existent out here, so we could just as easily have been looking at two white mice scurrying around a small black chicken with black flies buzzing overhead, as watching two arctic wolves gorging themselves on the freshly killed carcass of a muskox, with black crows circling and waiting their turn. As it happened on this particular day, it was the latter—confirmed by taking a quick photo using my 400-millimetre telephoto lens. Pumped with adrenalin and excitement, we redoubled our efforts to paddle to that far windward bank to get a look before the current whisked us past.

We were churning the water perhaps two-thirds of the way across—and still a good way upstream—when one of the wolves stopped eating and looked right at us. We stopped paddling, only to be instantly blown backwards again, so we hurriedly continued our vicious paddling while trying to maintain a passive, non-threatening atmosphere. The wolf then started trotting up the side of the river to meet us. She was in no hurry, and just loped gracefully to the exact point at which it looked like—if our arms didn't drop off from exhaustion first—we'd finally reach her side. There, the wolf simply sat down and waited, staring fixedly at us, fresh bloodstains down her chest, with a look that said more plainly than words: 'Mmm, very nice, and here comes dessert … '

Cameras ready, we nervously paddled on. When we were only perhaps 20 metres away she got up and trotted a little further up the bank and lay down, evidently happier to keep her distance but clearly burning with curiosity about us and our unwieldy craft. Then the other, larger wolf—his white face dirty with blood—left the carcass too and trotted over, fixing us with an unforgettable wolf-stare from those incredibly piercing eyes. He came perhaps within 10 metres, sniffing, watching, listening, inspecting, then joined his mate, and together they trotted off into the distance.

As 6 pm ticked past, we huddled around the GPS waiting for it to show us how far we'd come. Any moment now. *Beep.* We let out a cheer. A whopping 46 kilometres in just 24 hours!

## DAY 42: Speed and distance records smashed!

The night was bitterly cold. Try as we did—while we drifted along—we just could not sleep, and we both lay curled in the foetal position on our sides, balaclava and beanie pulled down tightly over our heads, feeling chilled to the core. Even the constant flow of hot drinks we administered only provided temporary relief, and in the end Clark took to sitting up and padding one side of the raft in pointless circles for hours just to try and generate a bit of body warmth, while I—apparently too worn out to shiver—had to resort to deliberately convulsing, repetitively tightening and releasing every muscle that my numb brain could command.

The hours seemed like days and while the kilometres were going well, it was a long, hard night, filled with multiple episodes of getting out and easing HMAS *Nugget* over ground so shallow it threatened to rip the tyres off. At about 3 am we found an excuse to heat up a full-on dehydrated meal, and that seemed to kick-start our day at last. As our rumbling stomachs were warmed by Chicken Tikka Masala, the sun—which since midnight had been rising in perfect synchrony behind a bank of cloud rising with it—finally started to pull clear. The sunlight leapt over the landscape ahead of us, visibly spreading from hill to hill towards us as the curtain of depression was withdrawn, until finally it was upon us, and we realised that perhaps we were going to survive the night after all. Having lost a few hours wind-bound at the start of 'today', the idea of trying to better yesterday's 46-kilometre effort seemed remote, but still we gave it everything we had.

We heard—even before we spotted—a rapid coming up around the corner a bit after lunch, and hurried to align HMAS *Nugget* as best we could with the chute of water funnelling through it. It looked like the height of the whole river had dropped by a good half-metre or more, and we certainly felt it. Half staring at the speed-over-ground reading on the GPS, and half watching the submerged boulders streak past horribly close beneath the wheel rims, we held on as we broke our PAC speed record, screaming along at 10.2 kilometres per hour, bouncing from one standing wave to the next. Beyond the rapid, the river became more contained, deeper and faster.

Losing sight of the bottom, sometimes it feels like we're only sluggishly drifting along but a glance at the GPS often reveals we are in fact scorching along at 6, 7 or even 8 kilometres per hour for minutes at a time. As 6 pm came and went, we again held our breaths looking at the GPS: 54.2 kilometres!! Not only did we break the 50-kilometres-a-day barrier, but we've also managed just over 100 kilometres in the last two days alone! At this rate, we'll get to our exit lake and strike out for the west side of the island around lunchtime tomorrow!

# DAY 43: The Kuujjua strikes back

So it seems the first half of the river was all sunshine and lazy drifting, purely to lull us into a false sense of security so that the last section—which we just travelled—would seem all the more traumatic. Day 43 started with us pinned, once again, to the side of the river by the wind, and so after yesterday's dinner we climbed the hill beside us to take a look at an ancient stone *inukshuk* (a stone cairn built by Inuit, often in the shape of a man) on the skyline, and to gaze down upon the upcoming quite serious rapid. In front of us, a branch river gushed into the main Kuujjua, sending the whole churning mess down through a rocky chute. It didn't look friendly, and, staring down upon it, I was starting to feel a little anxious. Unfortunately with the valley walls here far too steep to haul, we had little choice but to attempt the rapid. We couldn't even line it down on a rope as HMAS *Nugget* is anything but streamlined and there's no holding her back in a current. It looked like if we managed to keep ourselves in the very middle of the flow, we'd be okay. It looked deep enough that we shouldn't hit any boulders and none poked through the surface in view.

As soon as the wind died enough, we lashed the video camera to the bow to capture our experience, and pushed off. Critically, first we had to battle our way into the wind and try to get to the far bank where the chute started, otherwise the current would carry us past, right into the branch river's cascading flow.

We only just made it across in time, digging hard back strokes at the last moment to spin our houseboat lethargically around to face the flow (so that if we did strike a rock with our wheels, the tyre would absorb some of the impact, and then the PAC should roll up and over it, compared to striking anything side-on at speed, which would pull the tyre off the rim, smash the rim, and then probably break the whole wheel off the axle). Breaking up in the middle of a rapid doesn't even bear thinking about—some of our gear bags would sink out of reach, and the others would be washed away. Either way, we'd have nothing.

As the mouth of the chute started to suck us inward, HMAS *Nugget* still hadn't spun far enough around, and fear started to spike through our excitement. Glancing quickly from side to side with widening eyes, we tried desperately to see what was coming, all the while barking warnings and instructions at each other through teeth gritted hard by the exertion of paddling. 'Keep turning!' We managed to get ourselves aligned *just* before the chute really took off, and for a brief moment, it all looked like it was going to go smoothly.

We bucked over the first few standing waves without too much drama, our speed rising above 10 kilometres per hour, and then, part of our houseboat must have slipped out of the main flow of water, causing that corner to be pulled around by the slower water. To our absolute horror, we started to turn broadside in the middle of the rapid.

Adrenalin surging through our veins, we did all we could to counteract the spinning, but it was no use. We were travelling down the rapid, completely side-on, at about 11 kilometres per hour, when something hit one of the wheels. *Crunch!* Expletive! Terror.

A quick glance showed the wheel itself was still there, and as we were still being swept onwards we needed to remain focused. HMAS *Nugget* had been jolted around still further by the impact, and now our stern was facing more forward than the bow, so we switched directions of our frantic paddling and had almost aligned ourselves stern-first instead, when *CRUNCH!* Scraaaaape ... *CRUNCH!* This impact was even harder than the first and almost jolted us overboard. Clark—pale and very wide-eyed—shouted 'Puncture?!' to which I helpfully replied, 'Keep paddling!'

Hardly daring to prise my eyes off the situation still unfolding, I spared the wheel a quick glance—it didn't seem to be punctured, but there was certainly something odd about the way we were floating. But we were *still floating*, which meant things could yet get worse if we didn't pay attention, so I whipped my head forwards again, and helped to paddle, push off, swear and splash our way along, bouncing over more rearing stationary waves and sucking troughs, and ultimately ... we were spat out on the far side. While the rest of the flow charged onwards downstream, we were left spinning slowly in a side eddy. We scooped ourselves toward the bank until we were vaguely within standing depth and then leapt out in our drysuits, pulling the wounded HMAS *Nugget* to shore. Once alongside, we just stood there for a few silent moments, shaking.

A careful inspection of all four tyres revealed that somehow— unbelievably—there were no punctures. Next, I looked at all eight carbon-fibre/Kevlar half-rims, and the situation there was not as pretty—the edges of four of them had obviously been introduced to different rocks at some speed. The huge strength of the Kevlar strip reinforcing the rim's edge prevented the whole impact regions from actually crumbling away, but the damaged parts are now flexible as the epoxy resin bonding all the various carbon-fibre sheets has been pulverised. All in all, though, the strangling feeling around my chest relaxed a little; it was not as bad as I had feared. The rims themselves were vaguely okay, and would probably still perform their function quite well, especially if I mixed up some fresh epoxy glue to smear into the wounds and strapped it all with some spare carbon-fibre cloth that we brought along in the hope that 'what you prepare for never happens'—except on Victoria Island, clearly.

As after our billycart crash, our first action after this quick damage assessment was to walk away. Strangely, it just seems to be our subconscious way of dealing it. We both found ourselves with cameras in hand, walking towards the towering cliffs overhead, with a nut-break ration and thermos, as if we were merely on some photographic safari. After all, being about 1 am, the lighting was perfect—low and golden. A pair of rough-legged hawks repeatedly launched themselves from the top of the cliff and wheeled above us, screeching mournfully before alighting back on the crumbling skyline.

In the end, we both climbed back aboard HMAS *Nugget* and pushed off back into the river. It seemed the reason we'd been floating lopsidedly was just that the impact had pinched the air out of the submerged part of one tube, making it less buoyant. We soon fixed this, and continued on our merry way, around the next corner, to see another rapid.

And another. And another. The last 35 kilometres of the river was one rock garden after the next. These bank-to-bank sections of angrier, darker water—pock-marked with splashes of leaping white water—seemed to occur around every corner, and neither of us got a wink of sleep all day. Considering we'd only managed about two hours of sleep in the 24 hours prior, we were starting to feel spaced-out, big time. We were desperate for a section of calm water long enough for one of us to get some shut-eye, but it just wasn't to be.

The wind picked up, making even the sections in-between rapids an exhausting trial. At last we could cope no more, and after a few near misses and a few more minor rim-crunches that should have been avoidable, we dazedly pulled to the bank, tied off on a boulder, and—taking our Thermarests with us—staggered ashore and fell asleep on the ground. The novelty of 24-hour travel is wearing pretty thin. We awoke about an hour later—not feeling very revived, but at least conscious enough to realise that both kipping on the open ground in a place where we *knew* there were wolves and bears around was not the smartest idea. So, keen to get to the end of this nightmare where we could set up the tent and tripwire and climb into our sleeping bags for the first time in five days, we agreed to push on.

The 'end lake' where we'll exit the river—just before it swings south and turns into angry Class III white water with waterfalls— was only about 9 kilometres away by this stage, and with the river pulling along at about 5 kilometres per hour it could only be two hours away at most. We wearily walked HMAS *Nugget* out into the flow, Clark hopped on and I walked a few extra paces deeper, to ensure we were well clear of the rocks.

Just as I was about to heave myself up onto the deck, I felt the gushing rush of water pouring down into my pants. Either I'd just pissed my pants, or I'd forgotten for the first time in my life to pull closed the wee-zip in the front of my drysuit. Lamenting the fact that the water gushing in was by no means warm, I had to accept it was the latter scenario. Idiot! I had both my pairs of Icebreaker leggings on, and both were now drenched. I sat on the deck, seething with anger at my own carelessness. Clearly we did need more sleep—but *real* sleep was almost within reach, if we could just keep going …

We later broke the HMAS *Nugget* speed record *again*, ripping down a chute at 13.2 kilometres per hour, shortly before the flow did a sudden left-hand turn and then hard right. We almost had to lean into the corners, and the water's depth meant no risk of collisions, so it was actually quite fun.

We became well acquainted with what the GPS euphemistically refers to as 'unconsolidated ground', which translates in practical terms to what might be land, might be water, but is more likely a combination of both, just shallow enough to make us get out and walk the houseboat at 2 kilometres per hour while the water itself races past at 5 kilometres per hour. We hated it. The wheels crunched on the bottom if we stayed on, but trying to hold back HMAS *Nugget* when we got off was a drawn-out torture of slipping, sliding, and generally pummelling our already traumatised feet into all manner of slippery rocks, big and small. Wearing our rubber-soled Neoprene booties, we had the pleasure of intimately experiencing everything we stepped on, and by the end our feet were covered in bruises and aching terribly. Somehow we remained civil to each other, and just laughed weakly at each other's expressions when our feet copped another rock: a look of apprehension, followed by a wince of excruciating pain that dissolved into a look of utter helplessness and defeat.

And so it was that after several hours of this torture, the 'end lake' finally came into view. We just had to travel two final kilometres to where the river expanded enough to be called a 'lake' and then we'd stop. Naturally—in good old Victoria Island style—this wasn't as easy as it looked.

As usual, the wind prevented us from staying in the main flow, and we were constantly sucked broadside into any one of an endless series of side flows draining at right angles into a region of 'unconsolidated ground'. Frustratingly, we were forced to get out and haul the entire way through knee-deep water that covered a viscous, sucking muddy bottom. By the end, we weren't speaking at all; we had withdrawn into our own worlds, as ever growing swarms of mosquitoes billowed around us.

Over an hour later we got to the lake, pulled HMAS *Nugget* partly up onto the shore, tied her off, grabbed the tent, staggered up to the first patch of grass, set the tent up, put the bear alarm up, and crawled inside. After zipping up the tent and squashing countless hundreds of mosquitoes against the inside, we set our watch alarm for just two hours' sleep—the idea being that we'd then have dinner, write our already late website update to let people know we were vaguely alive—and then go back to sleep until tomorrow.

Utterly dead to the world, we awoke *eighteen hours* later, when the bear alarm went off.

## DAY 44: Hoist the sail, Mr Carter!

It turned out to be a false alarm—tripped by the wind—but without it, I think we may never have woken, ever. Cringing at the flood of concerned emails—including one from my dad, who believed something terrible must have happened to us—I wrote a website update as we began filling ourselves in on all the meals we'd inadvertently missed while unconscious.

After licking clean the packet of Mexican Chicken, we still had a few hours of the day left to utilise, and a few kilometres of lake still to cross before reaching our exit point. Packing up camp, I collected the bear alarm while Clark folded away the tent.

'Check this out,' Clark called. 'It looks like a sail!' It did indeed. Our special joining vestibule that we'd had made for us to join our two tents together (back in the days when we had the luxury of two tents) had caught the increasing wind and billowed out exactly like a yacht's spinnaker. It wasn't surprising, really, as the material we bought for it was in fact spinnaker rip-stop nylon.

'We should use it to pull us across the lake!' I suggested, throwing this ludicrous idea at Clark to see if he'd rise to meet it.

'You reckon?'

I gave the usual shrugging nod, translating as, 'No idea, but I reckon it'd be fun trying.' And that settled it.

We loaded HMAS *Nugget* up for one last voyage, pushed off into the now wave-filled lake, and hopped aboard. Clark clipped the front corners of the vestibule onto the bow, and tucked the rest of it under a strap of webbing, where it waited—trembling with anticipation in the wind—for us to release it.

'Hoist the sail, Mr Carter!'

PHWOOOOMP! The wind—by now 30 kilometres per hour and whipping the lake's surface into crumbling waves—leapt inside the tent vestibule and exploded it full of air. HMAS *Nugget* sagged to one side as we settled in on a course about 45 degrees to the wind, doing about 3 kilometres per hour. It was not bad at all, except that we quickly ran out of lake, and found ourselves now stuck on the downwind shore, and wishing we were much further along, up an inlet on the upwind shore.

'I'm sure we can do this!' I persisted, taking down the sail, and swapping ends. Now crouched on the stern—on top of the solar panels—I held up my end of the sail, while Clark stood in the centre cockpit (that'd be the middle of HMAS *Nugget*) and held onto his, erm, sheet rope (an over-length zipper, actually), and as the sail filled again we charged back across the lake and made it directly to the point from where we needed to turn up into the inlet. Brilliant! With the wind now blowing a slightly alarming 40 kilometres per hour and the breaking waves making the lake look more like the ocean, we set sail up the inlet. Our last bit of sailing just wasn't meant to be, though, and we ran aground with waves surging right across the deck. Oh, well. It was fun while it lasted.

We hauled the last bit and unloaded all the heavy bags, and carried them well up onto solid dry ground, and then rolled the empty houseboat up to meet them, ready for tomorrow's day of checking our food inventory and converting HMAS *Nugget* back into the 'original' land-based Nugget. After some much-needed repairs we'll then set out on what will hopefully be the final chapter in our epic tale of adventure—the 230 kilometres of lakes, mountains, and who knows what kind of new unseen horrors that lie between here and the western side of Victoria Island.

## DAY 45: Closed for stocktaking

Today was a day of preparations: converting HMAS *Nugget* back into permanent land mode, and readying us and our gear for the final stage of our adventure.

We split the jobs up and began ticking them off, one by one: repair damaged rims—tick; dry hiking boots—tick; put Kevlar wheel covers back on—tick (well, what's left of them. Two were such a tangled mess of bandages, rips and patches that we couldn't even work out how to unfold them, so we've decided to use our two 'spare' Kevlar covers—our original prototypes—for our front two tyres). Set hauling ropes back up—tick; make new fish-drying rack so Clark can have his hiking poles back—tick; plan route—semi-tick. (We have a vague idea that will see us through the next few days, after which we'll give this item the time it deserves.)

And, last but not least—check food inventory. Clark went through each and every food type, counting the number of rations we have left of each. As we have by mutual agreement been stealing the odd bit of extra food from time to time when we figured we deserved it, it is important to get a handle on what's left when planning the final stage.

The results were varied. Considering it's Day 45 and we packed

100 days' worth of food, we now should have 55 days left of everything. These were Clark's findings: lunch tortilla wraps, 51 days; sugar, 53 days; oats, 54 days; couscous, 51 days; milk powder, 63 days (extra creamy oats and coffee from now on!); protein drink powder, 34 days (whoops); hot chocolate powder, 51 days; cashews, 53 days; peanuts, 53 days; trail mix, 27 days (we lost heaps to water damage, remember); butter, 59 days (woohoo!!! yum yum); peanut butter, 50 days; chocolate, 53 days; dehydrated dinners, 42 days (and, horrifyingly, only three sets of Mexican Chicken left! Maybe Day 50 celebrations, end-point celebrations, and one for when we really need it?); instant coffee, 41 days (No!!! Clearly the number of days we can survive out here is dictated by the weakest link, and this is it); dried lake trout, three days; no, two days … chew chew chew … make that one day. Oh, okay, cross trout off the list.

So, we're all set to wake up tomorrow and haul. Our Nugget should be about 150 kilograms lighter than when we started, so that's only 350 kilograms. And in other breaking news, Clark just timidly turned on his iPod for the first time since it fell underwater, and—moment of truth—mercifully, it still works! All bodes well for the next section of the trip.

## DAY 46: Five punctures at once

Today—our first day of post-Kuujjua hauling—unfolded very well. We practised a little procrastination in the tent first, further pondering our best route. Glaring at the whiteish areas on Google Earth—which seem to span much of the route from here on after an initial stretch of green—we couldn't help but notice its similarity to the colour of Death Terrain.

We set off at a trot, full of energy and enthusiasm to get back into hauling, and the green terrain was great. By first nut break we'd passed the 2-kilometre mark, and we were almost at the second nut break when, passing over an old river bed, we heard the dreaded 'PSSSSSsssssssss!' Whirling around in our harnesses, we stared accusingly at the back left side of the cart as it sank to the ground, the tyre totally deflated— just like our optimistic outlook for the morning.

'Quick, let's get some load off this thing!' I called, noticing how our poor rims themselves were now bearing the load, and pinching the limp rubber inner tube into the ground.

It was a smooth operation: unloading, hoisting the back of The Nugget up onto our tripod as a stand to survey the damage. Not one, but *five* punctures, one after the other in a line, where a sharp corner of rock had snatched at the exposed side-wall of bare rubber, right where the Kevlar doesn't shield it. We both grinned and said, '*Ayuuknakmat*' (that's our new word, emailed to us the other day by an Inuit lady—it means 'It can't be helped').

It took just under one hour to make the repairs, and we decided to skip the nut break that was now long gone, and press on until lunch to try and recoup lost hauling time. The terrain remained favourable, and the kilometres trickled obediently past on the PAC-o-meter.

Lunchtime saw us chewing our peanut butter wraps from on top of a huge boulder overlooking an open expanse of grassy tundra that was literally smothered in colourful flowers—it was beautiful! Boulders—although smaller than the giant we were sitting on—are becoming alarmingly common, and with our rigid four-wheeled craft, steering to avoid them is something that requires a *lot* of forward planning. They're everywhere—it reminds me of a joke I overheard once about how God apparently created the world in six days, 'and then on the seventh day … he threw rocks at the Arctic'. It almost looks that way—gently rolling grassy hills, spattered with huge boulders resting on the surface.

In addition to flowers and boulders, we have also started to see heaps of mountain sorrel growing all around us—an edible plant which was an important food for the Inuit. Back in 2005 our good mate Brent had told us all about these tiny little weed-like plants with their red-green (and rather fleshy) heart-shaped leaves which taste amazingly like a wild berry—sweet and flavoursome. We kept our eyes out and found none in 2005, but today we have been pulling off the odd handful of juicy leaves as we haul past, and enjoying the novelty of fresh salad with our meals.

Passing a large lake we'd noted on Google Earth, we have apparently left the safety of the green zone, and entered the beginning of the 'whiteish' region of potential Death Terrain. Strangely, in front of us, it looked like the green continued on indefinitely. Perhaps it was just snow covered when the satellite took the photo? We dare not hope—we know Victoria Island too well. With 220 kilometres to go, we managed just over 10 kilometres today, which, if we could keep that up, could even mean we'd be at the far side in little more than twenty days! Obviously that's unlikely, but it's these whimsical little dreams that keep us going.

## DAY 47: Ditch Terrain

Frustratingly, the entire day from start to finish was an endless repetition of a routine that we now perform mindlessly and mechanically: both haul The Nugget for perhaps 10 metres, and then both unclip and walk around to the back ready to gradually ease it down into yet another ditch. Although only an average of 5 metres wide, each ditch is about 2 metres deep, making it quite a slope. Together we then dig our heels in, and with one drawn-out wince, we're dragged down, trying to restrain the beast until it reaches the bottom, our pre-bruised feet slamming into rocks before we have a chance to spot and avoid them. Once at the bottom, we then walk around to the front, re-clip our harnesses in and haul for all we're worth, front-pointing our boots into rocks and mud—even down on all fours—to try to get some kind of purchase as we inch upwards. By the time the cart is on the top of the crest, the person hauling in front is sometimes already partway down into the next ditch, unclipping to start the process again.

It's a real nightmare—bad for us physically and mentally—and is also not great for The Nugget's axles and wheels. The ground is increasingly spattered with large, ominously sharp rocks, forcing Clark—closest to the cart—to forever be calling out 'STOP!' and throwing his body against the wheels to prevent them rolling onto yet another lethally pointed spear. Crisis averted, but unable to steer the cart, we'd then kick, smash, or loosen the offending rock and cast it aside before proceeding. Many of the larger ones cannot be removed, and this requires us to roll The Nugget backwards—likely uphill—and perform a four- or even a six-point-turn, coaxing it to head gradually away from the rock as we push it forwards a few metres, then back, then forward, then back, all the while pulling it hard to one side. Ah, the joys of Ditch Terrain! We just coined that phrase today, elevating this special form of Victoria Island torture to join its compatriots Death Terrain and Mud Pits.

To add to our problems, our feet are now causing us some pretty serious grief. Apart from being generally pulverised, I seem to have pulled my Achilles tendon rather painfully, making it impossible to load my left leg unless I turn my foot out at right angles and side-walk 'like-an-Egyptian', putting the load instead on my heel (which itself has some interesting ailments, as do Clark's). 'We're like a couple of old men!' Clark snorted at our hobbling. I think I will join Clark in his morning dose of painkillers tomorrow, along with our daily multivitamin, vitamin C, vitamin D, zinc and calcium tablets that we take religiously. As we down this colourful array of pills each morning, we truly do feel like a couple of old men—we almost need one of those little weekly planner tablet boxes to keep track of it all.

Towards the end of the day we reached the base of a lake—which we had hoped to reach by lunch—and saw that the nice green tundra rim that we'd hoped to haul around was in fact made impossible by cliffs plunging directly into the lake a kilometre or so ahead.

Damn. With bitter scowls, we turned The Nugget hard left and heaved up a twisting route through still more rocks for over an hour, up to a ramp leading *above* the cliffs themselves, which we'll have to try and haul across the top of tomorrow. What torture. Up and down, up and down goes our cart, and—accordingly—our positive energy.

## DAY 48: Lesser of three evils?

Even as we set up camp last night, furtive glances around us revealed all was not well with our planned route for today. Matching up the terrain colours on Google Earth with what was around us, it seems the white area we have been aiming for ahead is actually an immense boulder field about 3 kilometres wide.

It was not even worth attempting. Our only option seemed to be to go all the way back down to the lake we'd just spent the previous afternoon climbing above, and just 'somehow' get around it. It was a depressing realisation. 'Unless …' I began, an idea forming. 'Just an idea—not saying it's possible …'

'Go on,' Clark urged.

'I wonder if we could haul over the floating ice on the lake—go directly across the whole lake, rather than around the edge?' Ice covered perhaps 95 per cent of this lake's surface, and we had no idea how thick it was, except that it had already melted well away from the shore by about 50 metres on all sides, was littered with quite large meltwater pools into the shimmering distance, and the first 10 metres or so seemed nothing more than bobbing fragments of ice, a semi-fractured floating carpet of unknown thickness that wobbled, rose and fell with the surface waves. It seemed rather dubious, but we agreed that we'd at least take a look this morning as we started our solemn journey around the 15-kilometre shoreline.

So, sooner than expected, we found HMAS *Nugget* back in service, as we began wade-hauling her along the 'shallows' which were, in fact, quite deep. It was also rather cold, and the idea of hauling around the entire shoreline was becoming increasingly appalling.

At the point where the giant pancake of floating, rotten ice seemed the closest to shore, I unharnessed, and swam out the 40 metres to the fluctuating edge of the ice. The water was icy, but it was the clearest I have ever seen in my life—the bottom, way below me, was clearly visible and my legs seemed to dangle almost as if in free space. Towards what I hoped was the solid edge of the ice, I swam through the floating hunks and shards, scooping them away to either side as I went, the little pieces tinkling and jingling against each other like a glass wind-chime.

'It looks good!' I yelled back to Clark. 'It seems to be over a foot thick, mostly.' Thumbs up. I swam back, and we hopped aboard HMAS *Nugget* and paddled over to the ice edge.

The next dilemma was how to get ourselves from our floating raft—held out a good metre by our tyres—over onto the ice. With Clark paddling us hard against the edge, and me using the paddle as a bit of a crutch onto the mushy ice, I shifted my weight off HMAS *Nugget* and found myself standing on the swaying, flexible zone of almost-ice. It seemed to be holding my weight for the moment, anyway. I grabbed a hauling rope and held it in as Clark also leapt off, and together, we heaved with all our might, scrunching the front two wheels up onto the ice, followed, at last by the rear wheels. It had taken us over an hour and a half to get to this stage, but after a nut break, we were able to set off hauling over the ice, directly towards the far side, 10 kilometres away.

It was fast hauling: scenic, easy under foot and even though it was by now raining and windy, with the sky blanketed in grey clouds and the temperature a mere 3 degrees Celsius, it was just fantastic. In the first hour we racked up 3 kilometres! Some of the meltwater pools were quite interesting—spattered with gaping holes through to bottomless blue water beneath. As our mate Brent in Cambridge Bay would say, 'particularly "religious"'. Breaks were kept short by the cold, and by 5 pm we'd reached the far side—a total of 11.88 kilometres by the PAC-o-meter. We are so happy with that! Even if the lakeside hauling option had been viable, and even if it had been good terrain (it was neither, we goggled up in awe at the cliffs and epic valleys that would have stopped us in our tracks as we hauled), even then, it would have taken a good two days to get around.

I just sent an update to our website, and as Day 50 is coming up and we want to cook an exceptionally tasty dinner to celebrate, we've posted a competition online for our supporters to come up with recipe ideas, using only the provided list of the 'ingredients' we have at our disposal. We're really looking forward to this!

## DAY 49: Valleys and more valleys—with lakes and more lakes

We knew today wasn't going to be much of a winner: the trend recently has been 'one good day, one bad', and so as yesterday was surprisingly good, when Clark returned from collecting the water for cooking last night, he said, 'There we go, guv, I got enough water to wait out tomorrow's cyclone or whatever else Victoria Island has planned for us.'

'Good thinking,' I nodded, grinning.

Turns out it wasn't quite *that* bad after all, but we did wake up to a depressingly glum morning. The thick grey blanket of cloud was more like a mattress, hanging very low, draping a heavy fog beneath it, and spitting rain. What's more, after a good long stare at our topographic maps and Google Earth, we realised that there was no obvious route forward from here. Unfortunately, we did not anticipate being so far south on the island—the Kuujjua itself being a last-minute decision—so we never downloaded this part of the island on Google Earth at high resolution. Hence we're stuck trying to interpret fuzzy pixelated daubs that cover hundreds of metres.

'Do you reckon that's a line of grass?'

'Dunno. Might be a river …' If only we had our good old super-dooper broadband out here—the idea of trying to download the local terrain images over Iridium's 9.6 kilobytes per second is, unfortunately, not a realistic one.

Once we'd picked a route and headed off, the region of white assumed 'boulders' that we had planned to skirt right around turned out to be white pebbles, and so, shaking our heads with frustration, we turned 90 degrees to the left and cut directly over it towards a long skinny lake we had to get around. As we hauled, the ground ahead of us gradually drew away, opening up a gaping valley beneath us, at the bottom of which lay the thin lake we'd seen on the map. It was a dangerously steep descent. We unloaded four of our heaviest Ortlieb bags from The Nugget, and then gradually eased it down the hillside.

Amazingly, nothing went dramatically wrong—no wheels fell off, no broken legs, nothing—and we saved ourselves several kilometres of hauling around the lake! At the following lake, we re-enacted yesterday's success by paddling over to what was left of the ice, and hauling across it—although more tentatively this time. At one stage I gave the ice a good hard stomp and my foot smashed right through. I guess being a smaller lake it's more melted.

Getting up the other side of the next dramatic valley was a slog and a half—even though we took it at an angle. Eventually we stood on the ridge, looking down into *yet another* identical valley containing the *next lake* we needed to cross. We simply rolled our eyes, went to the back of The Nugget and began lowering it into the valley.

We're now camped at the bottom, right in front of the lake, ready to paddle out to its floating icecap tomorrow morning. Unfortunately, while I wrote a website update and Clark busied himself with a bit of man-sewing—stitching up a tear in the tent—we heard a loud scrunching, grating noise. Poking our heads out, we watched, fascinated, as a huge region of the ice plate we were going to paddle out to tomorrow broke free from the main icecap and—swept by the wind—drifted over to the shore in front of us, where it smashed into a million pieces as it crumpled against the bank. I guess now we'll have to paddle a lot further out tomorrow to reach the ice.

# DAY 50: Half-century celebrations

Despite the weather gods' decision to quite literally rain on our parade, we awoke determined to make today—the 50th day we've been alone out here—a happy, successful milestone. As we enjoyed an extra-creamy, extra-sugary bowl of oats, we listened to the rain spit and then spatter in earnest against the taut tent fabric as we clinked our (plastic) mugs of coffee together in celebration. 'To Day 50!' As we drained the last trickle of coffee from our mugs and wiped them clean and dry with a repeatedly licked finger (standard practice out here, I'm afraid), we prepared to face the weather.

Considering we had a lake crossing coming up anyway, we figured our drysuits were better than any raincoat we could wish for, and sealed ourselves inside. Being in a drysuit in the rain reminded me of that old Nordic adage: 'There's no such thing as bad weather—just bad clothes', and we certainly have the best. The mozzies though—as we tried to pump up the two back tyres that had mysteriously deflated themselves overnight—were buzzing around in such incomprehensibly huge swarms that we couldn't help but pause and take photos of the billowing, humming grey clouds. There were millions of them—more than I have ever seen in my life. Beating ourselves up, continually slapping our itchy faces and banging our hands to dislodge them made concentrating on pumping nigh-on impossible. As soon as the tyres were vaguely inflated, we quickly rolled away. The mozzies simply followed, and even climbed inside Clark's mozzie head net, which soon filled up with squashed mosquitoes. From the next peninsula around, to our delight it was only a short paddle across to reach the ice, and, well practised at the manoeuvre now, we leapt onto its bobbing edge, hauled up HMAS *Nugget* and set off.

This ice was even thinner than the last, and we used our hiking poles as much for dubiously probing the 'ice' in front of us as for support and traction as we hauled. Several times we had to cross regions of 'rotten' ice that seemed to have been shattered into tiny fragments and were simply squashed back together by the surrounding pressure, giving the impression that if we were to dislodge a single piece of the puzzle, the whole jigsaw we were standing on would dismantle itself in a flash. Ominous creaks and groans sounded as we hauled. Fault lines shifted, cracks spread, and footfalls sounded suddenly hollow. It kept us on our toes for the full 3 kilometres across the frozen floating pancake. Then, when still several hundred metres from shore, not one but two gaping open-water 'leads' appeared in front of us.

We pushed The Nugget from behind until the front wheels broke through the thin ice at the edge, and we then rolled the back in after. The Nugget's front was now only a few metres from the other side of the lake, and, noticing a few drifting chunks, I ice-hopped across from one to the next, as they bobbed and sank beneath my every step. Once over, I threw Clark the paddle I'd used as an ice-hopping-stick, and he hopped over to join me. Together we then heaved The Nugget up and continued hauling. The second lead was narrow enough for the PAC to form a bridge to walk over, and not long afterwards we paddled the final crossing to the lake's shore.

I should explain the reason we are suddenly able to walk on these lakes again after they initially became too slushy when summer first set in. When we started out, everything was smothered in heaps of snow, and it was this snow cover on the lakes that melted and turned sloppy while deep underneath they were still almost solid ice. As summer progressed, the melted snow drained underneath the ice layer in the lake, allowing it to float to the top as an ever melting and thinning raft. Most of the lakes are ice free now, but the larger ones still have this thin sheet of ice floating in the middle.

We managed a respectable 8.2 kilometres today, and setting up camp beside some large, deep wolf tracks, I did another live TV interview with Sky News before our thoughts settled firmly on food.

'Day 50 Dinner' will go down in history as one of *the* tastiest meals ever prepared at these latitudes. We scrutinised each recipe idea sent in via our website, trying hard not to drool on the keyboard as our taste buds imagined all the vibrant flavours. In the end, considering some recipes cruelly required ingredients not on our list (like cheese and tomato), and others required—to be honest—more effort than we two weary explorers could muster, we selected 'Spicy Speckled Couscous Burritos' as suggested by Raoul Kluge and Marketa Skala:

*1. Rub butter in pot, fry six flatbreads (one at a time) until speckled with black flecks. 2. Melt 1 tbsp of butter and add salt, chilli powder, garlic powder and paprika to taste (but enough to make it spicy). Add 'Miscellaneous Spice #1 & #2' and fry spices for 1–2 minutes, then pour in water, bring to boil and remove from heat. 3. Add couscous, stirring constantly and wait for two minutes before adding the rest of the butter. 4. Spread couscous on burritos, sprinkle some nut-ration nuts on top, roll up and eat.*

Next we moved on to dessert, 'Peanut and Chocolate S'mores', submitted by Nicola Craig:

*1. Spread peanut butter on burrito. 2. Sprinkle peanuts and crushed chocolate ration over peanut butter. 3. Toast until chocolate melts and then eat.*

This amazing dessert was perfectly accompanied by Jennifer Eurell's 'Mountain Mocha':

*Heat two cups of milk. Add 1 tsp of instant coffee and 2 tbsp of hot chocolate. Shave chocolate on top using Leatherman!*

We went to sleep warm, happy, full and content in every way.

## DAY 51: The Grand Canyons

In the morning, we quadruple-checked the GPS, and reluctantly gave in to its unflinching arrow, heading off towards the menacing, crumbling hills made purely from boulders and fragments of jagged rock. It grew steadily more horrendous as we drew nearer. By the time we got into the thick of it, we were not so much horrified as amazed. It looked like a cross between a rocky version of the Grand Canyon, an open-cut mine, and a scene from a Road Runner and Wile E. Coyote cartoon. There were boulders everywhere—some placed in impossible positions, propped up high, cantilevered out into the air by ludicrously small stones under one edge, or teetering precariously on the very brink of crumbling cliff faces. The skyline was a ragged mess of spikes, spires and angled blocks between which splits of grey light made the whole place feel like an ideal setting for the foothills of Mount Doom from *The Lord of the Rings*. There was no way around it. Valley after valley, we literally inched our way forward, heaving the PAC up bit by bit, and then once reaching each ridgeline, we'd have to spend half an hour scouting to try and find a plausible way down into the next valley without risking death or completely destroying The Nugget in the process. It was incredibly full-on.

I spent the entire day hanging on to the back of the cart, either pushing it slowly up, leaning it to the left or right to help guide it around pointy rocks the size of cars, or trying desperately to slow it down as it bounced and scraped its way down into ditches and valleys. There were of course also repeated sessions of pulling the cart backwards and forwards for yet another twenty-point turn to try and change course by 90 degrees in order to follow less suicidal routes.

Clark spent all day at the front wheels doing the same thing. Forget about 'hauling'—we manhandled the cart all day, and we are now utterly, utterly exhausted, and our hands sprained and bruised, much like our feet. We forced our dilapidated Nugget over terrain today that we were both *sure* it would not survive, but we had no choice. We dropped it off ledges, we rolled it right up and over 70-centimetre spiky rock corners to avoid even more deadly ones, we lowered it down several landslide chutes filled with huge boulders, grimacing as the wheels bent this way and that, watching the whole metal frame skew and twist, both us and the cart squeaking and groaning in pain. It became a case of 'Just go for it … it's the best we've got. If it breaks, it breaks. We'll just have to find a way to fix it.' *Ayuuknakmat.*

Although the PAC-o-meter revealed a measly 4.22 kilometres (and only 3 kilometres by the GPS) we set up camp a little early tonight as we have zero energy left. Right in front of us is another torturous descent and climb, although there seem to be grassy patches we might be able to reach tomorrow. I really can't wait to get out of this terrain. It's pretty scary, stressful stuff.

Google Earth shows it gets greener ahead, and then it becomes strangely patterned with lines. Maybe it's a green, swishing grassy field, with a series of neatly mown pathways along it?

# DAY 52: Broken men

We waved the mouse pointer repeatedly around on Google Earth like the glass on a Ouija board, pretending we could divine some meaning from the blurred images, and magically devised a route for today that seemed to offer the smoothest, flattest, most PAC-friendly path possible. The result was, as it turned out, the most horrible, rough, boulder-filled, PAC-murdering terrain we've ever seen—yet, alarmingly, it probably was still the best option out there.

As we harnessed up, Clark pointed out a herd of muskox lazing around, lying beside the grassy riverbank down which we were about to haul. As we rolled towards them they begrudgingly got to their feet, and eyed us blandly for some minutes, great tufts of their woolly coats wafting and flapping from their unkempt, shaggy backs. Hemmed in by steep cliffs, we couldn't really divert from our path, so we edged closer until they began rubbing their eye glands on their forelegs in warning—and then we stopped. At a complete stalemate, we just had to wait until—possibly aided by a few of our wolf-like howls—they backed off a few paces, regained composure and lay back down and we managed to sidle past them.

Not five minutes after this, an arctic fox bounded up towards us, pausing every few seconds to sniff the air, cock his head inquisitively and leap a little closer, his bright little eyes sparkling with curiosity. Eventually he got close enough that our smell must have burnt his delicate nostrils and he scampered off.

As the wind died, the mosquitoes descended upon us in such numbers we just couldn't stand still. We slapped ourselves, shook them off our hands, snorted them out of our noses, spat them out of our mouths, and fished them out of our coffee with our grimy black fingers. More maddening still, The Nugget has recently developed a pronounced desire to always veer to the left of its own accord, which is particularly infuriating when, like today for instance, we really needed to arc right to avoid a slushy region. We strained sideways on our ropes, almost walking crab-like in the last few desperate metres before I flung my hiking poles down in disgust and went back to 'sort it out'.

Just as I was about to give the frame a shove to skew it back parallel, I caught sight of the rim on Clark's side. It was buckled on one edge. A crack had run down into the rim, splintering the epoxy bonding.

'Oh no—look at that!' My heart sank. It was exactly what I'd feared might develop after our incident with the rapids. We must have banged a pre-weakened part yesterday in all that hellish boulder terrain, and the damage had now spread. Our options for repair were very limited, and after assessing the situation we decided to leave it for today and see if it continued to worsen. 'We'll just make sure we take it easy over any rocks today.'

We hauled onwards, slowing down as a dramatic landscape slid into view around the corner. We shot tentative 'surely not' glances at each other as the scene deteriorated. We stopped.

Basically we were sealed between impossible cliffs on each side, with no option but to continue hauling right into a trap. We'd have to negotiate a shocking jumble of boulders (which had clearly once fallen from the cliffs on either side), and then descend through still more boulders into another valley. High on each side, the cliff faces were scattered with house-sized hunks of rock that looked like they'd been snap-frozen for no apparent reason in the middle of falling, while others teetered on the edge, and still more lay at the base, with a recently crumbled scar of shattered rock behind them. A lone rough-legged hawk cried its mournful wail above to complete the scene. Typical.

And so it became the kind of day where we just had to suck up our emotions and keep going, the terrain and boulders getting steadily worse and worse, until we found ourselves pushing and pulling the PAC over incomprehensibly stupid boulders. Bounce, bounce, slide sideways, bounce, grate, scrape, creak, groan, bounce, crunch, thud, bounce, creak, *SPLINTER*! I let out an agonised moan the instant the sound of our splintering rim reached my ears: even before I knew what had happened, I felt its pain.

We both hurried over and shook our heads, refusing to believe it. The edge of the rim had evidently landed heavily on a large boulder, sending splits and cracks right up through the structure of the rim like lightning bolts. It wasn't even the same rim as before. We still had several hundred metres of boulders to traverse ahead, and we had no option but to unload the cart and portage all our gear, one bag at a time, to the 'safe zone'—trying not to break a leg as we staggered around the boulder field. Not that breaking a leg and being flown out wouldn't have its advantages, we both mused, only half jokingly.

It was a real low point, and I accidently overheard Clark confiding into his video camera, 'It just keeps on going. I just want to go home. I've had enough. There are only so many bad things that we can try and overcome.' While I knew we both felt this way inside, it scared and shocked me to the core to hear Clark actually say it—if only privately to his video camera. The plunging effect it had on my morale was a real eye-opener as to the importance of maintaining our false optimistic exterior, just to help each other get through.

After the first portage we scrambled up a landslide chute to the top of the cliff to see what lay ahead: more boulders. Yay. On the way back to The Nugget, Clark set the GPS to point towards the far side of the island, still 168 kilometres away. He turned around and followed the arrow. 'At this speed ... walking ... it says it'll only take us 49 hours,' he announced pointedly. As we reloaded The Nugget, we seriously began considering the practicality of just shoving some food and safety gear into an Ortlieb bag and heading off, on foot. We could be there in a few days, bringing 30 kilograms instead of 300.

We hauled onwards. The rest of the day we were broken men, barely speaking. When we did, it was without energy or emotion, empty, just to confirm a direction, or to call a halt for a moment to recover. We each just put our soul into a little box somewhere inside us for safekeeping—to bring out again at some later date. For now, we merely stumbled onwards, gritting our teeth in anxiety as each boulder passed underneath, our stomachs knotting each time a wheel lurched down into a pit, threatening to further damage the rims or worse. The wheels aren't even round anymore.

The terrain got steadily worse, and at last beside a lake, we donned drysuits and, although we wanted to go almost 90 degrees to the right, we pushed the PAC into the water and hauled it, floating peacefully, the long way around the lake edge to give it a break. The lake bottom was also boulders—and covered in slime—so we were forever slipping over, our mangled feet sliding and wedging awkwardly into gaps between rocks.

'This stuff messes with your sanity!' Clark suddenly admitted.

'I think we're already pretty insane to be out here in the first place,' I replied, attempting humour.

'Yeah, well, I guess this is making me go sane then,' Clark mumbled, 'because I'm at last starting to think that … maybe this is crazy.'

We are going nowhere fast, our cart is breaking up, and so are we. To be honest, we are hating life out here today, and the far side feels impossibly far away.

## DAY 53: Gale force winds, rain, ice and … surf?

I woke as a particularly violent bullet of wind and rain struck the tent, the whole cart heeling slightly with the force. Squinting at my Citizen EcoDrive watch hanging above me, it took me a while to work out that the hands really were pointing at 9.45 am. That didn't seem to make sense as I was still dog-tired, but holding the watch up the other way gave an even less realistic time, so I woke Clark and we lay there, listening to the miserable weather raging outside.

We continued to lie there for another quarter of an hour, hoping it would ease, but it didn't. Even breakfast inside the tent was a challenge—milk powder blew right out of the mugs before we had a chance to add the coffee, and our titanium pot lifted off the MSR stove and hit me in the side of the head just as Clark started to pour water into it. There was nothing for it but to get out there and face the weather; we didn't want to stay crammed in the tent anyway. We squelched our feet into our boots, packed up camp, and headed off. Our thermometer showed 3 degrees Celsius, but a shocking minus 3.5 if we included windchill—our first sub-zero temperature in weeks, and mixed with rain it made the world quite unbearably cold. The wind was so strong! Hearing each other talk was impossible as the wind roared past our hoods, and our communications degenerated into a series of hand signals, nods and questioning looks of incomprehension. I got out our wind thingo (a Silva Atmospheric Data Centre Pro), and held it up: 50 to 60 kilometres per hour wind, gusting to 65 kilometres per hour. That's a new expedition record.

Mercifully, the wind and rain was at our back, and once we started hauling, it wasn't as bad as it could have been. Nor was the terrain—the boulders have mostly gone now, replaced by firm, short tundra grasses on long rolling slopes. Reaching the mountain pass we've been aiming towards for a few days, I surveyed the impassable landscape below. Rather than attempt to go down through the boulder-filled valley, Clark spotted a potential route that involved us hauling right up into the hills, but potentially led at last to a grassier, gentler slope down. It worked a treat, and a few hours later we found ourselves in front of a large lake that it looked like we'd have to haul around, as there was no floating pancake of ice visible.

Peering along the shoreline route, I saw some rather nasty terrain developing ahead, culminating in a boulder-filled ramp up to a jagged cliff that then plunged directly into the lake. Desperate not to subject ourselves to any more boulders, I looked around in vain for another option.

'If we push the PAC into the lake right here,' I began, 'the wind will blow us across to the other side, right past all these boulders and cliffs ...' Clark looked dubious; the idea of standing around in the rain getting changed into drysuits and booties wasn't appealing. 'We could just roll it in, hop on and push off with our paddles,' I encouraged. 'We could even stay in our hiking gear.'

We agreed, and six-point-turned The Nugget to face the water and rolled her in, leaping aboard just as the water crept up to boot height. A few hard shoves with the paddles against the bottom and we were afloat.

The screaming wind gripped us, and to our smug delight the GPS showed us accelerating directly towards the far corner of the lake where we wanted to exit at a nice grassy ramp perhaps a kilometre away. We jeered at the boulders as we passed. In response, Victoria Island increased the wind. The further from the windward shore we got, the larger the waves became. Whipped up by the wind, the surface of the lake transformed from scurrying ripples into ever-growing waves, crumbling into whitecaps. The crests of some of the larger waves even started to be blown clean off, the foam streaming across the surface like spindrift. It was—almost—like a mini version of the Southern Ocean. We looked at each other in a combination of awe, excitement, and a growing tinge of concern.

For reasons known only to herself, HMAS *Nugget* prefers to turn side-on in any wind and travel beam-on. As the waves grew, so did the rhythmic rocking of our raft, and with waves now smashing against the wheels and rims, some even emptied themselves right over onto the deck, threatening to wash away our gear.

The far side of the lake was getting closer and closer, and staring at it, I realised with increasing anxiety that our landing was not going to be as smooth as we'd imagined. The reason there was no floating pancake of ice on the lake was that the wind had blown it across into the corner we were now rapidly bearing down upon, smashing it into a billion fragments of ice—as well as a few sizeable chunks. As the waves crashed into the confusion of ice, they broke all over it like surf, and I watched, mesmerised, as each wave's energy passed through into the icy mixture, transmitting incredible surges of rising and falling hunks of ice through to the shore beyond.

My mind raced forward the 30 seconds or so it would be until our traumatised, swamped little raft struck this jumble of surf and ice, and what I saw terrified me.

'Hold this!' I yelled at Clark above the wind, flinging off my harness and snatching up my drysuit—something we should have done at the start—and racing to put it on. The gap was closing fast as I kicked off my hiking boots, one leg into the suit, two legs in … we could hear the ice grinding and breaking against itself just metres ahead.

*Expletive*. 'My zipper's stuck! Help me, will you!'

Clark freed the zip and I yanked it closed, slammed on one wetsuit bootie and didn't even have time to get my foot in the other, before I plunged over the side and—half swimming—grabbed a wheel, desperately fighting with all my effort to try and drag the PAC around to face the wind so that at least we'd 'roll' into the mess rather than collapse against it broadside.

I *just* managed it in time, and stood helplessly in the crashing, chest-deep, ice-filled water—with the wind blowing the spray into my face—and watched as the front of the PAC entered the fray. As Clark panicked to get into his drysuit, the wind drove HMAS *Nugget* further into the thick of it, and—buffeted by heaving ice boulders—I too found myself in that zone I'd seen earlier, where each rolling swell lifted up the suitcase-sized hunks of ice around me, and then dropped them—sometimes excruciatingly—onto my feet. If it wasn't for the fact that the ground was soft mud, I'm sure it would have crushed every bone in my feet.

HMAS *Nugget* eventually came to rest, jammed against a mess of compacted ice. We were stuck in the surging nightmare, 10 metres from shore, held off by all the jumble of ice pieces as wave after wave charged through. Clark, now in his drysuit, hopped in and we tried desperately to pull the PAC to shore but it wouldn't budge. In the end we actually backed it right out through the surf zone into the water again, out and around to a place where the ice was less built up. There, giving it our all, we at last managed to heave the PAC up and half onto the jumble of tumbling ice, and drag it across, finally, to shore.

It took us a while to collect our thoughts. The scariest thing about it was that we didn't see it coming at all. The terrifying half-hour just past was pure action and reaction—survival instinct kicking in. It could so easily have ended so badly. We didn't even feel up to jeering at Victoria Island for overcoming her latest hurdle—we were just mighty thankful that we did. Her games are getting serious.

Everything seemed to survive being swamped, including our battery and our drybags of food. 'All's well that ends well, I guess,' Clark shrugged.

'Maybe next time, though,' I grinned, 'we'll put our drysuits on a little earlier perhaps.' We nodded as the lesson sank in.

'I'm so glad you saw that coming and managed to get yours on in time, guv.'

## DAY 54: Rolling on broken rims

The silence when we woke this morning was so complete it was eerie. Something was missing. 'Hey, the wind's stopped!' The tent sides were motionless.

'Fantastic! Maybe we're finally going to get a good day.'

The terrain, although peppered with the odd boulder we had to multi-point turn to avoid, was, on the whole, brilliant. Firm dirt and dry mud—held together with a patchy covering of tundra and wildflowers—rolled ever onwards. By lunch, the sun had come out in full force, and with most of our electronics all but running on empty, we quickly had batteries charging left, right and centre. With 4 kilometres already clocked up, good terrain ahead, and a tummy full of lunch, everything was once again looking up in a big way.

Until I noticed something strange about the front right wheel. It was bulging oddly. Frustration mounting at the thought of yet another delay for more niggly repairs, I walked over to it as Clark watched with that now familiar 'what's broken this time?' expression.

It was far worse than I feared. 'Oh no!' I cried, slamming my fist down onto the hardtop in dismay. 'The rim! Look at it—it's *completely* buckled in!'

We didn't need this, not right now, when things were finally looking up. The poor rim—having been through so much—had finally given up. The entire side flange had collapsed in upon itself in two places, forming large pleats, the points of which were now sticking into the inner tube and about to puncture it. Wordlessly we unloaded the entire cart onto the tundra and steeled ourselves for another major repair job. It really needed to be popped back into shape, re-glued, and then reinforced with some spare aluminium riveted behind each tear.

We stared gloomily at what little was left of our epoxy glue, the few remaining pop-rivets, and the only bit of spare aluminium we had left—our mangled axle off-cuts. As we looked around for inspiration, Clark spotted that the other front rim was in a similar shape, also wielding a large buckle wound. We just didn't have enough stuff to attempt a repair of this scale.

'Maybe,' I began, voicing what we were both thinking, 'we should convert to two-wheel mode.' Apparently we've been independently thinking this over for some days. A quick, scribbled calculation of weights showed that if we piled everything into one cart now, it should *almost* (12 kilograms over) be equivalent to the original load carried by each single PAC at the start—a load we know the carts can handle, just. It was a big decision; it'd mean no more being able to sleep on top of the cart, no more water-mode, and no easy way to double-haul anymore as we'd need one person to haul, while the other walked at the back, balancing the load to stop it rocking on its axle. On the bright side, though, we'd be able to steer a two-wheeled contraption, it'd be lighter, and we'd instantly gain two spare inner tubes, covers, a spare axle and spare rims.

As I looked at the crumpled rim which was still trying to gouge a hole in the inner tube, I half-heartedly let some air out to relieve the pressure to stop it puncturing while we thought things over. As the air rushed out of the tube it shrank away from the rim, and amazingly the rim started to un-crumple itself. At a ludicrously low pressure, the rim was almost round again. Clark was also watching the rim 'repair itself' and we gazed at each other, wondering. 'We really shouldn't ditch the four-wheeler until we absolutely *have* to,' I thought aloud. 'We've still got more than 150 kilometres to go …'

Clark agreed. 'We may as well just go on, with ultra-low pressure,' I continued, 'until it does finally fall apart, and then we'll scrap it.'

It was agreed. 'You're on thin ice,' I warned the PAC, as Clark choked on another mosquito that flew into his mouth, 'Any more of this veering to the left nonsense—or *anything* else to annoy us—and you've had it. It'll be two wheels from then on!'

## DAY 55: Keep going, rain, hail or twister!

Today's terrain—a continuation of yesterday's firm grassy tundra—made for brilliant hauling, and as the temperature climbed to 17.2 degrees, we pushed up the sleeves on our Icebreaker tops, sweat pouring off us as we marched.

By our second nut break, we were well on our way to 5 kilometres, still sweltering away in the humid air. As we chewed a handful of peanuts and mosquitoes (there are so many out here it's getting ridiculous, I literally have to haul breathing through gritted, bared teeth to filter them out), I lazily gestured at a particularly impressive storm cloud curling and tumbling towards us, draping its grey curtain of rain below. 'Looks like we might be getting a spot of rain soon.' Clark nodded.

Moments later, the temperature plunged by an incredible 9 degrees (from 17 down to 8 degrees Celsius) as a cold front engulfed us. The sun withdrew, and we dived for our Gore-Tex pants and jackets, packed up our nut break and were about to shackle up and start hauling when I spotted something odd protruding from the cloud's dark base.

'Oh my God!' I pointed excitedly. 'A twister!?'

Sure enough, a long funnel cloud was reaching downwards, a tightly curling straw. Clark had the video camera rolling even before I got my camera out, and although the twister didn't even reach the ground, it was still pretty spectacular. Several minutes later it sucked back into the cloud, and we started hauling, just as the rain struck.

It was a full-on heavy downpour of astonishingly large drops, which then started bouncing off the ground around us—it was *hailing*! We grinned at each other through tightly drawn hoods, and as there was nothing else we could do, we started hauling. 'You can't break broken men!' Clark shouted at the sky. 'So up yours, Victoria Island!'

Besides repeated pauses to adjust and add more bandages to our shredded wheel covers, one last obstacle came our way before the end of the day—a sizeable river emptying a large lake system that we've been hauling below for days. The water was too deep for boots, so we threw on our drysuits, and waded in, towing The Nugget behind us. Our wheel covers were now so full of tears and tourniquet bandages that as we rolled through the water, each tear scooped up pocketfuls of water as the wheel turned, then emptied as it rolled past the top, like an enormous Chinese water-wheel garden feature.

Safe on dry ground on the far bank, we checked the PAC-o-meter: 13.40 kilometres—a new record! We both know what that means—an extra dehydrated meal for dinner tonight!

## DAY 56: A good day's hauling

After coffee and oats we spread out our various topographical and aeronautical maps, brought Google Earth up on our Eee PC and turned on the GPS, trying to ascertain what might be the path of least resistance for us and our Nugget. There are so many contour lines in this part of the world, all looping around each other, scribbling wildly hither and thither that sometimes it's impossible to work out if the slope should be going up or down. After an hour of this, we think we've settled upon a likely route from here to the west side of the island. Veering around the odd lake and avoiding the worst patches of mountains and cliffs, the route is still fairly direct, and we're confident it's the best we can do. However we look at it, though, it's going to be a nightmare of hauling up and down some terribly steep hills, and plenty of river crossings.

There was the lingering chance today of some real excitement. We'd received an email last night from a diamond mining exploration team who are temporarily camped on the island, saying they were actually intending to do some 'sampling' in our area, and might 'drop in for a coffee'!

'How crazy would that be!' Clark laughed. We've seen no other humans for 56 days, and the thought of having a helicopter roar down beside us is quite surreal. 'Oh, that'll be them, I'll pop the kettle on …'

Despite convincing ourselves we heard the drone of an approaching chopper several times during the day, we sadly had no visitors, and the whole day turned out to be a bit of a non-event. It's weird, actually; I can't even remember anything much about it at all. I feel a bit like I'm developing amnesia out here sometimes. We just … hauled, I guess, and the terrain (thankfully) stayed the same, the weather (unfortunately) stayed the same, and the hours and kilometres ticked past, and—amazingly—nothing serious broke.

## DAY 57: No more ice hauling

Unfortunately it seems our days of hauling over floating lake ice are behind us. While there were still small rafts of ice wandering around the surface of the large lake we came to today, the firm pancake has gone, even on a lake this size. We settled instead on following along the tundra shoreline, which to our delight was not too bad, despite the odd steep sideways slant and patch of boulders.

Except for a herd of muskox, we didn't see another living thing today, although quite frankly, we could have walked right past anything and not seen it—with the weather the way it is, we have just been 'existing' during the day, physically present hauling wearily onwards another 8 or 9 kilometres, but mentally already in the tent, waiting for warmth and dinner.

In order to extend the number of days we could potentially exist out here if we need to, over the last few days—even though we're still hungry—we have been cutting back on our rations. Instead of 125 grams of chocolate each per day, a few days ago we dropped to 100, then 50 grams. We have totally cut all the butter from our diet (about 50 grams each per day normally), and today we decided to also cease our daily couscous meal, so we're skimping now, but it will give us more options in the future. With less than 140 kilometres remaining, we figure that besides injury, about the only thing that could prevent us eventually getting to the far side would be running out of time, which is equivalent to food. Having come through so much to get this far, we owe it to ourselves to do whatever it takes—including volunteering to go extra hungry now—if it might improve our chances. We'll see how we go, anyway.

## DAY 58: The longest journey

Slowly but surely, we are getting more and more exhausted out here. Every morning for about the last week—despite our best efforts—we have inadvertently slept in, and risen feeling increasingly weary. This morning was even worse: we woke at each alarm: 7.30, 8, 8.30 and 9 am, but each time we faded away back into a daze of sleep.

Once we were finally out and about, we gave our two rear wheels some very much needed TLC, deflating and adjusting their 'covers' (if you could call them that—they are now nothing but a collection of rags held together with string and webbing). It's becoming incredibly frustrating—we have to spend almost as much time stopping and caring for our tyres as we are hauling. We're still managing to stagger about 8 kilometres each day, but we're now mentally traumatised by the paradox surrounding the burning question: how many more days? If the terrain holds up and we manage to maintain our speed, we could be there in as little as thirteen or fourteen days. But ironically, if our cart breaks, we could be there in just six or seven! Freed from this ungainly beast we have in tow, we could easily just put some supplies in a drybag and walk—if not run—to the end, and have the rest collected later by air. Surely the challenge we set ourselves was 'to cross the island', and for that we needed the PAC only to get this far—the challenge wasn't 'to drag this thing across the island'. For some inexplicable reason though, we'd feel guilty leaving it behind, unless we really had to.

'What about,' Clark said with a wry smile, 'if it just happened to break, you know, overnight?'

I couldn't deny having briefly thought of sabotage myself. Fuelled by this dilemma, our minds perpetually prey upon themselves as we inch ever so arduously onwards, feeling our inner strength fade daily.

Around lunchtime today this trip officially became the longest journey of our lives—it feels like it too. On Day 58 of our 2005 trip at 1 pm we were standing on a snow-clad esker as Willie Laserich flew in to collect us. We still have 125 kilometres left to go in a *direct* line. We just want to get there now—it's tantalisingly close, yet still so far.

## DAY 59: Visitors!

Well and truly submerged in a deep sleep, both Clark and I suddenly found ourselves being forcibly dragged upwards towards the surface of consciousness by a throbbing, growling noise getting closer outside. By the time we'd wrenched ourselves up into a dazed sitting position, the roaring, beating sound was unmistakably that of a helicopter, apparently about to land on the tent.

I ripped open the zip and shoved my head out, blinking in the bright light. It was indeed a helicopter, buzzing 100 metres away and banking around for another pass. We dived for our jackets and donned our stained, crumpled shorts, suddenly feeling rather self-conscious about our Icebreaker leggings and our dishevelled appearance as figures inside the chopper waved enthusiastically.

'Dammit!' Clark cursed. 'Why do we always oversleep these days?! Wish we were hauling!' I shoved my beanie over my serious case of bed-hair—my hair's so long that it gets in the way of my eyes now—and we both sprang from the PAC in bare feet, reaching for our cameras as the chopper came to a graceful landing about 50 metres away, just outside our bear tripwire alarm. Dazzling smiles were visible through the chopper's glass front even before the doors swung open and three figures stepped out and walked towards us, beaming. Our first contact with other humans in 59 days!

Hurrying over to disarm the bear alarm, we greeted them with a hearty, 'G'day,' shook their hands and then Clark politely ushered them into our tripwire enclosed 'yard'. Our visitors were from the De Beers temporary diamond mining exploration camp—two geologist students and a pilot—on their way to perform a site sample 20 kilometres away. Still half asleep, we found ourselves fielding a bunch of questions, explaining this and that about our cart and the expedition.

When we got a chance, we started asking our own questions,

about the terrain ahead. 'Yeah, it's really pretty to fly over—dramatic,' was their response. 'All these valleys and hills …'

Great!

They all produced cameras and posed for shots of themselves with the two crazy Australians. I then brought out my camera and tripod, and wandered around looking for the best place to set it up, trying to get the PAC, chopper and us all in shot, but the sun made it all back-lit.

'Yeah, if you'd just move the chopper over about … there,' Clark indicated jokingly, but the young pilot grinned and said, 'Sure. We'd best be on our way, but if you direct me where to go, we'll hover wherever—and then just wave us off when you're done.'

We did just that, and after a few more passes and much waving, the helicopter swung around and roared off back the way it'd come.

To our immense delight, the sun came out today, and the wind died also. Unfortunately this allowed the mosquitoes to plague us again as we wound our way around a few lakes, crossed the odd patch of boulders and even a short section of Ditch Terrain, before struggling up an almighty climb to the saddle where we are now. Ahead the terrain looks okay-ish for another kilometre or so, and then it looks quite terrifying: hills and escarpments, valleys and cliffs … But as ever, tomorrow's another day. We managed 7.11 kilometres on the PAC-o-meter today, which is reasonable, considering all the time wasted tending our wheel covers.

## DAY 60: Two months in …

After somehow managing—for once—to force ourselves to respond to our alarm at 7.30 this morning, we got off to a good start. A consistent breeze blew all but the hardiest mozzies away, and all in all, things unfolded well. I saw a few wolf prints and Clark spotted two arctic hares which promptly bounded away into the amazing jumble of boulders that hemmed one side of our route for much of the day. The geology of these crumbling mountains we're navigating is quite spectacular. It looks exactly like the whole landscape is made from regular stone bricks, all stacked upon each other—some having tumbled down while others remain, forming perfect walls and even flights of neat stone stairs leading into what resemble great ruined fortresses. It's amazing to look at—but hell to haul over. I guess we are getting there, though, just slowly. One or two punctures at a time.

## DAY 61: The last map

Although it's not over till it's over—Victoria Island has certainly taught us this, if nothing else—we're steadily getting more excited as we draw gradually nearer to the end of our journey. Our conversations are increasingly turning to discussing the things we'll do first, the things we'll eat, and the luxuries we'll enjoy as soon as we escape back into civilisation.

To our surprise, after a less than ideal morning's haul during which Clark lost his beanie, our afternoon's progress was great— slow but steady. The last few hours saw us facing the highest and longest hill climb for the entire expedition—an imposing gathering of three 100-foot contour lines on our map, an ascent which we have long been dreading. Rising to a lofty 400 metres above sea level, it marked the highest point on our route. It was a long, hot, mozzie-filled slog, and as breaks are awkward on such a slope with The Nugget wanting to roll back down, we just put our heads down and stuck it out, one step at a time.

We were almost at the top when I realised we didn't have any water with us for cooking dinner. There was a moment's awkward silence as we both gazed in dismay back out over the spectacular lake-strewn landscape now well below us several kilometres away, but thankfully a frantic search of the map revealed we should find a tiny lake right at the summit, and so we continued onwards, our day's energy ebbing fast. Almost there. Almost there.

Here we are! Camped beside the lake, on top of the world, having somehow racked up 9.8 kilometres today, and ceremoniously crossed onto our very last topographical map—showing us and the west side on the very same bit of paper! That—together with the knowledge that 'on average' it's all 'downhill' from here—is a real psychological boost.

# DAY 62: Under 100 kilometres to go!

Just before we fell asleep last night we agreed that in the morning, we'd get hauling as quickly as possible, and squeeze some serious kilometres to firmly put us within the '100 kilometres to go' boundary.

I must say it was a struggle to find last night's enthusiasm this morning, but once under way, the kilometres whipped past, despite the supposedly 'flat ground' promised by the topographical map actually being a series of hills and valleys which must have all cunningly stayed within the same 100-foot contour line limits, making them invisible to our route planning. Still, while the uphills slowed us, the flats were fast, and the downhills even faster.

With great ceremony we theatrically limped across the '100 kilometres to go' line mid morning, and ever since, it's been as if 'the end' is now somehow suddenly close enough to imagine—close enough for *the first time* to dare to hope. This excitement is what really drives us onwards now, rather than just the fear of not getting far enough from our start. Over our peanut butter flatbread we reminisced how so very often during the last 62 days we were both certain that the far side of the island was absolutely hopeless, that we wouldn't—couldn't—make it. As early as Day 6 when we realised our Kevlar covers were tearing, we have spent so many of the subsequent days hauling in despair after various setbacks—knowing we couldn't possibly get there—and wondering why we were still trying. It's incredible what you can do with a bit of perseverance, blind optimism and brute stubbornness.

# DAY 63: Suspiciously easy

Rain made breakfast a subdued, inside affair today, and after swallowing all our multi-vitamin tablets and cleaning our teeth, we ran out of procrastination ideas, looked at each other, groaned, and clambered out to face the day.

While the weather is again atrocious—raining and blowing 40 kilometres per hour—the terrain is still wonderfully agreeable. It has plenty of ups and downs, but most are rather gradual and rolling. The ground underfoot is mostly a hard, compacted earth, carpeted with a patchwork of green tundra clumps. Each little clump is perhaps only 20 centimetres across, yet contains an amazing array of tiny flowers. There are so many different colours—all sprouting through and around bright green moss, lichen, mountain sorrel, yellow poppies and more. Most plants are now starting to seed, and many of the flowers have started to wither and die. I guess the short Arctic summer is already on its way out. In fact, tomorrow at around midnight, the sun should dip below the horizon for the first time this summer—the end of our first 'day' that began the day we arrived in Cambridge Bay. It'll get chillier now at night, and the hours of daylight will reduce rather smartly, which isn't all bad—we might get a chance to see the Northern Lights if we're lucky.

We passed 6 kilometres by lunch, and everything kept going well all afternoon. Suspiciously well, in fact—what is Victoria Island playing at? I even undislocated my foot by accidently slamming it against a rock while lowering The Nugget down a hillside. Something structural has been hurting inside my foot for the last few weeks—enough for me to have developed an awkward limping gait to my hauling—but today whatever it was popped back into place. I'm cured!

Clark tells me we're only 82 kilometres from the end now. It's getting closer! But almost just as fast now, we're getting wearier, finding it harder to focus, harder to stand and continue after a nut break … So close—yet still so far. One day, (someday soon?), we are longing to catch a glimpse of the ocean on the distant horizon, beyond the never-ending hills.

## DAY 64: Let off lightly

It was a chilly start today: 3 degrees Celsius with windchill down to minus 2, and the usual delays didn't see us out of bed till about 8.30. My morning visit to the open-air toilet-with-a-view was somewhat more interesting today. Partway through I was interrupted by a giant arctic bee—like a normal honeybee, but bristling with fluffy hairs—buzzing agitatedly around my foot. As I looked down, it was joined by another. And then, another. Uh-oh! Then a fourth crawled out of a dark entrance hole under the very rock I was crouching on! Abort! Abort! It wasn't a dignified departure, but when you're caught with your pants down, escape is rarely a smooth operation. Peering back from 3 metres away, I saw that, thankfully, the gathering of bees hadn't attempted pursuit.

So much for our 'downhill from here' theory. It just means that there's slightly more downhill than uphill, but there's still plenty of both. Today started with a 3-kilometre uphill, and, reaching the top, we then looked down over 5 kilometres of gradual downhill—at least that's what our topographical map said it would be. A 'gradual sloping region of hills' might be a better description, however, and as we hauled along, up and down, I spotted an odd ridgeline running along beside us, drawing closer, in and out of view. While all our hills were a lovely, radiant golden colour—a mixture of earth and tundra—this 'other' ridge sidling up next to us was black. We thought it must have just been in shadow, but as it drew nearer we could see it was comprised entirely of large, dark, lumpy boulders poured on top of each other, completely obscuring whatever ground may have lurked beneath. It was incredibly ominous, and with the clouds above reflecting its drab gloom, it looked positively evil. Rather symbolically, a few black crows wheeled sinisterly above and with several boulders protruding tombstone-like against the skyline, we half expected a hooded figure holding a scythe to float past.

Inevitably—as we feared it must—the black ridge swung across our path, and there was nothing for it: we *had* to cross it somehow. Like all good traps, we were lured into it gradually. The boulders began as scattered obstacles, but increased in number until, almost before we knew it, we were trying to haul The Nugget over an ocean of the biggest boulders we have ever attempted—far worse than those which smashed our rims last time.

Pausing and looking back, I shook my head in disbelief at Clark harnessed in behind me—one corner of The Nugget was embedded against a bench-sized boulder, and the other corner tilted way up in the air at an absurd angle rolling on top of another. As I watched, the wheels of the cart passed over a giant protruding boulder, which scraped hard against the netting and drybags underneath, contorting and skewing the entire metal frame before the front left wheel slipped off its current pedestal and the whole cart sprang down, jolting Clark off his feet.

Ahead it just got worse. The Nugget hated it, the wheels hated it, and we—well, we were lucky to get through without breaking at least one of our legs. These huge boulders were simply jumbled upon others below, and it was a case of trying to hop from the random corner of one to the next, while trying not to slip down into gaping black voids between them, all the while attached to a lurching 300-kilogram cart by a length of quite elastic rope. I'd get one good footing, heave, remove my back foot, go to swing my body weight forward and just at that instant The Nugget's bulging tyres would usually absorb into the face of some other boulder and rebound, flinging us both off balance and bending our hiking poles. Ridiculously, we were even *below* The Nugget sometimes, while it clambered over boulders behind and above us. Occasionally it totally bottomed out on rocks and I'd have to sneak underneath and push upwards on the underside to free the netting while Clark kept hauling. It was full-on, and when we got to the far side, we could not believe we only had two punctures.

After crossing the black hill, the terrain mercifully returned to our favourite golden tundra. Shaken a little by this unexpected deviation from the ground we've come to know and love over the past few days, we hauled onwards until at last, up a few more hills, we arrived at a large river in our path. The GPS and 'topo' said it was 160 metres wide. We had been dreading it, but as we hauled down towards it, we found a crossing point where small rocks formed an ankle-deep path all the way across! I guess that's our trade-off for being smacked with the boulders. I'm happy with that.


## DAY 65 (1 August 2008): Eclipsed

We woke this morning to a crescendo of multiple alarms all set for 5.30 am, wolfed down a quick brekky and set up our cameras ready to witness the near-total solar eclipse due to occur at 6.15. The sun was blazing clearly in the sky as we set up, and we were pretty excited about what it would be like to experience our first bit of real darkness in 1800 hours since the perpetual daylight started when we flew into Cambridge Bay.

'I wonder what all the animals will do,' I said, looking around excitedly, 'and if we might even be able to see the aurora briefly?'

With about two minutes to spare, the sun suddenly dived for cover behind a thick blanket of dark cloud. Typical! We stood there, cameras rolling for about half an hour, and although it certainly became a little 'overcast' while the sun was behind the clouds, that seemed about the extent of our eclipse. Perhaps we got our time wrong or something? To be honest, we're pretty confused about what the 'real' time is these days, after so many clock adjustments.

'Oh well,' I shrugged, 'we'll just have to eclipse our hauling record instead.' Clark nodded with a 'you're on' kinda grin, and with nothing else to do, we packed everything away and were hauling by 7.15—well before we'd normally even hear and ignore our first wake-up alarm.

Extending our hauling day by two extra hours meant we'd naturally have to borrow some extra nut-break rations from some unfortunate day in the future, but it was definitely worth it.

We'd covered 8 kilometres by lunch, which we ate sitting atop a huge isolated square boulder that had inexplicably found its way to the very top of an otherwise perfectly rounded grassy hill. After that, it was up and down again, around this lake, along that ridge, down into that valley, climb out through the saddle to the left, skirt along the sloping side of the next mountain to the next lake, and so on. It was a real maze today, but picking our own path out here is part of the joy and freedom of it all. We are perpetually surrounded by this endless rumpled expanse of possibly unexplored land, dotted with lakes and animals, and we are free to go wherever we wish—so long as it's the fastest, straightest route possible to the far side, of course!

The excessive climbing today took its toll on my feet, and by mid afternoon I was hobbling around in my harness using both my hiking poles more as crutches than anything else, limping rather pathetically and wincing and grimacing with every step. With about half an hour still to go before our usual quitting time of 6 pm, I could haul no further, and we set up camp.

I was quite surprised at how debilitating what I assumed just to be a blister in the making felt—but when I at last eased my boot off, I discovered my foot had bypassed the blister idea. Instead, a wide region around the back and sides of my heel has been rubbed totally raw of skin, exposing that wonderfully sensitive, weeping base-layer that burns like fire when you touch it. I delved into our extensive first-aid kit—mercifully for the first time this trip besides for painkillers—and now just hope that the injury miraculously will have healed by the morning when I have to wedge my feet back into my boots and start hauling The Nugget up more mountains.

The PAC-o-meter reads ... wait for it ... 15.02 kilometres!! That's almost 2 kilometres further than we've hauled in a single day ever, and this was across the most jumbled set of contour lines we've faced yet. We're stoked with that. Eclipse hauling record—tick.

It's rather amusing to remember that 15 kilometres per day was the 'easy average' that we predicted in 2005 should get us to the far side within our guesstimated 65 days. I remember writing 'Hauling at a snail's walking pace of 3 kilometres per hour even for just five hours a day (which we could do before lunch if we really wanted to), should easily get us there in 65 days.' Ha ha! Yup, whatever you reckon, little boys! If you include those 58 days from 2005, we're now 123 days into the island, and we're still not there. If we'd been using PAC-1 today, though, we'd still be stuck back at the first few boulders near camp. We live and learn.

We've seen no sign of Inuit artefacts, stone tent rings or anything else for many days now: this really seems to be an untouched area, and the maze of hills might explain why. It's pretty cool pondering that we really could be the first people to ever walk through some of these valleys.

## DAY 66: A sight for sore eyes

After sending our update last night and finishing our various chores, the weather remained so pleasant, and the view outside so spectacularly beautiful, that we were both lured out for a few lazy hours of soaking up the experience. Lying down on the tundra, we watched the late evening sun cast its long golden rays over the strangely sculpted mountains around us, and the clear blue sky reflected vibrantly in the myriad of lakes below.

'Imagine having a house here,' Clark mused. It certainly was a million-dollar view, and we continued to watch as the odd herd of muskox trundled past on a distant hillside. While we have been absorbing and 'taking in' these scenes around us as we haul, up until the last few days we've always had that pressure in the back of our minds, forcing us to keep going, forcing us to keep trying— if only to convince ourselves that hope was not yet lost. Recently though—while we know it's not over till it's over—we are feeling, at long last, *confident*. It's hard to explain, but for once this confidence is no longer just a brave facade we display for ourselves and for each other to keep up morale. We now genuinely believe that, barring a serious accident, we will reach our goal. A huge weight has begun to lift from our minds, allowing moments like last night, where we were able to genuinely relax and properly absorb the serenity and splendour of it all.

Ever since about a week ago we have had the very real—and very tempting—option to dismantle and cache The Nugget, and simply walk to the far side of the island in a few days with only what we can carry. We have even gone so far as to write up an exact list of what we'd take with us. It's been a constant mental battle, but we have managed to resist the temptation to 'cut and run' and are determined to carry on as normal. We both know that as soon as we get back to civilisation, it won't take long before we just want to be back out here anyway.

After yesterday's epic efforts, we didn't manage to pull ourselves together until 8.30 am, so our day began a little late. Quite seriously, our Kevlar wheel covers are now beyond all help—they are nothing more than a series of rotten, frayed, torn scraps of fabric all bunched and wedged together, held vaguely onto some parts of the tyre by no less than eighteen bandage tourniquets. We have long since run out of spectra cord and webbing to make any more straps, and so the inner tubes bulge horribly in so many places. There are huge areas as big as a dinner plate of raw, exposed, abraded rubber, and with the low PSI pressure we need in order to not buckle the rims, all this hilly terrain makes the 'covers' slide around, overlapping the rim on one side and revealing a whole section of bare rubber on the other.

If we deflate, rearrange and reinflate the tyres, it takes at least half an hour per tyre, and about one hour later it's back how it was anyway. So for the last few days we've adopted a new tyre care strategy—the 'I don't care anymore' strategy—and we've been amazed at its success. In fact, the rubber holds its own so well that we've even given up trying to guide the immovable PAC around the more obvious rocks! Sure, we suffer the odd puncture, but they are few and far between, and being so close to the end now, we don't feel we need to conserve our puncture repair patches. So the secret to our improved kilometres for the last few days is not only the firm terrain, but that without having to avoid rocks and fix the covers every hour, we get so much more time to haul!

By mid morning, the weather had cleared into a *perfect* Arctic summer's day, and by lunchtime we even had our shirts off for the first time in ages, soaking up all the beautiful warmth. It was one of the most relaxing and pleasant lunch breaks we've ever had. Instead of mozzies, the air is now filled with fine tufts of cotton that are being released from billions of fluffy arctic cotton grass plants growing everywhere. We watched some rising and wafting around on invisible air currents until they disappeared from view.

We took a bit of a gamble with our route today. We had planned on a rather weaving, inefficient route that avoided some of the contour lines (thus hills and valleys) on our map, but instead—after cross-referencing with Google Earth—we decided to attempt a much more direct but hillier option. The gamble paid off, big time. There were some epic sections lowering The Nugget down mountainsides, and some trying climbs, but all were manageable, and it was interspersed with long open expanses of our favourite, firm terrain.

The kilometres flew past. As we lowered The Nugget down a particularly long hillside at some speed, a large boulder just in front suddenly transformed into a bull muskox that hastily stood up, shook himself, and then expressed his severe annoyance at being woken up by commencing the usual 'rub-eye-on-foreleg' warning manoeuvre as we bore down upon him, desperately trying to dig our heels in to stop. Seconds later, upon his realising that The Nugget was rather a lot bigger than he was, and that gravity was potentially going to make it a rather one-sided contest, he abandoned his warning and thundered off. 'That was lucky!' I panted, as the cart finally came to a stop.

Cresting the largest major hill between us and the end point, just above 300 metres high, Clark suddenly pointed to the horizon. 'Look! Is that … is that *the ocean*?!' Right in the distance, a thin blue band stretched behind the mountains.

'It is!!'

What a moment that was. The GPS indicated we had just over 50 kilometres to go. We've now descended the last epic slope, and are camped down beside a gurgling, crystal-clear stream. Ahead, the terrain for tomorrow continues to look ideal, and the weather is still perfect.

# DAY 67: Getting there …

We adopted another last-minute route-plan change today that was again more direct but hillier, and again, it seems to have paid off—at the cost of only two punctures. Twice during the day we heard the distant roar of a passenger jet passing way overhead, and both times we paused and looked up wistfully. Soon, my pretty, soon … Well, actually, we still don't have a confirmed pickup option, but like everything else at the moment, we've adopted the Inuit attitude that 'it'll be okay'.

To be honest, we're getting mighty sick of peanuts and cashews now. Nut breaks are no longer the radiant lights that once split up our days. We are starting to crave different foods now. Brekky, lunch and dinner are all still very much enjoyed, but oh, what we wouldn't give for a pizza, or a steak, or … trust me, there is a written list, and it is almost endless, under the heading 'Vancouver' in our notebooks. It won't surprise me if we gain 15 kilograms in the week or so we have planned in Vancouver before flying back to Australia!

There was one big surprise this afternoon, just after punting across another beautiful, cotton-lined stream—the far bank consisted of *trees*! Well, they were only perhaps 75 centimetres tall, but by Victoria Island standards, these were giants. We had to haul right over a full-on jungle of them—it was genuine old-growth scrub.

With 40 minutes left of our day, we found ourselves at the base of an alarmingly large hill towering above us. Rising over two contour lines on our map, there was no easy way around it so we bit the bullet and started to haul directly up its face. It was quite a trial—the humidity made the sweat literally run off the tips of our noses and at each step we shed a small shower of droplets, blinking to keep our eyes sweat-free as we fumbled and clambered for the next foothold. Eventually, to our dismay, it became just *too steep*, and we stopped moving. Despite our best efforts, The Nugget hung there, with the odd scraping, scrunching noise as it slipped back another few inches while we clung gecko-like to the mud slope.

We both carefully manoeuvred ourselves behind the front two tyres and managed to inch it up the last 100 metres by physically grabbing and rolling the tyre itself for a quarter of a turn in one massive synchronised heave, and then quickly wedging our knees in behind it to stop it rolling back and reclaiming our hard-earned altitude. We'd pause for breath, and then just before the weight of the cart threatened to telescope our knees through our lower leg bones, we'd then heave another quarter turn, and so on. It was the steepest ascent we've tried, and at long last we made it, thoroughly muddied.

We're now camped on a flat-topped hill, commanding spectacular views all around. There's a big mountain range off to the north, and to the south we can see the ocean in Walker Bay, and ahead, west, looks like—well, more hills. But we'll deal with those tomorrow.

Right now, though, it's time to celebrate. We just broke our daily distance hauling record, *again*! We managed 15.46 kilometres by the PAC-o-meter today, of which a whopping 14.7 kilometres was distance-made-good—such an amazingly direct route today.

## DAY 68: Aren't we there yet?

The world has again become so quiet up here, and we're both really noticing how far sound carries—bird calls, for instance. We'll hear what sounds like a duck honking right near us, and only after carefully scanning the landscape we'll track it down to a tiny speck on a distant lake. It's the same with talking to each other. The other day we were standing on two different mini hills, well over 100 metres apart both looking for route options ahead. After our attempts at communication by exaggerated hand signals, shrugging and pointing all became too confusing, I just tried shouting. It almost knocked Clark off his hill—it turned out we could just speak normally to each other.

After a delayed start, we set off into what began as more rolling hills of tundra, only occasionally having to ease our increasingly flimsy, creaking Nugget down into the odd steeper ditch. However, as we limped onwards, a jagged rocky hill came into view, and then another, and then more of them—we were surrounded. Considering the pitiful state of our tyre covers, we have been dreading being faced with any more rough rock sections, but it seems all good things come to an end, and so too must our favourite terrain.

We tried to pick the least savage route through the sea of serrated rocks, and with a final gesture of *ayuuknakmat*, we plunged in. As we staggered in ungainly fashion from rock to rock, we could hear the metal frame grating and grinding against the larger boulders and the rubber tubes twanging as they were nicked and snatched at by the sharp edges. It seemed like it would never end—one rock hill after the other—until suddenly we found ourselves lowering down the jumbled face of the last one, back onto our wonderfully earthy tundra.

Miraculously, we got through without a single puncture! It's hard to explain just how impossibly unlikely that was. One of our wheel covers has now slid off the inner tube almost entirely, exposing more than two-thirds of the rubber, flapping and flopping as the wheel lurches around. We're lucky The Nugget is so much lighter now, as without the covers to contain their squashy, ballooning form, our wheels are starting to become very 'flat' indeed and quite a drag to pull.

Our PAC really is on its last legs, and so are we. Now that the end is so close, I think our minds are letting our bodies start to shut down. We just can't cope with too much more. Mentally, I think, we are already there: we can picture it; we've lived that moment a thousand times in our minds, and really, all these days in between feel like they are just in our way, each one harbouring potential disaster.

We're tired, and we just want to be there, yet we know we can't let our guard down even for a second. Every kilometre, every day as we manhandle The Nugget through this convoluted terrain, something as simple as a stumble while heaving this wheeled mass up a steep hill (let alone those that slope down to a cliff) could so easily end everything. We're getting a little paranoid that *something* is going to happen before we get there.

This last section of the island we've been traversing—the last 60 kilometres or so—is quite technical navigation. There are just so many contour lines, so many hills and gullies and rivers and lakes and 'unconsolidated ground' and cliffs and false summits and hidden valleys, that picking a route through it at all—let alone trying to pick the most efficient one—is proving to be a real challenge. Helpfully, we're now onto a high-resolution satellite photo map we brought just for these last few days, but even though it shows wonderfully accurate 10-metre contour intervals, there are still surprises. Our debates often revolve around, 'Well, sure, there's a 120-metre contour line there, and the lake starts right next to it, but is the lake sitting at 111 metres and therefore ringed by a 9-metre impassable cliff, or is the lake at 120 metres also, with a nice broad walkway around it?' These details can clearly make all the difference, and we usually find out the hard way.

As we feel our way across this island, we've been keeping our eyes out for any 300-metre sections of flat, firm terrain that a plane could potentially land upon, and noting them down for René Laserich at Adlair Aviation back in Cambridge Bay. Considering we've only found about four of these sites across the entire island, it goes to show how invaluable knowledge of these places is. We found one more today—22 kilometres from the far side—and we're both desperately hoping that we can organise a boat pickup, so that we don't have to haul all the way back here and charter an expensive flight out—if we can even find anyone willing to do an off-strip landing, that is!

## DAY 69: She's determined to stop us

Last night we deflated each of our four tyres and did our best to rearrange their shredded bandages for what we hoped would be the last time. We went to sleep rather late—about midnight—too excited to sleep in the knowledge that if the good weather and good terrain continues, today might be our last full day of hauling!

We woke to pouring rain. Everything was wet. Water had seeped in through the tent, into our sleeping bags, and puddles of water had collected where the tent's material floor overhung The Nugget's hardtop. I tried to mop it up, and as I peeled back our Thermarests from the manky tent floor and wiped, a disgusting brown-grey bow wave sloshed in front of the rag—a foul bubbly mixture of almost 70 days of accumulated dust, bits of tundra, mud and various forms of body hair. Now that everything is damp, it has started to smell, too—it has become quite repulsive in what used to be our only sanctuary out here.

More than once this morning we shouted loudly at the sky in a mix of frustration and desperation: 'Get us out of here!!' Sharing a glance that said more plainly than words, 'I'm so ready for this to be over', we'd just have to laugh at our sorry selves, and get on with it.

We remembered the saying, 'When the going gets tough, the tough get going.' But as Clark pointed out, 'I don't see anyone tough around here anymore.' It's true; we're feeling pretty used and abused now. Any abnormal stretch or foot movement sends us—especially our feet and legs—into painful cramps, sometimes dropping us to the ground. I'm looking forward to a hot bath, I tell you what.

Mid morning we called a mate of ours in Holman (the only other community on Victoria Island, way down on a south-western peninsula) who has been trying to organise a pickup for us by boat—it all looked like it was happening, and this phone call was to confirm and lock in the date. It was the exciting moment we'd been looking forward to all morning ... but when I made the call, we learned that the boat's steering system is broken, and it can't be used for the pickup. He was still full of enthusiasm, though, and said he'd see if he can find someone else with a dinghy, and we're to call him back tomorrow night. We expect to *be there* tomorrow afternoon, so you can imagine how much this news crushed us. Visions of us waiting—stuck in purgatory at the end for weeks— were not encouraging.

Still the rain poured down, and after climbing yet another hill, we peered down over an angry expanse of cliffs, drop-offs and gullies—all made entirely from shattered rock. Our path blocked, we invented a new route, which involved an appallingly lengthy climb onto a side hill, but which would then reward us with a long stretch of what looked like our good ol' favourite: dry golden tundra.

We knew something was wrong as soon as we set foot on the hill. The nice dry earth was dry no longer. The top inch or so had absorbed all the rain, and transformed into a strange, ultra-dense and incredibly sticky variety of mud. Every step we took, the surface inch or two of mud adhered to the bottom of our boots and lifted with them, adding onto the next footstep of mud, and so on. Within three or four steps we'd literally be standing on great stilts of mud layers—including several rocks as big as a fist—all stuck to our boots and hiking poles, weighing us down as if we were wearing manacles.

Having survived that, we then came to an innocent-looking river. Rolling The Nugget in, we punted towards the far side, until—still a good 10 metres from the far bank—the weedy bottom became too shallow, and we were stranded. We almost broke a paddle pushing so hard against the bottom, but it was useless. Grabbing the wheels and trying to turn them by hand was similarly useless. Annoyingly, our drysuits were packed away under the hardtop we were standing on, and so with a withering look at Clark, I took my boots off, rolled my Icebreaker leggings up as high as I could, and eased myself into the icy water. The arches of both my feet instantly cramped in the cold, and the false bottom of weed sank me up to my waist, thoroughly wetting my rolled-up thermals. I'm really starting to tire of Victoria Island and her cruel tricks.

Just around our usual 6 pm quitting time, the rain—having done its job for the day—also stopped. Replacing it, a blinding fog descended all around us. About 13 kilometres from the far side of the island, and determined to bring it within striking distance for tomorrow, we decided to push on for another few hours. We were wet through, our cart and everything on top of it—including our tent—were all smothered in sticky mud flung everywhere by the tyres, and the thought of clambering back inside our dank, dripping hovel seemed even worse than continuing to haul.

We're glad we did continue on. As it turned out, Victoria Island had set up several nasty obstacles for what would have been our final day. River crossings flanked by towering multi-layered cliffs of 'moss'—literally forming thick rubbery walls we had to squelch up and over and then somehow manhandle The Nugget over too; sudden kinks and 8-metre drop-offs in the middle of what looked at a distance like pleasant grassy hills … strange new terrain in all directions.

Realising we hadn't gone to bed, the rain decided to return with vengeance to accompany the eerie white fog, just as we reached a large lake that wasn't on our map. We couldn't even see the far side through the swirling veil, and strange hills that also shouldn't have been there loomed ominously in and out of view around us.

Clark then pointed out half a muskox leg.

Yes. That's right. Just sittin' there; a hoof and the fur-covered lower portion of the leg, with the long bone protruding through the mess of tendons and muscle, ending abruptly where something fairly large had evidently crunched the bone in half. Umm … yikes! We both peered unseeing into the fog around us. 'This place is so creepy,' Clark whispered. I couldn't have agreed more.

We hurried on, down this valley that shouldn't exist, and on into the next, until the fog became so dense, and the random drop-offs so steep and sudden, that we figured we'd better call it a day. With only 9 kilometres to go, we figured it would be safer to negotiate this kind of madness tomorrow, hopefully during a lovely sunny day for our last day of hauling.

## DAY 70 (6 August 2008): The final steps

Having got to bed late at around 2.30 am, we woke feeling mentally and physically shattered this morning. It was still raining, the world around us was still veiled in thick fog, and everything was even more wet and disgusting than it was yesterday. Yet, the magnetic lure of the far side pushed all this from our minds as we prepared for what we so desperately *hoped* would be our last day of hauling.

That's the thing that's been tormenting us—even being *so* close, we still knew we couldn't take it for granted, and for the last week we've been forever having to stick a 'hopefully' or an 'if we're lucky', or 'maybe' onto the end of every potentially motivating thought or comment. While this frustratingly ate away at us now more than ever, it paradoxically also now spurred us on.

We wrung thick brown, putrid water from our socks, and squeezed on our hiking boots for the last time 'hopefully', and folded up the sopping bundle that was our tent and sleeping bags and wrapped it all in the blue tarp as usual and lashed it down to the top of The Nugget. Having packed up our bear alarm and done a last scout around to check we weren't leaving anything behind, we finally set off.

It was a good thing we stopped last night when we did, as negotiating The Nugget down into the last steep river valley was quite difficult, and only as the fog slowly lifted were we able to orchestrate a practical, safe descent. Our spirits lifted along with the fog, and soon afterwards the rain also cleared as we began power-hauling up the face of the last real hill (maybe), making excellent progress, despite the grotesque, wobbly wheels now rasping and grating against the side of the cart itself, great flapping folds of Kevlar slapping and catching on things as the covers finally gave up the ghost.

With about 7 kilometres to go, we watched three muskox lumber around the base of the hill several hundred metres away and then start charging up the hill directly for us. We stopped. 'That's weird,'

I commented, as they continued thundering towards us. We both unshackled, and went and hid behind our cameras and waited. Typical, we thought, we're going to be trampled and killed by a herd of rampaging muskox on the very last hill. It wouldn't have surprised us.

'Or, if they fail,' I laughed, 'Victoria Island will unleash a whole series of tornadoes from the clouds, ripping and churning their way towards us as we dodge and scramble to touch that far side.'

About 75 metres before impact, the big bull pimp muskox leading the charge of his two devout followers suddenly became aware of our presence and awkwardly slammed on his brakes, whirled around, and retreated a bit before swinging back to face us again, trying hard to maintain a nonchalant air of superiority, without success. 'How embarrassing!' We both laughed and hauled onwards, keeping our eyes on the clouds.

Much to our confusion, the top of our very last hill came easier than expected, and as we drew towards the crest, we could see the skyline falling further and further away in front of us, revealing an open expanse of ... nothing. There were, for once, *no more hills* on the skyline. Finally reaching the very top, we paused, and, looking down, exulted at the view we have both been so vividly imagining for the years since we started in 2005. Dead ahead through the wisps of fog we could see the west coast of Victoria Island—the wedge-shaped lake right against the shore that we'd both stared at so often on our maps, and slightly to the north of it, that little round lake marking the most westerly tip ... it was all there, just 4 kilometres in front of us.

We decided this was as good a place as any to have lunch, and nestled in to enjoy the view, but just before we took our first bite the fog came down like a curtain around us and visibility once again dropped to within a hundred metres. We just shook our heads, shook our fists in the air, and couldn't help but laugh at the almost comic injustice of it all.

Down we went, onto the flat coastal plain. The fog shielded us from any useful landmarks to aim for, and with Victoria Island clearly racking her brains to try and come up with some final obstacles to fling at us, we found ourselves climbing over some impossibly spongy ledges, faced with little rivers that were just the right width to neatly swallow and wedge our PAC's wheels, small lakes that appeared from nowhere on either side, forcing us to haul through their sloppy, weedy bottlenecks in-between, and even abrupt mud walls that we actually had to multi-point turn to go around. Against all odds, though, the kilometres kept reducing, and we could still see nothing ahead. We had long imagined this final sprint across the coastal plain, the sparkling blue ocean ahead, clear blue skies, and a nice gradual ramp leading into the lapping waves … ha ha. Whatever!

With only *one* kilometre to go, I put the GPS around my neck to guide us towards that all-important waypoint, determinedly following the little arrow into the fog as the excitement—and suspense—mounted. 'We're almost there!!!' We kept repeating this—and other variations on the theme—as we flung ourselves into our harnesses with all the feeble energy we had left. We were getting so close, so excited. We could now even hear the ocean thundering on the shore, and smell the salt in the air. With just under 500 metres to go—just as we were about to pull out the video cameras to capture the last (foggy) minutes—in a superb display of poor sportsmanship, Victoria Island parted the heavens and unleashed a torrential downpour of rain upon us. We flung on our Gore-Tex and resolutely marched onwards, with ever widening grins spreading across our faces. Two-fifty metres … 100 metres … the end was now drifting in and out of view through the billowing fog. We hauled faster, the surf in our ears, stupid smiles on our faces—'fifty metres!!!'—and then, we stopped.

'The ocean looks rather a long way down, doesn't it,' I said quietly. It certainly did. We unclipped and walked tentatively forward, our disbelieving gaze tracking downwards as we advanced towards the edge of … a cliff. A 10-metre cliff. Right at our end point, stretching in both directions as far as we could see, a 10-metre drop down onto a narrow, pebbly, rock-strewn coastline—our end point.

In complete exasperation, we threw a mock tantrum, water beading and flinging off us as we vented our frustration, and then at last we stood there, looking at each other in the rain, wet through, not wanting to move a muscle from our semi-hunched posture else wet, cold fabric would adhere to our clammy skin. Once again, we laughed at ourselves. What else could we do? The three of us started this trip together—Clark and I, and the PAC—and all three of us were going to finish it. There was no question about it, the PAC—good ol' HMAS *Nugget*—was going to celebrate with us, standing in the waves of the ocean. The question was: how to get it down there?

We eventually found an unlikely erosion gully running down to the shore—a near-45-degree slope comprised solely of slipping boulders. This would have to do. We unloaded some of the heavier items, set the video camera up, and began lowering the PAC down this boulder-avalanche-chute-of-death. As we accelerated down, realisation dawned. Even if we now broke all our legs, and tumbled head over heels downhill—even if we both had heart attacks or if Victoria Island struck us both simultaneously with lightning (I wouldn't put it past her)—it suddenly didn't matter anymore, because no matter what, we were now assured of reaching the far side, even if we fell the last couple of metres. This sense of inescapable destiny flooded us with euphoria, and with the PAC increasingly eager to get to the water too, we began running along behind it—more hanging onto it than lowering it—as the wheels finally scrunched onto the pebbles and burst against an incoming wave.

We'd done it. We were standing in the water, on the most extreme westerly tip of Victoria Island, after 70 days (128 if you count the first 58—that's more than a third of a year), not only with the PAC, but with all four wheels. We could not believe it.

It was pretty cool to think that three years ago we were standing across the other side of this, the ninth-largest island on the planet, about to try and walk across it at its widest point, with virtually no idea of what we'd face. And now, here we are … It's been a long-held dream, and it's become our lives. All the many things we've learned, experienced, feared, overcome and enjoyed between these two coastlines since Clark was 21 and I was 22 have made us who we are—they've shaped our personalities and values; taught us how to overcome, and if necessary, endure; and—above all—formed one hell of a friendship between us.

We had to wait a while down the bottom of the cliff for the rain to ease enough to grab some belated photos of 'the moment', and then we harnessed back up for 'definitely' the last time, and grunted our way back up the boulder-avalanche-chute-of-death to the flat, grassy tundra top, where we set up camp just as the rain set in again.

We enjoyed a celebratory mug of coffee (our last coffee ration!), and then dug into various other rations at random—not that we were particularly hungry, but just because we could. It was awesome.

As the drizzle continued, Clark had the ingenious idea of setting up the little blue tarp as a shelter, propped out from the side of the tent by our paddles (the tent itself was just too wet and manky to crawl into without totally killing the mood). We ate a few blocks of chocolate (yes, as opposed to 'squares' of chocolate), and then after a brief wander along the shoreline we came back and enjoyed our final Back Country Cuisine 'Mexican Chicken' dehydrated meal that we have been saving for this moment. Then, feeling at last content and secretly rather proud, we unwound the protective bubble-wrap from around our tiny little hotel minbar-sized bottle of Grand Marnier liqueur that we lugged all this way—just as we did in 2005. And—just as it did back then—having not had an alcoholic drink in so long, and with next to no body fat left (we shall remedy these issues in Vancouver), we both felt the effects of sharing this microscopic bottle. Good times. Good times. And still it rained.

'Do your worst, Victoria Island!' we jeered merrily. 'You're too late. We *got* there!' Let's readjust the scores now. Victoria Island: 0, Clark and Chris: 1.

Just before going to sleep, we gave our man in Holman a call, and to our delight, he had some good news. 'Call my friend,' he said. 'He has one of the biggest boats in Holman. He'll come and get you.'

I did just that, and after I'd explained our predicament, the man didn't hesitate: 'Oh, yes, sure. No problems.'

Even the clammy insides of our sleeping bags can't dampen our spirits tonight, and having set up the bear alarm and turned off our watch alarms, we're about to enjoy a very long and very well-deserved sleep.


## DAYS 70 TO 76: The great escape!

Only in the North could this happen. The last five days have been quite the experience. 'It's not over till it's over'—a truer phrase has never been uttered—and so the adventure continues from where we presumed it had ended: perched smugly on the most westerly tip of Victoria Island, glowing with satisfaction and Grand Marnier …

The following day (Day 70 + 1) brought with it equally unappealing weather, and we spent much of the day in the manky tent or huddled underneath the tarp shelter, enjoying forbidden pleasures like triple-ration servings, grinning all the while as we tried to shake the feeling of guilt at not hauling anywhere. But for the weather, it would have been perfect.

I kept calling our man with the boat in Holman, and each time I hung up with the news that, no, the waves were still too rough for him to attempt a pickup. We passed the time (Day 70 + 2) building a stone cairn propping up a small driftwood log into which we carved '1000 Hour Day Expedition—1000 km E > W—Chris + Clark—2008'.

We also explored several kilometres north and south along the coastline to look for a suitable place for a dinghy to land, and to our delight, about 3 kilometres south stretched a long pebbly beach. It looked perfect. When I called our man on the following morning (Day 70 + 3), he was already loading his boat with extra fuel for the twelve-hour, 300-kilometre return trip. We gave him the location of the beach, and after packing our campsite up, shouldered our harnesses for the last time 'definitely', and hauled south.

Re-energised by our two full days of food and rest, we basically ran all the way, covering the 3 kilometres in well under an hour. As we did, the sun burst through the clouds that had been smothering it since we arrived, and we were blessed with a perfect summer's day. The blue ocean sparkled, terns and seagulls wheeled and cried in the increasingly cloudless sky, and as we rolled The Nugget down onto the pebbles just metres from the lapping water, we unbuckled our harnesses and ceremoniously cast them aside and enjoyed the blissful sunny 'ending moment' that Victoria Island had denied us originally.

We spent the rest of the afternoon dismantling our PAC, reducing everything we had into a long line of yellow Ortlieb drybags, a few lengths of aluminium extrusion, and our carbon wheel rims—all stacked neatly inside each other. That was it. We were done. There was nothing to do now but kick back and twiddle our thumbs.

About an hour after our saviour's estimated arrival time, we grew bored of thumb-twiddling and I called his home to see if he'd radioed back any news. He had. In fact, he'd done more than radio it back; he brought it back in person: 'No, the weather out there was too rough. I had to turn back … I'm sorry.' Where we were, our coastline was protected by Banks Island (just visible on the horizon), whereas the first part of his boat trip from Holman would have been open sea. Having built ourselves up to the pickup all day, this news came as a bit of a letdown, but I guess there's no arguing with the weather when it comes to small boats, so we managed to laugh it off as just another classic Victoria Island moment.

'No worries,' I replied, grinning at Clark's comic eye-rolling, 'tomorrow?' I crossed my fingers.

'The weather is supposed to be better in the morning, yes. Call me in the morning.'

Unwilling to search through our sixteen identical yellow drybags for our tent, we set up our bear alarm and lofted our sleeping bags directly onto the tundra inside our newly formed paddock, rigged up a bit of a windbreak using the tarp and paddles, collected a pile of age-old driftwood from the shore and lit our first fire of the expedition. The sun skimmed lower and lower over the water, highlighting the clouds first pink, then orange, before painting the entire sky a spectacular mixture of reds, pinks and purples. It was just beautiful, and combined with the radiating warmth of our fire—and several curious arctic foxes that bounced right up to us and even played chasings with us—was the perfect evening.

As I peered idly through the super-telephoto zoom lens on my camera, scanning our surroundings, I paused on a tiny white dot on the far, far coastline—just where it curled around the horizon. I took a photo, and digitally zoomed right in. As I thought—just four white pixels—a rock. Scanning the horizon again, I trained the lens back on the microscopic white dot, and hesitated. Surely it was slightly to the left before? I took a second photo, more carefully this time, and again zoomed in. The group of white pixels now looked somewhat bulkier, and had four stocky white legs.

'Better get our act together,' I said, passing the camera to Clark. 'Looks to me like there's a polar bear headed our way!'

The next photo confirmed it, and we swung into action. The bear was downwind of us and was pacing towards us along the shoreline, getting bigger and bigger. We surrounded ourselves with shotguns, bear-bangers, bear spray, flares and a stockpile of extra ammunition—and waited.

Still the bear lumbered closer, and closer. We were both shaking with adrenalin. It was a huge bear, and having him pacing directly towards us without any kind of zoo fence in between was definitely 'one of those moments'. Then the bear made eye contact. Although he had been sniffing the air repeatedly as he ambled along, it was as though he suddenly realised we were there. Now looking directly at us he kept advancing, although more cautiously.

'Look at that …' I breathed, pulling myself away from my camera's viewfinder. 'He's just there …'

We both stared in awe across at him, absorbing the full experience without a lens in the way for once. It was incredibly humbling. About 250 metres away, he reared up, towering on his hind legs—well over twice my height—curiously trying to work out what we were. Arching his huge neck this way and that sniffing the air, he tried again to catch our scent. Considering neither of us had showered in 73 days, when he finally did cop a noseful, the effect was electric. In an instant he flung himself down and around, and with one horror-struck stare back over his shoulder, he began bounding away, back along the shore in a blind panic, his back legs flinging out sideways in what looked a rather awkward (yet alarmingly efficient) gait. He was terrified. After another petrified glance over his shoulder he promptly plunged into the icy water and began swimming powerfully away out to sea. Hiding as low as he could in the water, only the tip of his nose and eyes protruded above the surface. Occasionally he'd lift his head around well clear to glance back at us before resuming his frightened retreat.

It was a little sad, actually—not just because he'd fled before we'd got the photos we'd been hoping for—but because we felt a little offended and even slightly embarrassed by the depth of his terror. We certainly wished him no harm—we'd have been extremely reluctant to have even used our non-lethal deterrents—but seeing that moment of recognition in his eyes, and his blatant correlation between our being human, and therefore likely about to open fire on him, made me feel ashamed.

We spent another lovely day (Day 70 + 4) waiting for the dinghy to materialise, exploring our surrounds, and trying not to drink too much of the local supply of 'fresh' water. Every saucepanful looked like an illustration from a textbook on water-borne biological pathogens and toxic larvae. Once or twice I inadvertently scooped up a little character that looked like it belonged in the film *Aliens*— had I placed it on my hand, I'm pretty sure it'd have instantly buried itself under my skin and scuttled as a twitching lump all the way up to my neck.

At about 3 pm, I caught sight of a small dinghy motoring towards us. We were saved! I leapt into my drysuit and stood knee-deep in the water, ready to help welcome the boat in to shore, but they wouldn't come any closer than about 25 metres.

Perplexed, in the end I had to walk back ashore as I was shivering too much, and from there, it was eventually communicated that the waves were too rough on the beach, and they didn't want to come in. Fair enough. But as all our gear was in Ortlieb drybags anyway, I proposed that I'd just walk each bag out to them—swim if I had to. It was impossible to hold a conversation at that distance, but it became clear that they were going to head south to wait for better weather. With that, they waved, and took off back the way they'd come.

Hours passed, the weather got steadily worse, and then it started to rain. We found and erected our miserable little tent, and lay inside, feeling rather empty. How long were we to wait? While we had ample 'food' to last for over a week, much of our staples were running out: we had almost no milk powder, no peanut butter, sugar; hell, even toilet paper was thin on the ground. I kept checking the horizon every time I imagined hearing an outboard, but I checked less and less as the hours dragged on, and eventually—past midnight—we both fell asleep, utterly dispirited.

The next morning (Day 70 + 5), after a bowl of oats without milk, as much as I dreaded that they might be home to pick up the phone, I called their home.

'Hello, Chris!' They had indeed gone all the way home. 'The weather is bad again today ...' We knew what was coming next. 'Give me a call, maybe, tomorrow?'

After organising payment for the fuel already expended trying to reach us, I called Doug instead—a contact I'd got through Diamonds

North Resources—who was managing some mine cleanup work on Banks Island. We knew he had Twin Otter planes scheduled, and if they had tundra tyres, they could perhaps land somewhere nearby.

At the other end of the phone Doug pored over a map trying to work out where we were. 'We saw a big tugboat a few days ago towing three enormous barges past on the horizon,' I added in conversation.

'Oh, yes, that was ours, collecting a heap of mining gear and bringing it back to the mainland. Let me see now—Twin Otters ...'

It turned out he was actually chartering a plane that would pass nearby tomorrow, but it wasn't a Twin Otter. 'Let me see if I can change my booking to a Twin, then maybe you could do a side charter from us, and we could come and grab you guys. Call me back at three.' A faint flicker of hope rekindled inside us, only to be extinguished at 3 pm on the dot when I called him back.

Clark watched my eager expression fall. 'He couldn't change the booking,' I mumbled. The very next possible Twin Otter in the area wouldn't be for another three days, and might not have enough room to squeeze us in.

We stared glumly around for a while, and then Clark voiced what we were both wondering. 'What about the barge?'

It was a ludicrous idea, but we didn't have much to lose. I called Doug back. 'Sorry to pester you again, but that barge—is there any possibility of maybe, well, you know, could they maybe ...'

'They cost $40,000 a day,' Doug said as an answer. 'A side trip from that just isn't possible.'

'But if it's coming past anyway?'

To cut a long story short, Doug said that if I called the company that *owned* the barge, and they agreed, then fine.

I called them right away. 'You want to *what*? I don't understand. How did you *get* there?' It was quite a strange conversation, but in the end I was given the satellite phone number for the captain of the barge. And so I called Steve—the skipper of the *Jock McNiven*—and everything just fell into place.

'Sure, that won't be a problem. We're leaving here tonight, actually, just one more barge to load up ... give me a call about 9 pm and I'll give you an update on our departure.'

We couldn't believe our luck. 'We're going to Tuktoyaktuk, though,' he said, 'is that okay?'

My contagious grin spread to Clark beside me. 'Tuktoyaktuk? Sure. Wherever. Anywhere's better than the middle of nowhere.' Laughing, Steve agreed.

We spent the afternoon re-packing all our gear, our excitement mounting, filling in the time until 9 pm with servings of chocolate. I called Steve on the dot.

'We're already on our way,' he said. 'We should be near you guys about 3.30 am ... we'll start slowing her down a bit at, say, 3 am, as slow as we can, but it's hard with the tow. We'll come in as close as we can, maybe a mile off, lower an inflatable and nip in and grab you guys and just keep going.'

How's that for pure luck and timing, and good ol' Northern friendliness! Can you imagine standing on a beach near Sydney Harbour, calling the captain of a big ship heading out, and saying, 'Hi, I ... erm ... was wondering if you could take me to Melbourne? I'm standing on a beach ...'

As scheduled, at about 3 am (Day 70 + 6)—we were unable to get to sleep in any case after a second polar bear encounter—our campsite was lit up by an enormous floodlight streaming from a speck on the horizon. The *Jock McNiven* had seen our campfire. It was quite dark, and it was some time before we could see the looming outline of the enormous twin-smoke-stack tugboat (44 metres long, weighing 777 tons, with four engines totalling 4500 horsepower, and a crew of thirteen), towing the three huge, heavily loaded barges (each one 75 metres long, 17 metres wide and loaded with 1500 tons). We stood there on the beach watching as Steve orchestrated the entire thing into a 360-degree circle to slow it down without the barges running into each other, then veered in closer and lowered a little black dot into the water which came rocketing in towards us. It was one of those moments in life when you feel very small, and totally in awe of the magnitude of something that is going on around you—let alone because of you.

The weather was pretty foul by now, raining (typical), and the waves were really dumping on the beach, which made the Zodiac landing quite interesting, but before we knew it we were shaking hands with an enthusiastic man in a red drysuit: 'I'm Jeff, good to see you guys!' he said.

After only a few swampings of the Zodiac in the breaking waves, and a total of three trips out to the formidable tug which meanwhile re-enacted another giant circle to avoid it steaming right past us, eventually Clark and I clambered up a steel ladder and onto the vibrating deck of the *Jock McNiven*. It was done. We had escaped the clutches of Victoria Island, at last.

From the bridge-deck, Steve ushered us up and we stepped inside and sealed the door closed behind us. Instantly, the wind and rain stopped. There was warmth all around us. The ground was solid and dry. The air smelt like coffee. Nothing was flapping and flailing around. It was strangely quiet, still and calm. We couldn't stop smiling; it really hit us both right then.

'Well, Jeff'll show you guys around, you've got a twin cabin to yourselves, fresh sheets on the bed, there's a washing machine, two hot showers—guess you'll be wanting to use those—grab a coffee, some food, sleep … It's 48 hours before we get to "Tuk"… Make yourselves at home, boys!'

The first person we met down below was the ship's cook—an extremely gifted chef, Christina—who promptly started mothering us and pushed a steaming mug of coffee into our hands. From that moment on, we have been eating and sleeping and grinning, in no particular order. Sleeping on a soft, real bed with a white pillow, and eating breakfast (French toast, eggs, hash browns, bacon, sausages, toast, cereal, yoghurt—one after the other), lunch (chicken curry, stews, rice, salad), dinner (steak, shepherd's pie, roasted potatoes, asparagus, gravy), all interspersed with fresh fruit, and tray after tray of freshly baked treats (bran muffins, brownies, biscuits, scones, cup cakes, chocolate cakes, cherry tarts … ). Our poor deprived taste buds are going into overdrive! As Clark said, 'It's just one new sensation after another!'

I think, at last, it's safe to say that the iiNet 1000 Hour Day Expedition is 'over', and has turned out far better in every respect than either of us could ever have hoped for. Gotta run—that smells suspiciously like more chocolate brownies!

# PART FIVE

# STEPPING
# BEYOND

# ONWARDS

What do you do after such an expedition? After four years of inexorable focus, four years of passionately emptying our hearts, minds and souls—and our bank accounts—into such an eccentric, almost quixotic goal like walking across an island?

'What are you going to do now?' The gaggle of media at Sydney Airport had spun a web of questions even before Clark and I could reach our respective families waiting patiently in the background.

'Go home, chill out and enjoy a good ol' Aussie meat pie!' Clark laughed, squeezing through to hug his sister Alexis.

We had a fantastic welcome-home party hosted by the Canadian Consulate-General in Sydney, Clark and I did a national lecture tour, numerous interviews, were awarded the Australian Geographic Society's Spirit of Adventure Award and I was elected Chairman of the Australia and New Zealand chapter of the Explorers Club—but in those first few busy weeks, what we craved most was simply time off. Time to soak up the luxurious warmth of the Australian summer, to sleep in without the slightest feeling of guilt, and, for me, time to get to know Jess, who became my very real dream girlfriend.

As much as we both longed for the days of relaxation to last, we knew they could not. We were both in debt, had no job, Clark was already staring down the barrel of 'the next expedition'—his looming Indian Ocean row—and I too had plans on the boil. Exciting times; but in the back of my mind, I felt a growing unease.

'We can't just keep doing this …' I ventured during one of Clark's and my frequent catch-ups. He knew exactly where I was coming from: trying to scrape a living from adventure—living one hectic expedition to the next—would not only burn us out very soon, but it would mean we'd never accumulate any real capital, or have time for anything else in our lives. We also both acknowledged a sneaking desire to outdo our previous expedition—always one better, one bigger—or else we'd feel like our careers were going backwards. But in the high-stakes field of adventuring, constantly having to attempt something more extreme in order to chase sponsorship dollars seemed a sure-fire route to an early grave. Besides, we were really struggling trying to think of a better 'adventure' than the one we'd just completed.

'Adventure is always going to be part of our lives,' Clark stated firmly, and I agreed. 'But we do also need time for other things—such as our friends and girlfriends. And to achieve that—'

'To achieve that, we need to get our foot in the door of some kind of parallel career.' He nodded acceptingly as I finished his sentence.

Clark had yet to complete his film and media degree, and ultimately work out a way into his dream role: working on documentaries. I was left pondering how to break into a field that was my passion—the ever more competitive world of professional photography. With every second person these days having a fantastic digital camera and the image market saturated with cheap, amazing photographs just a mouse-click away, it was not going to be easy.

I'd been back from the Arctic for only two and a half months when Jess and I decided to give bicycle touring a try. We cycled right around Tasmania for three weeks, up until Christmas 2008. The very next morning, on Boxing Day, I left for Antarctica aboard a luxury cruise ship as a volunteer member of their Expedition Team. It was a role that I lucked into through a friend, aided by the fact that I had ice experience and could double as a guest speaker and official photographer.

To pass the time during the pounding five-day slog south to the frozen continent, I decided to put together a short lecture on photography basics. While most passengers were too seasick to attend, those who did loved it.

'Are you going to do any more of these when you get home?' one lady asked, at which several others also piped up: 'Oh, yes! Let us know—we'd all sign up!'

As I wandered around for the next week helping the guests take photos of penguins, seals and icebergs, I couldn't help but be struck by the number of amazingly powerful digital SLR cameras everywhere, all cripplingly left on 'auto-mode'. Forming a plan, as soon as I returned home I registered 'Chris Bray Photography' and challenged myself to turn it into a career.

Although I'd sold a handful of photos, owned great camera gear and had a fair bit of experience, I was by no means a professional photographer. Applying the positive, problem-solving mindset and self-confidence that my expeditions have taught me, however, I found the ensuing success of my photography business surprised even me. My theory was that instead of fighting for a place amongst the ever-rising tide of photographers, I'd embrace this influx and turn it to my advantage by teaching them. I'd show them how to unlock the huge creative potential of their cameras. I decided to make my photography course just one intensive nine-hour day, and to host the courses at zoo function centres, complete with boardroom-style venues for the theory sessions, along with great catering. We could then simply step outside for our practical sessions and immediately be surrounded by a diverse set of photogenic test subjects. As an outdoor and wildlife photography fan, my longer-term aim was to conduct photography safaris, enabling me to eventually mix my passions of adventure, travel and photography. It looked good on paper, and after doing copious research and preparation for several months, I compiled it all into something not dissimilar to an expedition document, and took a deep breath.

Still in debt from the Arctic, starting the photography business was a slow process but I had a few lucky breaks, including being sent on assignment for *Australian Geographic* magazine to Papua New Guinea, and also becoming Canon's ambassador for digital photography in Australia, hosting a series of 'how to' photography videos for their 'World of EOS' website which directed traffic to mine. Biting the bullet, I borrowed enough money from Jess to hire the Taronga Zoo Function Centre in

Sydney and held my very first one-day photography course in June 2009, and another two weeks later.

It was a huge success, and, spurred on by glowing feedback, I gambled all those proceeds on booking more venues in four other states around Australia—and the business took off. What started as just the occasional Saturday soon developed into Jess and me running sell-out courses on both days of every weekend in capital cities around Australia and even in Auckland, New Zealand. I spent all my free time learning and practising hard and promoting my photography, and to my humbled amazement people began describing me as 'one of Australia's leading outdoor photographers', asking me to judge competitions, write photography articles and give advice. Several of my beginner students even started winning international awards! I ran my own marketing campaigns, bought more equipment, redesigned my website and, before I knew it, Jess and I were running our first luxury photography safari down the east coast of Tasmania—complete with chartered helicopters and planes—which sold out within the first half-hour.

Scheduling time off for adventures—including cycling around New Zealand's South Island at the end of 2009—a mere eight months after starting up my business, I became the director of my own photography company which now employs Jess and myself.

Clark, already having committed to his ocean row, spent the ensuing months doggedly preparing for that with his housemate—building the rowboat and all—only to have their major sponsor pull out on them due to the economic downturn, mere months before the race started. It was a terrible blow, but allowed Clark to shift his focus back to university, and he graduated in 2010. Since then, he too has accelerated towards his dream career, initially filming and editing for the likes of Australian Geographic, and now working on our documentary film as well as at the ABC, gaining still more experience, contacts and funds to propel himself onwards to becoming a renowned expedition cameraman and specialist documentary maker. Of course, he too has scheduled in some more adventures; currently he's focusing on Papua New Guinea and, after that, he's determined to continue his crusade to row across the Indian Ocean, this time solo.

In the weeks after I finish this book, Jess and I have scheduled more time off in between photography courses and our upcoming photo safari (two by two-week trips to Kenya in January 2011) to embark on the first stage of our next, bigger adventure. Together we've just bought a little wooden 29-foot (8.8 metre) junk-rig yacht, renamed her *Teleport* and registered her as an Australian sailing vessel, home port Sydney. The only problem is that the yacht is in Halifax—on the east side (or 'wrong side'!) of Canada. Rather than sailing her home the 'normal' way down to the balmy Caribbean, through Panama and across the tropical Pacific Ocean, we've decided instead on a more exciting route. After this initial setup season of getting the yacht ready, teaching Jess how to sail and cruising 500 nautical miles north up closer to the Arctic, we'll fly home but return each subsequent Northern Hemisphere summer for a series of three-month yachting adventures. As the sea ice melts we'll sail *Teleport* up the coast of Greenland, over the top of Canada and through the Arctic's bitter Northwest Passage, to good ol' Cambridge Bay on Victoria Island—by which time the ocean will have frozen over again. Over the following years we'll sail onwards to Alaska, over to Siberia, down the Kamchatka Peninsula, maybe then onwards to Micronesia, Papua New Guinea and eventually home.

Clark and I brought almost nothing home from the Arctic. Having dismantled The Nugget into lengths of aluminium and inner tubes which the resourceful tug boat operators put to good use, and having distributed our outdoor gear to local fishermen in Tuktoyaktuk, our only tangible reminders were a few fossils, a genuinely unbreakable muskox horn spoon, 7000 photos and around 70 hours of video footage—however, the 1000 Hour Day expedition has stayed with us in so many ways.

I'm not talking about the fact that every so often I wake in a panic when my next-door neighbour inadvertently sets off his burglar alarm, because ironically it uses the exact same dual-tone siren that I built into our polar bear tripwire alarm. Or the fact that to this day as I walk along the beach sometimes, the sight of a large dog paw print splayed into the sand at my feet subconsciously snaps my wandering mind back to wolves. Ignoring these and other mental scars, the expedition really opened up the world to us both.

Having faced so many challenges which at the time seemed insurmountable—everything from crossing the island as a whole, down to the individual trucking strikes, axle breakages and lost paddles—we have learned how to calmly take life's difficulties in our stride, and to rationally problem solve to overcome them, piece by piece. Having faced enough failures that truly were impossible to remedy—everything from blowing up a video camera right through to not getting to the far side in 2005—we have subsequently learned how to recognise, acknowledge and accept things that cannot be fixed, and to stay focused and remain positive afterwards. With help often too far away, we learned the importance of teamwork and friendship, careful risk management and decision making, as well as the realisation that revenge, retaliation, grudges and blame can only ever make a situation worse. Having endured feelings of hunger, inescapable cold and at times seemingly unbearable physical and mental torment, we now find that we're able to dismiss these discomforts when we need to, and therefore have become so much more resilient. In a nutshell, the expedition has made us both realise that we are capable of so much more than we ever thought possible. As Sir Edmund Hillary once said, 'People do not decide to become extraordinary. They decide to accomplish extraordinary things.'

Unfortunately, in our increasingly risk-averse society, people—especially young people—are inadvertently being discouraged from learning these important life lessons that we discovered, and the profound ramifications of this upon their self-confidence, their motivation, their stress levels, and their overall physical, emotional, social and cognitive development are only just starting to be appreciated. With the western world progressively padded by comforts and conveniences, the notion of real risk and hardship is fast being forgotten. We're now seeing a world that is becoming increasingly demotivated and fearful, unable to make decisions or handle stress.

Scientists now understand why this is the case, and it relates to positive feedback in our brain's 'incentive–reward' system.

Challenge rewires the brain to be motivated and happy, and a lack of it encourages the opposite. Looking around us, we can't help but agree. People who challenge themselves—be that in sport, adventure, academically or any other field—often seem to be inexplicably enthused about what they do. It's their passion—their reason for being—and through this, they seem to gain a heightened appreciation for life in general. Compare this to someone who spends their time sitting around doing nothing, unchallenged and bored. They typically remain the least motivated, the least likely to be enthused about anything, and, significantly, are likely to be the most depressed. Broaden this logic across today's cotton-wool world, and it should not come as any surprise to learn that depression is actually the number one psychological disorder in the western world today. There is no paradox in the finding that those people living in the safest parts of the world—those with the least to worry about in terms of danger, hunger or disease—are among the most depressed and worried people on Earth.

All is not lost, however, and the fact that people still pick up and read adventure books like this one is testimony to the primal, subconscious instinct that is still there in our brains, reminding us that there is something exciting and worthwhile about a little responsible risk taking. You don't need to cross an Arctic island in order to experience an awakening; simply pushing back the limits of your own experiences is one of the most rewarding things you can do in life. I still remember the feeling that grew inside me during my first Tasmania hike—an inexplicably wholesome feeling of appreciation, accomplishment and motivation that has stayed with me. A strange sense that something had been missing from my normal convenient lifestyle back home, and that in some perverse way, a little hardship and responsible risk taking seemed to fill that void. People who have never set themselves such a challenge often fail to understand why we bothered, and the people who have, never need to ask. Clark and I discovered on our expedition how much we are capable of, and we learned the attitudes required to tackle life's challenges. More than this, though, throughout the expedition's dizzying highs and sickening lows, we experienced a level of satisfaction, contentment and happiness that neither of us had known before.

Adventure may not be the meaning of life, but without it life does start to lose its meaning. Comfort zones only exist so that we know where we must step beyond, when we want to feel alive.

# ACKNOWLEDGEMENTS

Special thanks to Clark Carter: being stuck in the middle of nowhere with only one other person, virtually never out of each other's sight for 24 hours a day, seven days a week, for months on end, under some of the most stressful and unpleasant conditions imaginable, it would be understandable for even the strongest, lifelong friendships to fail. As we know, they often do. How then we—having never even met before our 2005 trip—managed not only to tolerate each other but become the very best of friends I think is nothing short of extraordinary. Without a doubt the best thing to come from this entire four-year epic project is your ongoing friendship. Thanks for everything, mate—there's just no way any of this could have happened with anyone else, and had you not sent that email out of the blue asking if I wanted to plan a trip, my life would be very different now, that's for sure! We make quite a team, and I really look forward to conjuring up another expedition with you down the track.

And thanks so very much to all our sponsors and everyone who contributed personally to this expedition. Without so many enthusiastic people helping us—be that with donations, encouragement, support, time or ideas—this whole dream would have remained just that: a dream. I couldn't begin to list everyone to whom this credit should go, but in addition to our corporate sponsors, whose logos appear on the following pages, the names of a few people do immediately spring to mind:

Alan Brightman, Alejandro Rolandi, Alex and Tracy Stuit, Alexandra Darcy, Andreas Lombardozzi, Andrew Bray, Andrew, Ernest and Sue from Solazone, Anna Walmsley, Ann McFarlane, Anne-Claire Dejardin, Bea Harrison, Ben Charlton, Bob Heath,

Bob Iddles, Brad Gordon, Branko Celler, Brent Boddy, Bruce Lines, Buddy Robinson, Carmen Li, Cathy Kennedy, Chris Macleod, Christine Frith, Christine Heywood, Colette Vella, Dave Thomas, David Lyons, David Yates, Diane McDowell, Dick Smith, Don and Margie McIntyre, Doug Stern, Dr Richard Corkish, Dr Saxon Williams, Emidio Boto, Eric Philips, Fred Hamilton, Gavin Landers, Helen and Keith Smith, Ingrid Earle, Isabelle Alaban, Jack McCann, James Diamond, James Strumpfer, Jasper Timm, Jemima Robinson, Jeno Toppler, Jessica Taunton, Joanne Diver, John Booth, John Bridekirk, John Leece, Jonathan Selby, Josef Eberl, Karen Ward, Karl Toppler, Kate Ellis, Keith Lear, Keith Lear Sr, Ken Eastwood, Kendon Glass, Kylie Piper, Lachlan Welch, Laurie Geoghegan, Lawrence Otokiak, Liz McDougall, Luis Soltero, Margaret Bray, Margaret Donald, Matthew Searle, Max and Sandy Riseley, Melanie Berryman, Michael Ison, Michael Malone, Michelle Rowley, Michelle Wadham, Nancy Curry, Natalia Galin, Nick Simmonds, Nir Yaffe, Onno Benschop, Paul Mahal, Peter and Caroline Davidson, Peter Smith, Phil and Liz from Fine Tolerance, Rachel Francois, René Laserich, Richard Laffan, Rick McElrea, Rick Slowgrove, Robert Fox, Robin Kydd, Rohan Belliappa, Sacha Dench, Sandy Richardson, Sarah Bray, Simon Barrow, Sue Clothier, Steve Dalby, Todd Tai, Tom MacDonald, Tony and Tere Garland, Vicky Bray, Wave Vidmar, Wilfred MacDonald, and Willie Laserich.

And of course all our friends and family, and anyone else I have forgotten to name.

Thank you!

THANK YOU TO THESE SPONSORS
WHO SUPPORTED THE
FIRST EXPEDITION IN 2005

OCEAN FRONTIERS
**1,000 Hour Day**
Unsupported Across Victoria Island - The High Arctic

AIR CANADA

icebreaker.com
PURE MERINO

THANK YOU TO THESE SPONSORS
WHO SUPPORTED THE
SECOND EXPEDITION IN 2008